Myths and Milestones in the History of Sport

Also by Stephen Wagg:

THE NEW POLITICS OF LEISURE AND PLEASURE (*co-edited with Peter Bramham*)

CRICKET AND GLOBALISATION (*co-edited with Chris Rumford*)

SPORTING HEROES OF THE NORTH (*co-edited with Dave Russell*)

KEY CONCEPTS IN SPORT STUDIES (*edited, and co-written with Carlton Brick, Belinda Wheaton and Jayne Caudwell*)

SPORT, LEISURE AND CULTURE IN THE POSTMODERN CITY (*co-edited with Peter Bramham*)

AMATEURISM IN BRITISH SPORT: It Matters Not Who Won or Lost? (*co-edited with Dilwyn Porter*)

EAST PLAYS WEST: ESSAYS ON SPORT AND THE COLD WAR (*co-edited with David Andrews*)

CRICKET AND NATIONAL IDENTITY IN THE POST-COLONIAL ERA: Following on (*editor*)

BRITISH FOOTBALL AND SOCIAL EXCLUSION (*editor*)

BECAUSE I TELL A JOKE OR TWO: Comedy, Politics and Social Difference (*editor*)

THE SOCIAL FACES OF HUMOUR (*co-edited with Chris Powell and George E.C. Paton*)

THATCHER'S CHILDREN? POLITICS, CHILDHOOD AND SOCIETY IN THE 1980S AND 90S (*co-edited with Jane Pilcher*)

GIVING THE GAME AWAY: Football, Politics and Culture on Five Continents (*editor*)

COME ON DOWN? POPULAR MEDIA CULTURE IN POST-WAR BRITAIN (*co-edited with Dominic Strinati*)

BRITISH FOOTBALL AND SOCIAL CHANGE (*co-edited with John Williams*)

THE FOOTBALL WORLD: A Contemporary Social History

Myths and Milestones in the History of Sport

Edited by

Stephen Wagg
Professor of Sport and Society, Leeds Metropolitan University, UK

Editorial matter, selection, introduction and chapter 6 © Stephen Wagg 2011
All remaining chapters © their respective authors 2011

All rights reserved. No reproduction, copy or transmission of this publication may be made without written permission.

No portion of this publication may be reproduced, copied or transmitted save with written permission or in accordance with the provisions of the Copyright, Designs and Patents Act 1988, or under the terms of any licence permitting limited copying issued by the Copyright Licensing Agency, Saffron House, 6-10 Kirby Street, London EC1N 8TS.

Any person who does any unauthorized act in relation to this publication may be liable to criminal prosecution and civil claims for damages.

The authors have asserted their rights to be identified as the authors of this work in accordance with the Copyright, Designs and Patents Act 1988.

First published 2011 by
PALGRAVE MACMILLAN

Palgrave Macmillan in the UK is an imprint of Macmillan Publishers Limited, registered in England, company number 785998, of Houndmills, Basingstoke, Hampshire RG21 6XS.

Palgrave Macmillan in the US is a division of St Martin's Press LLC, 175 Fifth Avenue, New York, NY 10010.

Palgrave Macmillan is the global academic imprint of the above companies and has companies and representatives throughout the world.

Palgrave® and Macmillan® are registered trademarks in the United States, the United Kingdom, Europe and other countries.

ISBN 978–0–230–24125–1

This book is printed on paper suitable for recycling and made from fully managed and sustained forest sources. Logging, pulping and manufacturing processes are expected to conform to the environmental regulations of the country of origin.

A catalogue record for this book is available from the British Library.

Library of Congress Cataloging-in-Publication Data
Myths and milestones in the history of sport / edited
  by Stephen Wagg.
     p. cm.
  Includes bibliographical references and index.
  ISBN 978–0–230–24125–1 (alk. paper)
  1. Sports—History. I. Wagg, Stephen.
  GV571.M97 2011
  796.09—dc23   2011016953

10 9 8 7 6 5 4 3 2 1
20 19 18 17 16 15 14 13 12 11

Printed and bound in the United States of America

Contents

List of Figures   vii

Notes on the Contributors   viii

Introduction: Myths and Milestones in the History of Sport   1
Stephen Wagg

1   The Invention of Sporting Tradition: National Myths, Imperial Pasts and the Origins of Australian Rules Football   8
Tony Collins

2   From Evil to Expedient: The Legalization of Professionalism in English Football, 1884–85   32
Dave Russell

3   Peacefully at Wembley Stadium on 20 April 1974: The Quiet Death of Amateur Football in England   57
Dilwyn Porter

4   Rough, Manly Sport and the American Way: Theodore Roosevelt and College Football, 1905   80
Michael Oriard

5   Baseball, Invented Tradition, and Nationalistic Spirit   106
Gerald R. Gems

6   'Her Dainty Strength': Suzanne Lenglen, Wimbledon and the Coming of Female Sport Celebrity   122
Stephen Wagg

7   Before and After 1968: Reconsidering the Introduction of Drug Testing in the Olympic Games   141
Ian Ritchie

8   The 'Revolt of the Black Athlete': Tommie Smith and John Carlos's 1968 Black Power Salute Reconsidered   159
Maureen Margaret Smith

9   The D'Oliveira Affair: Cricket, 'Race' and Politics   185
Rob Steen

10	The Physical Activism of Billie Jean King *Jaime Schultz*	203
11	John L. Sullivan: The Champion of All Champions *Elliott J. Gorn*	224
12	The 'Packer Affair' and the Early Marriage of Television and Sport *David L. Andrews and Andrew D. Grainger*	239
13	All these Years of Hurt: Culture, Pedagogy and '1966' as a Site of National Myths *Michael L. Silk and Jessica Francombe*	262
14	The 1960 Rome Summer Olympics: Birth of a New World? *Barbara Keys*	287

Index   304

List of Figures

4.1 Hearst's *New York Journal and Advertiser*, November 7, 1897, describing 'How Young Hasche's Life Was Crushed Out,' 'How Von Gammon Was Killed by Concussion of the Brain,' and 'How Gordona Was Killed at Bayone, N.J., by a Fracture of the Skull.'   84

4.2 A two-page centerfold in the humor magazine *Judge* for November 4 portrayed the Football Slugger as just the latest of the many beasts – the Russian Bear, the Democratic Donkey, the Government Grafter, and the Spanish Monkey – tamed by President Roosevelt. *Harper's Weekly* had a similar cover on October 28.   86

4.3 *New York World*, November 20, 1905.   89

4.4 From the Sunday Magazine Section of the *New York World*, November 5, 1905.   96

4.5 *Judge*, March 10, 1906. *Life* ran a cover with a similar theme, appearing on November 8, 1906.   99

4.6 The 'new football' looked old in 1909: an injured player (fatally perhaps?) with teammates and distraught parents; a two-page centerfold in *Harper's Weekly*, January 1, 1910.   100

Notes on the Contributors

David L. Andrews is a professor in the Department of Kinesiology at the University of Maryland, USA. He edited *Michael Jordan Inc.: Corporate Sport, Media Culture, and Late Modern America* (2001) and *Manchester United: An Interdisciplinary Study* (2004) and co-edited *Sport Stars: The Cultural Politics of Sport Celebrity* (2001); *Sporting Dystopias: The Making and Meaning of Urban Sport Cultures* (2003); *Sport, Culture, and Advertising: Identities, Commodities, and the Politics of Representation* (2003) and *Corporate Nationalism(s): Sport, Cultural Identity, and Transnational Marketing* (2005). He is also co-editor of the *Global Culture and Sport* series for Palgrave Macmillan and is writing a book on late capitalist sport for Blackwell.

Tony Collins is Professor and Director of the International Centre for Sports History and Culture at De Montfort University, Leicester in the UK. He is the author of *Rugby League in Twentieth Century Britain* (2006), *Mud, Sweat and Beers. A Cultural History of Sport and Alcohol* (with Wray Vamplew; 2002), *Rugby's Great Split: Class, Culture and the Origins of Rugby League Football* (1998. New and expanded edition, 2006) and co-editor of *The Glory of their Times: Crossing the Colour Line in Rugby League* (2004). He has just completed a history of rugby union.

Jessica Francombe is a doctoral student in the Department of Education at the University of Bath, UK. Her research focuses on physical culture and how this intersects and articulates with young femininity. Particular areas of interest are the neoliberal subject, the female body politic and the healthification of popular culture. Her work has been published in *Television and New Media* and *Interactions*.

Gerald R. Gems is Professor of Health and Physical Education at North Central College, Napierville, IL, USA and a past president of the North American Society for Sport History. He is the author of *Windy City Wars: Labor, Leisure and Sport in the Making of Chicago* (1997); *For Pride, Profit and Patriarchy: Football and the Incorporation of American Cultural Values*

(2000); and *The Athletic Crusade: Sport and American Cultural Imperialism* (2006). With Linda Borish and Gertrud Pfister, he wrote *Sport in American History: From Colonization to Globalization* (2008) and, with Steven Reiss, he edited *The Chicago Sports Reader: 100 Years of Sports in the Windy City* (forthcoming).

Elliott J. Gorn is a professor of History and American Studies at Brown University, Providence, Rhode Island, USA. He is the author of *The Manly Art: Bare-knuckle Prize Fighting in America* (1989); *Muhammad Ali, The Peoples Champ* (1998) *A Brief History of American Sports* (2004) and *Sports in Chicago* (2008).

Andrew D. Grainger teaches at Liverpool Hope University in the UK. With David Andrews and Joshua Newman he wrote 'Sport the Media and the Construction of Race' in the recent *Handbook of Sports and Media*, edited by Arthur A, Raney and Jennings Bryant (2006).

Barbara Keys teaches history at the University of Melbourne in Australia. Previously she taught at California State University in Sacramento and was a research fellow at the Kennan Institute for Advanced Russian Studies at the Woodrow Wilson International Center for Scholars in Washington, DC. She is the author of *Globalizing Sport: National Rivalry and International Community in the 1930s* (2006).

Michael Oriard is Professor of English at Oregon State University in the USA and played American football as a professional. He is the author of *The End of Autumn: Reflections on My Life in Football* (1982); *Dreaming of Heroes: American Sports Fiction, 1868–1980* (1982); *Sporting With the Gods: The Rhetoric of Play and Game in American Culture* (1991); *Reading Football: How the Popular Press Created an American Spectacle* (1993); *King Football: Sport & Spectacle in the Golden Age of Radio and Newsreels, Movies and Magazines, the Weekly and the Daily Press* (2001) and *Brand NFL: Making and Selling America's Favorite Sport* (2007).

Dilwyn Porter is Senior Research Fellow in the Centre for Sport and Culture at De Montfort University, Leicester, UK and a Research Associate at the Business History Unit at the London School of Economics. He is author of 'Amateur Football in England 1948–63: the Pegasus Phenomenon', *Contemporary British History*, 14, 2000 and, with Ronald Kowalski, 'Political Football: Moscow Dynamo in Britain, 1945', *International Journal of the History of Sport*, 114, 1997. He edited, with Adrian

Smith, *Amateurs and Professionals in Post-War British Sport* (2000) and *Sport and National Identity in the Post-war World* (2004). He wrote *Mail Order Retailing in Britain: A Business and Social History* (2005) and most recently, with Stephen Wagg, he edited *Amateurism in British Sport: It Matters Not Who Won or Lost?* (2008). He is a former editor of the journal *Sport in History*.

Ian Ritchie is an associate professor in the Department of Physical Education and Kinesiology at Brock University in Canada. With Rob Beamish he is the author of *Fastest, Highest, Strongest: A Critique of High Performance Sport* (2006).

Dave Russell was Professor of History and Northern Studies at Leeds Metropolitan University, UK until his retirement in 2010. His principal publications are *Football and the English: A Social History of English Football 1963–1995* (1997) and *Looking North: Northern England and the National Imagination* (2004).

Jaime Schultz teaches at Pennsylvania State University in the USA. She researches issues of gender, 'race' and sexuality in the history of sport and is the author of 'The Legend of Jack Trice and the Campaign for Jack Trice Stadium 1973–1984' (*Journal of Social History* Vol. 41, No. 4, Summer 2008). She has also written for the *Journal of Sport History*, *The International Journal of Sport History*, the *Sociology of Sport Journal*, *The Journal of Sport and Social Issues* and *Sport & Society*. She is currently completing two books: *Moments of Impact*, concerning issues of race, cultural memory and football history, and *From Sex Testing to Sports Bras: Gender, Technology, & U.S. Women's Sport* (forthcoming).

Michael L. Silk is a senior lecturer in the Faculty of Education at Bath University, UK. His research and scholarship centres on the relationships between sport and physical activity, the governance of bodies, cultural pedagogies and identity politics within the context of neoliberalism. He has published across these areas in *Media, Culture, Society*, *Organisational Research Methods*, the *Journal of Sport and Social Issues*, the *Sociology of Sport Journal*, the *International Journal of Media & Cultural Politics*, *Cultural Studies ↔ Critical Methodologies*, *Social Identities*, *Studies in Ethnicity & Nationalism* and *American Behavioural Scientist*. He is co-editor, with David Andrews and C.L. Cole, of *Corporate Nationalisms: Sport, Cultural Identity and Transnational Marketing* (2003). With Andrews and Daniel Mason, he also edited *Qualitative Methods for Sports Studies* (2005).

Maureen Margaret Smith is a professor in the Department of Kinesiology and Health Science at California State University, Sacramento, USA and biographer of the great African American sprinter Wilma Rudolph (*Wilma Rudolph: A Biography*, Westport, CT: Greenwood Publishing, 2006). She is President Elect of the North American Society for Sport History.

Rob Steen is a cricket writer and Senior Lecturer in Sports Journalism at Brighton University, UK. He has written for *The Guardian*, the *Sunday Telegraph*, the *Sunday Times*, the *Independent*, the *Financial Times*, *The Observer Sport Monthly*, *India Today*, *The Wisden Cricketer* and *Cricinfo Magazine* and edited the short-lived cricket journal *The New Ball*. His books include biographies of the West Indian cricketer Desmond Haynes and England cricket captain David Gower, the latter winning him the Cricket Society Literary Award. He also wrote *500-1 – The Miracle of Headingley '81*. His investigation for *Wisden Cricketer*, 'Whatever Happened to the Black Cricketer?', won the UK section of the 2005 EU Journalism Award 'For diversity, against discrimination'. In 2007, his first textbook, *Sports Journalism – A Multimedia Primer* was published, and *Cricinfo*, the world's leading cricket website, began publishing his blog, 'Rob's Lobs'. His latest book is a biography of the heavyweight boxing champion Sonny Liston.

Stephen Wagg is Professor of Sport and Society at Leeds Metropolitan University, UK. He has been publishing work on sport and society since 1983 and is the author of *The Football World: A Contemporary Social History* (1984). He co-edited *British Football and Social Change* (1991), *East Plays West: Sport and the Cold War* (2007) and *Amateurism and British Sport* (2008) and edited *Giving the Game Away: Football, Politics and Culture Across Five Continents* (1995), *British Football and Social Exclusion* (2004), *Cricket and National Identity in the Postcolonial Age* (2005) and *Key Concepts in Sports Studies* (2009). He has also edited series for Leicester and Manchester University Presses and is currently co-editor for Palgrave Macmillan of the series *Global Culture and Sport*.

Introduction: Myths and Milestones in the History of Sport

Stephen Wagg

The immediate inspiration for this book came in the spring of 2004 when a number of historians and other academics convened at Oxford University to discuss the fiftieth anniversary of Roger Bannister's becoming the first athlete to run a mile in under four minutes. I had been six years old at the time of this race and, like millions of others, had grown up with what might be called the '*Newsreel* version' of Bannister's feat – that's to say, a simple record of heroic, individual achievement – a depoliticized account of what had taken place, bathed in a taken-for-granted triumphalism on behalf of late-imperial Britain. However, although the fabled mile of 1954 had been run at Oxford's Iffley Road track, the Bannister conference was certainly not an empty celebration of the event. Instead it showed the whole incident to have been politically contentious, in a variety of ways: Bannister had been the standard-bearer for a group of Empire loyalists, anxious to find circumstances in which this athletic barrier could be breached by a Briton, the mile, for them, being an imperial measure; there were reputed to be better and more deserving milers than Bannister – in Sweden, Australia and the United States; the record was disputed in international athletic circles because of the doubtful claim by two runners, who had appeared to act as Bannister's pace-makers, that they had been trying win the race. And so on. A great many of the specific arguments on this affair have been collated by John Bale.[1] But what principally matters here is the general point that arises from important work of this kind: that events defined as important – on the sports field or elsewhere – are greatly more complex than they are frequently rendered, be it by media spokespeople or by historians of a certain stamp.

Two equally important points arise from this recognition.

First, as the French writer Roland Barthes argued, purportedly key events in history have been converted into *myths*.[2] This is not to suggest – as in the conventional use of the word 'myth' – that these things never happened, or that they have been outrageously distorted. Rather, it means that – often for nationalistic reasons – these events have been made in some way sacrosanct and sealed off from any kind of critical discussion. Barthes himself used the word 'myth' to mean 'depoliticized speech'.[3] The distinguished historian Angus Calder deployed the concept to great effect, chiefly in relation to The Blitz – a series of German bombing raids on London in 1940 and 1941, around which an unassailable myth of the social classes of British society pulling together in adversity has been woven by historians.[4] Once again, it is important that these matters are opened up for discussion.

Second, the annals of sport have been unduly afflicted by 'Great Men Theory of History'. This is especially true if we accept the American publisher Philip Graham's suggestion that journalism is the 'first rough draft of history'. Too often sport history, most notably in the sport media, is rendered simply as the doings of great athletes, managers, coaches, owners and administrators. These people variously break records, lift trophies, win leagues, devise tactics, buy sports clubs and so on – invariably with no apparent social or political context. But sport historians, any more than historians of any other social sphere, cannot be content with these one-dimensional accounts.

This book therefore has three principal purposes.

First, it addresses the notion of *myth* in the history of sport in Britain, the United States and Australia and discusses in detail a range of specific myths – moments that have, for the most part, been viewed other than through a critical lens. The writing of 2004–6 rescued the Bannister moment from myth and rendered it in its social and political complexity; this book seeks to do likewise for a series of similarly important historical sporting moments and personalities.

Second, these moments and individuals have been chosen for their relevance to one or other of a range of important and established themes in the historical and sociological study of sport: social class, gender, 'race', state intervention, drugs and doping, celebrity, mediatization (simply, the conjoining of sport and the mass media) and commercialization.

Third, it has been written accessibly by some of the leading historians of sport in Britain and the United States in the hope that it provides an interesting book that moves beyond, and beneath, the 'newsreel' version of sport and instead renders a number of key sporting moments in the their social and political context.

The book is set out as follows.

In Chapter 1 **Tony Collins** casts a keen eye over the various circumstances in sport history when the academic and colloquial meanings of the word 'myth' come together – that is, in the fashioning of creation of myths in relation to particular sports. Collins shows how, following a pattern set out by Eric Hobsbawm and Terence Ranger in their influential book of 1983,[5] historians have invented a tradition for a particular sport that is resilient, despite the fact that it is supported by virtually no evidence. The chapter discusses these creation of myths in general and provides a specific analysis of the ongoing controversy surrounding the origin of Australian Rules football.

The second and third chapters are about social class myths and association football in England. The historic 'moment' covered by **Dave Russell** in Chapter 2 occurs in the period 1884–5 and the chapter surveys the politics, played out chiefly in the Northern and Midland regions of the country, which surrounded the emergence and sanctioning of professional football in England. Remarkable as it seems now, in a world wherein so many young people daydream of becoming professional footballers, professionalism was widely regarded as a curse by many of the pioneer administrators of association football. Moreover, as Russell shows, its acceptance came only as the result of a concerted campaign, which included a threat on the part of a number of clubs to break from the Football Association if they were not to be allowed to pay their players.

This chapter is followed by what is, in effect, a companion piece by **Dilwyn Porter**. Porter looks at the history of amateur football in England, organizing his argument around the final Amateur Cup Final at Wembley in 1974. This entails the examination of two important myths – that amateur footballers were always gentleman 'toffs' and that amateur footballers did not play for financial reward. As Porter shows, the amateur game had a strong and rich working class element and, as was widely acknowledged at the time, whether they were carpet fitters or Cambridge University graduates, most amateur footballers were 'shamateurs' who expected there to be money in their boots at the end of a game. The chapter shows the importance to communities, historically, of amateur football and analyses the circumstances that led to the demise of the Amateur FA Cup.

Chapters 4 and 5 are also, in a sense, companion pieces. Both are about the relationship between sport and the polity in the United States.

First, **Michael Oriard**, leading historian, and former player, of American football, writes about an important moment in the game's history: the political controversy that attended college football in America in the early twentieth century. In 1905, following a spate of deaths on the field of play, President Theodore Roosevelt, himself an imperialist and advocate of rugged pursuits, intervened and instigated a debate on the state of the game. As Oriard shows, this was not to emasculate the sport so much as to promote the 'necessary roughness' that Roosevelt – the political hero of Senator John McCain, Republican Presidential candidate in 2008 – wished to see in American life.

Next, **Gerald Gems** writes critically but with some affection about the relationship between baseball, American capitalism and the state. The essay is, once again, organized around a particular moment – in this case, the symbolic throwing of the first pitch of the American baseball season by the nation's president, initiated in 1910 by the Republican William Howard Taft. Gems, however, develops a narrative around this event that shows the way in which baseball was constructed as America's national sport, how it has served the needs of American capitalism and the American state and how successive American Presidents have related to the game.

Chapter 6, by **Stephen Wagg**, is essentially about female sport celebrity and is organized around the 'moment' when the spectators and public chroniclers at Wimbledon, the famous South London tennis tournament, first encountered the flamboyant French player Suzanne Lenglen in 1919. Women tennis players of the early twentieth century were expected to wear floor-length skirts, bodices, straw hats and even boots. Lenglen's light, chiffon tennis dresses rose almost to the knee and she played the game in an athletic and competitive way – an approach that shocked and enthralled in equal measure. This chapter relates Lenglen to the times in which she lived – which were undeniably changing times for women – and charts her development and treatment as, perhaps, the first sportswoman to be cast a celebrity.

Three essays now address sport events of 1968, each in its separate way shrouded in myth. In the seventh chapter **Ian Ritchie** discusses the 'war on drugs' inaugurated by the International Olympic Committee in that year. As Ritchie makes clear, his chapter does not dispute the principal historical events that constituted the introduction of testing for performance-enhancing drugs in the Olympics. But he does interrogate the central myths of drug-testing in the Olympic Games and elsewhere – namely that they are part of an ongoing campaign against 'cheats' and take place both for ethical reasons and to safeguard the health of athletes.

The following essay, by **Maureen Margaret Smith**, provides a rounded account of one of the most remembered *Newsreel* moments in sport history – the 'Clenched Fist Salute' raised by African American athletes Tommie Smith and John Carlos at the Mexico Olympics in October 1968. Smith renders this event in its proper complexity, discussing not only the political background to the salute itself and its immediate aftermath, but also the ways in which the gesture has been sanctioned by posterity, making the two athletes, who were widely vilified at the time, into heroes now frequently (and retrospectively) honoured for their stand.

In Chapter 9, **Rob Steen** discusses the 'D'Oliveira Affair' of 1968, in which Basil D'Oliveira, a cricketer born in South Africa but by then, following residential qualification, a prominent member of the England cricket team, was omitted from the party selected to tour South Africa during the forthcoming winter. Steen confronts a myth that has prevailed for much of the history of modern sport – namely that it can be, and largely has been, kept separate from politics. The D'Oliveira episode is, like the other moments explored in this book, shown in its full complexity but at least two things become clear from the chapter: first, that the very people who professed to be keeping politics out of sport were often the ones most zealously engaging in bringing the two together and, second, that in the post-colonial world those who wanted to see their country play international sport but who nevertheless practised state racism, would have to choose either one or the other.

Returning, in Chapter 10, to the theme of sporting females, the next essay considers an important four-year passage (1970–3) in the career of the American tennis player Billie Jean King. This period includes Billie Jean's televised Battle of the Sexes challenge match against the self-styled (and self-promoting) male chauvinist Bobby Riggs in 1973 – a somewhat kitsch moment in the history of sport since the Second World War. But the principal purpose of **Jaime Schultz** in this chapter is to place King in the context of the politics of women's tennis and, in that regard, to show King to have been an important exponent of, and campaigner for, physical feminism.

Chapter 11 by **Elliott Gorn** is once again about a period of time in the life of a particular sportsperson, rather than about a specific moment. The objective here, as with Chapter 6, is to portray the early days of sport celebrity – this time, in relation to males. The United States of America was the first society to commercialize sport on a grand scale and it was perhaps to be expected that the first male sport celebrities would emerge there. Moreover, it was probable that such a person would be drawn from the 'fight game' with its deep roots in the migrant-descended American working class. This chapter describes the social world of the Irish American boxer John L. Sullivan, widely regarded as the first sportsman to be recognized, via the nascent mass media, to be a 'star'. (This chapter is the only one in the book to have been published before. It first appeared in the *Virginia Quarterly Review*, Vol. 62, No. 4 (Fall, 1986), pp. 614–33. Permission to re-publish it here is gratefully acknowledged.)

Chapter 12, by **David Andrews** and **Andrew D. Grainger**, provides an important and perceptive analysis of the 'Packer Affair' in Australian cricket. In 1977, Kerry Packer, a newspaper magnate, angered that his Channel Nine TV station had been denied the right to broadcast the coming Test cricket series in Australia, resolved to run his own tournament and to employ many of the world's leading cricketers to play in it. This was a vital moment in the growing relationship between sport and television and, as the writers show, an important example of the growing 'Disneyization' of sport – a key feature of sport under late capitalism. Following this episode cricket began to become a brand.

The penultimate chapter, by **Michael L. Silk** and **Jessica Francombe**, provides important insights into the regular re-visitation in English life of '1966' – the year in which England won the football World Cup. Silk and Francombe argue that the recurrent invocation of 1966 – seen again in the media 'build-up' to the South Africa World Cup in 2010 – as a kind of jogger of the national memory is an important example of 'cultural pedagogy' – that is, teaching through culture: what we sing, what we remember, what we like and so on tell us who we are. They suggest that contemporary corporate merchandising of '1966' (the flags, the bags, the T shirts...) has mobilized a kind of Englishness that, in the early twenty-first century, calls up a simpler English time when men were men, jobs were for life and England (supposedly) dominated world football. This has served to reconcile the English working class to the new market realities: unopposed neoliberal ideology and drastic cuts in public expenditure. The (currently 44) 'years of hurt' since England won the World Cup have merged with the comparable 'years of hurt' that followed the deindustrialization and privatization of the Thatcher, Major, Blair and Brown administrations.

The final essay, by **Barbara Keys**, is particularly apt. It demonstrates the inadvisability of trying to tie key changes in sport culture to a particular moment. In this instance the writer David Maraniss recently claimed that the Olympics of 1960, which were held in Rome, were 'the Games that changed the world'.[6] In a patient and eloquent analysis, Keys shows that there is little ground for believing this, the principal moral of her argument being that sport culture changes not through single, one-off seismic events, but steadily over time, in relation to social processes and developments.

I'd like to express my grateful thanks to Stuart Whitmore and to a number of contributors for their help in the development of this book.

Notes

1. See John Bale, *Roger Bannister and the Four Minute Mile: Sports Myth and Sports History*, London: Routledge, 2004; John Bale (ed.), *Sport in History*, Special Issue: 'The Sporting Barrier: Historical and Cultural Interpretations of the Four-Minute Mile', Vol. 26, No. 2, 2006.
2. See Roland Barthes, *Mythologies*, London: Paladin, 1973 (first published 1957), p. 143.
3. Ibid.
4. See Angus Calder, *The Myth of the Blitz*, London: Jonathan Cape, 1990.
5. Eric Hobsbawm and Terence Ranger (eds.), *The Invention of Tradition*, Cambridge, at the University Press, 1983.
6. See David Maraniss, *Rome 1960: The Games That Changed the World*, New York: Simon and Schuster, 2008.

1
The Invention of Sporting Tradition: National Myths, Imperial Pasts and the Origins of Australian Rules Football

Tony Collins

The history of sport has become a palimpsest. Meanings, interpretations and purposes are written and rewritten over that history as people seek to give a broader significance to the act of play. Details and fragments are reassembled and rearranged to create a story that meets the desires and demands of different generations, social groups and ideologies.

These stories have been fashioned around particular incidents, such as Babe Ruth's 1932 supposedly 'called' home run; artefacts, like W.B. Wollen's 1895 'Roses Match' painting of a northern English rugby match; or philosophies, for example de Coubertin's reinvention of the Greek Olympics as a beacon of amateur sport.

But the most powerful re-imagined narratives are the creation stories of particular sports. William Webb Ellis' picking up that ball and running with it for the first time at Rugby School in 1823 and Abner Doubleday's invention of baseball at Cooperstown in 1839 have little to commend them as examples of historical accuracy.[1] Yet their resonance lives on, not least in the name of rugby union's world cup and at Doubleday Field, Cooperstown's ball park. These invented traditions acquired their power and resilience because they articulated the desires of each sport for special social significance. For rugby union, Webb Ellis demonstrated that this was a game created by and for the middle classes. For baseball, Doubleday confirmed that this was a uniquely American game.

In 2008 a ferocious debate broke out in Australia about the origins of Australian Rules football (AFL), ignited by the publication of a lavishly illustrated official history, *The Australian Game of Football: Since 1858* that aimed to celebrate the 150th anniversary of the first Australian football match.² The code was founded and has its centre in Melbourne. Its national competition, the Australian Football League, was until 1990 named the Victorian Football League, and outside of New South Wales and Queensland it is Australia's most popular code of football.

Two of the opening chapters in the book detailing the formative years of the code were written by the widely respected Melbourne historian Gillian Hibbins. The first, 'Men of Purpose' recapitulated much of her earlier detailed work on the individuals who drew up the first rules of football in Melbourne in 1859. A second, much shorter, piece scrutinized and dismissed as 'a seductive myth' the popular belief that the sport had its origins in Aboriginal ball games and dismissed it as a 'seductive myth'.³ Nothing in these chapters was new or unknown to historians. Yet it attracted the wrath of many Australian Rules supporters and writers across the game's heartlands. Accusations of inaccuracy, insensitivity, poor scholarship and even racism were raised. Throughout the middle of 2008 a battle raged across newspapers, radio, television, the Internet and even literary magazines over what seemed to be the minutiae of the football rulebook.

For historians, it was a rare moment. Like astronomers witnessing the birth of star, they were observing a new sporting tradition in the process of being invented.

Inventing an Australian tradition

The major charge against Hibbins' work was that she had ignored the influence of Aboriginal ball games, and especially one called Marn Grook, on the sport's early history. Her adversaries argued that Tom Wills – the man who had written *Bell's Life in Victoria* in July 1858 suggesting the formation of a football club and who had been one of the four men who drew up the first set of football rules in Melbourne in 1859 – was heavily influenced by Marn Grook when he drew up the rules of Australian football. The reason for this influence was, in the words of Martin Flanagan, author of *The Call*, a novel based on Wills' life:

It's recorded that games of Aboriginal football, commonly called Marn Grook, were played at the Victorian gatherings and that one of the groups that attended the meetings, or corroborees, were the Tjapwurrung. Wills grew up in Tjapwurrung country, his father being the first white settler in the Ararat area, arriving in 1838 when Tom was three.⁴

According to nineteenth-century descriptions of Marn Grook by white European colonists, the game featured high kicking and leaping for a ball. 'The ball is kicked high in the air, not thrown up by hand as white boys do, nor kicked along the ground, there is general excitement who shall catch it, the tall fellow stands the best chance,' wrote James Dawson in 1881. 'When the ball is caught it is kicked up in the air again by the one who caught it, it is sent with great force and ascends as straight up and as high as when thrown by hand.'[5] Descriptions such as this were combined with accounts of Wills' boyhood friendships with Aboriginal children to claim that the true origins of Australian football were to be found in Aboriginal ball games.

There are a number of significant problems with this idea. Firstly, there is no evidence to suggest Wills was the primary force behind the drawing up of the 1859 set of football rules. He was merely one of the men who drew up a code of rules for the Melbourne Football Club on 17 May 1859.[6] Secondly, there is nothing in the historical record to suggest that Wills, who despite being born in New South Wales was educated at Rugby School in England, was in the least influenced by Aboriginal ball games. As Gregory de Moore has found during his exhaustive biographical research, there is not a single mention of the subject in any of Wills' private or public writings. Quite the opposite in fact, as Wills favoured rules that bore a closer resemblance to those of Rugby School, such as a crossbar on the goalposts and a designated kicker to take kicks at goal.[7]

Moreover, all supporters of the 'Wills/Marn Grook tradition' shared a common misapprehension, best expressed by Ciannon Cazaly in the literary magazine *Meanjin*. She quoted James Dawson's 1881 account of the ball being kicked high in an Aboriginal game and concluded by saying 'to me, that sounds a lot like what happens at the MCG most weekends' (Melbourne Cricket Ground is the sport's premier stadium).[8] The problem, of course, is that this is an anachronism – the description may sound like what happens at the MCG *today* but it does not sound like an Australian Rules match during the sport's formative period.

Indeed, its now characteristic 'high mark', where a player leaps above an opponent to catch the ball in the air, seems only to begin to become a significant feature of the game in the mid-1870s, almost 20 years after the first rules were drawn up. In its 1876 edition the handbook of the game, *The Footballer*, advised players to avoid 'jumping for marks' because of its danger.[9] Rugby-style loose scrummaging was a more important part of the game in its early years than the high mark. Such was the importance of scrummaging that the 1874 Victorian rules of football laid down that 'a scrummage commences when the ball is on the ground, and all who have closed round on their respective sides begin kicking it'. Even as late as the 1890s complaints were made in Melbourne that the game had become dominated by scrummaging in which sides would often each have ten players competing for the ball. Indeed, AFL in its formative years bore little resemblance to either Aboriginal ball games or its modern self.[10]

Characteristics of invented sporting traditions

This type of anachronistic misinterpretation is a feature of all forms of invented tradition. As Eric Hobsbawm and Terence Ranger noted in their introduction to their 1983 collection, *The Invention of Tradition*, 'the peculiarity of "invented" traditions is that the continuity with ("a historic past") is largely factitious... they are responses to novel situations which take the form of reference to old situations, or which establish their own past by quasi-obligatory repetition'.[11]

Moreover, we can go further and identify four other key characteristics shared by invented sporting traditions.

The first of these is that the 'founding father' of the sport must have had minor rather than extensive involvement in it. Webb Ellis had no association with football after he left school. Doubleday built a career in the US military apparently undisturbed by participation in baseball. Similarly Wills' major contribution to the development of football in Victoria occurred while he was secretary of the Melbourne Cricket Club. The lack of substantive long-term engagement with the sport is an important factor in such invented traditions due to the 'narrative space' it leaves open for speculation and supposition.

Secondly, the weight of evidence to support the invented tradition is based largely on hearsay or personal affirmation, usually of one person. Thus Webb Ellis's role was founded on nothing more than the testimony of Matthew Bloxam, an old boy of Rugby School who based his case entirely on his 'enquiries'. The Doubleday story was predicated on a letter written by Abner Graves, who had been a five-year old child in Cooperstown in 1839. Wills' famous claim that Australia now had 'a game of our own' is based on the recollections of his cousin H.C.A. Harrison written some 60 years later. Claims that his boyhood interaction with Aboriginal youths provided the inspiration for his innovations in football rules lack any supporting evidence.[12] Again, the plasticity of the evidence allows the story to be fashioned according to the needs of the advocate.

It is also worth noting that the idea that Tom Wills picked up for AFL as a boy is one that can also be found in the mythology of William Webb

Ellis. It has been claimed variously that he got the idea for picking up the ball and running with it during childhood visits to Ashbourne, where a form of mass, folk football is played, or from boyhood visits to Ireland (his father was a British Army officer based at Tipperary) where a football game based on handling was played. There is no evidence for either assertion.[13]

The third common feature is that these traditions emerge at pivotal moments in each sport's history. Thus the Webb Ellis myth came to prominence at the time when rugby union felt itself to be under the threat of working-class domination. This resulted in the split in the rugby code of 1895, the same year that the Old Rugbeian Society's inquiry into the origins of the game decided that Webb Ellis was its inventor. Similarly the Doubleday myth emerged in the mid-1900s, at the same time that baseball was emerging from the turmoil of labour relations' and intra-league disputes, which had led to the National League's acceptance of the American League as partner major league and the first World Series in 1903. In Australian Rules, the Wills/Marn Grook tradition emerged as the sport sought to position itself as the national football code of all Australia, highlighted by the transformation of the Victorian Football League into the Australian Football League in 1990 and its subsequent national expansion.

Fourthly, supporters of the invented tradition ultimately base their position on an unverifiable act of faith rather than on the historical record. Thus the official 1970 history of the Rugby Football Union says of those who wanted proof of the Webb Ellis story, 'what these materialists are unable to understand is that not only are we unable to prove it, but also that this fact does not bother us at all'.[14] In a similar vein, the exhibit on Doubleday at baseball's Hall of Fame museum in Cooperstown reads: 'in the hearts of those who love baseball, he is remembered as the lad in the pasture where the game was invented. Only cynics would need to know more.'[15] Writing in defence of the idea that Australian Rules derived from an Aboriginal game, Jim Poulter wrote that 'we should reverse the onus and accept the indigenous origins to our game, unless somebody can clearly prove otherwise', putting those who disagree in the position of having to prove a negative.[16] All three statements serve to seal off their arguments from critical inquiry, elevating the invented tradition to an article of faith for followers of each particular sport. Once more, the history of sport becomes the tablet on which to use the metaphors of play to write about contemporary society.

And finally, the invented tradition projects back into the past a picture of how the inventors would like to see the world. For rugby union followers, Webb Ellis confirmed their belief that theirs was a game for the middle classes. For baseball, Doubleday supported their ideas of American exceptionalism. And for Australian Rules, the Wills/Marn Grook story of cultural exchange through sport between European colonists and Aboriginal peoples offers a sanitized view of the bloody genocidal reality of race relations in nineteenth-century Australia.

However, like all Australian sports, Australian football was no less racist than the society that nurtured it. One of its most famous clubs, Essendon, was for the early decades of its history known as 'the bloodstained niggers'. Aboriginal football clubs were often excluded from local competitions and even the greatest of Aboriginal footballers faced racist taunts and humiliations.[17] Doug Nicholls, who in 1976 was to become governor of South Australia, transferred from Carlton FC to struggling Northcote FC in the late 1920s, because the other Carlton players claimed that he smelled. The Marn Grook story views Aboriginal involvement in Australian Rules football through the rose-tinted spectacles of the late-twentieth century.

In fact, the AFL's record of racial equality is no better than that of its major rival, the National Rugby League. The percentage of Aboriginal footballers in the National Rugby League (NRL) in 2009 stood at 11 per cent, the same as in the Australian Football League, although a further 29 per cent of NRL players were of Polynesian heritage, a group with little representation in the AFL. Moreover, some of the arguments used to support the Wills/Marn Grook story are based on racially stereotyped conceptions of the 'natural affinity' of Aboriginal players for Australian Rules. 'They express themselves both on and off the field, to watch them play is exhilarating at times', claimed Essendon coach Matthew Knights in 2008, a racially inflected view that is unlikely to be expressed about 'European' players.[18]

Since the 1950s the debate on the historical roots of Australian Rules football has been a barometer of changing ideas about Australian national identity. In 1958 the journalist C.C. Mullen published a history of the game which speculated, on the flimsiest of evidence, that the sport had been popular in Scotland in the years before World War One, reflecting the prevailing sense of 'different but equal' Britishness then prevalent in Australia.[19] In the 1960s and 1970s, after Harold Macmillan's government had effectively broken the imperial link by ending free entry into Britain for all Commonwealth citizens and applying to join the European Common Market without consulting Australia, a more radical nationalist outlook became fashionable, bringing comparisons with Ireland to the fore. In 1967 an Australian Rules side undertook a short tour of Ireland, where 'Waltzing Matilda' was played before matches instead of 'God Save The Queen' (still the Australian national anthem at the time). The idea that Australian Rules was derived from Gaelic football also became fashionable, despite the fact that Melbourne rules were codified 25 years before those of the Gaelic game.[20]

Today, the dominant liberal (and largely official) view of Australian national identity is based on reconciliation between European and Aboriginal Australians, as highlighted by Prime Minister Kevin Rudd's 2008 apology to the country's Aboriginal population for what he described euphemistically as 'mistreatment'. Thus it has now become popular to imagine that Australian Rules has its roots not in Australia's imperial past but within its native Aboriginal culture. The invention of an Aboriginal pre-history for the sport therefore plays the role of, as Hobsbawm and Ranger point out for different contexts, 'establishing or symbolizing social cohesion or the membership of groups, real or artificial communities' and 'legitimizing institutions, status or relations of authority'.[21] For the AFL, it plays a crucial role in authenticating its claim to be Australia's true national football code.

The Imperial world of football

The case of Wills highlights a broader problem in the writing of the history of sport, that of *assumed* traditions. A series of assumed traditions in the history of football in Australia are accepted by almost all historians, regardless of their acceptance or otherwise of the Wills' mythology. First and foremost among these historical assumptions is the belief that, to quote Richard Cashman, 'the invention of new sports and sports culture is indisputably linked to national pride'.[22] Yet, like an invented tradition, this assumption projects backwards into history's current thinking about the role that sport plays in expressing national and regional identity.

If we look at the context of football in Melbourne in the mid-nineteenth century, we find that there is nothing uniquely Australian about the rules of football played in the colony at that time. As Hobsbawm noted, sport was 'one of the most significant of the new social practices of this period, for the middle classes as much as the working classes', because 'it provided a mechanism for bringing together persons of an equivalent social status otherwise lacking organic social or economic links'.[23] Wills, Thompson and the rest of the Melbourne football pioneers were merely emulating the activities of their equivalents in Britain. 'Football' in its generic sense at that time was a cultural expression of middle-class British nationalism. 'It is the very element of danger in our own out-of-doors sports that calls into action that noble British pluck which led to victory at Agincourt, stormed Quebec and blotted out the first Napoleon at Waterloo,' wrote one Australian commentator, echoing the widespread imperial belief that football was one of 'those important elements which have done so much to make the Anglo-Saxon race the best soldiers, sailors and colonists in the world'.[24]

In the mid-nineteenth century, all organized or codified forms of football were seen as part of this Muscular Christian cult of games. Football was played not merely for recreational enjoyment, but also for a moral purpose. The sport, whatever its rules, was played for the lessons it taught and the examples it set. It was part of the socialization of young men and boys across the British Empire, and the wider English-speaking world. Muscular Christianity, and the football codes based on its principles, was an expression of British cultural nationalism. And the colonies of Australia were nothing if not British. Indeed, as the economist and noted Australian Rules historian Lionel Frost has noted, such was the integration of the Australian colonies with the economy and culture of the British Isles that 'nineteenth century Australia may therefore be thought of as a "suburb of Britain"'.[25] It should therefore not be surprising that when we examine those features of early Australian Rules football that are held to be uniquely Australian, we can find their equivalents in the wider Imperial world of football.

To modern eyes, perhaps the most distinctive feature of the game is the lack of an offside rule. For Rob Pascoe this is the first of the 'basic laws of Australian Rules which distinguish it from Rugby and reflect Melbourne's different social history'.[26] Attacking players can advance beyond the ball-carrier, and indeed their opponents, at will and without restriction. In contrast, the rugby codes allow no player to advance beyond the ball carrier and even soccer has an offside rule.

But in the primordial soup of football's early evolution in the 1850s and 1860s, offside rules were fluid and changing. Although the major public school codes of football had rules regulating offside play, the rules of the Sheffield Football Club, formed in 1857 (two years before the first Melbourne rules were drawn up), had no offside rule at all until 1863. Sheffield FC had a considerable influence on early football in England and by 1867 enough clubs played under its rules for it to form the Sheffield Football Association. The Sheffield FA eventually merged with the London-based Football Association in 1871.[27] It should also be noted that Gaelic football and basketball, although both codified after the Melbourne rules (in 1884 and 1891, respectively), did not and do not have offside rules, suggesting the possibility that dissatisfaction with offside restrictions was not uniquely Australian.[28]

The second distinctive feature of Australian Rules is the mark. Robin Grow's belief that 'if there is one aspect of the Australian game that distinguishes it from all other codes, it is the mark' is shared by almost all historians of the sport.[29] Yet the mark was commonplace across almost all football codes. Commonly known as a 'fair catch', the rule allowed a player who caught the ball cleanly before it touched the ground to claim a 'free kick', the right to kick the ball unimpeded by his opponents. The second edition of C.W. Alcock's *Football Annual* in 1868 outlined in some detail the widespread use of this rule:

Catching the Ball

At Harrow, Rugby, Winchester, Marlborough, Cheltenham, Uppingham, Charterhouse, Westminster, Haileybury, Shrewsbury [public schools], Football Association, Sheffield Association and Brighton [College], catching is allowed, but at Eton, Rossall and Cambridge the ball must not be touched with the hands.

Privileges obtained by a Catch

At Harrow and Shrewsbury, 'free kick' with a run of three yards is allowed. According to the Football Association, Sheffield Association, Charterhouse and Westminster, the ball must be kicked at once. Rugby, Westminster, Marlborough, Cheltenham, Haileybury, Brighton and Uppingham allow running with the ball, on certain conditions. At Winchester a player may run with the ball as long as one of the other side follows him: at Uppingham until he is stopped or held.[30]

The original 1863 rules of the Football Association specified that 'if a player makes a fair catch he shall be entitled to a free kick, provided he claims it by making a mark with his heel at once'. Even the Cambridge version of football originally allowed the ball to be handled, as an 1863 description of a game under Cambridge rules highlights: 'any player may stop the ball by leaping up, or bending down, with his hands or any part of the body'.[31]

Although its use disappeared from the London and Sheffield Football Associations by the late 1860s, the fair catch was already a major feature of the Rugby game. Indeed, the definition of a fair catch was rule number one in Rugby School's 'Football Rules' of 1845.[32] The 1862 rules of Blackheath FC, a founding member of not only the Rugby Football Union (RFU) but also of the Football Association, defined a fair catch as

> a catch direct from the foot or a knock-on from the hand of one of the opposite side; when the catcher may either run with the ball or make his mark by inserting his heel in the ground on the spot where he catches it, in which case he is entitled to a free kick.[33]

This was essentially the definition adopted by the RFU in its 'Laws of the Game' at its foundation in 1871. It was not until 1892 that the RFU rules specified that a mark could only be made by a player catching the ball on the ground, thus outlawing what in Australian Rules would be called a high mark, when the mark is awarded to a player who catches a ball while airborne.[34]

The third distinctive feature of Australian Rules football is the fact that the player in possession of the ball can only run with it if it is bounced or touched on the ground regularly (current rules specify that this must be done at least every 15 metres, although it was originally 'five or six yards').[35] Again this can be found in Gaelic football, although given the limited state of scholarly research into the history of that code it is impossible to assess how much the Irish game was influenced by the Australian. Nevertheless, bouncing the ball to advance it was not unknown in English codes of football in the 1860s. Indeed, the 1864 rules of football as played at Bramham College, a private school in West Yorkshire, explicitly incorporated this rule. Carrying the ball by hand was not permitted, but the college's football rule 14 stated that 'the ball may "bounced" with the hand, and so driven through the opposite side'.[36] It is worth noting that this rule was in use at least two years *before* it was introduced into the Australian game in 1866.

Some historians, such as Gillian Hibbins, have argued that Melbourne footballers' distaste for 'hacking' in the Rugby School game was uniquely Australian and that the Melburnians' ban on hacking was 'the chief decision which was ultimately to give rise to a distinctive Australian football game'. Most famously, J.B. Thompson claimed in 1860 that he and his fellow rule-framers forbade hacking because 'black eyes don't look so well in Collins Street [Melbourne's commercial centre]'. But again, this concern was also widespread in Britain. The FA outlawed hacking and many rugby-playing clubs also forbade hacking, Rochdale and Preston Grasshoppers being two of the more prominent sides to do so. The reasons were exactly the same as those expressed by J.B. Thompson. Before the first Lancashire versus Yorkshire rugby match in 1870, the Yorkshire captain Howard Wright sought an assurance that his opponents would not hack, because, echoing Thompson, 'many of his men were in situations and it would be a serious matter for them if they were laid up through hacking, so it was mutually agreed that hacking should be tabooed'.[37]

Alongside the technicalities of playing the game, those who assert that Melbourne football rules were distinctively Australian also point to broader features of the sport. The most sophisticated of these historians is Richard Cashman in his outstanding *Sport and the National Imagination*. Cashman argues that there are also participatory and spatial issues in Australian Rules that reflect the uniqueness of Australian society in the mid-nineteenth century:

> Australian football is an expansive game both in terms of the size of the playing field, the number of players – originally there were 25, then 20, then, in modern times, 18 – and the length of play. In the early years play continued until a goal was scored or dusk intervened.... Some of the large Australian football grounds are approximately twice the size of rugby, soccer or American football grounds.... The character of Australian football reflected this abundance of cheap land in close proximity to cities and suburbs. It is a practical demonstration that Australia has abundant space for sport.[38]

But, again, such features were not unique to Melbourne. Neither the original rules of the FA nor of the RFU specified the number of players in a team. Until 1876, when it was reduced to 15, the usual number of players in an adult rugby team was 20, although schoolboy sides would often number far in excess of 20. At Rugby School, 'Big-Side' matches, as described famously in *Tom Brown's Schooldays*, regularly had 60 players on each side.[39] Nor was there any fixed period of play specified in the rules of the RFU, the FA or the Sheffield FA. As in Melbourne, teams generally decided that a game was won when one side had scored a specified number of goals. Perhaps the most famous example of this elasticity is in the 1862 football rules of Rugby School, of which rule 39 stated that: 'all matches are drawn after five days, or after three days if no goal has been kicked'.[40]

The question of the dimensions of the Australian Rules' playing area is regularly highlighted as having a distinctively Australian character. Rob Pascoe in his simultaneously evocative and provocative *The Winter*

Game argues that Australian Rules' 'oval and rather carelessly measured' playing field distinguishes the pre-capitalist mind-set of English football codes from that of Antipodean 'post-feudal society'.[41] There are two problems with this assumption. Firstly, as Geoffrey Blainey has demonstrated, most football grounds in the first 15 years of the Australian code were not oval but rectangular, exactly the same as every other football code. The first published diagram of player positions, in the Melbourne yearbook *The Footballer* of 1876, shows a rectangular playing area. Indeed, as late as 1903, the *Laws of the Australasian Game of Football* published by the New South Wales Football League also showed a rectangular pitch.[42]

The second problem is that the English football codes were similarly imprecise in their specifications. The Melbourne rules of 1858 and 1860 stated that 'the game shall be played within a space of not more than 200 yards wide'. The 1866 revised version of the rules was the first to define the length and width of the playing field. Rule one stated that

> the distance between the goals shall not be more than 200 yards; and the width of the playing space, to be measured equally on each side of a line drawn through the centre of the goals, not more than 150 yards.[43]

This sounds uncannily similar to the original rule number one of the FA, which stated that 'the maximum length of the ground shall be 200 yards, the maximum width shall be 100 yards', as did that of the Sheffield Association. The difference in dimensions was quantitive, not qualitative. What is more, and in contrast to the English soccer-style codes and the Melbourne rules, the RFU did not originally specify *any* measurements for the size of the rugby pitch. It was not until 1879 that an amendment was added to rugby's 'Laws of the Game' that laid down that 'the field of play must not exceed 110 yards in length nor 75 yards in breadth'.[44]

Cashman also points out that in Melbourne 'matches were sometimes held up so that players and officials could debate the rules', as an example of the democratic nature of the Australian game.[45] Yet, again, this was no different to football in Britain, where negotiation between captains over disputed points had become so common by 1870 that it was accepted practice to add time on to the length of a match to cover the time lost for play through arguments. As York rugby club captain Robert Christison admitted, 'the more plausible and argumentative a player was, the more likely he was to be considered as a captain'. As in

Australia, a referee or umpire was not initially part of either the rugby or soccer codes.[46]

Thus in the context of the mid-nineteenth century 'British world' of sport, the set of rules developed in Melbourne in the 1850s and 1860s was simply one of many dozens of variations in the playing of football throughout the British Empire. As a correspondent to *Bell's Life in London* wrote in 1861, football's 'rules are as various as the number of places in which it is played'. The Melbourne rules were no more indicative of Australian nationalism than the Sheffield FA's rules were of an aspiration in the north of England for independence from the south. J.B. Thompson's famous remark that the Melbourne rules would 'combine the merits of both [Eton and Rugby football codes] while excluding the vices of both' did not express antagonism towards British football but was merely an echo of the wider debate going on in British football circles about how to develop a common set of rules for all adult football clubs. Many sides in England had gone down the same path as the Melburnians: Lincoln FC, for example, described their rules as 'drawn from the Marlborough, Eton and Rugby rules'.[47] The impetus for the drawing up of the Cambridge football rules in 1848 was also based on this desire to transcend the divisions between Eton and Rugby rules, and the formation of the Football Association in 1863 was based on an unsuccessful attempt to take the best from each variant to create a unified football code.[48]

Thus Wills' alleged remark about developing 'a game of our own' had nothing to do with national pride but was just one more example of commonplace frustrations felt towards the existing rules of football. With its own code of rules Melbourne did indeed have a game of its own – just like English public schools had games of their own, like Cambridge University had a game of its own and like the city of Lincoln too had a game of its own.[49]

The 'Britishness' of Australian rules football

Commonly underlying the assertion that Australian Rules was created in opposition to football as played in Britain is the assumption that there is a parallel between the Australian game and Gaelic football. Scholars such as Patrick MacDevitt in his *May the Best Man Win* have suggested that the impetus behind the anti-British political sentiment of the Gaelic Athletic Association (GAA) could also be found in Australian football.[50] However, this view is supported by no other evidence than the fact that

Australian Rules is different to other football codes played in Britain. No substantive example of a GAA-style political stance has been found in Australian sport.

That is because the culture of Australian Rules was firmly British. Its terms of reference were entirely within a British, Muscular Christian framework. Thus the motto on the masthead of the house organ of the Victorian Football League (VFL), the *Football Record*, first published in 1912, was the unashamedly British 'Fair Play is Bonnie Play'. Nor, despite the significant Irish presence in Victoria, was the VFL the slightest bit hesitant in its monarchism. 'It is the law of the game that there must be matches on the day when all the English-speaking world is celebrating the anniversary of the birthday of our King,' the *Football Record* informed its readers in June 1914.[51] In Sydney, where the sport was not strong, the New South Wales Football League published in the early 1900s a guide to the sport titled *The Australian Game*, which described football as being 'the British boy's training'.[52] These sentiments were not merely for public consumption. Internally, the leadership of Australian Rules resorted to British values and principles in organizational debates. Thus, when in 1911 a dispute broke out between the South Australian National Football League and the Australasian Football Council, Charles Brownlow of the AFC defended his position by saying that 'it was only British fair play to hear both sides of the question'.[53]

Of course, the sport promoted itself as uniquely Australian, not least when contrasting itself to other codes of football. But this was not counterposed to being British. Like cricket in Yorkshire or rugby union in Cornwall, the promotion of a strong regional identity that thought itself superior to the metropolitan centre did not threaten, nor seek to threaten, its essential underlying Britishness.

This can be seen in the famous address by Australian Prime Minister Alfred Deakin to the sport's 1908 Silver Jubilee carnival, in which he stated that 'the game is Australian in its origin, Australian in its principle, and, I venture to say, essentially of Australian development. It and every expression of the sporting spirit go to make that manhood which is competent for a nation's tasks.' This is often interpreted by Australian historians to be a clear expression of a distinct Australian national sporting identity. But in fact the speech was an example of the widespread use across the British Empire of sport as an auxiliary to the growing martial patriotism that had emerged since the Anglo-South African war and which was to become increasingly shrill in the years leading up to 1914. Not only did Deakin quote Newbolt's British militaristic poem

Vitai Lampada, the final sentence of his speech made it clear that the 'nation's tasks' were preparation for future wars conducted by *Britain*:

> And when the tocsin sounds the call to arms, not the last, but the first to acknowledge it will be those who have played, and played well, the Australasian game of football before they play the Australian game of nation-making and nation-preserving *to stand by the old land*. [author's emphasis][54]

Unsurprisingly, the outbreak of World War One saw the leadership of Australian Rules follow the lead of football organizations in Britain. As in Britain, defenders of amateur sport sought to halt professional sport now that the 'greater game' was under way. In Victoria, the chief proponents of this view could be found in the Metropolitan Amateur Football Association (MAFA). Its president L.A. Adamson declared in 1914 that Victorian Football League (VFL) players who continued to play during the war should receive the German Iron Cross instead of a premiership winner's medal for their services to the enemy. In 1915 the VFL's rival league, the Victorian Football Association, voted to stop playing for the duration of the war. The VFL itself split down the middle. In 1915 it voted narrowly to cease playing but the season continued because its constitution required a majority of three-quarters for binding decisions. In 1916 only four VFL clubs took to the field, a number that increased to six in 1917. Both sides of the debate looked to Britain for justification of their stance. The MAFA pointed to the actions of the Rugby Football Union in cancelling all rugby for the duration of the war.[55] Those in the VFL who sought to carry on used the example of soccer in England and Scotland. South Melbourne official L. Thompson explained 'they did not put off football playing in England', while an editorial in the *Football Record* commented:

> I saw by the cable messages the other day that in Scotland they were going about business as usual, and had given out that their sporting affairs would go on too, notwithstanding the war. Consequently I see no good reason why the same sort of confidence in regard to the ultimate issue of the greatest war in history should not be expressed in Melbourne.[56]

The appeal to Britishness was repeated during World War Two. Writing in its annual report of 1941, the VFL's secretary L.H. McBrien wrote that 'the history of the British race is replete with evidence of the value of sport to prepare men for the fighting front'.[57]

It proved difficult for the sport to cut its umbilical cord to Britain and its imperial trappings. As late as 1970 the Melbourne *Herald Sun* published a guide to the 1970 VFL season entitled *Football '70: the Royal Year*, the first five pages of which consisted of photographs of Elizabeth II and her family. Perhaps most telling is the fact that 'God Save The Queen' was still being sung at the VFL Grand Final in 1980, despite 'Advance Australia Fair' having become the official Australian national anthem (at least on non-regal occasions) in 1974.[58]

The only example in Australian Rules of an anti-British political opposition is that of J.J. Simons, the secretary of the Western Australia Football League in the decade before World War One and founder of the quasi-militaristic Young Australia League. Simons promoted the Rules game over what he saw as 'British' soccer, not least because he suspected that the British government favoured unrestricted Chinese immigration that would undermine white Australia. *Australia Junior*, the magazine of the Young Australia League, featured racist cartoons of Chinese people to highlight to its young readers the supposed threat to Anglo-Saxon Australia. Even this opposition was based on racial fears commonly held across the British Empire and reflected in many ways what Humphrey McQueen described as the desire of many emigrants Down Under to create a 'New Britannia'.[59] And sadly, as we have seen, racism in Australian Rules was not confined to the fringe activists of the sport. An editorial in the *Football Record* in 1912 congratulated players for their performances in recent games with the words 'the work was high class. No Chinese factory stamp on it. Pure White Australian'.[60]

But in general it appears that it wasn't until the 1960s that the idea that Australian Rules football could represent an overt cultural *opposition* to Britain became commonly accepted. Westminster's abrupt shift in its relationship with Australia, exemplified by Britain's undermining of the economic link with Australia in favour of the European Common Market and the 1962 Commonwealth Immigrants Act's restrictions on Australian visitors to the UK, forced Australians to rethink their relationship with the culture of the 'Mother Country'. This was reflected strongly in sport. In both rugby league and cricket, Australian attitudes moved from a rivalry underpinned by an ultimate deference to a distrust that bordered on hostility.[61] Although Australian Rules football had no organizational link with British sports, something of this changing relationship can be seen in its attempts to build an alliance with the Gaelic Athletic Association and its abandonment of 'God Save the Queen' on the 1967 tour of Ireland. Indeed, lacking cricket and rugby league's heritage of colonial tours, it was much easier for Australian Rules to be seen as a symbol of the spirit of independence that had become popular in Australia. Today, the AFL's continual focus on the heritage of the sport, real or imagined, is a conscious part of its strategy to portray itself as the uniquely Australian national sport.

Historiography and the invention of sporting tradition

As in all historical disputes, the debate over the origins of Australian football raises a number of historiographical questions.

The first of these is the extent to which historians accept the assumed traditions of a sport. Those who take the *a priori* viewpoint that the sport's origins are uniquely Australian naturally look for points of difference with those football codes based in Britain. Thus evidence of the similarity between the various types of football, such as the widespread use of the mark, is overlooked or dismissed. The differences that are taken as the point of departure are largely drawn from football as it played today, not in the 1850s and 1860s. Commonplace assumptions are taken as self-evident and historical research starts from these premises, rather than beginning with an interrogation of them.

Moreover, because differences are automatically assumed, there is little rigour applied to the logic by which those differences are affirmed. Thus Australian Rules is seen as both an older form of football than those in Britain – Bill Murray describes it as 'the code of football that is closest to nature, the game of the noble savage' – and a new sport that reflects the modernity of its Melbourne birthplace – Rob Pascoe believes that it 'reflects the liberal social democratic milieu in which it was formed'.[62] Other examples of one-sided logic can also be seen, such as the claim that the use of cricket ovals for Australian Rules football matches demonstrates the unique abundance of space in Australia. Yet it could also be argued that this shared use of pitches, far from highlighting an abundance of space, could be taken to suggest restricted space for sport, forcing cricket and football to share the same playing area.

This is related to a second problem, that of hindsight. By assuming that the configuration of the football codes in their formative years is essentially the same as exists today, non-contextual or ahistorical meanings and significance can be ascribed to events or actors. Thus the phrase 'a game of our own', which was unexceptional in the football context of 1860, now assumes the importance of 'a radical proclamation' from the perspective of modern Australian nationalism.[63] By looking the wrong way through the telescope of history, those facts that support the beliefs of today will be confirmed and those details that do not will appear inconsequential.

By way of illumination, it is instructive to examine a British colonial football code that did not survive. In Cape Town, South Africa, a unique set of football rules developed in the 1860s and 1870s based on a variation on Winchester College rules. Known locally as 'Gog's Game', after the nickname of Canon George Ogilvie, the headmaster of Cape Town's Diocesan Collegiate School where it originated, it was codified in 1873. By 1876 the *Cape Times* could refer to it as the 'well-known game which has grown up in the colony... its principles are generally understood by young South Africa'.[64] It was only in 1879 that the local game began to be eclipsed by rugby. But these South African rules of football were not an expression of English-speaking South African nationalism, simply an attempt to find the most enjoyable way to play the game. Yet the logic underlying the assumptions of Australian Rules' historians should lead them to suggest that Gog's Game was a nascent nationalist project that reflected the character and particularities of the local population.

This also raises a third methodological issue, that of comparative perspective. Because the creation and sustenance of invented tradition is based on a sport's claim to be unique and exceptional, origin stories exclude meaningful comparisons with other sports. Indeed, for Australian Rules the British-based football codes are the 'other' against which it defines its origins. Yet without a comparative perspective, any research into the history of football, of whatever code, becomes a form of 'tunnel vision' that can only confirm the premise from which one started.

But, of course, this is not simply a debate about historical evidence or research methodology. Invented traditions today play an important commercial role in the business of sport. Rugby union's world cup is fought for the Webb Ellis trophy. Well-heeled spectators at Twickenham can enjoy luxury corporate hospitality in the stadium's exclusive 'Webb Ellis Suite'. Visitors to Cooperstown can stay in Doubleday-inspired hotel suites, visit the Doubleday exhibit in the Hall of Fame and watch a game at Abner Doubleday Field.[65] Heritage is now part of the 'revenue stream' of all commercial sporting organizations. Presenting a complex and often uncomfortable view of the past that challenges existing and often cherished notions of sporting history is rarely compatible with 'revenue-generating' schemes.

So, while the AFL's campaigns since the 1990s to stamp out racial vilification in the sport are highly laudable, its use of heritage for commercial and public relations purposes is no different from any other sporting body. Martin Flanagan's rhetorical yet actually plaintive question – that if the Wills/Marn Grook story is wrong, 'the AFL has got no more claim to having a connection with indigenous culture than rugby union does and so all these big games it has like the Marn Grook Trophy and "Dreamtime at the G", what are they? Are they just marketing exercises?' – has to be answered largely in the affirmative.[66] Commercial exigency today plays a major role in the shaping of sporting history and heritage. The refashioning and even the falsification of history for commercial, publicity or political reasons is just as likely in sport as it is in any other public activity. Indeed, the shallow reach and narrow focus of much of the current historical research into sport means that commercialism faces little challenge when its misapprehensions enter the public arena.

In many ways, this is only to be expected. The contemporary importance of sport to commonplace, 'everyday' nationalism increases the power of the invented traditions of sport.[67] As we have seen in the case of Australian Rules football, the stories that are re-woven from the historical fabric of sport are not merely narratives about sport, but are projections of how contemporary Australian nationalism wants to view its national history. As Hobsbawm commented in regard to the invented traditions of the USA, they became important because 'Americans had to be made'.[68] So too did Australians in the final third of the twentieth century, as the umbilical link with 'Mother' Britain was cut. Just as the culture of 'football' in the mid-nineteenth century offered supporters of the British Empire, whether at 'home' or in the colonies, the reassurance of the superiority of the middle-class British male, so too today each football code provides comforting confirmation of its ideology and values to its supporters. In the constant reinvention and revitalization of national identity, sport occupies a central position.

And that means that if, in Ernest Renan's words, getting its history wrong is part of being a nation, so too is inventing its history a part of every sport's cultural function.

Acknowledgement

The author thanks the Menzies Centre for Australian Studies at King's College, London, for their generous granting of an Australian Bicentennial Fellowship in 2007 that enabled the research for this article to take place. I am grateful to Professor Carl Bridge for his support and to

Professor Graeme Davison for asking the question 'what about Aussie Rules?' in response to a paper given by me on Britishness and Australian rugby league.

Notes

1. For Doubleday, see Harold Seymour, *Baseball: The Early Years*, Oxford: Oxford University Press, 1960, pp. 8–12 and James A. Vlasich, *A Legend for the Legendary: The Origin of the Baseball Hall of Fame*, Wisconsin: Bowling Green State University Press, 1990, pp. 162–8. For Webb Ellis, see Tony Collins, *Rugby's Great Split*, London: Frank Cass, 1998, pp. 5–8 and William Baker, 'William Webb Ellis and the Origins of Rugby football', *Albion*, Vol. 13, No. 2 (Summer, 1981), pp. 117–30. Douglas Booth in his The Field, Abingdon: Routledge, 2006, Ch. 6, pp. 111–26, discusses sporting myths but in the spirit of post-modern agnosticism draws no distinction between actuality and invention.
2. Geoff Slattery (ed.), *The Australian Game of Football*, Melbourne, 2008. Controversially, the book was published to mark the match between Melbourne Grammar School and Scotch College on 7 August 1858, which, as Gillian Hibbins pointed out, was definitely not played under any type of 'Australian' rules. See Hibbins, 'Are We Celebrating a Year Too Early'?, *The Age* (Melbourne), 2 August 2008 and Martin Flanagan's defence, 'Football Ebbs and Flow with Tide of Society', The Age (Melbourne), 9 August 2008.
3. Hibbins, pp. 31–45 in *The Australian Game of Football*. Her views had already been widely disseminated in 'The Cambridge Connection: The English Origins of Australian Rules Football' in J.A. Mangan (ed.), *The Cultural Bond*, London: Frank Cass, 1993, pp. 108–27, and (with Anne Mancini) in *Running with the Ball: Football's Foster Father*, Melbourne: Lynedoch Publications, 1987. For a useful overview of the 'Football History Wars' as they were dubbed, see Bob Stewart, 'Myth-Busting in Australian Rules Football', *Bulletin of Sport and Culture*, No. 30 (September 2008), pp. 3–5.
4. Martin Flanagan, 'A Battle of Wills', *The Age*, 10 May 2008. The general outline is also suggested in David Goldblatt's *The Ball Is Round: A Global History of Football*, London: Viking, 2006, p. 93.
5. James Dawson, *Australian Aborigines: The Language and Customs of Several Tribes of Aborigines in the Western District of Victoria, Australia*, Melbourne: George Robertson, 1881, p. 85.
6. See Hibbins and Mancini, pp. 23–4.
7. Greg de Moore, *Tom Wills: His Spectacular Rise and Tragic Fall*, Sydney: Allen & Unwin 2008, pp. 161 and 283–6. As Rob Hess has pointed out, Wills involvement in the 1868 Aboriginal cricket tour of the UK make it unlikely he would disguise any Aboriginal influences. Rob Hess and Matthew Nicholson, 'Beyond the Barassi Line' in Bob Stewart (ed.), *The Games Are Not the Same*, Melbourne: Melbourne University Press, 2007.
8. Ciannon Cazaly, 'Off the Ball', Meanjin, Vol. 67, No. 4 (2008) at http://www.meanjin.com.au/editions/volume-67-number-4-2008/article/off-the-ball/ (accessed 11.23, 28 May 2009). The quote is from James Dawson,

Australian Aborigines: The Language and Customs of Several Tribes of Aborigines in the Western District of Victoria, Australia, Melbourne, 1881, p. 85.
9. Geoffrey Blainey, *A Game of Our Own*, 2nd Edition, Melbourne: Information Australia, 2003, pp. 118–22.
10. Blainey, pp. 64–5 and 227. For scrummaging, see Robin Grow, 'From Gum Trees to Goal Posts, 1858–76' in Rob Hess and Bob Stewart (eds), *More Than a Game*, Melbourne: Information Australia, 1998, pp. 15, 30 and 78.
11. Eric Hobsbawm and Terence Ranger (eds), *The Invention of Tradition*, Cambridge: Canto, 1983, p. 2.
12. In reality it was J.B. Thompson, one of the four Melbourne rule-framers who used the phrase in the *Victorian Cricketers' Guide for 1859–60*. See Hibbins and Mancini, p. 18.
13. On Ashbourne, see R.T. Rivington, 'William Webb Ellis and Ashbourne Football', *International Journal of the History of Sport*, Vol. 8, No. 1 (May 1991), pp. 133–9. On Ireland, see Edmund Van Esbeck, *100 Years of Irish Rugby*, Dublin, 1974, p. 7. I am grateful to Dr. Liam O'Callaghan for bringing this to my attention.
14. U.A. Titley and R. McWhirter, *Centenary History of the Rugby Football Union*, London: RFU, 1970, p. 9.
15. Quoted in Stephen Jay Gould, 'The Creation Myths of Cooperstown' in his *Triumph and Tragedy in Mudville*, New York: Norton, 2003, p. 199.
16. Jim Poulter, *From Where Football Came*...(September 2007) at www.sportingpulse.com/assoc_page.cgi?client= 1-5545-0-0-0&sID=75914&news_task=DETAIL&articleID=5854332&sectionID=75914 (accessed 13.05, 25 May 2009).
17. For example, see the accounts of Aboriginal footballers in the 1920s and 1950s in Richard Broome, *Aboriginal Victorians: A History Since 1800*, Sydney: Allen and Unwin, 2005, pp. 224–5. For a post-war example, see Peter Read, *Charles Perkins, A Biography*, Melbourne: Penguin revised edition, 2001, pp. 51–2.
18. For participation rates, see Roy Masters, 'League's Polynesian Powerplay Muscles in on Indigenous Numbers', *Sydney Morning Herald*, 24 April 2009, and Antonia MacGee, 'Sports Stars Embrace Rudd Apology', *Herald Sun* (Melbourne), 13 February 2008, which also includes the Knights' quote.
19. C.C. Mullen, *History of Australian Rules Football from 1858 to 1958*, Carlton, 1958. The Scottish link is examined in John Williamson's *Football's Forgotten Tour*, Applecross: Williamson, 2003.
20. For the tours to Ireland, see Peter Burke, 'Harry and the Galahs' *ASSH Bulletin*, No. 29, December 1998, pp. 9–17. Barry O'Dwyer, 'The Shaping of Victorian Rules Football', *Victorian Historical Journal*, Vol. 60, No. 1, pp. 27–41, argues the case for the Irish origins of the game, but see Blainey, pp. 187–96 for a debunking of this myth.
21. Hobsbawm and Ranger, p. 9.
22. Richard Cashman, *Sport and the National Imagination*, Sydney, 2002, p. 43.
23. Eric Hobsbawm, 'Mass Producing Traditions: Europe, 1870–1914' in *The Invention of Tradition*, pp. 298–9.
24. Quoted in Leonie Sandercock and Ian Turner, *Up Where Cazaly?*, Melbourne: Granada, 1981, p. 33. Yorkshire Post, 29 November 1886. See also W.F. Mandle 'Games People Played: Cricket and Football in England and Victoria

in the Late-Nineteenth Century', *Historical Studies*, Vol. 15, No. 60 (April 1973), pp. 511–35.
25. Lionel Frost, *Australian Cities in Comparative View*, Victoria: Penguin, 1990, p. 4.
26. Rob Pascoe, *The Winter Game*, 2nd Edition, Melbourne: Mandarin, 1996, p. xiv.
27. For the Sheffield FA, see *Rules, Regulations & Laws of the Sheffield Foot-Ball Club*, Sheffield: The Club, 1859, Brendan Murphy, *From Sheffield With Love*, Sheffield: Sports Books, 2007, pp. 37–41, and Adrian Harvey, Football: *The First Hundred Years*, London: Routledge, 2005, pp. 11 and pp. 162–3.
28. See Joseph Lennon, *The Playing Rules of Football and Hurling 1884–1995*, Gormanstown: NRC, 1997, p. 10.
29. Grow, p. 21.
30. C.W. Alcock (ed.) *Football Annual*, London: John Lilywhite, 1868, p. 74.
31. Rule eight, reprinted in *The Rules of Association Football 1863*, Oxford: Bodleian Library, 2006, p. 49. John D. Cartwright, 'The Game Played by the New University Rules', reprinted in Jennifer Macrory, *Running with the Ball*, London: Collins, 1991, p. 164.
32. *Football Rules*, Rugby: Rugby School, 1845, p. 7.
33. Percy Royds, *The History of the Laws of Rugby Football*, Twickenham: RFU, 1949, p. 6.
34. RFU rules of 1871, reprinted in O.L. Owen, *The History of the Rugby Football Union*, London: Playfair, 1955, pp. 65–72. Royds, pp. 7–8.
35. Rule eight of the 1866 rules, in Blainey, p. 225.
36. 'Bramham College Football Rules, October 1864' in *The Bramham College Magazine*, November 1864, p. 182.
37. Hibbins, 'The Cambridge Connection', p. 114. Thompson in the *Argus*, 14 May 1860, quoted in Blainey, p. 45. For hacking in Britain, see Collins, *Rugby's Great Split*, pp. 10–12.
38. Richard Cashman, *Sport and the National Imagination*, Sydney: Walla Walla Press, 2002, p. 45.
39. See, for example, the reminiscences of Arthur Pearson in 'Rugby as Played at Rugby in the 'Sixties', *Rugby Football*, 3 November 1923.
40. 'Football Rules of 1862' reprinted in Jennifer Macrory, *Running with the Ball*, London, 1991, p. 101.
41. Pascoe, pp. xv–xvi.
42. Blainey, pp. 49–50. Thomas P. Power (ed.) *The Footballer: An Annual Record of Football in Victoria and the Australian Colonies*, Melbourne: Henriques & Co., 1876, p. 126. NSWFL, *The Laws of the Australasian Game of Football*, Sydney: NSWFL, 1903 in the E.S. Marks Collection at the Mitchell Library, Sydney, shelfmark 728.
43. For pitch dimensions see the respective rules reprinted in Blainey, pp. 222–4.
44. For the FA and Sheffield FA, see C.W. Alcock (ed.) *Football Annual*, London, 1869, pp. 40–1. For rugby, Royds, p. 1.
45. Cashman, p. 46.
46. See Collins, p. 13.
47. *Bell's Life in London*, 8 December 1861. J.B. Thompson in the *Victorian Cricketers' Guide, 1859–60*, quoted in Hibbins and Mancini, p. 27. *Bell's Life*, 21 November 1863.

48. Harvey, p. 48.
49. 'A game of our own' was first attributed to Wills in the 1923 autobiography of fellow rule-framer H.C.A. Harrison, *The Story of an Athlete*, Melbourne, 1923, reprinted in Hibbins and Mancini, p. 119. For a broader discussion, see also Roy Hay 'The Last Night of the Poms: Australia as a Post-Colonial Sporting Society' in John Bale and Mike Cronin (eds), *Sport and Postcolonialism*, Oxford: Berg, 2003, pp. 15–28.
50. Patrick McDevitt, '*May the Best Man Win*': *Sport, Masculinity, and Nationalism in Great Britain and the Empire, 1880–1935*, London: Palgrave, 2004, pp. 11–12.
51. *Football Record*, Vol. 1, No. 1 (27 April 1912) and Vol. 3, No. 9 (13 June 1914).
52. NSWFL, *The Australian Game*, Sydney, undated, unpaginated, in the E.S. Marks Collection at the Mitchell Library, Sydney, shelfmark 728.
53. Australasian Football Council, minutes of meeting August 1911, p. 81.
54. Deakin's speech of 28 August 1908 is reprinted in full in Richard Cashman, John O'Hara and Andrew Honey (eds), *Sport, Federation, Nation*, Sydney: Walla Walla Press, 2001, p. 111–13. For similar sentiments expressed by British rugby union writers in the years before 1914, see Tony Collins, 'English Rugby Union and the First World War', *The Historical Journal*, Vol. 45, No. 4. (2002), pp. 797–817
55. Joseph Johnson, *For the Love of the Game: The Centenary History of the Victorian Amateur Football Association*, South Yarra: HylandHouse, 1992, p. 50. For the war and Australian Rules in general, see Richard Stremski, *Kill for Collingwood*, Sydney: Allen and Unwin, 1987, pp. 63–5; Dale Blair, 'War and Peace 1915–1924' in Hess and Stewart, *More Than a Game*, Ch. 4 and Michael McKernan, 'Sport, War and Society: Australia 1914–18' in Richard Cashman and Michael McKernan (eds), *Sport in History*, Queensland: University of Queensland Press, 1979, pp. 1–20. For a British perspective see Colin Veitch, 'Play up! Play up! And Win the War!' Football, the Nation and the First World War 1914–15', *Journal of Contemporary History*, Vol. 20 (1985), pp. 363–78.
56. Thompson in *Football Record*, Vol. 4, No. 1 (24 April 1915) Editorial by 'Wideawake', *Football Record*, Vol. 3, No. 20 (29 August 1914).
57. McBrien quoted in Keith Dunstan, *Sports*, Melbourne, 1973, p. 184.
58. *Australian Football Yearbook 1990*, Melbourne, 1990, p. 157. I am grateful to Roy Hay and Dave Nadel for their help and advice on this issue.
59. See Simons' magazine *Australia Junior*, Vol. 2 (undated, c. 1907), in the J.C. Davis Collection, Sydney: Mitchell Library.
60. *Football Record*, Vol. 1, No. 5 (25 May 1912).
61. For a discussion of this change see Tony Collins, 'Australian Nationalism and Working-Class Britishness: The Case of Rugby League Football', *History Compass*, 3 (2005) AU 142, pp. 1–19.
62. Bill Murray, *The World's Game: A History of Soccer*, Aldershot: Scholar Press, 1994, pp. xiii–iv. Pascoe, p. xvi.
63. See Martin Flanagan's 2001 Alfred Deakin lecture *Sport: Touchstone of Australian Life* transcribed at http://www.abc.net.au/rn/deakin/stories/s291489.htm, accessed 14.06, 31 May 2008.
64. *Cape Times*, 18 July 1876, quoted in Floris van der Merwe, 'Gog's Game: The Predecessor of Rugby Football at the Cape, and the Implications Thereof' paper presented to the 35th Conference on Social Science in Sport, Ljubljana,

Slovenia, 24–27 August 2006. I am grateful to Prof van der Merwe for providing me with a copy of his paper.
65. The importance of the Doubleday myth to baseball's Hall of Fame is described in Vlasich.
66. Flanagan interviewed on ABC television's 'The 7.30 Report', 22 May 2008, transcript available at http://www.abc.net.au/7.30/content/2007/s2253142.htm (accessed 14.21, 20 September 2008).
67. See Michael Bilig, *Banal Nationalism*, London: Sage, 1995. I have avoided the word 'banal' as it carries the assumption that this type of nationalism is harmless.
68. Hobsbawm, p. 271.

2
From Evil to Expedient: The Legalization of Professionalism in English Football, 1884–85

Dave Russell

'One of the most radical changes which has taken place in football since the game was first brought into the prominence which it now enjoys'. The *Athletic News*'s analysis of the Football Association's decision in July 1885 to legalize professionalism in the English game captures well both the significance of the ruling and the sense of new possibilities that it engendered.[1] Three years later, the need to provide the regular and genuinely competitive fixtures that would render the newly accepted professionalism a viable commercial proposition led to the formation of the Football League. While many individuals found the commercial face of professional football unacceptable, by 1905–06 some 5 million spectators were being drawn to the games played in the 20-strong First Division of an organization that was, in Matthew Taylor's words, 'possibly the most influential sporting competition in England'.[2] Perhaps only the reforms to wages and transfer policy in the early 1960s and the launch of the FA Premier League in 1992 are comparable in their importance within English football history to these events of the 1880s.

Unsurprisingly, then, the emergence of professionalism and the conflicts it generated, particularly in the period 1884–85, have produced thoughtful and informative commentary from historians of sport.[3] However, a number of key aspects remain understudied and, while in no sense staking claim to fundamental revisionism, this study seeks to provide a rather more nuanced account than we currently possess.[4] It commences with a short but necessary descriptive account of the emergence of professionalism and the FA's response to it; many existing accounts are rather selective and, in particular, exclude the critical FA rule changes of early October 1884. It then moves on to discuss the specific contribution of the British Football Association, an organization whose contribution to events has often been alluded to but rarely examined, and, finally, considers the interplay of social, cultural and sporting factors that underpinned both the shape and the outcome of the conflict.

The road to professionalism

As organized association football began from the mid-1870s to extend its social base and popular appeal, it would have been strange indeed if outstanding footballers from working-class backgrounds had not accepted financial inducements from the most ambitious clubs. The idea of being paid to play was deeply embedded in popular sport and, for that matter, in other forms of popular recreation.[5] Football 'professionalism' in its early forms covered a multitude of activities in which payment, sometimes only for appearances in specific games, might be combined with or replaced by, such inducements as the provision of paid work outside the game or the awarding of public house tenancies or similar business opportunities. It is difficult to identify the first paid footballer, although Peter Andrews and James Joseph Lang, arriving from Scotland to play for the Sheffield-based Heeley and Wednesday clubs, respectively, in 1876–77, appear to have been amongst the earliest examples; Andrews had come south for business reasons but Lang was found a suitable sinecure in a knife-grinding workshop.[6] The arrival at Turton FC in 1878 of Fergie Suter, later of Darwen and Blackburn Rovers, almost certainly began the flow of 'Scotch professors' into Lancashire that was to place the county at the heart of the professionalism debate.

The ferocity of that debate must not be allowed to obscure the point that importation and financial remuneration were not actually illegal until the early 1880s. It was the challenge to the supposed spirit of the game that led to initial concern. There was certainly never a 'pure' amateur game in England in which the extrinsic pleasures of 'playing the game' entirely overrode financial considerations. Public school old boy sides expected substantial expenses payments on their provincial tours, while the receipt of justifiable travel expenses and compensation for lost wages, so-called 'broken time', was accepted practice amongst clubs competing in the FA Cup. However, many critics claimed increasing abuse of such practices and demanded action. Hostility towards emergent professionalism took many forms, genuine practical concerns mixing, often within the mind of the same individual, with social unease and varying degrees of snobbery. Some critics stressed the negative impact on the competitive balance of the game, suggesting that wealthier clubs would take the best players, others the social and moral problems that would flow from the existence of men paid only to play and whose extensive leisure time would open opportunities for drinking, gambling and the setting of the worst kind of example to the wider working class. The loss of social status experienced by 'gentlemen' amateurs as mere 'players' encroached on their previously largely exclusive social space, gave further cause for anxiety.[7]

Although it was the upper-middle and upper-class players and administrators associated with sides from London and the Home Counties that set the social and moral tone of amateurism in early association football, leading clubs in most other parts of the country seemed, at least initially, broadly to have shared their philosophy. Many of those who eventually advocated the legalization of professionalism had initially opposed importation and payment. Again, there was no significant campaign for legalization until 1884, merely an ever-growing number of clubs prepared to flout existing conventions and nascent legislation to gain a competitive advantage, eventually large enough to make conflict inevitable. The detailed geography of that process is hard to capture due to the necessarily secretive nature of proto-professionalism, but it seems to have been effectively non-existent in London and the south where the social demography of the game still largely excluded the types of player most likely to have adopted it, strongly resisted but undeniably in existence in provincial centres such as Birmingham, Nottingham and Sheffield, and increasingly accepted in Lancashire. When, in 1884, the fiercely anti-professional Scottish FA named over 50 *émigré* players unable to play in Scotland without its special dispensation, a clear accusation of professionalism, only one, Aston Villa's Archie Hunter, was located outside Lancashire.[8] As will be seen, these regional variations were fundamental to the nature of the debate that followed.

As early as 1881, FA secretary Charles Alcock accurately prophesied that 'there is no use to disguise the speedy approach of a time when the subject of professional players will require the attention of those on whom devolves the management of Association Football'.[9] January of that year had already seen the banning of 11 players in Sheffield for taking part in matches for the Sheffield Zulus, an exhibition side declared to be professional by the hostile local FA the previous year, and the pace and extent of controlling legislation and policing activity at both local and national level began to increase.[10] As Tony Mason has argued, much initial concern focused on the importation of players as much as payment itself, with the Lancashire FA imposing, in May 1882, a two-year county residence qualification on any player involved in the Lancashire Cup.[11] However, the issues quickly elided for, in the words of one contemporary journal, players could not be expected 'to forsake home and kin without any tangible means of support'.[12] 1882 thus saw the FA introduce its Rule 16, stating that:

> Any member of a club receiving remuneration or consideration of any sort above his actual expenses and any wages actually lost by any such player taking part in any match, shall be debarred from taking part in either cup, inter-Association or International contests, and any club employing such a player shall be excluded from this Association.[13]

Following the example of the Birmingham, Lancashire and Sheffield Football Associations, the national body also established a subcommittee charged with seeking out illegal practices. Little action followed, although in early 1883 the Birmingham FA banned three local players on the grounds that they had previously been paid in Lancashire while, in November, Accrington FC was expelled from the FA for making illegal payments.[14]

Events following an FA Cup tie between Preston North End and the London side, Upton Park, in January 1884, gave the matter new prominence and urgency. Accused before the FA Committee in London of using paid professionals in the game – the club frequently fielded nine Scots at this stage – Preston secretary, William Sudell, admitted to importation by finding work, but argued that this was standard practice throughout Lancashire and the midlands and not in breach of regulations.[15] Although the club was consequently expelled from the FA (it was reinstated in October 1884), this confession from a highly respected figure focused the attention of the senior administrators. Alcock felt that the introduction of properly managed and controlled professionalism, of the type that he knew in his parallel role as secretary of Surrey County Cricket Club, represented the solution to what was clearly a growing problem. On 11 February, supported by Dr Ebenezer Morley of Blackburn Rovers and seconded by Norman Bailey of Clapham Rovers and the then England captain, he succeeded in passing a resolution at the FA Committee stating simply that 'the time has come for the legalization of professionalism'.[16] However, stiff opposition had been expressed during the debate, not least from the Birmingham delegates, and by the time that a General Meeting of clubs took place to discuss the resolution on 28 February, it had been mobilized sufficiently for an amendment to be tabled defining 'veiled professionalism' and importation as 'serious evils' and asking for the establishment of a subcommittee to seek suitable strategies 'for the repression of these abuses'.[17] This amendment, moved by N.L. 'Pa' Jackson, Assistant Secretary of the FA and founder of the rigorously amateur Corinthians club, was passed by a large majority. The tortuous journey towards July 1885 had begun in earnest.

The subcommittee recommended a substantial body of punitive measures, which were agreed to by a special meeting of the FA on 24 June 1884. Special meetings with powers of suspension and expulsion were to be convened, with suspected clubs and individuals players expected to prove their innocence. Broken-time payments were to be allowed for only one day of the week (receipts as proof) and all training expenses not paid by players were deemed to fall outside of Rule 16 and defined as illegal. Finally, in a major blow against importation, only English players were to be allowed to play in the FA Cup.[18] However, the targeted clubs appear to have taken a relaxed attitude, with *Athletic News* commenting on the number of new Scottish arrivals in Lancashire at the start of the season.[19] At the August Annual General Meeting, a particularly vocal opponent of professionalism, Charles Crump of the Birmingham FA, backed by Jackson, succeeded with a condemnatory resolution stating that 'all clubs which are enrolled in the Association be strongly recommended not to make arrangements with clubs which are openly setting the rules of the Association at defiance'.[20] A small number of Lancashire sides including Great Lever and Halliwell, the latter with six Scots in its team, declined to enter the FA Cup rather than risk sanction and deeper investigation of their mode of operation, but there was little sign of concern.[21]

The situation changed dramatically when, on 6 October, the FA introduced three new measures bringing English football at elite level into a full-blown crisis; this, far more than the better known incident between Preston and Upton Park, was the defining moment in the protracted debate. Under a new Rule 25, it was announced that any club entering the FA Cup that organized fixtures with any other club *'whether belonging to the Association or not'* [author's emphasis] that employed 'imported players or players of different nationality to that of the club itself whose names have not been submitted to and approved by the Association Committee, or remunerating their players in any way beyond that permitted... shall be excluded from the competition'. Rule 26 decreed that the qualification period for players whose names were to be thus submitted to the FA for approval should be backdated until 1 September

1882. Finally, Rule 27 demanded that all club secretaries complete a form in regard to players 'of different nationality' or who had joined the club 'from another district' that gave full details of their length of residence, occupation and wages both at their previous and current clubs and provided a reason for a player's most recent change of residence.[22]

'Consternation has been rampant among Lancashire clubs since Monday evening. The blow at professionalism and importation has been struck at last,' announced the Bolton-based *Football Field*. The threat posed to the proto-professional game was severe indeed. Rule 25 presented the most immediate problem by undermining the pre-arranged fixture list and, ironically, not least for those FA member clubs accepting the new framework. Not only were they forced to avoid fellow affiliates whose arrangements they suspected, but also the substantial number of clubs that were believed to be paying players but were not FA members – Darwen FC, for example, keen FA loyalists – immediately found themselves facing six consecutive cancellations.[23] Rule 26, in its turn, badly affected clubs with large numbers of recent imports while Rule 27, as well as demanding a potentially disastrous level of disclosure, was so loosely worded, with the key term 'district' left undefined, that some clubs genuinely did not know what constituted a legitimate player. On 10 October, 17 individuals representing 9 Lancashire clubs met in Bolton to discuss the issue. The meeting was reconvened five days later in Blackburn, with 17 clubs in attendance, and once again on the 23rd at which point the group designated itself the 'British Football Association' (BFA). Finally, in Manchester on 30 October, under the chairmanship of Bolton Wanderers' George J. Healey, 70 delegates representing 37 clubs attended a BFA meeting called 'to promote and consolidate a powerful organization which will embrace clubs and players of every nationality'.[24]

The Football Association now beat a remarkably swift retreat. On 3 November, after what *Athletic News* termed 'warm discussion', the FA Committee accepted a resolution brought forward by the Lancashire FA secretary, R.P. Gregson, calling for the suspension of Rule 25, established yet another investigative subcommittee and called a 'special general meeting to consider the whole question of professionalism and importation'.[25] At a meeting in Manchester on 12 November, the subcommittee voted by 7–4 that 'it was now expedient to legalise professionalism under stringent conditions'. The patient Alcock was once again the proposer, supported by N.L. Jackson, now moving away from his previous opposition on the grounds that repression simply was not working. The full FA Committee endorsed this position by 13 votes to 5, agreeing to a set of conditions for the control of professionalism very similar to those eventually endorsed in July 1885; a clause excluding professionals from the FA Cup, unsurprisingly unpopular in Lancashire, was dropped in early December.[26] The proposal now came before a special meeting at the Freemasons Tavern in London on 19 January 1885, drawing representatives from over 60% of the FA's member clubs and an even higher proportion of its affiliated county associations.[27] While Alcock spoke powerfully and Sudell's speech acknowledging that Preston paid its players, but could never be proved to be doing so, was a key contribution, probably the most important intervention in the long term was the public conversion to professionalism of Aston Villa secretary, William McGregor, and his acknowledgement of the existence of illegal payment within Birmingham football. Crump, in conjunction with his Midlands compatriot W.H. Jope and Sheffield's William Peirce-Dix and W.F. Beardshaw, were amongst the main speakers for the opposition. After vigorous debate, the Alcock–Jackson proposal was carried by 113 votes to 108, but fell comfortably short of the two-thirds majority required for rule changes. Finally, in scenes suggestive of considerable confusion and uncertainty in the minds of the delegates, a subsequent motion from Peirce-Dix, stating that 'Professionalism in football is an evil, and as such should be suppressed', was passed by 125 votes to 68, only three short of the binding majority.[28]

The situation could hardly be allowed to stay in this chaotic state, and a subsequent special meeting was held in London on 23 March 1885, billed by *Football Field* as 'A second rehearsal of that highly popular farce "The Professional Difficulty".' While an attempt by the Lancashire FA to replace the necessity for a two-thirds majority with simple majority voting, a device good enough for Parliament as Gregson waspishly argued, was heavily defeated, the supporters of managed professionalism much improved their position, winning the vote on this occasion by 106–69. The two-thirds majority was again elusive, but was now clearly in sight. McGregor's speech in January had signalled that the more ambitious provincial clubs outside of Lancashire were increasingly alert to the benefits of legalization and others were presumably now following his lead; three leading Derby clubs, for example, also now voted in favour.[29] Peirce-Dix, rather than reprise his oppositional motion, now preferred to call for the establishment of a subcommittee dedicated to finding a compromise.[30] It was at this moment and with this decision that legalization in some form became a certainty. The nine-man subcommittee circularized all affiliated associations with a number of questions, but the poor response received suggested a tired constituency, happy to be led and largely sure of the outcome.

At the third and final special meeting on 20 July, the number of delegates was much reduced. This partly resulted from a rule change successfully mooted by Lancashire representatives at the March meeting reducing representation, in the interest of economy, to one per club, but it also reflected a general acceptance of the inevitable; while 85 clubs attended in March, only 35 were present now.[31] Morley of Blackburn and Robert Lythgoe of the Liverpool FA moved for professionalism under strict management. Professionals seeking to play in the FA Cup would have to have been born or lived for two years within six miles of the ground or headquarters of their club and all professionals were to be registered with the FA and could not play for more than one club in a season without permission. There was no debate amongst the sparse gathering and in barely ten minutes this divisive chapter came to a close. Many contemporary sources, including *The Times*, record the vote as 35–12, while Geoffrey Green's 1953 official history of the FA rendered it 35–15. However, *Football Field* claimed 35 in favour with 5 against and 7 abstentions; given the latter's close reporting throughout the controversy, it is these figures that are accepted here.[32] Whatever the mathematics, controlled professionalism was now in place and a crucial moment on football's modernization had been reached.

The British Football Association

Given the British Football Association's emergence at such a critical stage in the process outlined above, it is slightly surprising that it has not received fuller investigation in published works. Two central, inter-related questions emerge in regard to the organization: to what extent did its establishment represent a serious attempt at a breakaway from the parent body, a potential precursor of rugby's split in August 1895, and what was its role in the final victory of the pro-professional lobby? Contemporary accounts tend to be highly coloured by personal history. J.J. Bentley, in 1885 secretary of Bolton Wanderers, one of the organization's most fervent affiliates, later claimed that the BFA, if now long forgotten, had 'once played a very important part in the history of the game'. N.L. Jackson, however, very much an FA insider in 1884–85 and consequently reluctant to acknowledge the role that external threats might have played, saw it as at best a minor element in the unfolding events. The 'loss of these clubs would have been of small moment to the parent body', he confidently assured his readers in 1900.[33]

Overall, it is difficult to see the BFA, certainly as constituted in 1884–85, as possessing anything resembling the clarity of purpose demonstrated by the northern rugby clubs at the heart of the 1895 breakaway. As noted, its largest meeting attracted some 70 delegates from 36 or 37 clubs, along with a representative of the Bolton and District Charity Cup Association. (The uncertainty as to the exact number of clubs stems from the disputed status of two Aston Villa delegates, noted in some press accounts as formal delegates, but firmly declared to be unofficial representatives by the club.) Not all of these clubs, however, joined the organization, with the *Football Field* declaring that 10 additional clubs had enrolled at the meeting, taking membership to 25.[34] With all due allowance for the newness of the body, this was a very modest number in comparison with the 165 affiliated to the FA and the 104 to the Lancashire FA. Again, only Aston Villa, officially or not, Sunderland and Walsall Swifts attended from outside Lancashire, rendering the organization's geographical base extremely narrow. Moreover, a number of the clubs attending the Manchester meeting were fairly minor in terms of playing record (of the 34 Lancashire clubs present, only 15 were FA affiliates, then a reasonable index of status and ambition), and, while most of the county's leading clubs were attracted, a few avoided it with greater or lesser degrees of ostentation. Blackburn Olympic and Blackburn Rovers, winners of the FA Cup in 1883 and 1884, respectively, were notable FA loyalists, completing the new paperwork and remaining in the Cup, as was Darwen FC, one of the few clubs formally to decline an invitation to the Manchester meeting.[35] A desire to remain at the heart of football's major competition, the role of senior officials from these clubs within the FA nationally and, especially in the case of Darwen's secretary, Thomas Hindle, personal prejudice against professionalism, all played a part. Whilst it is undoubtedly the case that other clubs might well have joined the BFA if the FA had not compromised so swiftly, it is difficult to believe that it would have received much support from outside Lancashire; the *Athletic News*, far from unsympathetic to the professional cause, certainly used this point as part of an editorial argument against the foundation of the BFA in November 1884.[36]

It is also unclear as to whether the BFA ever established a fully developed strategy with regard to its relationship with the FA. The idea for what became, effectively, its initial meeting on the 10 October 1884 came from John Roscow and Stephen Tillotson of Great Lever and Burnley, respectively, and was rooted in specific problems arising from Rule 25. A fixture between the two sides was scheduled but, given that Burnley FC, at that stage not an FA member, was clearly a proto-professional team, Great Lever risked FA sanction if the game went ahead. Burnley, in its turn, risked loss of revenue if the game was cancelled. The meeting, chaired by Sudell, was called to gauge the level of support Great Lever could expect if the game went ahead and punitive measures followed. The clubs eventually decided to play the match at their own risk, the meeting, in a less-than-radical stance, 'declining to commit itself'.[37] At the Blackburn meeting the following week, called, presumably, to discuss the general principles raised by the Great Lever problem, firmer action was taken. Following proposals from Bolton Wanderers, the seven clubs present who had entered the FA Cup agreed to withdraw from the tournament and, after much debate, all clubs represented agreed not to complete the new form introduced under Rule 27.

These, however, were both defensive measures, designed to disguise the clubs' financial procedures and to limit the FA's scope for punitive action. Moreover, Sudell, again in the chair, initially spoke against both of the measures eventually taken and counselled against the 'formation of a Northern Association'.[38] Only at the third meeting on 23 October, chaired by the apparently more radical Healey, was a formal body established with both a properly constituted committee and, 'the Chairman having pointed out the advisability of a title being adopted', a name. Even at the Manchester meeting, the emerging BFA appears to have viewed itself more as a pressure group than a potential new governing body. It is significant that the major outcome of the meeting was the sending of a deputation to the Lancashire FA calling for the latter to hold an emergency general meeting. Formal breakaway was not apparently an immediate objective.[39] The short-lived nature of the BFA as an effective force also needs to be stressed; indeed, its period of direct influence only lasted for perhaps two or three weeks in October and November 1884. Although there were brief references to its committee meetings in the sporting press from that point, it appears to have been content largely to monitor events. Rather inconsistently, given its initial stance on the organization, *Athletic News* actually criticized it for being 'too quiet' in the approach to the March general meeting, suggesting that it might need to 'take up the cudgels with more vigour...if the sham amateurs again carry the day'.[40]

For all these limitations, however, the BFA exerted influence in two critical ways. At the 15th October meeting, when only in its most nascent form, it agreed to take legal advice on the FA's new rulings.[41] The resultant view, taken by G.W. Heywood of the Northern bar, that the FA had no jurisdiction over the organization and management of games beyond the FA Cup, clearly justified opposition to Rule 25. The BFA's decision to circulate this finding immediately to all FA member organizations must have played a significant role in the FA's virtually immediate suspension of the new rulings.[42] The FA was never to admit to this, arguing that it was the detrimental consequences for clubs remaining loyal to the ruling body that had led to the rapid reversal.[43] There was undoubtedly some truth in this, but the FA clearly protested too much. The *Nottingham Daily Express*, no friend of the BFA, which it saw as a narrow Lancastrian pressure group, acknowledged that 'we should thank them for obtaining counsel's opinion' and met FA denial of the significance of this with the rejoinder 'oh no, not at all, neither! as says that "artful Dodger", immortalised by Charles Dickens'. Again, as *Athletic News* pointed out, the risk of damages claims against the FA that might follow a successful court action was a problem of which the organization was only too aware.[44]

Perhaps more important still was the pressure exerted by the BFA within Lancashire. Initially hostile to both importation and payment, despite their growing presence in the very clubs that its members represented, the Lancashire FA (LFA) leadership seems gradually to have accepted the inevitability of professionalism and the desirability of controlling it. It certainly tried, generally unsuccessfully, to provide some support for member clubs that fell foul of the national body on the issue, challenging the legality of Accrington's expulsion in 1883 on a procedural point and asking to see the evidence used to expel Preston North End from the FA Cup in 1884.[45] The committee also took swift action in October 1884, declaring that FA interference in games other than FA Cup ties was illegal and telling members that, as Rule 25 interfered unjustly with the county association's own regulations, clubs were to fulfil their Lancashire Cup games whatever the nature of the opposition.[46]

It was, however, ultimately committed to the national body. During the height of the crisis in late October, it tried hard to persuade local clubs to accept the other new regulations. In a letter to the *Athletic News* of 29 October, committee member Daniel Woolfall, of Blackburn Rovers, tested the political skills that eventually led to his being the first ever British President of FIFA, by suggesting that while Rule 25 was absolutely wrong, compliance elsewhere might prove less painful than assumed. He asked how many clubs that had completed registration forms had received challenges to individual players, and suggested that Rule 26 backdating registrations of players from different 'districts' to 1 September 1882 may prove not to be quite the obstacle some clubs believed it to be. There was no need for a breakaway, he argued, merely a clear decision in favour of professionalism. His implication that a strong LFA presented the best vehicle for bringing about change was probably correct, and there is little doubt that the organization would have fought for Lancashire interests within the FA where necessary. However, the emergence of a potential rival body undoubtedly gave even greater urgency to its activities. While the loss of the BFA clubs might have been of 'small moment' to the FA, the defection, partial or complete, of 34 clubs (30% of its membership), with the possibility of more to follow, would most certainly not have been so to the LFA; it moved on to the offensive and held the BFA in check because it simply had no alternative.[47] The fact that, immediately after the departure from the room of the BFA deputation, Gregson was empowered both to submit a resolution to the national body challenging Rule 25, and to call an emergency meeting of all affiliates if it fell, speaks very loudly indeed.[48]

As events unfolded from 30 October, the LFA, thus galvanized, became, alongside Alcock and his FA committee supporters, the critical grouping in the move to professionalism. Its key individual was secretary R.P. 'Dick' Gregson. A Blackburn Rovers committee member and a photographer by profession – he was to become the FA's official photographer and, more significantly, a pioneer of hospital X-ray photography in northern England – he had become the LFA's secretary in a highly competitive election in 1882.[49] He proved an effective public speaker, but probably his most significant role was as an organizer of proxy votes, a task given to him officially by the LFA.[50] Having himself had to persuade the organization to increase his secretarial stipend and allowances to attend FA business in London, he appreciated the importance of maximizing votes at meetings which many delegates often found expensive and inconvenient to attend. He worked tirelessly in approaching clubs, with *Football Field* claiming that 83 of the 106 votes cast in March 1885 were 'found' by Gregson. He was also adept at finding the actual proxies: several of the Preston North End team that had played the Corinthians in London days before, served in this fashion at the January 1885 special meeting, a rare example of professional players exerting influence within the political structures of Victorian football, albeit at one remove.[51] With Gregson as its representative, Lancashire football needed the BFA, at best, as a background presence to be invoked in times of crisis: it had played a vital role but had been denied a larger one by the flexibility of the game's existing organizational structures.

Taking sides

Historians have long acknowledged the complexity of the conflict over professionalism, with the best analyses consistently refusing to posit simple oppositions between classes or regions and prepared, as social and cultural historians are not always willing to do, to look for autonomous, 'sporting' reasons for decision-making.[52] As Matthew Taylor has argued, to explore these complexities in greater detail it is essential to know far more about the electoral geography and politics displayed, especially in the three general meetings between January and July 1885, and to look in greater detail beyond Lancashire, which has, understandably, been the focus of much scholarship.[53] Although this section attempts to pursue these issues in various ways, there are quite significant problems, often source-related, with which to contend. Not the least important is the fact that voting at general meetings was by head count, with no written record of individual club and association votes; a full record of the votes is thus unobtainable. More generally, many potentially valuable manuscript sources are not available – the FA minute books for 1884 and 1885, for example, are not currently traceable – and press reports, whether at local or national level, are often extremely thin, providing a record of decisions made, but little of the vital discussions that led to them. *Football Field*, which gave extensive coverage to the three key meetings and recorded full lists of all clubs (with numbers of delegates) and associations attending them, is an invaluable exception as are some other specialist football and sporting titles. Even when voting behaviour can be identified, the process of trying to equate (or not) attitudes to professionalism to particular social, cultural and geographical groupings is made difficult by a relative paucity of biographical data and by the fact that individual delegates may not necessarily be representative of the wider social status of the organization they represented. Yet again, delegates might not always have spoken for all sections of their local or regional football community. While the leading sides of both Wolverhampton and Nottingham, for example, were initially strong opponents of professionalism, the football correspondents of at least one newspaper in each town were not.[54] The discussion that follows is conducted in full acceptance of these current limits to our knowledge.

As has been clear throughout this study, geography mattered greatly to this debate and the simplest method of analysing it is to consider voting patterns at the general meeting in January 1885, when divisions of all kinds were at their sharpest.[55] Most press commentators agreed that clubs from Birmingham (Aston Villa apart), Nottingham and Sheffield were universally opposed to legalization at this stage, and the size of their combined delegations as listed in *Football Field* would suggest that these areas delivered about 50 of the 108 'anti-votes'. The Lincolnshire and Berks and Bucks FA contingents, representing associations that had both formally voted against professionalism, provided approximately another ten votes each.[56] Of the 113 votes cast in favour of Alcock's motion in January 1885, about 50 emanated from Lancashire, the area with the single largest body of representatives. Amongst clubs from the county, only Darwen FC passed into the anti-professionalism lobby. The personal opposition of the club's secretary, Thomas Hindle, was so deep that he, thinly disguised in the *Football Field*'s unfavourable report of his action as 'the ex-secretary to the most important provincial Football Association', was cited as one of the five delegates willing to vote against professionalism even as late as July 1885.[57] By far the best-represented region outside Lancashire was London, with its 21 clubs and local FA officials controlling about 40 votes.[58] This made them, alongside other upper-middle class and ex-public school sides in the south of England, critical power brokers and there is every reason to believe that a substantial number of them used this position to support professionalism; indeed, it would have not been possible for the pro-lobby to have found another 60 or so votes outside Lancashire without support from the metropolis. Now, and over the following six months, Lancashire and London together changed the shape of English football.

This is far from being a new argument. Geoffrey Green, writing in 1953, argued for the central role of the London and district clubs in the legalization process, noting the apparent anomaly by which the 'pure' South became 'the leading advocate for legalized professionalism while itself remaining entirely amateur'.[59] However, such an analysis has only rather faint echoes in modern sporting historiography, most notably in the work of Graham Williams.[60] Tony Mason has noted 'the presence of ex-public schoolboys' , often, irrespective of their actual birthplace, 'proxy' southerners in this debate, on 'both sides of this controversy' and the critical role of key FA personnel such as Old Harrovian Charles Alcock and Old Etonian Arthur Kinnaird in supporting professionalism has long been acknowledged.[61] Nevertheless, the implication has tended to be that southern amateurs were largely enemies of professionalism. Having established Lancashire as the key supporters, Mason states that 'it would not surprise us to find the bastions of southern amateurism in the opposing camp'. In a more specific argument, Derek Birley argued for N.L. Jackson who, as has been seen, was actually the seconder of the January 1885 pro-legalization resolution, as 'an implacable opponent' of professionalism and as the man who 'led the diehards in a long rearguard action'.[62]

Such views are completely understandable precisely because southern amateurs, and not least Jackson, were indeed often intensely critical of professionalism in the early 1880s and even more so from later in the decade, a process that culminated in the formation of the breakaway Amateur Football Association in 1907.[63] For a brief moment in 1884–85, however, a substantial number thought differently. The picture has also been clouded by the deep tensions between north and south, provinces and metropolis. These were, of course, hardly confined to the sporting arena, but sport was a particularly highly charged space for the reinforcement and contestation of territorial allegiances; *Football Field*'s query as to why Lancashire clubs 'should eternally bow the knee to southern opinion' captures a sentiment so commonly expressed as to become a *cliché*.[64] Moreover, the standard resort to wider pro-provincial, anti-metropolitan discourses sometimes had the effect of constructing an apparently common bond between regions that, while often sharing a general mentality in broad terms, were antithetically opposed in the specific arena of association football. 'Why should everything affecting English clubs be transacted in London? Are not Birmingham, Sheffield, Nottingham, and Manchester equally important to the football world?' *Football Field* once again pointed up the existence of major disagreements between core and periphery – the article included a plea for a northern location for the FA Cup Final in preference for 'handing over something like £200 to the Surrey Cricket Club' (the Cup Final was played at Surrey's ground, The Oval) – but in the context of 1884–85, Birmingham, Sheffield and Nottingham were hardly friends of Manchester and Lancashire more generally.[65] Against such a context, one in which a local Lancashire newspaper could identify 'the South' as a key opponent to professionalism in a report that included Jackson's speech in favour of professionalism, it is hardly surprising that historians have not reached the somewhat more counter-intuitive reading of events actually required.[66] Matthew Taylor has argued that the professionalism issue 'can hardly be reduced to simple north–south or Lancashire–London rivalries' but even a considered judgment like this does not go far enough.[67] The 'North', notoriously troublesome to define, but, in this context, effectively industrial Lancashire and the Sheffield region, was irrevocably divided. The 'South' had supporters in both camps but London eventually provided a critical block of support for legalization. Following standard compass bearings in this case leads largely in the wrong direction.

London-based support for professionalism clearly existed from the early 1880s, as evidenced by sympathy for Alcock's resolution in February 1884 within the FA Committee, undoubtedly dominated at this stage by southern clubs. There then followed a period of some six months when the Committee appeared to be moving firmly in the opposite direction. Even during this period, however, there was a sense within the Committee that professionalism was inevitable, but not possible in the current climate. Jackson, for example, admittedly perhaps attempting to explain his inconsistencies over the two years, argued a decade later that repression was accepted in the short term 'chiefly because of the argument of representatives from the districts more closely affected by the evil as it was then called'. Unaffected by the issue themselves, the 'leading Southern members of the Council were anxious not to be too precipitate in their actions'.[68] The speed with which the FA Committee acted in the face of the October 1884 crisis, 'making concessions which three months ago would have appeared ridiculous to contemplate', certainly lends some weight to Jackson's contention.[69] The FA was constantly accused of vacillation but it may have had a more consistent underlying position than was immediately apparent.

From late autumn 1884 southern support became ever more obvious. *Sporting Life* had claimed as early as September that 'the chief supporters of recognising professionalism are in the south' while, as Jackson later pointed out, in the critical 13–5 Committee vote in November 1884 proposing legalization, 'ten of those voting in the majority [were] southerners'.[70] The London Football Association column in *Athletic News* was generally supportive of the cause throughout the period from late 1884 to July 1885 and clearly some of its delegates went into the 'yes' lobby. *Football Field*, a publication unlikely to overplay the role of the South, noted that 'many Londoners' voted for professionalism in January 1885 and also recorded the support of Mr Hardman of the Oxford University team.[71] Alcock's connections also allowed him to generate support elsewhere in the Home Counties with the Surrey FA, on whose committee he served, coming out for professionalism at the end of 1884.[72] Other prominent southern representatives declared for legalisation as events unfolded, most notably Old Harrovian Morton Petto Betts. An FA Committee member and, under the *nom de plume* 'A.H. Chequer', scorer of the first ever FA Cup Final goal in 1872, for Wanderers, he announced his conversion at the March 1885 meeting, at which another London delegate from the West End FC also spoke of a change of heart.[73] At the July 1885 meeting, London was the best-represented geographical region, its Association providing 14 of the 40 club delegates in attendance. Although argument can only be speculative here, most opposition votes and abstentions can probably be accounted for by the presence of delegates from provincial clubs with long histories of hostility to professionalism, suggesting that the majority, and perhaps even all the London clubs, voted in favour of legalization.[74]

If neat regional patterns resolutely refuse to appear, the same might be argued in terms of social class. Class discourses were certainly present. *Football Field*'s description of Great Marlow delegate, Mr Ranson, as 'a clean-shaved, horsey-looking gentleman', captures both the northern cross-class hostility to the southern upper-middle classes that was possibly the most frequent trope on display and the sometimes slightly euphemistic manner of its articulation; the publication's reference to 'Cockney Swelldom' was clearly a little more pointed.[75] There are undoubtedly hints of an homology between class and attitudes to professionalism. In their pioneering history of rugby football, Dunning and Sheard argued that association football survived its crisis in 1884–85 because the FA's essentially aristocratic and upper-middle class leadership had a social confidence in its dealings with working- and lower-middle class footballers far greater than that displayed by the slightly less socially elevated leadership of the Rugby Football Union; the sheer scale of the social gap made them less likely 'to have perceived the working class as a threat' or to fear for loss of status.[76]

Although this necessarily speculative interpretation has not found much favour amongst historians, it may provide some clues. Certainly, while John Lowerson was undoubtedly correct in arguing that 'sheer physical distaste for the working classes' was an unspoken factor behind some forms of amateurism, relationships between upper-class footballers and their less favoured counterparts were often quite cordial and generative of considerable mutual respect.[77] Upton Park, for example, denied bringing the accusations of professionalism against Preston North End in January 1884 and paid the club's expenses when Sudell appeared before the FA.[78] Again, leading southern amateurs were much in demand as referees in Lancashire, with M.P. Betts, Norman Bailey and C.W. Woolaston (of the Wanderers) invited to officiate at key Lancashire FA Cup matches in February 1885.[79] Above all, the northern tours made by the Corinthians and, to a lesser extent, other southern amateur sides such as the Casuals, along with the return fixtures, were amongst the most widely awaited features of the contemporary game. Both Corinthians and Casuals toured Lancashire in the winter of 1884–85, hardly an indication of a breakdown in class or any other relations, with the former drawn through Bolton in a coach pulled by four greys. Indeed, the matches played between Preston North End and the Corinthians in 1884–85 were used by amateur supporters of legalization to demonstrate that, in Alcock's words, 'gentlemen do not object to meeting' professionals. The delegate of West End FC, whose conversion was noted above, implied that it stemmed from attendance at an outstanding game between the two sides in January 1885.[80]

It is also possible to identify individuals who might fit Dunning and Sheard's interpretation, with Charles Alcock and Arthur Kinnaird, FA treasurer from 1878, the clearest and best-known examples. However, personal history, geography and beliefs were possibly more important here than any general class behaviour. Keith Wood has argued that Alcock's experience of growing up in the north-east, the son of a Sunderland shipbuilder turned marine insurer, followed by schooling at Harrow, 'made it easier for him to reconcile the conflicting approaches of the amateur and the professional'.[81] His experiences at Surrey County Cricket Club and his work as a professional sports journalist and publisher, trades that brought him into contact with professionals in many guises, were also important ingredients. Again, Kinnaird's extensive involvement in a remarkable variety of philanthropic bodies suggests that individual generosity of social vision (albeit one imbued here with a decidedly puritanical streak) might be a crucial factor.[82] It is also the case that many who voted for legalization in 1885 were only lukewarm in their support and grew increasingly uncomfortable with the professional game and its impact upon the FA. N.L. Jackson provided the most extended critique of the post-1885 developments, claiming that the 'game as a sport was almost forgotten at headquarters, so much had the authorities to do in promoting the business of football'.[83] While the parvenu Jackson, notoriously coy about his education, was hardly a representative member of the public school-educated upper class, it is likely that such an analysis was shared by Major Marindin, President of the FA at the time of legalization, N.C. Bailey and others who retired from active involvement in the FA during the 1890s.[84]

The problem of aligning sporting position with class position is made equally plain when looking somewhat lower in the social scale. William Sudell, a mill manager, and Charles Crump, Superintendent of the Great Western Railway works in Wolverhampton, appear to have enjoyed remarkably similar occupations and levels of social status and yet were absolutely diametrically opposed during the conflict.

It is likely that the gathering of more detailed collective biography would generate many other similar pairings. It is also significant that (in contradistinction to many of its upper-class supporters noted above) some of the most vehement opponents of professionalism accepted the changed situation and remained loyal to the FA after July 1885: J.H. Cofield (Birmingham), Charles Clegg (Sheffield), eventually an FA President, Crump and W.H. Jope (Wednesbury), are striking examples. Such changes of attitude do not seem compatible with a sporting belief system deeply rooted in social class. Rather, they suggest the behaviour of individuals who had lost a tactical battle over how best to control professionalism. Tony Mason's view that the division of 1884–85 was 'really in essence a tactical one' and Rob Lewis's labelling of the rival camps within the FA as footballing 'liberals' and 'conservatives' signpost the best interpretative routes.[85] Although coloured by social and cultural factors at every turn, the debate over professionalism is arguably best interpreted as something shaped as much, and probably rather more, by the autonomous sporting space than the wider social one.

There can be little doubt that at least some of the antagonism towards change, particularly from Sheffield and Birmingham clubs, stemmed from a fear that they, as pioneers of the game, would become secondary within the football world to *arriviste* clubs from Lancashire operating with an unfair advantage. Sheffield FC was founded in 1857, and 16 of the clubs affiliated to the Sheffield FA in 1880 had been founded in the 1860s. The city had its own cup tournament, the Cromwell Cup, from 1868 and the Sheffield Football Association, dating from 1867, was the first regional football association, playing an important role in establishing the game's rules and, until at least the early 1870s, administering a larger number of clubs across a far wider territory than the national body. As leaders of a game with such a pedigree and as individuals who had fought so hard against creeping professionalism in their own locality, they were hardly likely to enjoy the possibility that the leadership of the game was going to pass to an area where the game had only really emerged in the mid- and later 1870s – the Lancashire FA was only founded in 1878 – and where the veil drawn over professionalism was thin indeed. W.H. Chambers, one of the Sheffield delegates to the January 1885 special meeting and a pioneer within the city's football world, commented tellingly that the game had prospered well enough in the early days without Lancashire's involvement and argued that if the Lancashire clubs 'had not the courage to repress professionalism, let them go on as they liked outside the Association'.[86] The loss, actual and potential, of local players to Lancashire was also a great cause for concern.[87] Birmingham, while a little later in its growth than Sheffield, could also claim a lead over Lancashire; one study has found 155 extant football teams in Birmingham as early as 1879–80.[88] On the other side of the debate, clubs from London and the south had no experience of professionalism in their local game or expectation that it would arise; it thus commanded little fear. Lancashire, for its part, producers of the first non-public old boys FA Cup finalist side in 1882 and the first such winners in 1883, had gone too far in the direction of payment and importation to consider turning back.

A similar balance between socio-cultural and sporting contexts can be seen in the eventual resolution of the conflict. As a number of commentators have observed, in comparison with rugby, football faced its crisis in a relatively calm political atmosphere. When *Athletic News* called for football to show the same spirit of compromise that had been 'the modern means of satisfying all radical differences of opinion' and argued that 'it has been frequently used in English politics during the last twelve years', it undoubtedly indulged in a certain degree of artifice. Nevertheless, it was probably correct in implying that in the relatively quiescent political atmosphere of the mid-1880s, compromises by social elites in one area of life need not be seen as a sign of weakness in others or an encouragement of wider social and political inclusiveness. Working men could be paid to play without serious consequence.[89] The Rugby Football Union, however, faced its battles over professionalism in the far more problematic 1890s when, in Tony Collins' phrase, 'relationships between classes had changed profoundly' and 'industrial conflict and class antagonism were to the fore'.[90] The industrial militancy of the period, coupled with the early possibilities of labour as an independent political force, were hardly conducive to measures that could be interpreted as a major concession to a working-class constituency.

Once again, however, factors within the narrower football world played a critical role. It must be remembered that organized football was still a relatively new and modest phenomenon. The Football Association had really only established itself as the ruling body within the previous ten years and had only 165 members in 1885. It is difficult to be precise about its strength in comparison with rugby, the more frequently played of the codes on a national scale in the late 1870s, but it was certainly still at a point of development where leading figures were unwilling to undermine its future health. The rapidity with which most FA Committee members abandoned opposition to professionalism in November 1884, and the self-denying actions of Pierce-Dix and his colleagues in March 1885, suggest high levels of commitment to the game above all else. The main protagonists on both sides were also relatively young, mostly in their early 30s and 40s and often still active as players and/or officials, and perhaps this shared engagement helped create a spirit of compromise.

Moreover, and the initial rancour of the debate in the 1880s can disguise this, the central problem was at a manageable level. The actual number of professionals playing football was fairly small; in January 1885, *Athletic News* believed that 'in practice, nearly a hundred players are paid for taking part in the game on behalf of other clubs'.[91] The full consequences of July 1885 simply could not be known at that stage. They were, of course, much better known by 1895, when opponents of professionalism in the Rugby Football Union could point to the abandonment of some of the controls – residence clauses were removed in 1889, for example – and the disillusionment of some of those who had countenanced change. The legalization of professionalism was crucial in helping secure association football's place as the country's leading winter team sport. Surmounting its problems so promptly, it was spared the divisions and dissension that beset rugby football and culminated in its 'Great Split' in 1895. By providing genuine case history to discuss, it also served to make those divisions and dissensions far worse.

Notes

1. *Athletic News*, 28 July 1885.
2. Matthew Taylor, *The Leaguers: The Making of Professional Football In England, 1900–1939* (Liverpool: Liverpool University Press, 2005), p. xii.
3. Tony Mason, *Association Football and English Society, 1863–1915* (Brighton: Harvester), especially pp. 69–81; Stephen Tischler, *Footballers and Businessmen: The Origins of Professional Soccer in England* (New York: Holmes and Meier, 1981); Matthew Taylor, *The Association Game: A History of British Football* (Harlow: Pearson Education, 2008), pp. 44–52.
4. Geoffrey Green, *The History of the Football Association* (London: Naldrett Press, 1953), pp. 95–109, still provides the most detailed narrative history.
5. Neil Wigglesworth, *The Evolution of British Sport* (London: Frank Cass, 1996); Dave Russell, *Popular Music in England: A Social History, 1840–1914* (Manchester; Manchester University Press, 2nd edn, 1997), pp. 278–81, for brass bands.
6. Graham Curry, 'Playing for money: James J. Lang and emergent soccer professionalism in Sheffield', *Soccer and Society*, 5, 3, 2004, pp. 336–55.
7. Richard Holt, *Sport and the British: A Modern History* (Oxford: Clarendon Press, 1989), pp. 74–134 remains an outstanding introduction.
8. Robert W. Lewis, 'The genesis of professional football: Bolton-Blackburn-Darwen, the centre of innovation, 1878–85', *International Journal of the History of Sport*, 14, 1, 1997, pp. 26–7, 54. *Football Field*, 13th December 1884.

9. *Football Annual*, 1881.
10. Curry, 'Playing for money', pp. 345–7.
11. Mason, *Association Football*, pp. 71–2.
12. *The Sportsman*, 20 January 1885.
13. Lewis, 'Genesis', p. 25.
14. Green, *Football Association*, pp. 98–9.
15. David Hunt, *The History of Preston North End F.C. the Power, the Politics, the People* (Preston: PNE Publications, 2000), pp. 53–4; Neil Carter 'Football's first northern hero? the rise and fall of William Sudell' in D. Russell and S. Wagg (eds.) *These Sporting Lives: Sport, Heroism and the North of England* (Newcastle-upon-Tyne: University of Northumbria Press, 2010).
16. Green, *Football Association*, pp. 100–1; N.L. Jackson, *Professional Football* (London: George Newnes, 1900 ed.), p. 97.
17. Green, *Football Association*, p. 101.
18. Ibid., pp. 101–2; Jackson, *Professional Football*, pp. 99–100.
19. *Athletic News*, 27 August 1884.
20. The full resolution was recorded in *Athletic News*, 3 September 1884.
21. *Athletic News*, 17 September 1884.
22. *Football Field*, 11 October 1884.
23. Ibid., 11 October, 25 October 1884
24. Ibid., 1 November 1884. See Lewis, 'Genesis', Appendix B, p. 49, for clubs in attendance at the meetings. See also, C.E. Sutcliffe and F. Hargreaves, *History of the Lancashire Football Association, 1878–1928* (Blackburn: Toulmin and Co, 1928), pp. 163–70; *Football Field*, 18 and 25 October 1884.
25. *Athletic News*, 5 November 1884; *Times*, 5 November 1884.
26. *Football Field*, 22 November and 6 December 1884.
27. Green, *Football Association*, p. 103. Twenty-one associations and 102 clubs were represented.
28. *Football Field*, 3 January 1885, for the various motions on the agenda paper, not all of which were called, and 24 January 1885, for the meeting. See also *The Sportsman*, 20 January 1885. For Peirce-Dix, a stockbroker, Graham Curry, 'Degrading the game: the story of the Sheffield Zulus', *Soccer History*, 24, 2009. His surname appears in reports as both Peirce-Dix and Pierce-Dix.
29. *Football Field*, 24 January 1885; *Derby and Chesterfield Reporter*, 23 January 1885.
30. *The Sportsman*, 24 March 1885; *Football Field*, 28 March 1885.
31. *The Sportsman*, 24 March 1885
32. *Times*, 21 July 1885; Green, *Football Association*, p. 107; *Football Field*, 25 July 1885.
33. Quoted in Lewis, 'Genesis', p. 40; Jackson, *Professional Football*, pp. 100, 103.
34. *Football Field*, 1 November 1884. Unfortunately, no membership list exists although, as signatories to the 30th October memorandum to the Lancashire Football Association, Accrington, Astley, Bolton Association, Bolton Wanderers, Burnley, Burnley Union Star, Clitheroe, Great Lever, Halliwell, Padiham, Preston Zingari and Turton comprised 12 of the number. *Football Field* was extremely sympathetic to the BFA at this stage and one of its journalists, William Fairhurst, acted as its first secretary.
35. *Football Field*, 1 November 1884.
36. *Athletic News*, 5 November 1884.

37. C.E. Sutcliffe and F. Hargreaves, *History of the Lancashire Football Association, 1878–1928* (Blackburn: George Toulmin, 1928), pp. 163–4.
38. *Football Field*, 18 October 1884.
39. Minutes of Lancashire Football Association, 31 October 1884, Lancashire Record Office, Preston, DDX 2708/1.
40. *Athletic News*, 17 March 1885.
41. Interestingly, this course of action was not pursued dissatisfied rugby clubs in the lead up to the schism of August 1895. I am grateful to Tony Collins for this point.
42. *Football Field*, 18 October, 1 November, 8 November 1884.
43. See, for example, Charles Crump's speech to the Birmingham FA, *Football Field*, 8 November 1884.
44. *Nottingham and Midland Counties Express*, 1, 8 November 1884; *Athletic News*, 5 November 1884.
45. Minutes of Lancashire Football Association, 6 December 1883, 30 January 1884.
46. Ibid., 13 October 1884.
47. Green, *Association*, p. 103.
48. *Football Field*, 1 November 1885; Minutes of Lancashire Football Association, 31 October 1885.
49. Sutcliffe and Hargreaves, *Lancashire*, pp. 167–70; Minutes of Lancashire Football Association, 15, 27 May 1882.
50. Minutes of Lancashire Football Association, 15 January, 25 February 1885.
51. Ibid., 9, 13 October 1884; *Football Field*, 4 April, 24 January 1884.
52. Mason, *Association Football*, pp. 74–7; Lewis, 'Genesis', pp. 25, 37; Taylor, *Association*, pp. 50–2.
53. Taylor, *Association*, p. 51.
54. 'Mercutio' of the *Nottingham and Midland Counties Daily Express*, supported legalization with some reservation; 17 January 1885. 'Captain Coe' of Wolverhampton's *Midland Counties Express*, however, claimed to have been a supporter for six years; 28 July 1885.
55. Approximately 35% of clubs and associations present came from north of Sheffield, 25% from between Sheffield and Birmingham and 40% from south of Birmingham.
56. For example, *Bell's Life in London*, 21 January 1885; for the decision of the Lincolnshire FA to oppose, *Sheffield Daily Telegraph*, 16 January 1885. It is presumed here that all affiliated clubs followed this ruling. For Berks and Bucks, *Athletic News*, 31 March 1885.
57. *Football Field*, 25 July 1885. The two Blackburn Rovers representatives, Ebeneezer Morley and John Lewis, crossed the floor to vote for Pierce-Dix's anti-professionalism resolution in January 1885, but this appears the only other diversion from the dominant path. For this and the full list of clubs and associations attending the January meeting and the number of votes they could cast, *Football Field*, 24 January 1885.
58. *Football Field*, 24 January 1884; *The Football Annual*, 1884, p. 73.
59. Green, *Association*, p. 108. Also, pp. 100, 103.
60. *The Code War* (Harefield: Yore Publications, 1994), pp. 88–93, provides an excellent and adumbrates many of the arguments offered here.
61. Mason, *Association Football*, p. 75.

62. Ibid., p. 75; Derek Birley, *Sport and the Making of Britain* (Manchester: Manchester University Press, 1993), pp. 273–4. (Tischler, p. 45.)
63. W.E. Greenland, *The History of the Amateur Football Alliance* (Amateur Football Alliance: Harwich, 1966). More widely see also Richard Metcalfe, 'The Origins, Development and Impact of the Football Association Amateur Cup, 1893–1915' (unpublished MA (by research) thesis, Leeds Metropolitan University, 2010).
64. Jeff Hill and Jack Williams (eds.), *Sport and Identity in the North of England* (Keele: Keele University Press, 1996); Dave Russell, *Looking North: Northern England and the National Imagination* (Manchester: Manchester University Press, 2004), especially pp. 236–66. *Football Field*, 1 November 1884.
65. *Football Field*, 25 October 1884.
66. *Preston Guardian*, 21 January 1885.
67. Taylor, *Association*, p. 51.
68. Jackson, *Professional Football*, p. 99.
69. *Athletic News*, 10 December 1884.
70. *Sporting* Life, 15 September 1884; Jackson, *Professional Football*, p. 103.
71. *Football Field*, 24 January 1885. For claims of support from London clubs, see also *Bell's Life in London*, 21 January 1885.
72. *Football Field*, 27 December 1884; *Football Annual*, 1884, p. 88.
73. *Football Field*, 28 March 1885.
74. The Birmingham, Lincolnshire, Nottingham and Walsall FAs, along with Darwen, Great Marlow, Queen's Park (the sole Scottish representatives), Reading, Stafford Road, Sheffield and The Wednesday are particularly likely candidates.
75. *Football Field*, 28 March 1885. The paper did not name him but see Jackson, *Professional Football*, p. 106 for his identification. *Football Field*, 25 October 1884.
76. E. Dunning and K. Sheard, *Barbarians, Gentlemen and Players* (New York: New York University Press, 1979), p. 189.
77. J. Lowerson, *Sport and the English Middle Classes, 1870–1914* (Manchester: Manchester University Press, 1993), p. 183.
78. Hunt, *Preston North End*, p. 54.
79. Minutes of Lancashire Football Association, 19 February 1885.
80. *Football Field*, 20 December 1884, 10 January, 24 January and 28 March 1885.
81. K. Booth, *The Father of Modern Sport: The Life and Times of Charles W. Alcock* (Manchester: The Parrs Wood Press, 2002), p. 261.
82. *New Dictionary of National Biography* (Oxford: Oxford University Press), Vol. 31, pp. 732–4.
83. Jackson, *Professional Football*, pp. 107–31.
84. Ibid., p. 120; Dave Russell, *Football and the English* (Preston: Carnegie Publishing, 1997), p. 40.
85. Mason, *Association Football*, p. 75; Lewis, 'Genesis', p. 25.
86. *The Sportsman*, 20 January 1885; *Football Field*, 24 January 1885.
87. Curry, 'Playing for money', p. 346; *Sheffield Daily Telegraph*, 30 September 1884.
88. Tischler, *Footballers and Businessmen*, p. 35.
89. *Athletic News*, 7 April 1885.

90. Tony Collins, *Rugby's Great Split: Class, Culture and the Origins of Rugby League Football* (London: Frank Cass, 1998), p. 112. See also, Dunning and Sheard, *Barbarians*, pp. 191–200.
91. *Athletic News*, 13 January 1885.

3
Peacefully at Wembley Stadium on 20 April 1974: The Quiet Death of Amateur Football in England

Dilwyn Porter

It was an interment attended by 30,500 paying customers. 'Amateur football in England', *The Times* reported, 'was quietly buried without ceremony at Wembley on Saturday'.[1] In some ways this was misleading. While it was true that the last ever match in the 80-year history of the Football Association Amateur Cup competition had been played on 20 April 1974, thousands of footballers continued to turn out for fun on park pitches up and down the country, many of them on the Sunday morning immediately following the match at Wembley. The Football Association (FA) would thereafter categorize all footballers simply as 'players', abandoning the distinction between those who were paid ('professionals') and those who were unpaid ('amateurs'). Relatively few, however, would have reason to notice that anything had changed. Moreover, if the competition had become 'redundant', as *The Times* claimed, it was largely because the amateur status of participant clubs – especially those that were most successful – had been in doubt for many years. It was familiarly referred to as the 'Amateur Cup', but 'shamateurs' (or 'sham-amateurs'), usually carried it home.

Not that this would have mattered to those who lined the streets to greet the cup-winners a few hours after the match. Bishop's Stortford, representing a market town 29 miles north of London, had triumphed on the day, beating Ilford, from an outer East London suburb, by four goals to one. For some weeks, the local newspaper had been reporting an outbreak of 'cup fever' as the 'Blues' progressed to the final. Three special trains carried 1500 supporters to Sunderland for the semi-final, the first time that 'football specials' had been arranged for a Bishop's Stortford match. Others made the 250-mile journey by road. Once a Wembley final was in prospect it was predicted 'that the trek from the town and district... [would] reach massive proportions'.² The homecoming followed a pattern that would have been recognized by football supporters everywhere.

> When the blue-and-white coach finally came in sight several thousand fans gave the Blues a tumultuous reception. They spilled from the footpaths into the road, slowing the progress to such an extent that, despite the valiant efforts of the police escort, it took an hour for the coach to travel from the Co-op corner to the Half Moon public house.

The mayor compared the scene to Trafalgar Square on VE-Day. 'It was,' he declared, 'probably the greatest day in the history of Bishop's Stortford.'³

Accounts of senior amateur football's last big day at Wembley suggest two narratives that might usefully be pursued.⁴ The first relates to what the Amateur Cup competition meant to players, clubs and the communities that they represented. In 1893–4, when the Cup was first contested, it attracted 81 entries and the final, between the Old Carthusians and the Casuals, drew an estimated 3500 spectators to the Athletic Ground, Richmond. By the 1950s, when the public's interest peaked, the Amateur Cup final had become a major event on England's sporting calendar. A total of 428 clubs entered in 1950–1, their names indicative of small town, suburb, neighbourhood and workplace across the land, and testifying to the importance of voluntary association in English social life.⁵ The competition supplied a national stage for Barnet, Bedford Avenue and Billingham Synthonia, 'the only club in Britain named after a fertiliser'.⁶ Bishop Auckland and Pegasus met in the 1951 final at Wembley, attracting a capacity crowd of 100,000. 'If you want to book a ticket for next year's final you'd better book now', joked the Pathé cinema newsreel commentator, though it was good advice.⁷ In terms of English popular culture the Amateur Cup competition was an annual event of some significance and merits more attention than historians have given it to date.

It is also important to recognize the Amateur Cup as one of a number of sites where a struggle for the ownership of English football took place, and it is here that the second narrative emerges. For 20 years or so after the FA had been founded in 1863, English football was run by and for the privately educated middle class, buttressed by an element of aristocratic support. Public school and 'varsity' influences were to the fore, along with the ethos of gentlemanly amateurism with which they were associated. This hegemony was undermined from the 1880s onwards by those who regarded football primarily as a form of commercialized entertainment. As a 'true blue' amateur later explained, representatives from clubs in the North and the Midlands 'made it clear that they looked upon the game as a business proposition and were determined to assume a leading part in its administration'.[8] On the field of play, gentleman amateurs, who had once dominated without undue effort, found it increasingly difficult to compete with working-class professionals, employed by the new football businesses to entertain paying customers. The tensions that these developments generated led to a schism between 1907 and 1914 when the gentlemanly element broke away to form the Amateur Football Association (AFA). They saw themselves 'as the David of pure amateurism standing up to the Goliath of professionalism and business football'.[9]

The FA initiated the Amateur Cup competition in an attempt to reconcile these conflicting interests. It created a space where the gentleman might yet prevail without risk of his world being turned upside down. Within a few years, however, it was clear that this strategy was not working. Though there were early successes for Old Carthusians (winners in 1894 and 1897) and Old Malvernians (1902), there were also wins for teams from the industrial North-East – Middlesbrough (1895, 1898), Bishop Auckland (1896, 1900) and Stockton (1899, 1903). Denied supremacy at the highest levels of the game by the rise of working-class professionals, the 'old boys' now found themselves thwarted by the rise of working-class amateurs, who were said to play in a different spirit. A second-round tie between Old Etonians and Middlesbrough in February 1894, when the Middlesbrough captain was sent off for raking an opponent's shin with his studs, set the tone for much of what was to follow. Crowd trouble at Chatham on the same day, where the locals greeted the gentlemanly Casuals with a singular lack of deference, was also ominous.[10] After 1902–3, the public school old boys clubs simply defected, preferring to compete against each other for the Arthur Dunn Cup.[11]

Such incidents signified a clash of football cultures that often left both sides nursing grudges. This manifested itself in various ways throughout the entire history of the competition, often in the form of disputes relating to the amateur status of participant clubs and players. Old-style amateurs retained sufficient influence at the FA to mount a defensive campaign against shamateurism for almost a century. Yet, despite their efforts, covert payment, usually in the form of liberal 'expenses', became a defining characteristic of senior amateur football. Tony Pawson, who was playing his club football at the time for Pegasus, a 'true blue' club in every sense, comprising undergraduates and recent graduates from Oxford and Cambridge, recalled in his memoirs:

> In soccer 'money in the boot' was rife... as I experienced with Great Britain's [Olympic] soccer team in Helsinki in 1952. In informal talks with the others in the party of twenty, only three proved to be genuine unpaid amateurs.[12]

The last Amateur Cup final in 1974 signalled defeat for those seeking to uphold what FA Secretary Stanley Rous, with England's international rivals in mind, called 'our more purist view of amateurism'.[13] They did not concede with good grace. 'Unhappily, the Amateur Cup did not die a natural death; it committed suicide,' noted a terse obituary in the *FA Yearbook* for the following season. 'The players themselves – especially those attached to our leading amateur clubs – have made a mockery of their status, until the FA has been compelled to yield and admit that the amateur game was no more.'[14]

Local heroes: amateur football and community identity

Much of the popular appeal of sport – football and other team sports in particular – lies in its capacity for making imagined communities real. It is clear that this works at a number of levels – local, regional and national. As Martin Johnes has argued, it was possible for a South Wales miner in the 1930s to identify with the team representing his village, with the Welsh League club from his valley, with a major professional club in Cardiff, Newport or Swansea, along with the Welsh national side on international day. Moreover, it was possible to identify with two or more of them simultaneously, while prioritizing one over another as the occasion demanded.[15] This has important implications when considering amateur football in England, where the professional game was so firmly embedded in popular culture. Thus a Durham miner, for example, might follow Newcastle United or Sunderland while retaining an attachment for Bishop Auckland, Crook Town or another Northern League club. Growing up in East London in the 1950s and 1960s, my primary attachment was to Leyton Orient, the local professional club, but I also identified with Leytonstone of the Isthmian League, following them to Wembley in 1968.

The popular appeal of the Amateur Cup competition derived from its capacity to deliver occasions when it was natural to support a team with which it was relatively easy to identify, generally on account of locality, neighbourhood or workplace. A successful cup run, with excitement growing round by round, effectively strengthened and extended the imagined community. Progress to the final supplied an opportunity to validate its existence at an event that registered nationally. In addition, where communities were peripheral in a geographical sense, or where they regarded themselves as marginalized, the Amateur Cup competition made them, albeit temporarily, more visible. It was *because* Cockfield was an obscure pit village in remote County Durham that the achievement of its team of out-of-work miners in reaching the 1928 final was culturally – and politically – significant. It allowed a community which saw itself as neglected to make a point. For a while, it was possible to speak of Cockfield as 'the wonder village', the bitter aftermath of the General Strike and the privations that came with long-term unemployment notwithstanding.[16]

Arguably, community identification with a particular team was facilitated by the accessibility of the players. The Amateur Cup was *the* competition for local heroes, usually working men with everyday jobs, who were touched by the excitement that a cup run could generate in an unremarkable town or an anonymous suburb. Amateur football's most prestigious competition brought players and the communities that their clubs represented together. Naturally, it helped if players lived and/or worked locally. When Wycombe Wanderers reached the final in 1931, an estimated 4000 supporters went with them to the Arsenal Stadium at Highbury, including at least one 'chairboy' who carried an example of local craftsmanship, suitably decorated in the club's colours, onto the terraces. The team was greeted by an estimated 10,000 people on its triumphant return and the brake which met them at the station was pulled by enthusiastic supporters to the Guildhall, where speeches were delivered. This display of local patriotism and civic pride was entirely fitting, not least because all but one of the victorious team lived within five miles of the town centre.[17]

Even when players were recruited from outside the immediate locality, it remained possible to identify with them, provided that they remained accessible, the kind of person one might meet in the street or at work. 'After every home match', recalled Harry Young of Bishop Auckland, 'some of the players would walk over to Gregory's Cafe in Newgate Street and have pie and chips and a cup of tea and then I would catch the bus from the market square to Newcastle'. There was, no doubt, some enjoyment to be derived from being a local celebrity, along with financial 'perks' and the occasional treat. Young, a printer by trade, travelled mainly by bus but arrived at the 1939 final at Sunderland in a Rolls Royce laid on by the club.[18] Laurie Topp, a Hendon regular and England amateur international in the 1950s, spent his entire working life at a local engineering company which allowed him time off for football. In return, his club supplied complimentary tickets for big games, thus enabling the firm to identify itself with its success. 'When we won the cup in 1960', Topp remembered, 'I spoke to the managing director as I was going up the steps to the Royal Box'.[19] A working-class local hero was something to be and the Amateur Cup helped some players live the dream.

The cultural significance of the competition was especially evident in small towns whose inhabitants discovered in it a focus for local patriotism. Its capacity for changing the way in which communities saw themselves and were seen by others is very apparent when tracking local press coverage of Evesham Town's progress from preliminary round to final in 1922–3. Evesham was a small market town in rural Worcestershire, an area more famous for its fruit than its football. 'When the Town scored the first goal,' claimed the *Evesham Standard*, commenting on the second-round victory over West Auckland, 'the yell which went up, they say, shook next year's crop of plums from the trees'.[20] Having negotiated the qualifying rounds, Evesham reached the final via a series of home victories over opposition from County Durham. In these circumstances, with travelling support for the away teams minimized, steadily increasing attendances – 3300 in round two, 4000 in round three, 5110 (a ground record) in round four – were a reliable indicator of burgeoning community self-awareness. 'Many who have never troubled to see a football match before,' the *Standard* observed when it was all over, 'have been attracted to see the Town play.'[21] It is possible also to detect a sense of satisfaction in having put Evesham on the map. 'A few weeks ago,' it was noted, 'they knew very little of Evesham up there [the North], but the experience of West Auckland made them rub their eyes some.'[22]

The final, played at the Crystal Palace in London, where many FA Cup finals had been contested, provided an opportunity to project sentiments that were essentially parochial to a wider audience, enhancing their apparent significance. A substantial proportion of the 14,132 crowd had travelled up from Evesham by special train, 'many of them arrayed in fantastic costume'.[23] Coverage of this expedition indicated a self-confident sense of local identity which had been enhanced by what 'the Robins' had achieved. One old-timer, making his first trip to the metropolis, was reported to have said: 'My word, there will be a lot of people in London today with all these folks going up.' Behind this story, artfully constructed to make local readers smile, lurks a sense of what it meant to belong to Evesham at that moment and the idea that it was as good, if not better, to be from there as from anywhere else in the land. 'No other team,' the *Standard* reflected, '[had] ever played through all the qualifying rounds of the English Amateur Cup and much fame and glory have been brought to the town by Evesham's remarkable achievements.'[24] In April 1923, Evesham (population 8688 in 1921) could look the rest of the country proudly in the face.

When the Robins returned to Evesham they were greeted by the town brass band, a cheering crowd and a civic reception. Such homecoming rituals were by then well-established, having been honed to perfection at Blackburn in the 1880s when the FA Cup had been won and duly celebrated at the end of each of four consecutive seasons: 'Once more there were the wagonettes, the brass bands, the milling crowds, the streamers, and there, most important of all, the "little tin idol" glittering again in the hands of the Rovers' captain as he held it aloft.'[25] In this respect the amateurs simply followed the example set by the professionals on a reduced, but still impressive, scale. Football, as Brad Beaven has observed, 'gave working-class males a new medium in which to express a civic pride'.[26] The Amateur Cup helped to ensure that this phenomenon was as likely to be encountered in Bishop Auckland or Bishop's Stortford as in Blackburn or Birmingham.

It may have been especially important in places struggling to establish an identity. Arguably, winning the Amateur Cup in 1927 (and again in 1928) was almost as significant for the otherwise nondescript working-class London suburb of Leyton as winning the FA Cup had been for neighbouring Tottenham a few years earlier. Leyton, like Tottenham, had mushroomed rapidly, its population growing from 27,068 in 1881 to 128,430 in 1921, and there was little to relieve 'the prevailing monotony of brick'.[27] Having only recently attained borough status the mayor and corporation were no doubt delighted when the 'Lilywhites' provided its citizens – most of whom had come from somewhere else – with an occasion when they could sense that they belonged to a community. Returning from the 1928 final at Middlesbrough, the team was greeted at King's Cross by civic worthies and a crowd estimated at between three and four thousand. On reaching Leyton, they were met by the borough's prize-winning silver band which accompanied the conquering heroes to the pub that served as the club's headquarters. 'So great was the crowd,' reported a local newspaper, 'that the traffic was stopped.'[28] This enthusiastic response seems especially significant when the presence of professional clubs in neighbouring boroughs – Clapton Orient, Tottenham Hotspur and West Ham United – is taken into account. Even when the connection between club and community was tenuous, an Amateur Cup final victory could prompt a temporary surge of local pride as the town claimed the trophy for itself. The Casuals, having previously played at a number of grounds in and around London, were relative newcomers to suburban Kingston upon Thames when they won in 1936. Nevertheless, a crowd gathered to see them bring the cup 'home'. 'At last the club had done something really great,' said a club official, 'and he was glad that the people of Kingston wanted to share in their success.'[29]

If winning the Amateur Cup ever was 'something really great', it was in the late 1940s and 1950s when football and other mass spectator sports enjoyed enormous popularity. Trevor Bailey, better known as a Test cricketer, had been awarded a soccer 'blue' at Cambridge and went on to play for Leytonstone and Walthamstow Avenue, the leading amateur clubs in East London at that time. Reflecting on this experience, Bailey could not recall a home match for either where the attendance was below 5000; Amateur Cup games regularly attracted 9000 or more. Spectators at Leytonstone's ground in January 1949 were asked 'to give every assistance to those officials who are responsible for packing the crowd to the best possible advantage'.[30] The crowd of 15,580 for Wycombe's quarter-final against St Albans in February 1950 set a ground record for Loakes Park that was never beaten.[31] In 1949, an attendance of 93,000 for the first final to be staged at Wembley justified the FA's decision to use English football's most prestigious venue. Amateur finals filled English football's national stadium to its 100,000 capacity from 1951 to 1955 before attendances began to decline. Even then, it continued to prove a significant attraction. A crowd of 41,000 for the penultimate final in 1973 was perhaps a little disappointing, but was beaten on the day only by Arsenal and Liverpool.[32]

As the popularity of the competition peaked, so did media interest in amateur football generally. In addition to extensive local press coverage, some national newspapers employed specialist amateur football correspondents, like Norman Ackland of the *Daily Telegraph*, whose previews and match reports supplied generally sympathetic publicity. Senior amateur football – the Amateur Cup in particular – also attracted some radio and television coverage. The first live football on BBC television when it resumed after the Second World War was a match between Barnet and Tooting in October 1946.[33] With access to Football League matches denied in the early 1950s, Amateur Cup ties were an acceptable alternative. 'We are not unmindful,' a Romford match programme noted rather quaintly in 1953, 'that we also enjoy the company of many thousands of Viewers through the wonderful medium of Television.'[34] When live coverage of the final ended in 1963, the FA's Amateur Cup committee claimed that it was 'a great disappointment' for football enthusiasts in the provinces who could not get to Wembley.[35]

Some idea of the excitement that the competition could generate is conveyed by a compelling visual source, newsreel footage of the quarter-final between Oxford City and Pegasus played in March 1951, which shows crowds queuing outside the ground and highlights of a robust contest watched by a very full house of 9500 enthusiastic spectators.[36] Oxford City versus Pegasus was a local derby with the additional spice of 'town versus gown' thrown in for good measure. 'There was a tremendous demand for tickets to see this all-Oxford fourth round cup-tie,' Ken Shearwood of Pegasus later recalled; it had been 'the talk of Oxford.'[37] Matches between local rivals, always a strong possibility in the early rounds, were a particular feature of the competition and could generate fierce passions, even in a famously sedate seaside resort. A bad-tempered preliminary round encounter between Eastbourne and Eastbourne United in September 1954 'kept sections of the crowd on their toes, and, at times, almost at fever pitch'.[38] In towns where the local favourites were serious contenders, travelling support could be impressive. As Wycombe Wanderers progressed to Wembley in 1957, 160 coaches and three special trains were required to transport 5000 supporters to Ilford for the quarter-final.[39]

By the early 1960s, however, it was clear that conditions were changing. When Leytonstone, where Bailey had played in front of crowds of 5000 or more, played Penrith in the Amateur Cup in 1962, the club struck an apologetic note. Admission prices had been raised, it was explained, 'simply because of economics'. A gate of 2000 would leave only a very small margin once match expenses had been met. What was clearly worrying was 'that only once during the past two seasons have we had a gate of 2,000'.[40] An Ilford match programme three seasons later testified to 'the general drop in gates of most amateur clubs in recent years'.[41] It was not just that the English people were falling out of love with senior amateur football; they were falling out of love with football generally. Football League attendances had fallen from almost 42 million in 1948–9 season to just under 28 million in 1961–2, and were declining particularly rapidly in the early 1960s.[42] In an era when all sports that relied heavily on gate money were feeling the pinch, those clubs described by Geoffrey Green of *The Times* as 'merely poor imitations of their professional brothers' were especially vulnerable.[43] For senior amateur football to remain attractive in an increasingly diverse and competitive leisure market it was imperative to invest in ground improvements and floodlights at a time when income from gates was falling. In these circumstances, building a side capable of achieving a lucrative run in the Amateur Cup was especially important, but finding the right players – and keeping them – was an expensive business. As clubs struggled for survival the tensions generated by shamateurism and other sharp practices were increasingly evident.

In pursuit of the shamateur

The first draft of an article that Dr Harold Thompson, writing as president of the Oxford University Football Club, sent to *The Times* in January 1964, recalled the comment of a leading FA official after Pegasus had defeated Bishop Auckland in the 1951 Final. 'What a magnificent game,' he had said, 'and how refreshing that a truly amateur team has won the Amateur Cup after so many years.'[44] Thompson had been a member of the FA Council since 1941 and was the driving force behind Pegasus when the 'Oxbridge' club made such a huge impact on the competition in the late 1940s and early 1950s. A distinguished research scientist and highly ambitious, his influence at the FA was considerable and was generally exercised at this time on behalf of amateur football as played by the old universities, old boys clubs and others with a similar outlook. He was later vice-chairman of the FA from 1967 to 1976, and then chairman until 1981.[45] As far as he was concerned in 1964, 'the canker of sham-amateurism' was one of a number of problems that English football would have to resolve if it was not to wither at the roots.

It seems likely that Thompson's letter to *The Times*, published to coincide with the first round of the Amateur Cup under the headline 'Competition Under a Cloud', was designed to shock. He used it to urge the FA to abolish the distinction between amateurs and professionals that had been a feature of English football since 1885. This intervention was especially surprising in view of Thompson's recent endorsement of the report of a committee set up by the FA in February 1963 to investigate the nature and extent of shamateurism in the amateur game. This had recommended a number of measures that included requiring the officials of clubs entering the Amateur Cup competition to sign a statutory declaration that, to the best of their knowledge, no player

...is receiving or will receive either directly or indirectly any payment or any expenses over and above those which are permitted by the Football Association Rule 25 and [that] there is no arrangement whereby any player or member of his family or anyone on his or their behalf or for his or their benefit can receive any such payment or expenses or benefit in kind.[46]

Thompson had endorsed the report reluctantly, 'allowing sentiment to overcome my proper conviction', and did not believe that the proposed measures would be effective.[47] 'Surely,' he explained to readers of *The Times*, 'it is more appropriate to have done with it now, and call them all footballers.'[48] He had changed his mind because he recognized that shamateurism was so deep-rooted and so widespread that a radical solution was required.

'In a world divided by the FA into two categories, amateur and professional,' as Richard Metcalfe has observed in his study of the competition in its early years, 'a great deal of effort went into maintaining the purity of the Amateur Cup.'[49] This was part of a wider campaign undertaken by the FA and its affiliated associations to enforce the rules regarding amateurism. The most celebrated case in the late nineteenth century concerned Royal Artillery (Portsmouth), favourites for the Amateur Cup in 1899, but suspended shortly before their semi-final because they had breached the rules of the competition by preparing for their quarter-final at Harwich with a week's training on the Suffolk coast. Various expenses run up at the White Lion Hotel at Aldeburgh were disallowed, the Royal Artillery was removed from the competition and its players suspended for the remainder of the season.[50] Such cases set the pattern for what was to follow. Payment of expenses beyond the strict limits indicated by the FA put the amateur status of both clubs and players at risk.

Securing a level playing field for its amateur showcase supplied a rationale that could be used to justify a strict interpretation even when this was at variance with local custom and practice. In the North-East, for example, one of the regional strongholds of senior amateur football, most clubs reimbursed expenses via flat-rate payments ('tea money'). Though often no more than a few shillings, these were usually in excess of what players actually spent on travel and subsistence. This contravened FA rule 29 but does not appear to have been questioned until 1928 when Bishop Auckland protested that Crook Town, who had just knocked them out of the Amateur Cup, was 'not a properly constituted amateur club'. Crook, some of whose officials had been punished a year earlier for failing to keep their books in order, was immediately suspended by the Durham FA. In response the club secretary sent a dossier to the FA, comprising sworn statements from players relating to the payment of flat-rate expenses at 20 other North-Eastern clubs, including Bishop Auckland. Engaged at the time in a dispute with FIFA over the legitimacy of 'broken time' payments, the FA could hardly ignore this evidence and maintain its credibility.

The ensuing commission of inquiry dispensed some spectacularly rough justice; 337 players were declared to be professionals and suspended for various lengths of time according to the nature of their offence. Numerous club officials suffered a similar fate. 'The FA had to take action in those Durham cases,' its secretary later explained, 'because of wholesale breaches of rules: payments in excess of expenses permissible, and the players never giving, nor the clubs demanding, receipts as required by the regulations.'[51] The view from Crook and other towns and villages in the North-East was rather different. It was strange, observed Cockfield's captain, 'that pit Durham, of all England the area where industrial depression is the blackest, should be the one district rich enough to subscribe its amateur football players'.[52] The implication was that the FA was imposing standards that might reasonably apply in the affluent south on working-class amateurs in the impoverished north, for whom a few shillings a week over and above 'expenses permissible' was a fair reward for providing an afternoon's entertainment.[53] Not that the FA could afford to be complacent about irregularities in the South. A few months after their Amateur Cup triumph a cloud of suspicion settled over Leyton when the club was fined £50 and its officials suspended after failing to produce the books required by a commission appointed to look into its financial affairs.[54]

The FA's pursuit of the shamateur persisted into the post-war period, though with indifferent success. For a few years, booming attendances meant that the senior amateur game was awash with cash and the FA found itself swimming against the tide. 'Most successful amateur clubs', Bailey recalled, reflecting on his playing career with Leytonstone and Walthamstow Avenue, 'were "shamateur" in practice'. He had not been looking for money but it was clearly not hard to find and he saw no reason to turn it down. 'My own view of the situation was realistic', he explained. 'I enjoyed football so much that I would have played for nothing, but certainly had no objection to receiving extra pocket money'.[55] 'Boot money' and other forms of disguised payment helped make senior amateur football an attractive option for many talented players who realized that they could work in a secure job or pursue a career while earning a part-time income from their efforts on Saturday afternoons. For many, this was preferable to and carried less risk than full-time employment with a professional club, especially in the era of the Football League's maximum wage restriction before it was abolished in 1961. Jim Lewis, Bailey's teammate at Walthamstow Avenue, a much-capped England amateur international who was sufficiently talented to play for Chelsea's championship-winning team in 1955, recalled that he had once been approached by a representative of a professional club who appeared at his home with a suitcase crammed with £5 notes, 'which was to be my signing on fee'. Lewis was able to resist the temptation to relinquish his amateur status, not least because he already had a well-paid job, but the money on offer at Avenue may also have been a factor.[56]

From time to time the authorities would act where the abuse was flagrant and sufficient evidence was available, though such interventions were often resented. In January 1950, 139 current and former players of Grays Athletic, along with several club officials, were suspended for offences relating to expenses payments going back to 1946–7.[57] It was a judgement that made the FA very unpopular at Grays and at other clubs for whom ex-Grays players were now registered. 'The unfortunate part, so far as Grays is concerned', thundered the *Essex and Thurrock Gazette* as the storm broke, 'is [that] they have been doing what we are told most amateur clubs do'.[58] Letters from supporters took a similar line, arguing that the FA had been unduly harsh. 'I must agree,' one correspondent wrote, 'Grays are unlucky to be the one club found out. This pretence of amateur football has been going on for years, and everybody knows it.'[59] John Norman, who covered football for *Amateur Sport*, noted that much press comment suggested that Grays, an ambitious but unfashionable club, had been penalized 'for doing what 90 per cent of the Big Boys do every Saturday'.[60]

Though covert payments were endemic in senior amateur football, there were important exceptions. Some players, like Bob Hardisty, possibly the outstanding English amateur footballer of the 1950s, 'always refused even legitimate expenses, never mind the extras', though it seems likely that many of his Bishop Auckland team-mates were more pragmatic. 'We were amateurs but all the clubs paid the players to turn out for them...expenses, you see,' recalled Bob Thursby. When he joined the club in 1956, he had made it clear that he expected 'the going rate'.[61] Douglas Insole, who was staunchly defending the role of the amateur in first-class cricket as late as 1960, also claimed the moral high ground. He had been offered money by two amateur clubs while captaining the Cambridge University soccer team in the 1940s but had turned it down.⁶² Insole, however, was associated with Corinthian Casuals, one of a small number of clubs – Dulwich Hamlet and Northern Nomads also come to mind – whose *raison d'être* was to maintain amateur purity. This embraced rather more than a self-denying ordinance regarding liberal expenses. Playing the game in what was believed to be the 'right spirit' was also expected, not least because it was necessary to set a good example. 'What an important lesson the Casuals have to teach other amateur sides,' purred one match reporter in 1953 after an encounter with Leytonstone. 'They play the game as it should be played, in a happy, carefree way – regardless of their need for points.'⁶³ On the whole, it must be said, this was not a recipe for success in either the Isthmian League or the Amateur Cup, their appearance in the 1956 final notwithstanding.

The most important, and briefly the most successful, of these clubs in the post-war period was Thompson's beloved Pegasus, founded in 1948, at a time when football at the old universities was benefiting from an influx of relatively experienced players whose education had been interrupted by war service. Granted exemption from the qualifying rounds on its first entry into the Amateur Cup after some energetic canvassing by Thompson, Pegasus quickly made a significant impression in senior amateur football, winning the trophy in 1951 and 1953, while playing a fluent version of the 'push-and-run' style pioneered by Arthur Rowe's Tottenham team of the same era. For Thompson, and for many of the club's supporters, Pegasus was a reincarnation of the famous Corinthians club that had helped to sustain the hegemony of the classes over the masses on the field of play in the late nineteenth century. They also saw it as part of a crusade to purify a game that had been corrupted by commercialism and professionalism.⁶⁴ Pegasus, by winning the Amateur Cup, had 'demonstrated that England's foremost sport need not... depend for its future vitality on players receiving money'. Its victories were also seen as representing a symbolic triumph over shamateurism, against which the 'Pegs' were said to be waging 'a not unsuccessful war'.⁶⁵

Ten years later, however, a wave of negative publicity sent out a clear signal that this war had been lost. In the early 1960s, as ideas and institutions associated with Britain's 'Establishment' were subjected to critical scrutiny, it was hardly surprising that the FA's inconsistent and outdated policy on amateurism should attract attention. The Wolfenden Committee's report on *Sport and the Community* in 1960, had drawn attention to sports where amateur rules and the way in which they were interpreted '... permit, or even invite, what looks to the outside world very much like hypocrisy or even plain dishonesty'.[66] This seemed to encapsulate the situation in senior amateur football where clubs that chose not to pay their players, and felt themselves thereby disadvantaged, became increasingly frustrated by the FA's inability to enforce its own rules.

Even when it did, the outcome was not always satisfactory. A commission of inquiry in 1963 into flat-rate payments at Ashton United, which resulted in 21 players from the Lancashire club forfeiting their amateur status and *sine die* suspensions for the club chairman and treasurer, uncannily echoed the Durham tea money scandal and suggested that little had changed since 1928.[67] Yet, though rumour was widespread, proof remained hard to find, especially as much of the cash seemed to be supplied by third parties, such as supporters clubs. Eventually, Insole, by then chairman of Corinthian Casuals, supplied compelling details to the *Daily Mail*. 'The average weekly amounts to players in the big amateur leagues', he claimed, 'are £5 or £6 with the top clubs paying up to £10 plus bonuses'. Over a full season, a star player at this level could expect to earn around £400 free of tax. Insole also revealed that he had heard of bonuses of £100 per man being offered to teams for reaching the Amateur Cup final. 'Is there any amateurism left?', asked the chairman of the Athenian League, quoted in the same article. 'It's plain to all that shamateurism exists. I expect the balloon will go up one day.'[68] In reality, it was already drifting skywards.

Extra time: 1963–74

From this point on our two narratives merge and, in coming together, help to explain the FA's decision to abandon amateurism, and with it the Amateur Cup, in the early 1970s. When surveying the football landscape at this time, it is important to keep shamateurism in perspective. The vast majority of the 35,000 affiliated adult male clubs catered for recreational footballers who paid to play.[69] It was the relatively small number of players attached to clubs in elite amateur leagues who constituted the problem. Most of them, it was clear, were not averse to receiving payments over and above the expenses that they were permitted to claim when they played a match or attended a training session. However, whereas at one time it had been possible for their clubs, especially if they were successful, to operate profitably, or at least to break even, this situation no longer applied. With public interest declining sharply from the early 1960s – 45,000 for the 1961 final was less than half the attendance of six years earlier – clubs that paid their players often struggled to meet their commitments. At the same time, those senior clubs where a different tradition prevailed were also in difficulties. 'With a few exceptions,' claimed a spokesman for Dulwich Hamlet, 'our players refuse to accept expenses'; he then admitted that the club's playing record was disappointing, that it was impossible to retain promising youngsters and that crowds were diminishing fast. The only consolation was that 'it doesn't cost us £100 a week to field a losing team'.[70] In these circumstances the recent demise of Pegasus – which had closed down in June 1963 – was ominous. Neither amateurism nor shamateurism, it seemed, were financially sustainable.

Ironically, this meant that achieving success in the short term – especially in the Amateur Cup – became more rather than less important as senior clubs battled to survive in their rapidly shrinking sub-sector of the entertainment market. One long-established feature of the game at this level was the existence of an unofficial transfer market which parodied that operating more transparently in professional football. Though some players remained loyal to one club, others took advantage of their amateur status and moved around, often acquiring 'more clubs than Jack Nicklaus' and arousing suspicions that they were looking for a better deal. The frustration that led Insole to talk to the *Daily Mail* in 1962 was fed by irritation at the impending departure of Corinthian Casuals club captain John Robertson for Tooting and Mitcham. Casuals believed that Robertson had been illegally approached (or 'tapped up'), though the FA could not be persuaded to take action. 'This', notes the club's historian, 'was symptomatic of the growing problem of shamateurism'.[71] Mass defections, which occurred from time to time, created bad feeling, especially when the clubs concerned were local rivals. Hendon, having won the Athenian League title in 1960–1, lost most of its team to Enfield during the following close season and this was much resented.[72]

The recommendations of the FA's Amateur Status Committee, adopted in December 1963, aimed to discourage such practices and to crack down on shamateurism generally. Amateurs who accepted what some of them referred to as 'wages' would now be charged with 'misconduct', thus risking a *sine die* suspension; they would be permitted to play for only two clubs in a season; and an attempt would be made to restrict players to clubs within a 50-mile radius of their home or business address. New forms, carrying printed warnings of the dire consequences that would ensue if players or officials breached the rules, were issued to all clubs competing for the Amateur Cup. The aim, it seemed, was to strangle the shamateur with red tape, though this approach cut little ice with those who had pressed the FA to take action. What the *Mail* referred to as 'The Anti-Sham Charter' found few friends. Insole believed that it would fail mainly because most under-the-counter payments were made by supporters clubs which were effectively beyond the FA's jurisdiction. He also feared that the residence qualification would simply encourage clubs to find jobs for players, an aspect of shamateurism that was already a cause for concern. Taking his line from Insole, Brian James, the *Mail*'s football correspondent was unimpressed. The new regime would 'harass the "shamateur" wanderers and embarrass the clubs who pay them to move. But it won't stop "shamateurism" – perhaps nothing can'.[73]

The limitations of the new regime were quickly exposed. It may have played a part in persuading Wimbledon (1964) and Barnet (1965) to turn professional but, for most senior clubs, it was 'business as usual'. A Sutton United official complained in 1965 that 'quite a number of clubs' had been willing to cooperate at first – hardly surprising in view of the financial pressure that many were now under – but they had grown disillusioned when flagrant abuses went unpunished. Walton and Hersham were known to be an excellent club but eight first team players had recently left in suspicious circumstances. 'The Football Association apparently did nothing to enquire into the matter,' he observed. In these circumstances, clubs could hardly be blamed for reverting to their old ways. 'We have tried to stand out,' a nameless club official had told him, 'but now we realise that we must do what everyone else is doing'.[74] In the North-East, the Northern League was anxious for clarification, its ranks having been boosted by clubs seeking to cut their expenses by abandoning part-time professional for amateur football. In 1968, at a meeting of county associations, the Durham FA proposed substituting 'non-contracted players' for 'amateurs' in the FA's rule book but received insufficient support. Thompson urged them privately to 'persist in their campaign to get something done about this matter'.[75]

The FA's policy of categorizing players as either 'amateur' or 'professional', though losing credibility after Thompson's *volte face* in 1963, remained in place until 1972. By this time both cricket (1963) and tennis (1968) had abandoned the distinction, so football's relatively slow movement in this direction requires explanation. The Amateur Cup competition was significant here. Though it had lost some of its lustre, it was still a national competition with a relatively high profile. As Ford United, an Aetolian League club linked to the Ford motor works in Dagenham, recognized when entering the 1963 tournament, a good run would strengthen their case for entry to a better league.[76] The Cup still retained some of its old capacity for engaging communities in support of their local team, especially when a small club punched above its weight, as when Worcestershire Combination side Alvechurch reached the semi-final in 1965–6. Chesham United's 17-match run from the preliminary round to Wembley two seasons later re-emphasized the point.[77] The 1967 final between Enfield and Skelmersdale, from a Liverpool 'overspill' community that had been granted 'new town' status only six years previously, attracted 75,000 to Wembley and a further 55,388 to the replay at Maine Road, Manchester. While there was some life and potential profit in the tournament, it was difficult to persuade clubs to abandon the amateur status that they often honoured only in the breach. 'The only reason why some clubs *pretend* to be amateur,' the *FA Year Book* observed as the system entered its last days, 'is that there is an advantage to be gained: that of dominating the amateur world, and in particular the Amateur Cup.'[78]

There were, however, always going to be more losers than winners and this was not a position that many could sustain for long, especially as a radical formula to deal with the ambiguities that had plagued amateur football amateur for so long had now emerged. The Wolfenden report in 1960 had acknowledged a minority view in favour of abolishing 'quite simply and straightforwardly, the formal distinction between amateur and professional, and to allow any participant, if he needs or wishes it, to be paid as a player without stigma, reproach or differentiation'.[79] This was the preferred option of Tony Pawson, now a football writer for *The Observer*, who had been a member of the committee, and also of many important figures in the senior amateur game. 'I'd call them all players and be done with it', was the view of Wimbledon chairman Sydney Black.[80] In June 1969, Thompson appears to have realized that he could move decisively to achieve the outcome he favoured when he was presented with a dossier of evidence relating to Enfield, which amounted to 'a severe indictment of a so-called Amateur club'.[81] The allegations were potentially embarrassing, not least for the FA, who regularly selected Enfield players to represent England in amateur international matches and had presented the club with the Amateur Cup at Wembley a few weeks earlier.

It was the beginning of the end. Thompson was rewarded for exercising his discretion when the Amateur Status Committee called representatives of county associations and senior amateur leagues to a meeting in January 1970. This allowed his friends in the North-East to restate the case for referring to all footballers, paid and unpaid, as 'players'.[82] A recommendation to this effect was provisionally endorsed by the FA Council in May 1971 and finally approved in November 1972. Clubs were given time to adjust to the new dispensation, which was to run from season 1974–5.[83] The consensus of press opinion was that the decision should have been taken at least a decade earlier but had been delayed by the unwillingness of the *blazerati* on the FA Council to face reality and the determination of amateur football's big fish to swim in their own small pool for as long as possible. Modernization had been frustrated, according to Geoffrey Green, because 'certain voices of authority [had] clung blindly to the ideals and values of another age'; these had now 'been swept away'.[84] It was ironic, nevertheless, that the pursuit of the much-maligned shamateur should end in this way, with the simultaneous demise of amateur football. At last, the disease had been eradicated, but the cure had cost the patient his life.

Notes

1. *The Times*, 22 April 1974.
2. *Herts & Essex Observer*, 22 March, 12 April 1974. 'Cup fever' was also reported in Ilford as the final approached; see *Ilford Recorder*, 28 March 1974.
3. *Herts & Essex Observer*, 26 April 1974.
4. The designation 'senior' in English amateur football related to status rather than age. In practice, it was applied mainly to clubs whose playing record allowed them to compete in elite amateur leagues, such as the Athenian, Isthmian and Northern Leagues, where money was taken at the gate. 'Junior' clubs played mainly in local league competitions.
5. For entries, matches and results see Fred Hawthorn, *The F.A. Amateur Cup Complete Results: Qualifying Rounds and Rounds Proper 1893/4 to 1973/4* (Nottingham: SoccerData Publications, 2009); also Richard Samuel, *The Complete F.A. Amateur Cup Results Book* (Cleethorpes: Soccer Books Ltd, 2003); Bob Barton, *Servowarm History of the F.A. Amateur Cup* (Newcastle upon Tyne: author, 1984).
6. Harry Pearson, *The Far Corner: A Mazy Dribble Through North-East Football* (London: Warner Books, 1994), p. 49. Synthonia was a trade name for synthetic ammonia.
7. Newsreel footage of the 1951 final can be previewed at http://www.britishpathe.com/record.php?id=33374 (accessed 20 June 2010).
8. W.E. Greenland, *The History of the Amateur Football Alliance* (Harwich: Standard Printing and Publishing, 1965), p. 13. Greenland was the secretary of the AFA.
9. Tony Mason, *Association Football and English Society, 1863–1915* (Brighton: Harvester Press, 1980), p. 249n. See also Dilwyn Porter, 'Revenge of the Crouch End Vampires: the AFA, the FA and English Football's "Great Split", 1907–14', *Sport in History*, 26 (3), 2006, pp. 406–28; also Matthew Taylor, *The Association Game: A History of British Football* (Harlow: Pearson Longman, 2008), pp. 82–5; Dave Russell, *Football and the English: a Social History of Association Football in England, 1863–1995* (Preston: Carnegie Publishing, 1997), pp. 22–9, 38–42.
10. Richard Metcalfe, 'The Origins, Development and Impact of the Football Association Amateur Cup, 1893–1915', unpublished MRes thesis, Leeds

Metropolitan University, Leeds, UK, 2009, pp. 25–6; Rob Cavallini, *A Casual Affair: A History of the Casuals Football Club* (Surbiton: Dog N Duck Publications, 2009), pp. 39–40.
11. See Greenland, *Amateur Football Alliance*, pp. 39–40; Ian Sorenson, 'The Arthur Dunn Cup', in A.H. Fabian and Geoffrey Green (eds), *Association Football* (London: Caxton Publishing Co., 1960), Vol. 2, pp. 142–6.
12. Tony Pawson, *Indelible Memories: Playingfields and Battlefields* (privately published, 2006), pp. 177–8.
13. Sir Stanley Rous, *Football Worlds: A Lifetime in Sport* (London: Faber and Faber, 1978), p.123.
14. *The Football Association Year Book 1974–1975* (London: Heinemann Ltd., 1974), p. 96.
15. Martin Johnes, *Soccer and Society: South Wales, 1900–1939* (Cardiff: University of Wales Press, 2002), p. 210.
16. Mike Amos (ed.), *Northern Goalfields Revisited: The Millennium History of the Northern Football League, 1889–2000* (privately published, 2000), pp. 133–5; see also Pearson, *Far Corner*, p. 210.
17. Dave Finch and Steve Peart, *Wycombe Wanderers F.C. 1887–1996: The Official History* (Harefield: Yore Publications, 1996), pp. 35–7.
18. Alan Adamthwaite, *Glory Days: The Golden Age of Bishop Auckland* (Manchester: Parrs Wood Press, 2005), pp. 29–30.
19. David Ballheimer and Peter Lush, *Hendon Football Club: The First 100 Years* (London: London League Publications, 2008), pp. 157–8.
20. *Evesham Standard and West Midlands Observer*, 27 January 1923.
21. Ibid., 27 January, 24 February, 10 March, 28 April 1923.
22. Ibid., 24 February 1923.
23. *The Story of the London Caledonians Football Club, as told by an Old Member* (Harefield: Yore Books, n.d.), p. 28; reprint of a booklet first published in 1924; for photographic evidence see *Berrow's Worcester Journal* (Gratis Supplement), 28 April 1923.
24. *Evesham Standard*, 28 April 1923.
25. Geoffrey Green, 'The Oval: 1884–1892', in Fabian and Green (eds), *Association Football*, Vol. 3, p. 17. Blackburn Olympic won the FA Cup in 1883; Blackburn Rovers in 1884, 1885 and 1886.
26. Brad Beaven, *Leisure, Citizenship and Working-Class Men in Britain, 1850–1945* (Manchester: Manchester University Press, 2005), pp. 72–81; see also the comments on rugby and civic pride in Tony Collins, *Rugby's Great Split: Class, Culture and the Origins of Rugby League Football* (London: Frank Cass, 1998), pp. 23–4.
27. W.R. Powell (ed.), *The Victoria History of the Counties of England: A History of Essex* (Oxford: Oxford University Press, 1973), Vol. 6, pp. 175, 182. For Tottenham see Dilwyn Porter, ' "Coming on with Leaps and Bounds in the Metropolis": London Football in the Era of the 1908 Olympics', *London Journal*, 34 (2), 2009, pp. 117–18.
28. *Walthamstow, Leyton and Chingford Guardian*, 20 April 1928.
29. See Cavallini, *Casual Affair*, pp. 175–7.
30. Trevor Bailey, *Wickets, Catches and the Odd Run* (London: Willow Books,1986), p. 199; match programme, Leytonstone v Walthamstow Avenue, Essex Senior Cup, first round, 8 January 1949 (author's collection).

31. Finch and Peart, *Wycombe Wanderers*, p. 40. Wycombe Wanderers played at Loakes Park from 1895 to 1990.
32. 'The Amateur Cup Final', *FA Year Book 1973–1974*, p. 94.
33. Maurice Golesworthy, *The Encyclopaedia of Association Football* (8th edn.) (London: Robert Hale, 1967), p. 187.
34. Match programme, Romford *v* Crook Town, FA Amateur Cup, second round, 23 January 1954 (author's collection).
35. The Football Association, Wembley, Minutes and Proceedings, [hereafter FA Minutes and Proceedings], Meeting of Council, 29 June 1963, attached report of Amateur Cup Committee, 7 June 1963.
36. http://www.pitchero.com/clubs/oxfordcityfc/?section=videos_photos_views &video_id=1370 (accessed 25 July 2010).
37. Ken Shearwood, *Pegasus* (Oxford: Oxford Illustrated Press, 1975), p. 72; *Hardly a Scholar* (Ormskirk: Tyger & Tyger, 1999), p. 396.
38. *Eastbourne Gazette*, 22 September 1954.
39. Finch and Peart, *Wycombe Wanderers*, p. 43.
40. Match programme, Leytonstone *v* Penrith, FA Amateur Cup, second round replay, 10 February 1962 (author's collection).
41. Match programme, Ilford *v* Woking, Isthmian League, 23 January 1965 (author's collection).
42. See Russell, *Football and the English*, pp. 131–8.
43. Geoffrey Green, *Soccer: The World Game: A Popular History* (London: Pan Books Ltd., 1953), p. 79.
44. The Royal Society Centre for the History of Science, London, Sir Harold Thompson MSS, [hereafter Thompson Papers], E.371, draft typescript headed 'Illegal Payments in Amateur Football, [January 1964]. This sentence is scored through and did not appear in the version published in *The Times*, 11 January 1964.
45. See 'Sir Harold Warris Thompson', in H.G.C. Matthew and Brian Harrison (eds.), *The Oxford Dictionary of National Biography* (Oxford: Oxford University Press, 2004), Vol. 54, p. 438.
46. FA Minutes and Proceedings, Council Meeting, 2 December 1963, attached paper, 'Amateur Status: Report of the Sub-Committee'.
47. Thompson Papers, E.369, letter from Thompson to Denis Follows (FA Secretary), 11 November 1963 (copy).
48. *The Times*, 11 January 1964. For more on this episode see Dilwyn Porter, 'Amateur Football in England, 1948–63: The Pegasus Phenomenon', *Contemporary British History*, 14 (2), 2000, pp. 24–6.
49. Metcalfe, 'Amateur Cup', p. 62.
50. Ibid., pp. 57–60.
51. Sir Frederick Wall, *Fifty Years of Football: 1884–1934* (Cleethorpes: Soccer Books Ltd, 2006), p. 120; first published in 1935.
52. Cited in Amos, 'Storms in a Teacup', in Amos (ed.), *Northern Goalfields*, p. 488.
53. For the most detailed account of the Durham 'tea money' affair see David Johnson, *The Durham Sham-Amateur Affair of 1928* (Nottingham: SoccerData Publications, 2009); see also Amos, 'Storms in a Tea Cup', pp. 484–90; Pearson, *Far Corner*, pp. 216–9.
54. See *The Times*, 27 August, 27 September 1928.

55. Bailey, *Wickets, Catches and the Odd Run*, p. 200; see also Jack Bailey, *Trevor Bailey: A Life in Cricket* (London: Methuen, 1993), p. 27; also 'Strolling Down the Avenue', *The Non-League Paper*, 9 July 2000, pp. 21–5.
56. *Walthamstow Guardian*, 29 December 1989. For interviews with other players of this era who decided to combine amateur football with a more conventional career see Ballheimer and Lush, *Hendon*, pp. 166–7, 216–9.
57. See FA, Minutes and Proceedings, Council Meetings, 13 February, minute 46(i); 28 April 1950, minute 63(m).
58. *Essex and Thurrock Gazette*, 19 November 1949.
59. Letter from A.J. Johnson, *Essex and Thurrock Gazette*, 18 February 1950.
60. *Amateur Sport*, 11 February 1950.
61. 'Bobby topped them all', *Non-League Paper*, 16 July 2000; Adamthwaite, *Glory Days*, pp. 142–3.
62. See Insole's interview in the *Daily Mail*, 22 January 1963; for his views on amateurism generally see Douglas Insole, *Cricket from the Middle* (London: Sportsmans Book Club, 1961), pp. 34–48.
63. *Walthamstow Guardian*, 24 April 1953.
64. See especially Edward Grayson, *Corinthians & Cricketers* (London: Sportsmans Book Club, 1957), pp. 173–4.
65. Jerry Weinstein, 'University Soccer – A Mission', *Varsity* (Cambridge), 22 November, 1952. For the history of Pegasus, see Porter, 'Amateur Football in England', pp. 1–30.
66. *Sport and the Community: The Report of the Wolfenden Committee on Sport* (London: Central Council of Physical Recreation, 1960), p. 67, para. 168.
67. FA Minutes and Proceedings, Council Meeting, 7 June 1963, attached paper, Interim Report of a Commission appointed to investigate alleged breaches of rules by Ashton United FC.
68. *Daily Mail*, 22 January 1963. £400 in 1962 was the equivalent of £6244 in 2009, a significant part-time salary. See http://bankofengland.co.uk/education/inflation/calculator/flas/index.htm (accessed 31 July 2010).
69. Estimate based on figures in Taylor, *Association Game*, p. 253.
70. *Daily Mail*, 23 January 1963.
71. Rob Cavallini, *Corinthian Casuals: The First Seventy Years, 1939–2009* (Surbiton: Dog N Duck Publications, 2009), p. 78.
72. Ballheimer and Lush, *Hendon*, p.159.
73. *Daily Mail*, 3 December 1963. Thompson Papers, E.373, for cuttings supplying further examples of press criticism.
74. Thompson Papers, E.373, letter from Mr A.W. Letts to Denis Follows, 15 July 1965 (copy).
75. Thompson Papers, E.372, letter from Thompson to J.B. Blenkinsopp (Durham FA), 3 January 1969 (copy); see also Amos (ed.), *Northern Goalfields Revisited*, p. 291.
76. *Daily Mail*, 26 January 1963.
77. Barton, *FA Amateur Cup*, pp. 198–9, 204–5.
78. 'The End of the Amateur', *FA Year Book 1973–1974*, pp. 90–1.
79. *Sport and the Community*, p. 68, para. 170.
80. *Daily Mail*, 23 January 1963; for other examples see Porter, 'Amateur Football in England', p. 26.

81. Thompson Papers, E.24, letter from Thompson to Dr Andrew Stephen (FA chairman), 20 June 1970 (copy).
82. FA Minutes and Proceedings, Council Meeting, 2 March 1970, attached report of Amateur Status Committee, 16 January 1970; Amos (ed.), *Northern Goalfields*, p. 291.
83. FA Minutes and Proceedings, Council Meeting, 7 May 1971, minute 66(s); 27 November 1972, minute 46.
84. *The Times*, 28 November 1972.

4
Rough, Manly Sport and the American Way: Theodore Roosevelt and College Football, 1905

Michael Oriard

'It was the flying wedge, football's major offense in 1905, that spurred the formation of the NCAA.' Thus opens the brief history of the organization posted on the website of the National Collegiate Athletic Association. It continues:

> The game's rugged nature, typified by mass formations and gang tackling, resulted in numerous injuries and deaths and prompted many institutions to discontinue the sport. Others urged that football be reformed or abolished from intercollegiate athletics.
>
> President Theodore Roosevelt summoned college athletics leaders to two White House conferences to encourage such reforms. In early December 1905, Chancellor Henry M. MacCracken of New York University convened a meeting of 13 institutions to initiate changes in football-playing rules. At a subsequent meeting December 28 in New York City, the Intercollegiate Athletic Association of the United States (IAAUS) was founded by 62 members.[1]

The IAAUS (or ICAA, as it's usually called) became the NCAA in 1910.

Unlike baseball, whose origins were long entangled in the creation myth of Abner Doubleday, the origins of American football have always been straightforward: a first intercollegiate (soccer-style) game played by Princeton and Rutgers on 6 November 1869; the formation of the Intercollegiate Football Association by Harvard, Yale, Princeton, and Columbia in 1876 around a rugby-style game; the evolution away from rugby toward a distinctive American version in the 1880s; the founding of the forerunner of the NCAA to oversee the sport in December 1905.

80

Out of the new rules formulated for the 1906 season came, most significantly, the forward pass, which completed the break from rugby and, over time, completely transformed the American version. The other aspect of the 1905–6 moment that has resonated most strongly was the involvement of Theodore Roosevelt, among the most mythologized of American presidents. Some accounts of the 1905–6 moment over the years have noted that *even* President Roosevelt, the young sport's most exalted champion, was prepared to abolish it for its excessive brutality. Actually, Roosevelt summoned 'college athletics leaders' to the White House, not to threaten but to impress upon them the need for reforms lest antagonistic college presidents or an alienated public demand abolition of the game.

The 1905–6 moment, then, has long had a privileged place in histories of American football, but a simple morality play such as the synopsis on the NCAA's website – collective outrage against the sport's unchecked mayhem, the game saved from itself only by radical reform – misses a messier and more revealing drama.[2]

In a minor key, the creation of what became the NCAA foretold the organization's limitations as a regulatory body. Conspicuously missing from the meetings out of which the NCAA was born were Harvard, Yale, and Princeton, not just the leading American universities but also the jock powerhouses – the Texas, USC, and Ohio State of the era. In 1905–6, the Big Three (particularly Harvard) were unwilling to surrender their autonomy to the collective will of lesser institutions. In recent decades, the current football powerhouses have been asserting *their* autonomy through the creation of divisions and subdivisions within the NCAA, through a College Football Association that successfully challenged the NCAA's television monopoly on anti-trust grounds, and the various arrangements culminating in the current Bowl Championship Series (BCS), all of which served to guarantee more and more revenue for fewer and fewer top programs. Since 1905–6 (and before), regulating college football for the collective good has been like regulating Wall Street: the most powerful institutions always manage to have their way.

In the major key, the moment of 1905–6 opened a window into football's place in American culture, particularly its deepest connections to notions of manliness. A 'crisis of masculinity' in the late nineteenth and early twentieth centuries has been so well-documented (and challenged) that it warranted an entry in a 2003 historical encyclopedia of 'American masculinities.'[3] Gail Bederman has argued persuasively that 'masculinity,' or 'manliness' (the term that it began to replace in this period) was an ideological construct in continuous process of evolution. Although the term 'crisis' may overstate it, the years from 1880 to 1910 were a period when men 'were actively, even enthusiastically, engaging in the process of remaking manhood,' in response to the profound social and economic changes in the decades since the Civil War. The extraordinary growth in the popularity of college football in the 1880s and 1890s, a time when a tiny minority (3 or 4 percent) of Americans went to college, was part of the 'remaking' that resulted. By the 1890s, as Bederman puts it, 'College football had become a national craze; and commentators like Theodore Roosevelt argued that football's ability to foster virility was worth even an occasional death on the playing field.'[4] Bederman's interest is in middle-class manhood, but gender issues also engaged the elites, who felt their own power and authority being usurped by a new self-made commercial and professional class. College football was an elite sport in its origins, but by the turn of the century it had already extended its reach well into the middle and lower classes.

Concern about brutality in football was nothing new in 1905, having erupted intermittently since the mid-1880s. Rugby football was rough, but Americans made it rougher, partly through the unintended consequences of revising the rules. Awarding the ball to one side at a time, to be advanced five yards in three attempts ('downs'), led to the creation of set plays and distinct roles for backs and linemen. 'Interference' (blocking) by linemen had to be permitted when it proved impossible to eliminate it, with the result that, in a typical play, a mass of offensive players collided with a mass of defensive players. The obvious alternative was for a speedy ballcarrier to run around the defenders, but when tackling below the waist was legalized (to take away the ballcarrier's advantage), end runs became useless. The cleverest tacticians now took advantage of the absence of anything like the modern rule limiting the number of backfield men and forbidding them to move toward the ball before it was put in play. The result was the various formations and mass-momentum plays represented by the 'flying wedge': beefy guards and tackles lining up in the backfield along with the fullbacks and halfbacks, all moving toward the line of scrimmage before the ball was put in play for a violent collision with stationary defenders – over and over, ad nauseam (and ad mayhem).[5]

The rules themselves were a problem in 1905, then, but so was the players' observance of them. One factor was an American spirit of 'gamesmanship' as opposed to British 'sportsmanship': recognition of the letter but not the spirit of the rules.[6] The rules of American football evolved, after all, as a continuous process of modifying existing rules that clever coaches and players had figured out how to circumvent. The other factor was the common practice of simply ignoring the rules if you could get away with it, specifically the rules against unnecessary roughness – slugging, kneeing, pulling – that were never consistently enforced.

Beyond the rules, and their circumvention or violation, lay a third crucial element: a desire that football be rough, just not too rough. Football's roughness was what made it a test and training ground for a generation in danger of losing its 'manliness.'

The crisis

The 1905 season opened, then, in a continuation of ongoing controversies, of which brutality was just one. 'Commercialism,' 'professionalism' (hiring coaches, recruiting and subsidizing athletes), overemphasis, and the spirit of a sport that valued brawn over brain and winning by any means possible were as regularly denounced as the sport was celebrated.[7] Brutality was the only issue capable of arousing the broad public, but whether the game was indeed too violent, or 'newspaper hysteria' wildly exaggerated the violence, was yet another source of controversy. This was the era of 'yellow journalism' and the circulation war in New York between Joseph Pulitzer and William Randolph Hearst. A sudden death, or three, on the football field, such as those in 1897, was always good for sensational prose and ghoulish illustrations, staples of the penny press in Britain and the U.S. since the 1830s (Figure 4.1).

The 1905 season was no more brutal than many preceding it, but several events came together to create a sense of crisis.[8] In June, President Roosevelt (Harvard class of '80) gave a commencement address at his alma mater that became the narrative frame for the incidents that transpired a few months later. Only a portion of his address on 'The Harvard Spirit' dealt with sport – his topic was the essential functions of a great university – but this was the portion seized on by the popular press. In words that would be quoted over and over during the season to come, the President expressed his belief in 'rough sports' and his 'hearty contempt' for those who wrung their hands over broken collarbones, but he reserved his 'heartiest... contempt' for any player guilty of mere brutality. He spoke at greater length about the proper spirit of the game: for the rewards of participation over spectatorship and of 'the effort to win' over victory itself; and against overemphasis, sensationalism, and the 'semi-professionalism' that perverted it.[9] Roosevelt had no legal authority over coaches and college presidents, but the popular press gave him a vast audience for his 'bully pulpit.' It also so happened in 1905 that

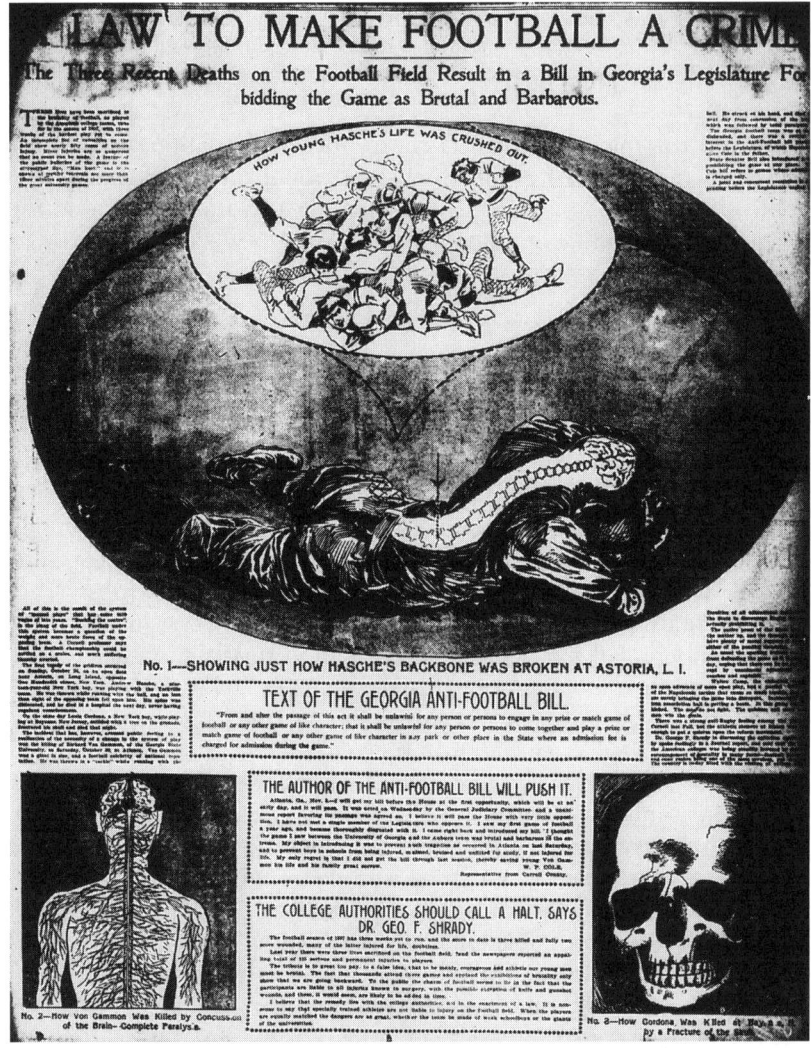

Figure 4.1 Hearst's *New York Journal and Advertiser*, November 7, 1897, describing 'How Young Hasche's Life Was Crushed Out,' 'How Von Gammon Was Killed by Concussion of the Brain,' and 'How Gordona Was Killed at Bayone, N.J., by a Fracture of the Skull.'

Roosevelt's son Ted was an undersized end on the Harvard freshman team, a coincidence from which the press made much more. The President of the United States who valued 'rough sports' was also the father of a young football player subjected to the battering tactics of the game.

The latest campaign for reform began in June and July, when the muckraking journal *McClure's* published a two-part *exposé* of commercialism and professionalism in college football, prompting Roosevelt to meet with their author, Henry Beech Needham, that summer.[10] Roosevelt took the initiative in early October, when he summoned representatives from Harvard, Yale, and Princeton to the White House to discuss how to make the game less violent. By agreement, Yale's Walter Camp issued a brief statement to the press, announcing that the representatives from the three schools had 'agreed that we consider an honourable obligation exists to carry out in letter and in spirit the rules of the game of football relating to roughness, holding and foul play,' and that the coaches present had pledged 'to carry out that obligation.'[11] Though remarkably bland, this statement prompted the press to proclaim that the trust-busting president was now taking on Big Football along with the rest of the nation's and world's problems (Figure 4.2).

What might have transpired, had the 1905 season played out uneventfully, cannot be known. Much talk of reform had preceded this meeting, though never emanating from the White House, but the 1905 season concluded with a shocking death that made inaction unthinkable. Football seasons had a distinct rhythm in these years: the major teams scheduled weaker opponents through October and into November, then played their Big Games in the final weeks, while second-rank teams scheduled around them. New York had only second-rank teams, in Columbia and New York University (NYU), but also many alumni from Harvard, Yale, and Princeton, whose season-ending contests received the most extensive coverage. A series of incidents marred several early-season match-ups. Police had to restore order after Columbia players charged onto the field when a Wesleyan player kicked one of their teammates. Its game with Harvard left a Swarthmore player with a bloodied face that was captured by a photographer. Against Penn, a Harvard player was ejected after slugging an opponent in the face in retaliation for being kneed repeatedly. These incidents prompted local criticism but were just the warm-ups for the big contests.[12]

The freshman game on November 19 between Harvard and Yale received unusual attention in 1905 because of Harvard's 145-pound end bearing the same name as the President of the United States. Early reports out of Cambridge about Ted, Jr's progress on the freshman team

Figure 4.2 A two-page centerfold in the humor magazine *Judge* for November 4 portrayed the Football Slugger as just the latest of the many beasts – the Russian Bear, the Democratic Donkey, the Government Grafter, and the Spanish Monkey – tamed by President Roosevelt. *Harper's Weekly* had a similar cover on October 28.

had described him as a 'strenuous' young athlete who 'falls on the ball with an earnestness that warms the heart of the freshman coach.' Over the next month, young Roosevelt, though 'a slender, wiry little chap,' worked in scrimmages 'like a demon for victory,' his facial features flashing 'a resemblance to a square-faced man with a big jaw and lips that part over teeth that seem able to bite through a tenpenny nail.'[13] The Harvard freshmen played only one game that really mattered, and against Yale's behemoths Ted, Jr proved himself truly his father's son. The writer for Hearst's *New York American* pulled out all the stops in describing young Ted as 'beaten down until there wasn't a bone in his body that didn't ache, and until he wasn't sure whether he was playing football or just suffering in a bad dream. But he wouldn't quit.' The writer also noted that the President's son disdained the shin protectors, nose guard, and head covering that might have softened the blows, and he left with the game (unwillingly) with both eyes closed and his nose flattened.[14]

The Harvard and Yale varsities played the following week, a contest marred by a Yale player's blatant foul that went unpunished. But the biggest game of the season was eclipsed by a minor one on the same day between NYU and Union College, when a Union player was killed. 'Another college student yesterday gave up his life on the gridiron as a startling proof of the brutal tactics of modern football,' the *New York American* began its account. A Union defensive halfback, Harold Moore, collided head-on with an NYU back, dropped to the ground 'writhing in convulsions', and died shortly after with his father ('one of the best-known men up-state') looking on. Before the game, according to the *World*, young Moore had told his teammates: 'Fellows, I am going to play the game of my life to-day, because my father is in the grand stand, and he has never seen me work before'.[15]

The response was immediate. In chapel the next day, NYU chancellor Henry MacCracken told the students that he would push to drop football, a once-worthy sport now degraded by its 'homicidal features,' its 'exaltation of bulk and brawn over brains,' and its 'exaltation of money-making.'[16] On Tuesday, a faculty committee at Columbia (with the full support of President Nicholas Murray Butler) announced that Columbia was also dropping football. Having appealed unsuccessfully to Harvard president Charles Eliot, the most distinguished academic critic of the sport at the time, for his leadership of the reform movement, NYU's MacCracken invited the 19 schools it had played over the past ten years to a conference. Twelve (plus NYU) ended up sending representatives to a meeting on December 8 at which an 8–5 majority voted to reform rather than abolish the game. (Columbia, NYU, and Union voted for abolition.) A second meeting on December 28 drew 60 schools (again without Harvard, Yale, and Princeton) and produced a proposal for a new rules committee to work with the existing committee (dominated by the Big Three) to reform the game. The two committees met over the winter and spring, while Harvard also weighed in with its own proposals. Eventually, and in time for the 1906 season, the various groups agreed on a set of rules, the most important of which increased the yards needed in three downs from five to ten (to reduce the incentive for plunges into the line); created a 'neutral zone' between the opposing lines (to eliminate slugging before the ball was put in play); limited to five the number of players who could line up in the backfield, with one of them required to be flanked outside the widest lineman (to reduce mass plays); shortened the game from 70 to 60 minutes (to lessen fatigue); and legalized the forward pass (to open up play) but with major restrictions that would inhibit the development of the passing game until the rules were modified again in 1910. Pushing and pulling the ballcarrier was not banned – the new rules were meant to create opportunities for open play, rather than to ban mass play altogether – and the groups did nothing to address the larger issues of eligibility and the place of the game within institutions of higher education. The source of the immediate crisis was brutality, and the new rules were intended to make the game less violent.[17]

Teddy and Ted

But not too much less. Harold Moore's death from football was far from the first, but it happened in New York, in the presence of the New York press, near the end of a season in which the President himself had declared a need to make the game less brutal. The fatality was the catalyst that forced university leaders throughout the country to decide whether to reform or abolish the game. Reform won out, but it won out with a narrow focus on unnecessary roughness, and even here with an important unstated condition: that the roughness not be eliminated altogether.

The tension between necessary and unnecessary roughness was as old as the game, and in 1905 it was framed by the comments of the President of the United States. Key lines from Roosevelt's Harvard commencement address were repeatedly quoted by journalists as the season played out.[18] 'I have no sympathy whatever with the overwrought sentimentality which would keep a young man in cotton and wool,' Roosevelt had declared, 'and I have a hearty contempt for him if he counts a broken arm or collar bone as of serious consequences when balanced against the chance of showing that he possesses hardihood, physical address and courage.' But the President also said this: 'Brutality in playing a game should awaken the heartiest and most plainly shown contempt for the player guilty of it, especially if this brutality is coupled with a low cunning in committing it without getting caught by the umpire.' Among the places these words were quoted was the front page of the New York *World* on November 20, in a box under the headline, 'What the President Said of the Game His Son Plays,' accompanying an illustration of the 'President's Son as Sample "Victim" of Football Game'. Arrows pointed to each of the injuries that Ted, Jr suffered two days earlier against the Yale freshmen: Both Eyes Discolored, Cheek Swollen and Mouth Cut, Battered Head, Nose 'Swollen', Shoulders Twisted and Covered With Bruises, Fingers Stiffened, Right Leg Injured, Both Shins Barked. The illustration alongside the President's words raised an obvious question: how much of this damage to his son was acceptable? (Figure 4.3)

Figure 4.3 New York World, November 20, 1905.

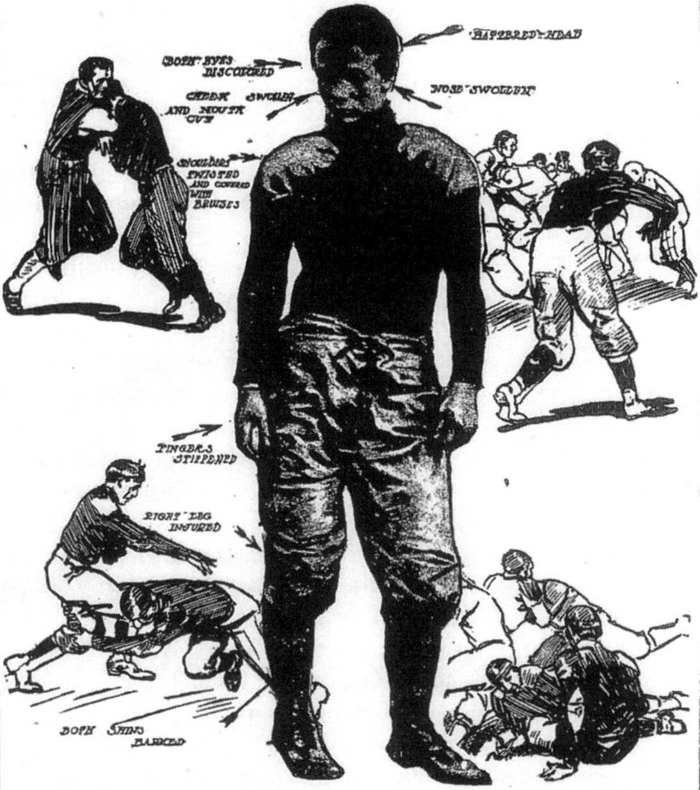

We can surmise Roosevelt's answer from his letters to Ted, which reveal the President, with his oft-professed views representative of his position and class, not as a cartoon figure with a Big Stick but as a father applying those views to his own son. After young Ted suffered a breakdown around the age of 10, Roosevelt took to heart the suggestion that his own 'excessive expectations' were the cause.[19] He continued to want his son to challenge himself, but within reason. In May 1901, when Ted was in prep school at Groton, his father wrote after a visit that he was 'entirely satisfied' with his son's standing in both sports and studies. 'I always believe in going hard at everything,' he wrote, 'whether it is Latin or mathematics, boxing or football, but at the same time I want to keep the sense of proportion.' That fall, after Ted broke a collarbone in a football game, father wrote his 'Blessed Ted' that he was sorry about the injury, 'but I am glad you played right through the game, and that you seem to have minded it so little. It is hard luck to lose the rest of the football season, but still you have had four good weeks and must have improved a great deal.'[20] A few months later, without telling his son ('Ted would have a fit if he knew I were writing') he also wrote the school's headmaster, Endicott Peabody, to express deeper concern that his son could not withstand the beating from much larger players.[21]

Roosevelt's letters convey no sense of 'excessive expectations.' He knew himself to be no great athlete – 'I am simply a good, ordinary out of doors man,' he would write to Henry Beech Needham after their meeting in July 1905[22] – and he knew that his son was no great athlete, either. The following season, responding in a jocular mood to an amusing note from Ted about some hunting adventure, the President/father wrote, 'So, killer of the buck and shooter of the prairie chicken, I hereby grant you unconditional permission to play on the third Eleven. Now do not break your neck unless you esteem it really necessary. About arms and legs I am less particular, although on the whole I prefer that even they should be kept reasonably whole.'[23] Behind the joking about matters he took very seriously clearly lay a desire that his son develop manliness, but not at too high a cost – the sort of ambivalent, competing, perhaps contradictory desires that make Roosevelt the father seem more familiar than strange.

The President's letters to his younger son Kermit reinforced his advice to his eldest. When Ted was a junior (fourth former) at Groton, his father wrote to Kermit that 'I would rather have a boy of mine stand high in his studies than high in athletics, but I would a great deal rather have him show true manliness of character than show either intellectual or physical prowess; and I believe you and Ted both bid fair to develop just such character.'[24] Writing two days later to Ted, Roosevelt responded to his son's disappointment over being demoted from the second eleven with his fullest elaboration on the role of rough football in a boy's education (along with a bit of self-deprecation, to bolster his son). 'I am proud of your pluck, and I greatly admire football – though it was not a game I was ever able to play myself, my qualities resembling Kermit's rather than yours. But the very things that make it a good game make it a rough game, and there is always the chance of your being laid up.' A worthy goal – a place on the school team or on his class team when he should enter Harvard – would justify the risk. 'But I am by no means sure that it *is* worth your while to run the risk of being laid up for the sake of playing in the second squad when you are a fourth former, instead of when you are a fifth former. I do not know that the risk is balanced by the reward.'

Beyond such cost/benefit calculations lay the value of the game itself, as played at any level:

> I am delighted to have you play football. I believe in rough, manly sports. But I do not believe in them if they degenerate into the sole end of any one's existence. I don't want you to sacrifice standing well in your studies to any over-athleticism; and I need not tell you that character counts for a great deal more than either intellect or body in winning success in life. Athletic proficiency is a mighty good servant, but like so many other good servants, a mighty bad master...I am glad you should play football; I am glad that you should box; I am glad that you should ride and shoot and walk and row as well as you do. I should be very sorry if you did not do these things. But don't ever get into the frame of mind which regards these things as constituting the end to which all your energies must be devoted, or even the major portion of your energies.[25]

After Ted arrived at Harvard in the fall of 1905, the President/father was less concerned about his son's prowess at football than about the hounding he received from the local press. A letter on October 2 offered advice about ignoring 'the newspaper men, camera creatures, and idiots generally,' as far as he was able, along with the hope that they would grow bored and disappear. He ended with a pat of encouragement: 'This is just an occasion to show the stuff there is in you. Do not let these newspaper creatures and kindred idiots drive you one hair's breadth from the line you had marked out in football or anything else. Avoid any fuss, if possible.'²⁶ A few days later, he reminded Ted what football should mean in the context of his college experience: not winning renown or even a place eventually on the varsity eleven, but 'showing that in athletics you mean business up to the extent of your capacity.'²⁷

Roosevelt senior also commented on Ted's prospects in several letters to younger brother Kermit, still at Groton: first, that Ted would not likely make Harvard's freshman team but he was giving it a good try; later, that Ted was sticking it out but still expected to be dropped before the Yale game; finally, that Ted had won his numerals after all and had 'evidently played a skilful and plucky game' against Yale. To this he added: 'Now he'll have to buck up about his studies! or I am afraid he'll have trouble.'²⁸ At no time did the famously bombastic President express disappointment when Ted's prospects seemed dim, and he had no expectation that his son would eventually play on the varsity.

Necessary roughness

Roosevelt the father wanted for his son what Roosevelt the president wanted for the nation: the moral and physical courage to take on life's and the world's challenges. In the concluding paragraph of one of his most famous speeches, 'The Strenuous Life' (1899), Roosevelt had posed the challenge that life offered:

> The twentieth century looms before us big with the fate of many nations. If we stand idly by, if we seek merely swollen, slothful ease and ignoble peace, if we shrink from the hard contests where men must win at hazard of their lives and at the risk of all they hold dear, then the bolder and stronger peoples will pass us by, and will win for themselves the domination of the world. Let us therefore boldly face the life of strife, resolute to do our duty well and manfully; resolute to uphold righteousness by deed and by word; resolute to be both honest and brave, to serve high ideals, yet to use practical methods. Above all, let us shrink from no strife, moral or physical, within or without the nation, provided we are certain that the strife is justified, for it is only through strife, through hard and dangerous endeavor, that we shall ultimately win the goal of true national greatness.²⁹

In his public pronouncements the President spoke for his age, most pointedly for his own gender and class. National strength began with personal manliness. As the most 'manly' of American sports, football would provide tonic for the erosion of manliness elsewhere in American life, but to provide its tonic benefits, the game must be physically and mentally demanding.

By 1905, the value of necessary roughness was a given. Arguments for reform during and after the season often began with a reassurance – 'Nobody is worrying about hard play,' 'No one proposes to "mollycoddle" any boy or to make a "Miss Nancy" of him' or turn football into a 'pink tea' – before addressing the need to reduce brutality.[30] Selfless struggle on behalf of alma mater and 'manly' forbearance amidst the strife embodied the values of 'muscular Christianity'.[31] For the more secular-minded – including distinguished statesmen such as Henry Cabot Lodge and Oliver Wendell Holmes, Jr as well as President Roosevelt (all Harvard men) – a football game was both itself a struggle and an ideal training for the more momentous struggles that awaited young athletes upon graduation.[32] That football in its ruggedness and its fostering of both physical and moral courage trained young men for life was sufficiently a commonplace by this time that it could be mocked by a writer in *The Independent* with confidence that his readers knew the arguments he was debunking. Yes, football provided training for life, but here were its lessons: it cultivated 'indifference to the sufferings of other people,' it provided the 'best possible training in trust methods' by teaching 'how to combine against an individual,' it taught 'blind partisanship' and 'self-sacrificing devotion to an irrational ideal,' and so on. In sum, 'Football is the epitome of our competitive commonwealth, the real national game, the symbol of our civilization, the rehearsal of the drama of life, and it is very irrational to object to the students practicing in miniature the game they will afterward play in earnest.'[33]

In his address at Harvard in June, Roosevelt distinguished between necessary and unnecessary roughness as a matter of intentions, not consequences. For the one who withstood it, a broken collarbone would be a badge of 'hardihood, physical address and courage.' For the one who administered it, it might have been unintentional or it might have been the result of 'low cunning.' A gentleman, of course, would not resort to 'low cunning,' and the rules and their enforcement could reduce the number of injuries. But collarbones would be broken in any case, as happened to the President's own son in prep school. The cost was acceptable, but sometimes it was higher, as Harold Moore's father discovered at the Columbia–Union game in 1905. Moore was not a victim of 'low cunning' but died from a legal blow.

In his Harvard address Roosevelt denounced the spirit of 'semi-professionalism, of which 'low cunning' was one expression.

'Professional sport is all right in its way,' he conceded. 'I am glad to say that among my friends I number professional boxers and wrestlers, oarsmen and baseball men, whose regard I value, and whom in turn I regard as thoroughly good citizens. But the college undergraduate who, in furtive fashion, becomes a semi-professional is an unmitigated curse.' Unlike the boxer or oarsman, 'the college graduate ought in after-years to take the lead in putting the business morality of this country on a proper plane, and he cannot do it if in his own college career his code of conduct has been warped and twisted.'[34]

In speaking of professionals and semi-professionalism, Roosevelt touched on issues that had vexed college football since the 1880s along with its twin evil, 'commercialism.' Much of the criticism in 1905 focused on these two problems. Needham's muckraking articles on 'The College Athlete' in *McClure's* in June and July were subtitled 'How Commercialism Is Making Him a Professional.' Edward S. Jordan's four-part *exposé* in *Collier's* in November and December of practices at Midwestern universities was titled 'Buying Football Victories.'[35] A writer in *Outlook* pointed to 'The Money Power in College Athletics' as the factor that compromised 'the strenuous physical effort and discipline which in many respects are good.' An editorial in the *World* echoed the President's comments at Harvard in condemning 'the cold knavery of the long preparation, of hiring semi-professional players, of corrupting high-school students to get "material," of fixing even college entrance exams in favour of fierce unstudious giants who can be hired or cajoled to "play." '[36] Like President Roosevelt, Stanford president David Starr Jordan and Caspar Whitney, sporting editor of *Outing* magazine, conceded the legitimacy of frankly professional sports. It was the blurring of the distinction between amateur and professional that undermined the particular value of college football.[37]

As in Britain, the distinction touched on fundamental issues of class. Early defenders of college football, a 'sport' often indistinguishable from a brawl, had outraged boxing promoters such as Richard Kyle Fox, editor of the *National Police-Gazette*, for denouncing prize fighting as brutal and immoral. College football players were supposedly gentlemen, while prize fighters were lower-class thugs. By 1905, prize fighters represented for increasing numbers of middle- and upper-class men a new ideal of rugged manhood (yet another sign of the search for models of revitalized masculinity).[38] Midway through the football season, before the shocking climactic games, the Sunday magazine section of Pulitzer's *World* posed the question, 'Can a Gentleman Play Football?' and enlisted recently retired heavyweight boxing champion Jim Jeffries (the future

Great White Hope who would fail to dethrone Jack Johnson in 1910) to make the case against the college game. Jeffries judged football 'ten times as dangerous as fighting, even if the rules were followed,' and no game for gentlemen. 'It's a funny thing,' Jeffries wrote. 'The fight crowd, whom some people like to describe as ruffians, won't stand for rough work that fine society people applaud and cheer for all they're worth.' (Weakly defending the college sport was an unknown Yale sophomore. Presumably, Walter Camp and perhaps others of like stature declined to participate in the sensation-mongering.) TR's words from his Harvard address about broken collarbones and low cunning also appeared in a box on this page, along with another box documenting 'Football's Harvest of Death and Wounds Since 1900' (45 deaths along with 95 assorted injuries). (Figure 4.4)

A month later, after young Moore had been added to the death toll and as college leaders nationwide were debating whether to reform or abolish football, an editorial in the *World* echoed the President in declaring prize fighting to be more ethical because its competitors were 'frankly professional.'[39]

The quarrel between football and prize fighting exposed a class bias that was losing relevance. Behind both the rapid rise of college football in the 1880s and 1890s and the new legitimacy enjoyed by prize fighters was a shift from a Victorian ideal of 'manly self-restraint' to a new model of 'primitive masculinity,' a multilayered response to the sense that, while modern civilization was humankind's highest achievement, it was also emasculating modern men.[40] The influential psychologist G. Stanley Hall found a solution to this dilemma in the era's widely held 'recapitulation theory,' which held that the individual 'recapitulates' the stages of human evolution from the primitive to the civilized. Here was a rationale for rough sports such as football. For the boy, football indulged his natural instinct to relive his ancestors' primitive experiences. For the adolescent (ages 14–24), it prolonged those experiences into powerful manhood.[41]

Both an intellectual and a popular cult of primitivism thrived in these years, in manifestations ranging from President Roosevelt's efforts to conserve the American wilderness to the extraordinary popularity of Western novels and Jack London's Yukon tales, as well as the dramatic growth of sports. Civilization remained humankind's highest achievement and the individual's ultimate goal; primitive experiences (such as football) assured arriving at that goal intact and prepared to assume leadership. But pop Darwinism cut both ways. What if football, in all of its primitive bloodiness, was instead a sign of 'arrested development

96 *Rough, Manly Sport and the American Way*

Figure 4.4 From the Sunday Magazine Section of the *New York World*, November 5, 1905.

of the man's moral nature', as Thorstein Veblen (an anti-football faculty member at the University of Wisconsin) argued in *The Theory of the Leisure Class* just a few years before the 1905 crisis? Veblen saw in football 'a rehabilitation of the early barbarian temperament,' but without 'the redeeming features of the savage character.'[42] The sporting editor of Hearst's *New York American* reluctantly came to a similar conclusion following the death of Harold Moore. In the most remarkable statement to emerge from the crisis (at least I have seen none to match it), writer and journalist Julian Hawthorne (son of the famous author Nathaniel) conceded that college football remained a splendid spectacle, but this did not alter the fact that football fans had seemingly become as callous as the spectators at bullfights and the gladiatorial contests of ancient Rome, for reasons perhaps deep in human nature. 'We are not normally bloodthirsty – are we?' Hawthorne asked rhetorically, ' – and yet there is a savage latent in us all; and if we are not on our guard against him, and do not erect cautious barriers against his emergence, he will declare himself in some moment of excitement and carry all before him for a few tingling moments, and then, perhaps, leave us with a corpse on our hands.'

In a remarkable passage Hawthorne recalled a 'nice-looking girl who sat near me' at the Harvard–Yale game and who at one point 'exclaimed, between her pretty teeth, "I hope they'll break every bone in the Harvard team's bodies!"' Hawthorne knew that 'she didn't mean it,' but 'later on, when the redoubtable Mr. Shevlin, of Yale, being angered at the turn things were taking in his vicinity, reached into a scrimmage, seized a smaller Harvard man by the neck, and threw him headlong with such violence as to stun him, this nice girl said, "Good! I hope he killed him!"' Again, Hawthorne knew that 'she did not mean it; she was greatly excited; her side seemed to be losing; her blood was up; but there was an expression on her face as she uttered the words which might have surprised her had she seen it in a glass.'[43]

Sportswriters since the 1880s had paid particular attention to the females attending intercollegiate football games. Women were emblems of propriety and respectability; their presence alone redeemed the rough new sport from association with such sporting activities as prize fighting. For Julian Hawthorne, the female instead represented a dark warning: 'If the nice girl could look thus, and speak thus (even without really meaning it), what are we to expect from the nice man, not to mention the other people who are not quite so nice? What has come over us?'

Hawthorne seems his father's son here, translating his father's brooding about original sin into his own brooding about 'the savage lurking in all of us,' as psychology had replaced theology in explaining human nature. There were two sides to the primitive. This was the age that produced *McTeague* (1899), Frank Norris's novel that drew on psychological theories of degeneracy to portray a working-class man who, through hardship and hard drink, descends into the savagery that always lurked within. This was also the age that would produce Tarzan (in 1912), the son of an English gentleman who gets deeply in touch with his inner ape without losing the instincts of a gentleman.

Football tapped into the latter fantasy. McTeague was a proletarian; Tarzan (Lord Greystoke), an aristocrat. College football supposedly differed from prize fighting on the same terms, but the games sometimes played out in McTeague-like ways.

The aftermath

Columbia and NYU dropped football after the 1905 season, as did Northwestern and a few lesser teams. Stanford and the University of California gave up American football for rugby for the next 13 seasons. But most American colleges and universities opted for reform rather than abolition, and when college football resumed in 1906 the new rules were generally applauded for opening up the game and making it safer. The dean of sportswriters, Caspar Whitney, judged the 1906 season to be 'American play at its best,' as well as 'the most satisfying year I have known in football, and the first in which I saw no unclean play.' A writer in *The Independent* declared the 'new football' to be a spectacular success, more visible and comprehensible for spectators, safer for the players – fatalities down 80 percent, non-fatal injuries down by a third.[44]

But not eliminated. That preserving a proper element of roughness in football remained a cultural imperative is perhaps most clearly illustrated in the humor magazines *Life* and *Judge*. A cover of *Judge* in March looked toward 'Football in 1906 Under the New Rules.' Beribboned, resplendent in dotted powder blue for Yale and striped pink for Harvard's crimson (with the face of the Harvard man resembling its currently most distinguished alumnus, Teddy Roosevelt), and equipped with all of the necessities (face powder, Vichy water, cigarettes, and matches), the rival players doff their hankies and bow courteously to each other. At their feet, Football Rules 1906 are inscribed on a scroll: No Pinching, No Slapping, Hug Easy, No Yelling. Humor depends on the readers' common understanding, which in this case was that no one wanted football to become a 'pink tea.' (Figure 4.5)

Football seemed measurably safer in 1906. The number of deaths at all levels in 1905, variously reported as 18 or 19, dropped to 11, then 11 again in 1907 and 13 in 1908 before jumping to 26 in 1909.[45] A new crisis (see Figure 4.6) led to another revision of the rules, which this time largely completed the evolution of American football. (Most importantly, the restrictions on passing were loosened.)[46] But not the

Figure 4.5   *Judge*, March 10, 1906. *Life* ran a cover with a similar theme, appearing on November 8, 1906.

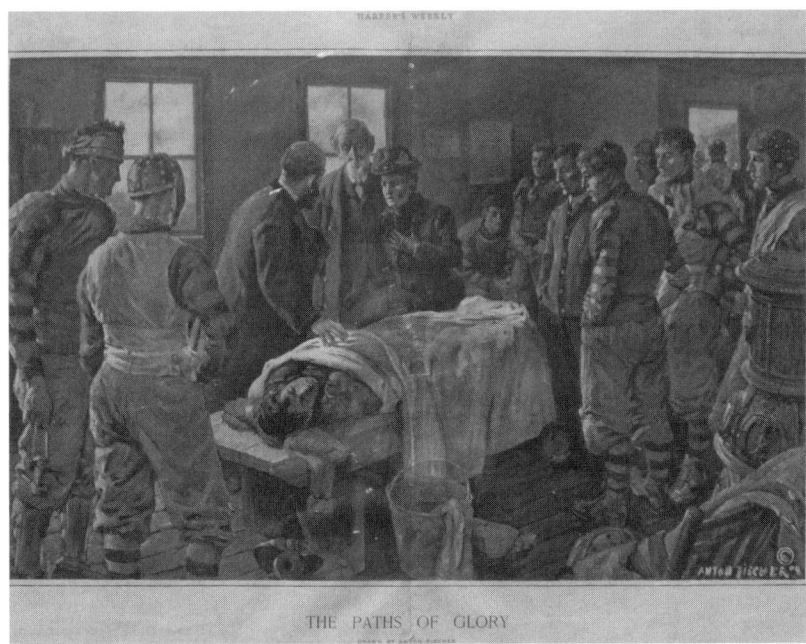

Figure 4.6 The 'new football' looked old in 1909: an injured player (fatally perhaps?) with teammates and distraught parents; a two-page centerfold in *Harper's Weekly*, January 1, 1910.

elimination of serious and fatal injuries. Over 200 players (at all levels) died in the 1930s, with a high of 31 in 1931. Between 1931 and 1965, an average of 17 players died each year directly from football injuries, another 8.5 indirectly. From 1966 through 2008, the annual averages were 9.4 and 9.2. At the college level, since 1969 no more than three players have died directly from a football injury in any year, but death remains an ever-present possibility.[47]

The numbers are small – many more college students die from binge drinking – but the deaths are always shocking. A sudden rash of injuries periodically provokes a media frenzy, but it always passes.[48] Developing better equipment to make the game safer – padding for shoulders, hips, and knees; plastic helmets – has in some ways made the game more rather than less dangerous. Padded shoulders are like the padded gloves mandated by the Queensberry Rules, which protect the boxer's knuckles so that he can smash the opponent's face with more force. Helmets were not required in college football until 1939, in the National Football

League until 1943. The plastic suspension helmet – a hard shell with webbing inside to absorb the blow – also introduced in 1939, became a weapon over time, making it possible to launch oneself head-first in blocking and tackling, causing more damage to both the opponent and oneself. (Hard shells and interior webbing provide no protection for necks and spines.)

Periodic revision of the rules has made football somewhat safer. 'Spearing' (leading with the head in blocking or tackling) can be outlawed, as can 'clotheslining' (tackling by extending the arm so that it catches the opponent in the neck) and 'head slaps' (defensive linemen swinging a taped fist to the side of an offensive lineman's helmet). But collisions are collisions, their impact a simple product of mass times velocity. Neither rule changes nor improved equipment has kept up with the athletes' gains in size, speed, and strength.

And the violent dance of that size, speed, and strength is what makes football Americans' favorite spectator sport. College football remained the premier version of the game into the 1950s, as a rough sport contested for the honor of alma mater, draped in the rituals and pageantry of mascots and fight songs, bands and cheerleaders. It bound students and alumni to their schools and schools to their communities, states, and regions. Professional football, on the other hand, was violence unredeemed by the spirit and trappings of collegiate sport. In the 1950s, however, what had long made pro football marginally respectable at best became its most celebrated feature: mere brutality became 'sanctioned savagery,' as a writer in one of the era's magazines termed it, an antidote for life in a drab, passionless world.[49] It was the 1890s and early 1900s all over again, on slightly different terms.

Professional football first passed baseball as Americans' favorite spectator sport in 1965, and it has held that position ever since, by an increasing margin in recent years (college football comes in #3 in surveys).[50] Concern about brutality continues to erupt periodically, prompted by a sudden rash of injuries or when aging ex-pros came forward to describe the long-term consequences of those injuries.[51] Surveys reported that nearly two-thirds of former NFL players have permanent disabilities, yet these same players typically insist that they would do it all again.[52] As I write, the most recent news from football's dark side – research connecting concussions and even routine head blows to later brain damage – may in fact put an end to the belief that 'necessary roughness' is possible without unacceptable consequences. 'Sanctioned savagery' remains at the heart of the game for fans, its current appeal seemingly magnified by the most recent gender revolution but also by a longing for intense experience such was described in the 1950s. Scholarly writing about football and masculinity has proliferated in recent decades, often with a view that football simply represents something pathological in American males.[53] A major unwritten book on American football would come to terms with the data from surveys that repeatedly reveal roughly 40 percent of the NFL's audience to be female.

As in 1905 so today: football violence has always generated conflicting viewpoints, and the periodic reminders of its consequences have always discomforted the game's fans. The 1905 moment ultimately did not change all that much. It did not alter the unique and extraordinary role that athletics in general and football in particular continue to play in American higher education. It did not address the 'professionalism' and 'commercialism' that seemed incompatible with educational missions. It took crucial first steps to open up the game for the pleasure of spectators without making it truly safer for the players. What it mostly did was open a window into football's place in American life and culture in a way that continues to reverberate today. And it may presage a moment in the not-too-distant future when 'necessary roughness' is fully confronted.

Notes

1. 'The History of the NCAA', at www.ncaa.org.
2. The NCAA's brief summary also misnames the source of the problem. The flying wedge was not an issue in 1905 because it had been banned after the 1893 season. (After Harvard introduced it for the Yale game at the end of the 1892 season, several teams worked variations off it the following year, prompting the rules committee to ban it for 1894.) The term, however, captures the problem more succinctly than listing 'guards back,' 'tackles back,' and similar formations, which along with various other mass momentum plays were doing the actual damage to players in 1905. The NCAA indulges in poetic license, not mythologizing, here.
3. Thomas Winter, 'Crisis of Masculinity', in *American Masculinities: A Historical Encyclopedia*, ed. Bret E. Carroll (Thousand Oaks, CA: Sage, 2003), pp. 117–19.
4. Gail Bederman, *Manliness & Civilization: A Cultural History of Gender and Race in the United States, 1880–1917* (Chicago, IL: University of Chicago Press, 1995), pp. 11, 15.
5. I trace the development of the rules more fully in *Reading Football: How the Popular Press Created an American Spectacle* (Chapel Hill, NC: University of North Carolina Press, 1993), pp. 25–56.
6. See my *Sporting with the Gods: The Rhetoric of Play and Game in American Culture* (New York: Cambridge University Press, 1991), pp. 10–16.
7. On the early decades of college football, see Ronald A. Smith, *Sports & Freedom: The Rise of Big-Time College Athletics* (New York: Oxford University Press, 1988); John Sayle Watterson, *College Football: History, Spectacle, Controversy*

(Baltimore, MD: Johns Hopkins University Press, 2000); and my own *Reading Football*.
8. On the 1905 crisis and the controversies over brutality preceding it, in addition to the books on early college football cited above, see John Hammond Moore's early seminal essay, 'Football's Ugly Decades, 1893–1913', *Smithsonian Journal of History* 2 (Fall 1967): 49–68; and Allen Guttmann, 'Civilized Mayhem: Origins and Early Development of American Football', *Sport in Society* 9 (October 2006): 533–41.
9. Theodore Roosevelt, 'The Harvard Spirit', *Harvard Graduates' Magazine*, September 1905, 1–9.
10. Watterson, *College Football*, p. 66.
11. 'President Put Coaches on Honor to End Brutality', *World*, October 11 1905.
12. Watterson, *College Football*, p. 70.
13. 'President's Son in His Gridiron Armor', *World*, October 4 1905; 'Teddy, Jr., Wins Celebrity at Football', *World*, November 5 1905.
14. ' "Teddy" a Hero in Fast Game of Football', *New York American*, November 19 1905.
15. 'Student Is Killed in Football Game', *New York Herald*, November 26 1905; 'Football Kills College Hero', *New York American*, November 26 1905; 'Union Halfback Killed in Football Scrimmage', *World*, November 26 1905.
16. 'Football Denounced', *Evening Post*, November 27 1905.
17. Watterson, *College Football*, pp. 101–2.
18. See, for example, 'The President Calls for Fair Play', *Congregationalist and Christian World*, October 21 1905; 'President Roosevelt's Sporting Philosophy', *Town and Country*, October 28 1905; J. William White, 'Football and Its Critics', *Outlook*, November 18 1905.
19. H. W. Brands, *T.R.: The Last Romantic* (New York: Basic Books, 1997), p. 336.
20. *Theodore Roosevelt's Letters to His Children*, ed. Joseph Bucklin Bishop (New York: Charles Scribner's Sons, 1919), p. 25 (May 7 1901); *The Letters of Theodore Roosevelt*, ed. Elting E. Morison, 8 vols. (Cambridge, MA: Harvard University Press, 1951–4), III: 178 (October 19 1901).
21. *Letter of Theodore Roosevelts*, III: 216 (January 4 1902).
22. *Letters*, IV, 1281 (July 19 1905).
23. *Letters*, III: 372 (October 31 1902).
24. *Letters to Kermit from Theodore Roosevelt, 1902–1908*, ed. Will Irwin (New York: Charles Scribner's Sons, 1946), pp. 42–3 (October 2 1903).
25. *Letters to His Children*, pp. 62–5 (October 4 1903).
26. *Letters of Theodore Roosevelt*, V: 43 (October 2).
27. *Letters to His Children*, p. 141 (October 11).
28. *Letters to Kermit*, pp. 118 (October 17), p. 122 (November 12), p. 125 (November 27). The President also repeatedly commiserated with Kermit for having to drop football after a month, to concentrate on his studies. See pp. 119–20, 122, 125.
29. Theodore Roosevelt, 'The Strenuous Life', *The Strenuous Life: Essays and Addresses* (New York: Century, 1900), pp. 20–1.
30. Caspar Whitney, 'The View-Point', *Outing*, December 5 1905; 'Reformation in Football', *New York Observer and Chronicle*, November 23 1905; Ralph D. Paine, 'The School and College World: View-Points of the Pacific Coast', *Outing*, December 1905.

31. See, for example, Clifford Putney, *Muscular Christianity: Manhood and Sports in Protestant America, 1880–1920* (Cambridge, MA: Harvard University Press, 2001).
32. Kim Townsend, *Manhood at Harvard: William James and Others* (New York: W. W. Norton, 1996), pp. 97–120.
33. 'Football as a Training for Life', *The Independent*, November 30 1905.
34. Roosevelt, 'The Harvard Spirit', pp. 5–6.
35. The series ran in *Collier's* from November 11 through December 2.
36. Clarence Deming, 'The Money Power in College Athletics', *Outlook*, 1 July 1905; 'Educated Brutality', *World*, November 30 1905.
37. David Starr Jordan, 'The Future of Football', *Collier's*, December 9 1905; Caspar Whitney, 'The View-Point', *Outing*, January 1907.
38. See Elliott J. Gorn, *The Manly Art: Bare-Knuckle Prize Fighting in America* (Ithaca, NY: Cornell University Press, 1986), pp. 194–206.
39. 'Football and Prize-Fighting', *World*, December 7 1905.
40. See particularly Bederman, *Manliness & Civilization*.
41. On Hall and primitivism, see Bederman, *Manliness & Civilization*, pp. 77–84. And see G. Stanley Hall's monumental *Adolescence*, 2 vols. (New York: D. Appleton, 1904), I, pp. 202–36, for his discussion of play, sports, and games. His specific comments on football and other team sports (pp. 221–2) also address the issues of character-building and the concerns about professionalism and media sensationalism typical of current opinion.
42. Thorstein Veblen, *The Theory of the Leisure Class: An Economic Study of Institutions* (1899; New York: Macmillan, 1911), pp. 256, 262.
43. Julian Hawthorne, 'Evils in American Game of Football Cannot Be Purged', *New York American*, November 28 1905.
44. Caspar Whitney, 'The View-Point', *Outing*, January 1907; Arthur B. Reeves, 'Football Safe and Sane', *The Independent*, November 22 1906;
45. Watterson, *College Football*, Appendix One, p. 401.
46. Watterson, *College Football*, pp. 110–29.
47. The National Center for Catastrophic Injury Research, under the direction of Frederick Mueller, compiles annual reports. For the data since 1931, see Frederick O. Mueller and Bob Colgate, 'Annual Survey of Football Injury Research, 1931–2008', online at http://www.unc.edu/depts/nccsi/FootballAnnual.pdf.
48. On the 1931–32 crisis, for example, see 'Football's Death Roll', *Literary Digest*, December 12 1931; 'Football Deaths: What Shall We Do to End Them?'; *Literary Digest*, December 26 1931; 'Making Football Safe for Men on the Gridiron', *Literary Digest*, 5 March 1932; 'Football and Health', *Literary Digest*, October 8 1932; and 'Football Casualties from a Medical Viewpoint', *Literary Digest*, January 30 1932. (The *Literary Digest* reprinted items from various newspapers and magazines.) In recent decades *Sports Illustrated* periodically announces a new crisis of brutality.
49. Thomas B. Morgan, 'The Wham in Pro Football', *Esquire*, November 1959.
50. Professional football first officially passed baseball in a Harris Poll in October 1965. See Michael MacCambridge, *America's Game: The Epic Story of How Pro Football Captured a Nation* (New York: Random House, 2004), p. 212. In the most recent Harris Poll (January 27, 2009), 31 percent of respondents named pro football as their favorite sport, followed by baseball (16 percent) and

college football (12 percent). For rankings since 1985, see 'Professional Football Continues Dominance Over Baseball as America's Favorite Sport', online at harrisinteractive.com.
51. See, for example, John Underwood, 'An Unfolding Tragedy', *Sports Illustrated*, August 14, 1978, and 'Punishment Is a Crime', *Sports Illustrated*, August 21, 1978; Paul Zimmerman, 'The Agony Must End', *Sports Illustrated*, November 10, 1986; and William Nack, 'The Wrecking Yard', *Sports Illustrated*, May 7 2001.
52. See, for example, Bob Glauber, 'Special Report: Life After Football', a five-part series in *Newsday*, January 12–16 1997.
53. In what Michal Kimmel in a recent book calls 'Guyland', football and other sports are said to offer a refuge from, and evasion of, 'the complexities of life', particularly those that involve women. Kimmel acknowledges the 'harmless and even positive experiences' of young male sports fans, along with the 'dominance bonding', but on balance Guyland is a pretty sad place. See the chapter 'Sports Crazy' in Michael Kimmel, *Guyland: The Perilous World Where Boys Become Men* (New York: HarperCollins, 2008), pp. 123–43. The sociologists Michael Messner and Donald Sabo are the leading scholars in this area. I attempt to historicize and complicate these issues in my *Reading Football* (esp. Chapter 4: 'Versions of Manliness'), *King Football* (esp. Chapter 4: 'Sanctioning Savagery' and Chapter 10: 'Masculinity'), and *Brand NFL* (esp. Chapter 5: 'Football as Product').

5
Baseball, Invented Tradition, and Nationalistic Spirit

Gerald R. Gems

On April 14, 1910, President William Howard Taft threw a baseball from his seat to a player on the field to commence the opening of the professional baseball season in the United States. In doing so, Taft began an invented tradition, a yearly ritual that symbolized the merger of sport, politics, and nationalism, a process that had been under way for more than half a century. The act gave sanction to baseball as the national game, a wholesome activity, and a utilitarian pastime that extolled American beliefs and virtues.[1]

Taft seemed an unlikely candidate for the role. An avid golfer despite his girth, his 300+ lb body was not that of a baseball player (although he had been a baseball pitcher as a young man). Still, Taft was a devoted fan of the game and his brother became the owner of one of the professional teams in Chicago. Taft's interest in the game led Clark Griffith, the owner of the Washington team, to devise a marketing ploy to generate interest in his franchise. Griffith's team had not performed well in previous years, and fans' interest in the team began to wane. He reasoned that a presidential invitation would draw much needed attention to his enterprise. Other presidents had declined offers to attend the games in Washington, and none had appeared since Benjamin Harrison in 1892. Taft's appearance guaranteed publicity and promotion, which generated a record crowd to witness the opening day ceremony. Taft's continued attendance throughout the 1910 season and his re-enactments of the opening ball toss in subsequent years established the presidential ritual.[2]

The ascendance of baseball as the national game had not been uncontested. Throughout the colonial era and well into the nineteenth century, cricket held great interest and the British game competed for the attention of Americans. Baseball had evolved with various sets of rules until the version developed in New York gained precedence.

Alexander Cartwright, secretary of the New York Knickerbockers baseball club, recorded its rules in 1845, for which he is considered the 'father of American baseball.' When Cartwright moved to Hawaii in 1849 he was astonished to learn that American missionaries had already taught the game to the indigenous population. By 1855, the Knickerbockers already referred to the sport as 'America's national game,' and a year later a Currier and Ives print declared baseball to be 'America's pastime.' That designation assumed general agreement, largely through the promotion of Henry Chadwick, a British transplant and an early New York sportswriter. The New York version of the rules gained great impetus with the advent of the Civil War, where soldiers played the game in camps, and spread it to other regions of the country. A virtual explosion ensued in the aftermath of the war as teams competed on a local, regional, and even a national basis. Whereas 62 clubs composed the membership of the National Association of Baseball Clubs in 1860 before the war, 91 clubs from ten states had joined by 1865 at the war's end. Only a year later 212 clubs attended the annual convention in New York City.[3]

A year later Charles Peverelly published the Book of American Pastimes, in which he remarked that '...it [baseball] has grown with giant strides until its organizations are the pride of numberless villages, towns, and cities, all over the land... Having no debasing attribute, and being worthy of the presence of the good and the refined, it has everywhere been countenanced and encouraged by our best citizens; and of the thousands who gather at important matches, we have always noted with sincere gratification that the ladies constituted an honored proportion.'[4] Thus early in its history did baseball purport to assume the perceived qualities of the nation. For many, baseball exemplified Americans' perceptions of themselves as a good and wholesome people.

The evolution of baseball coincided with ideological and economic transitions in American society. In the late 1850s, the concept of 'Muscular Christianity' emanated from British boarding schools and found root in the United States as well. The Young Men's Christian Association (YMCA) had been founded in London in 1844 as a means to counter urban ills through moral education. The YMCA appeared in the United States in 1851. Following a lead taken by senior boys at Thomas Arnold's Rugby, headmasters of other British public schools began to adapt the ideology to sport as a wholesome means of building one's character through the demonstration of manliness, leadership, courage, and fair play. By the end of the decade, American ministers, such as Thomas Wentworth Higginson, began extolling the benefits of sport in the melding of body and soul to combat perceived physical and spiritual weakness. Baseball provided a wholesome alternative to the urban temptations of the bachelor subculture, which centered on saloons and emphasized more carnal and brutish pleasures as cities amassed ever larger populations throughout the latter half of the nineteenth century. William Alcott, a prominent physician, warned against gambling, but noted that for young men, 'Recreations they must have; active recreation, too, in the open air...Some of the most appropriate are playing ball...but in no case for money.'[5]

The urbanization of America was accompanied by a transition in its economy from an agricultural to an industrial basis. Baseball seemingly eased that transition. Some proponents of the game relished its nostalgic rural images as it was played on open fields; or the fact that it was not relegated to a time limit in an industrializing economy ruled by the clock. Others charged that the game was more suitable for the fast pace of American life. Whereas a game of cricket could take two days to complete baseball took only two hours. Baseball also seemed to be a more aggressive sport, which matched the youthful mentality of the vibrant, growing, and assertive nation that ascribed to the notion of 'manifest destiny.' The jingoistic term, coined in the 1830s after American settlers in Texas revolted against their Mexican overlords, found widespread usage a decade later when the United States usurped more territory in the Mexican–American War of 1848. Throughout the remainder of the nineteenth century, 'manifest destiny' rationalized American imperial ambitions as a Social Darwinian obligation to spread American democracy throughout the world. By the time Taft initiated the 1910 competition, American missionaries and military forces had expanded both their ideology and their national game to global proportions.[6]

Before the globalization of baseball could ensue the promoters had to first consolidate the game and its ties to a particular ideology within the national boundaries. Sport, and baseball in particular, assumed the mantle of meritocracy and social mobility, key components in the American mantra of equality and opportunity as the sport began to professionalize in the 1860s. Clubs began to pay their top players to assure their loyalty and better their chances in heavily wagered matches against rival teams. By 1869, the businessmen of Cincinnati garnered a fully professional team, with salaries that ranged from 600 to 2000 dollars, which they sent on a national tour as marketing strategy in the rapidly expanding American economy. Chicago, one of Cincinnati's rivals for the hinterland trade in the Midwest, formed its own team the following year. By 1876, there were enough fully professional teams to establish the National League. As the premier circuit in the country, it attracted the most media attention, while myriad regional associations, known as minor leagues, offered additional opportunities for young men to be paid for their physical prowess. At a time when only the wealthy managed to obtain anything beyond a rudimentary education, baseball provided another means for the uneducated to gain a measure of social mobility.[7]

The children of the early ethnic immigrants, especially the Irish and the Germans, readily availed themselves of such opportunities. Mike 'King' Kelly, the son of immigrants, not only earned the highest salary but gained celebrity status to become one of America's first sports heroes in the 1880s. His athletic feats were lauded in a popular song and adoring fans packed the ballpark to marvel at his colorful antics. Kelly and the entire Chicago team were even invited to the White House by President Grover Cleveland in 1885. All players, however, labored under the dictates of the team owners, who maximized their own profits by paying the players as little as possible. Players likened themselves to the 'wage slaves' of the industrial factories, and finally revolted in 1890, forming their own league based on socialist principles. Fans divided their loyalties between the competing teams in the same cities. The revolution lasted only one year, as the wealthy owners, led by Albert Spalding in Chicago, were able to absorb greater losses, forcing the players to return on the owners' terms. Still, by 1908, Honus Wagner, the son of German immigrants, earned a salary of 10,000 dollars, far in excess of the common laborer. The game had already achieved iconic status when, in 1908, vaudevillian Jack Norworth and composer Albert Von Tilzer penned 'Take Me Out to the Ball Game,' which became one of the country's most popular songs, an invented tradition still sung at every game today.[8]

Baseball had a primary role in the assimilation and acculturation of ethnic groups. American presidents had recognized its ties to citizenship as early as 1883, when President Chester Arthur had invited two teams to the White House and announced that 'Good ballplayers make good citizens.'[9] The entitlement of citizenship and its responsibilities were soon questioned as more than 23,000,000 immigrants flooded American shores between 1880 and 1920, and many brought radical European sympathies with them. The industrialization process pitted workers against employers and exacerbated ideological conflicts. Progressive reformers of that era attempted to alleviate social tensions by employing a three-step process: remove the children from the workplace, require education, and utilize physical education as a teaching strategy. The latter proved particularly effective for non-English speakers, and baseball, as the national game, proved a mainstay of the educational process. Baseball taught competition, the basis for the American capitalist economy. It also rectified some of the apparent contradictions for immigrants, many of whom came from communal societies. Baseball required all nine teammates to play together when on defense for the good of the team, a lesson in democracy, and one familiar to communal societies. Yet on offense, each player batted as an individual, and earned rewards based on his performance, similar to employees in the commercialized economy and individualistic American society. Moreover, baseball taught deference to authority in the form of a team manager or umpire. Arguing with a game official might result in banishment from the game. Even Mike Kelly was sold to another team when his boss, Albert Spalding, deemed that his drinking affected his productivity. Employers especially relished such lessons, and many formed their own company teams and industrial recreation leagues. Other wealthy benefactors sponsored urban playgrounds, parks, and interscholastic leagues where the children of immigrants learned to become 'good citizens' and compliant employees. Fifteen thousand spectators attended the 1907 high school championship game in New York. By that time the Germans, Czechs, Poles, and Jews all incorporated baseball teams within their ethnic associations to retain the interest of their own youthful element. Despite their differences with employers, workers found some agreement in baseball. Even non-players might supplement their salaries by wagering, and 115,000 appeared to witness a 1914 national playoff game in Cleveland between two industrial teams (the highest spectator figure ever recorded for a baseball game in the USA).[10]

Baseball stretched across some social boundaries as it reinforced others. Female baseball teams began forming in the women's colleges as early as the 1860s. By the end of the nineteenth century, a number of barnstorming women's teams travelled throughout the United States, but baseball still served to combat the growing feminization of culture in its public displays of masculine prowess. African Americans too formed their own teams and leagues, having been barred from the National League after 1884. Despite whites' claims that blacks were incapable of performing at the highest levels, African Americans continued to play in the minor leagues and even won championships in integrated urban leagues, where they consistently beat the white teams. By 1910, when Taft delivered his pitch, baseball had clearly assumed the sobriquet of the national game, a commercialized enterprise that extolled largely white, Anglo-Saxon, Protestant capitalist values of individualism, work ethic, and productivity, as measured by the increasing fascination with team and individual records and statistics.

Albert Spalding, a former star player who had gained ownership of the Chicago team and consequently leadership of the National League, exemplified the opportunities and social mobility possible in the American sporting culture. Unlike the British, many American athletes eschewed the amateur ideal, and working-class athletes in particular found no philosophical or ethical conflict in earning their means through their physicality. Spalding ventured into a lucrative sporting goods business that made him a millionaire. After the culmination of the 1888 season, he organized a global adventure designed to introduce American baseball to an international audience and broaden his own market for equipment. Spalding's baseball tour encompassed Hawaii, Australia, Ceylon (now Sri Lanka), Egypt, Italy, France, England, Ireland, and Scotland, but had little success in supplanting cricket in the British Empire. When the British judged baseball to be no more than a mere British boys' game, unworthy of modern masculinity, Spalding embarked on a project that culminated with another invented tradition. In 1905, he organized the Mills Commission, which included two United States senators, to research the origin of baseball. Two years later, the commission came to the conclusion that baseball was a purely American invention, originated in 1839 by Abner Doubleday, a Civil War hero, in an obscure New York village. Consequently, the Baseball Hall of Fame was established in that location in the centennial year of 1939. Although sport historians have conclusively disproved the 'Doubleday myth,' baseball broadcasters continue to reaffirm its authenticity throughout each baseball season.[11]

The American belief in manifest destiny assumed national proportions and fostered widespread debate in the aftermath of the Spanish–American War of 1898. The United States had already surpassed Great Britain in its industrial output and endeavored to join the great nations of the world. A quick victory in the war provided the United States with an instant empire in the form of the Philippines, Puerto Rico, Cuba, Guam, American Samoa, and the annexation of Hawaii. As Americans debated the incongruence of empire and democracy, Senator Albert Beveridge asserted that

> He [God] made us master organizers of the world to establish a system where chaos reigned. He has given us the spirit of progress to overwhelm the forces of reaction throughout the earth. He has made us adept in government that we may administer government among

savage and senile peoples. Were it not for such a force as this the world would relapse into barbarism and night. And of all our race He has marked the American people as His chosen nation to finally lead in the redemption of the world.[12]

Beveridge's self-righteous sense of nationalism and manifest destiny held sway and the United States joined Great Britain, France, and Germany among the imperial powers of the world. In some cases, baseball had preceded the American military forces throughout the Pacific and Caribbean regions, spread by missionaries, businessmen, the YMCA, and students who had learned the game in American colleges. Like the progressive reform agenda of the American mainland, education and sport would be introduced to colonized subjects to propagate the American value systems. In the Philippines, where William Howard Taft served as Governor-General from 1901 to 1903, baseball served as a surrogate form of warfare, as American administrators tried to quell an insurrectionist guerrilla movement by transferring Filipino nationalism against the baseball teams of Pacific rival Japan in international competition. General Franklin Bell, military commander in the Philippines, claimed that 'baseball had done more to civilize Filipinos than anything else.'[13] The American-owned *Manila Times* newspaper was even more effusive in its almost religious faith in the game. It declared that 'Baseball is more than a game, a regenerating influence, or power for good.'[14]

Under the presidency of Theodore Roosevelt (1901–1909), perhaps the most nationalistic and athletic of American presidents, sport assumed great influence in the lives of Americans and their colonial subjects.[15] American naval vessels carried baseball all-star teams as they travelled the earth, and in 1907 Roosevelt sent his Great White Fleet around the world to demonstrate the growing American might. Roosevelt enthusiastically supported sport as character building and essential to American citizenry. He stated that

> ...In any republic, courage is a prime necessity for the average citizen if he is to be a good citizen; and he needs physical courage no less than moral courage, the courage that endures, the courage that will fight valiantly alike against the foe of the soul and the foes of the body. Athletics are good, especially in their rougher forms, because they tend to develop such courage. They are good also because they encourage a true democratic spirit, for in the athletic field, the man must be judged not with reference to outside and accidental attributes but by that combination of bodily vigor and

moral quality which go to make up prowess... the weakling and the coward are out of place in a strong and free community... the governing class is composed of strong men... if you are too timid... you become one of the governed... one of the driven cattle of the political arena.[16]

Roosevelt further elaborated on his credo at the Sorbonne in Paris in 1910, where he pronounced that

The credit belongs to the man who is actually in the arena, whose face is marred by dust, and sweat, and blood; who strives valiantly, who errs and comes up short again and again because there is no effort without error and short-comings; but who actually strives to do the deed, who knows the great devotion, who spends himself in a worthy cause, who at the best knows in the end the high achievement of triumph and who at worst, if he fails while daring greatly knows his peace shall never be with those timid and cold souls who know neither victory nor defeat.[17]

American politicians and American educators had a particular faith in the lessons of baseball. Baseball proved so popular, in fact, that a second major circuit evolved in 1901 as a challenger to the National League. The organizers dubbed their enterprise the American League, a nationalistic nomenclature that was proclaimed as a moral alternative that disavowed both gambling and beer in its stadiums. Fans welcomed the new league, which competed with the older association for star players. Unable to drive it out of business as it had its previous competitors, the National League acquiesced, agreeing to a three-man ruling body to govern the sport. In 1903, the two league champions faced each other for national honors in a spectacle that they presumptuously called the World Series, indicative of Americans' growing belief in their global influence. Taft's initiation of the 1910 season occurred on behalf of the Washington Senators, an American League team. Despite the increasing commercialization of the sport, Taft claimed that 'the game of baseball is a clean, straight game.'[18]

Woodrow Wilson succeeded Taft as president in 1912. Wilson had been the team manager for both the baseball and football squads as a student at Princeton, and he continued the precedent set by Taft of delivering the opening pitch of the baseball season, After the 1913 baseball season, Charles Comiskey, owner of the Chicago team in the American League, and John Mc Graw, manager of the New York team in the National League, combined their forces in a further attempt to globalize America's national game. Following in the footsteps of Albert Spalding, they organized another international venture that included a national tour of the United States, followed by an ocean voyage to Japan, the Philippines, Ceylon (now Sri Lanka), Egypt, Austria, Italy – where they had an audience with the Pope, France, and England, before returning to New York to start the 1914 baseball season. Despite their own beliefs in the values of baseball they had little more success than Spalding in their international efforts to promote the game.[19] Such early efforts to proselytize American culture would assume greater significance after World War I.

Initially the US government took an isolationist stance when the war broke out in Europe, but the baseball players soon marched in military drills before the games to demonstrate their readiness for military service. The government used baseball during the war as a form of social control. The US Army baseball league eventually engaged more than a million soldiers as a moral deterrent to French prostitutes.[20] During the first game of the 1918 World Series the Star Spangled Banner was sung as part of the intermission known as the seventh inning stretch. The overwhelming and patriotic response of spectators and players, who joined in the singing of the tune, resulted in its continued playing at subsequent games. Although the song would not become the official national anthem of the United States until 1931, the invented tradition that began in 1918 provided a further nationalistic link between baseball and politics. The tradition has since extended beyond baseball to include virtually all athletic contests in the United States, including intercollegiate and interscholastic contests.[21]

The allied victory in World War I, aided by the late entry of the Americans, gave great impetus to the United States' ascendance as a world power. President Woodrow Wilson's plan for a League of Nations, adopted by the European countries, failed to pass the United States Congress. Although the United States temporarily assumed an isolationist stance, it continued to pursue sporting options to spread American culture and American commerce. The 1920 census indicated that urban dwellers outnumbered those in the countryside for the first time, indicating the transition from a rural, agricultural economy. Cities soon gained increasing power and influence, vying with each other for stature. For the remainder of the twentieth century, professional baseball franchises symbolized that hierarchy (between the haves and the have-nots) and presented particular civic images (winners and losers) within the American society.

Before that strategy could be pursued in earnest, however, the country had to confront the devastating Black Sox scandal of 1919, in which eight players from the Chicago White Sox team, the American League champions, were accused of purposely losing the World Series to the National League champions from Cincinnati in collusion with gamblers. The revelation destroyed Americans' faith in their national game as the symbol of pride and goodness. The national anguish proved short-lived as Americans found a new hero in Babe Ruth, a player whose amazing feats changed the nature of the game and spawned even greater interest. Ruth, an incorrigible youth, had been sent to an orphanage by his parents, where he had learned to play baseball so well that he soon joined the professional ranks. His hedonistic lifestyle gained him celebrity status and a salary greater than that of the President of the United States. For the poor and downtrodden Ruth resurrected the dream of an American meritocracy, where one might succeed regardless of pedigree.[22]

Ruth's emergence coincided with a period of dire government corruption during the presidency of Warren G. Harding, who had been the owner of a minor league baseball team in Marion, Ohio. Harding apparently ran his baseball team better than he did the government, as several of his associates extorted money, took bribes, and accepted kickbacks while in office. During Harding's term the national government greatly aided the baseball owners when a disgruntled owner of a nascent third professional league sued Major League Baseball as a monopoly. The case reached the US Supreme Court in 1922, which oddly ruled that baseball was not considered to be interstate commerce, and was therefore exempt from antitrust legislation. Baseball team owners enjoyed that privilege for the remainder of the century.

Harding's successor, Calvin Coolidge, noted the clear relationship between the baseball teams and civic identity. After the Washington Senators team won their first American League championship in 1924, he invited the team to appear on the White House lawn, where he congratulated the team while a mass of fans observed his announcement that '...By bringing the baseball pennant to Washington you have made the National Capital [sic] more truly the center of worthy and honorable national aspirations.'[23] Throughout the remainder of the century politicians courted professional sports teams as a marketing tool for their cities and as a means to boost their own popularity.

The explosion of sport in the United States during the 1920s (termed the Golden Age of Sport) did not go unnoticed by the US government. Sport might be a useful and more subtle vehicle for transmitting

American culture, and to that extent the US State Department formulated plans to capitalize on the popularity of swimmer Johnny Weissmuller and the Olympic Games to market American sporting goods abroad. With an ultimate faith in the powers of sport, President Hoover declared that 'Next to religion, baseball has furnished a greater impact on American life than any other institution.'[24]

Hoover's optimism was soon tempered by the Great Depression. Baseball entrepreneurs overcame the economic malaise by inventing new traditions to entice fans to the games. They offered doubleheaders (two games played consecutively on the same day for the price of one game), night baseball games to attract those who had daytime jobs, and an all-star game that brought the best players from all teams together in one place for interleague competition. The innovative strategies proved so successful that administrators adopted them as regular traditions thereafter. Despite the economic woes all-star teams of professional players continued to travel to Japan. In one such venture during 1934 the government even employed the multilingual catcher Moe Berg as a spy to photograph Japanese installations, presciently aware of possible future conflict between the two nations. That tension had been apparent since the 1890s when Japanese university teams began to challenge American residents in baseball games. American universities sent their own teams to compete with their Japanese counterparts throughout the early twentieth century, and by the 1930s the Japanese clamored for a true World Series between the international powers.

When the hostilities erupted into open warfare in 1941, many of the professional players joined the military service. Their exodus so depleted the team rosters that owners considered suspending major league play until the cessation of the war. On January 15, 1942, President Franklin Delano Roosevelt responded to baseball commissioner Kenesaw Mountain Landis, urging him to continue play for the morale of the nation. During the war, baseball games forged an even closer bond with the nationalistic spirit by featuring marching soldiers, military bands, and fundraising drives for war bonds, as well as the Army and Navy Relief Funds. Baseball also travelled with the troops, as a means of exercise, training, and recreation. American engineers constructed baseball fields in the far-flung regions of Europe, Africa, and the South Pacific. The war even provided an opportunity for women, as the All-American Girls Baseball League provided professional opportunities for women in the Midwestern states. Originating in 1943, the league proved so popular that it lasted until 1954, well after the troops had returned home.[25]

The primacy of baseball within the American culture might also be seen in the fact that even the Japanese-Americans, interned in concentration camps by the American government during the war as possible enemy aliens, formed baseball leagues. At the Gila River Camp in Arizona the young men fielded 28 teams in three leagues, while another 4000–5000 attended as spectators.[26] The so-called 'war for democracy' also called into question the exclusion of African-Americans from mainstream American society, and from major league baseball, the most visible sporting symbol of the American culture. That glaring omission was rectified after the war with the entry of Jackie Robinson into the National League in 1947. Despite persecution, Robinson prevailed in spectacular fashion; opening the way for a multitude of black talent that followed. Perhaps more importantly, Robinson's heroic desegregation of baseball presaged by seven years the historic Brown *v.* Board of Education ruling that legally ended segregation in American society.

The allure of baseball extended throughout the land and encompassed other American heroes. Rocky Marciano (Marchegiano), the only heavyweight boxing champion to retire undefeated, and an ethnic hero of the 1950s, embarked on a boxing career only after he had failed as a baseball player. Dwight Eisenhower, commander-in-chief of the Allied forces in Europe during World War II and subsequently the 34th president of the United States, remarked that 'Not making the baseball team at West Point [the US military academy] was one of the greatest disappointments of my life, maybe the greatest.' Eisenhower also related a childhood story. 'When I was a small boy in Kansas, a friend of mine and I went fishing and as we sat there in the warmth of the summer afternoon on a riverbank, we talked about what we wanted to do when we grew up. I told him that I wanted to be a real major league baseball player, a genuine professional like Honus Wagner. My friend said that he'd like to be president of the United States. Neither of us got our wish.'[27] Such was the hold of baseball on American males.

Eisenhower's vice-president, Richard Nixon, who was elected president in 1968 and again in 1972, proved to be an even bigger fan. In 1972, Nixon fled a national conference of governors to attend the baseball all-star game instead. Nixon was star-struck by professional athletes, especially baseball and football players, to whom he offered advice and tried to befriend. Nixon even offered the media his own selections for an all-time all-star team.[28]

An affiliation with baseball became almost a presidential requisite. Ronald Reagan began his career as a broadcaster for the Chicago National League team in the 1930s. On a trip to California he abandoned his duties to the team to obtain an audition in Hollywood, which set him on a different career path as an actor, a profession that served him well as president. During his tenure in office, he invited 32 former baseball stars to the White House for a luncheon. It was the Bush family, however, that had the closest alliance with baseball. George H. Bush had captained the Yale team to the national intercollegiate championship game in 1948. His son, George W. Bush, gained part-ownership of the Texas Rangers professional baseball franchise, where he served as managing partner during his father's presidency. His mother, the wife of the president, threw out the first ball for the 1989 season in Texas. The younger Bush desired to govern all of baseball as its commissioner, but having failed to achieve that position he set his sights on politics, winning elections as the Texas governor in 1994 and the US presidency in 2000.[29] The second Bush presidency included the September 11, 2001, attack on the World Trade Center, war in the Mideast, the devastating Hurricane Katrina that demolished the city of New Orleans in 2005, and a dramatic collapse of the US economy; yet a telling interview conducted at the end of his tenure revealed an overriding concern about his baseball performance. The interviewer asked 'Which moments from the last eight years do you revisit most often?' Bush replied 'I think about throwing out that pitch at the World Series on [October 30] 2001. My heart was racing when I got to the mound. Didn't want to bounce it. Didn't want to let the fans down...I never felt that anxious any other time during my presidency, curiously enough.'[30]

Despite Bush's misgivings, and misplaced values, baseball had already lost some of its lustre. The attraction of baseball began to change in the 1950s as American football began to surpass baseball as the national game. The martial spirit, aggressiveness, and brutality of the gridiron game better exemplified American needs and values in the Cold War; but Taft's gesture in 1910 marked a significant moment in both sport and American culture. Taft's imprimatur signalled not only the ascendance of a game, but the progress of a nation. The growth of baseball had coincided with the resolution of the slavery question. It fostered mutual ties between towns, cities, and regions in baseball associations as it symbolized mutual beliefs in what it meant to be an American. In distancing the sport from its British antecedents, Americans constructed a separate national identity, what Benedict Anderson has termed an 'imagined community.'[31] The baseball narrative incorporates racial, ethnic, gender, religious, and social class factors in the ongoing construction and deconstruction of the American story, as more baseball books are published annually in the United States than any other sporting genre. Newly constructed baseball stadiums invoke the nostalgic elements of the past and increasing numbers of baseball halls of fame attract tourists to the artifacts and relics that serve as places of remembrance for the education of American citizens and others interested in American culture. As historian Jacques Barzun once remarked 'Whoever wants to know the heart and mind of America had better learn baseball...'[32]

Notes

1. Eric Hobsbawm and Terence Ranger, eds, *The Invention of Tradition* (Cambridge: Cambridge University Press, 1983).
2. Christine L. Putnam, 'A President Inaugurates a Remarkable Tradition,' Baseball Almanac, 2003 at http://www.baseball-almanac.com/articles/president_taft_opening_day.shtml (December 7, 2008); http://www.baseball-almanac.com/prz_qca.shtml (December 11, 2008); *New York Times*, April 15, 1910, *Chicago Tribune*, April 15, 1910, 13. John Sayle Watterson, *The Games Presidents Play: Sports and the Presidency* (Baltimore, MD: Johns Hopkins University Press, 2006), 84, claims that Taft was such a fan that on May 4, 1910, shortly after delivering the inaugural pitch, he attended two games, one in each professional league, on the same day.
3. George B. Kirsch, *Baseball and Cricket: The Creation of American Team Sports, 1832–1872* (Urbana, IL: University of Illinois Press, 1989); Frederick Ivor-Campbell, 'How Knickerbocker Baseball Became America's National Game,' at http://www.sabr.org/sabr.cfm?acms,c,1286,3,158 (December 10, 2008), http://www.19cbaseball.com (December 10, 2008); Ronald Story, 'The Country of the Young: The Meaning of Baseball in Early American Culture,' in David K. Wiggins, ed., *Sport in America: From Wicked Amusements to National Obsession* (Champaign, IL: Human Kinetics, 1995), 121–32; Benjamin G. Rader, *American Sports: From the Age of Folk Games to the Age of Televised Sports* (Englewood Cliffs, NJ: Prentice Hall, 2004), 54; William Wood, *Manual of Physical Exercises, Comprising Gymnastics, Calisthenics, Rowing, Sailing, Skating, Swimming, Fencing, Sparing, Cricket, Base Ball, Together with Rules for Training and Sanitary Suggestions* (New York: Harper & Bros., 1867), Vol. 2, 191–2.
4. Gerald R. Gems, Linda J. Borish, and Gertrud Pfister, *Sports in American History: From Colonization to Globalization* (Champaign, IL: Human kinetics, 2008), 102.
5. Gems et al., *Sports in American History*, 69–72 (quote, 69).
6. Story, 'The Country of the Young,' Steven A. Riess, ed., *Major Problems in American Sport History: Documents and Essays* (Boston, MA: Houghton Mifflin, 1997), 90–2.
7. Gems, et al., *Sports in American History*, 158. The National League differed from the National Association of Professional Base Ball Players which had been established in 1871, in that the former was organized and controlled by team owners rather than players.

8. Gems et al., *Sports in American History*, 148; Daniel M. Pearson, *Baseball in 1889: Players vs. Owners* (Bowling Green, OH: Bowling Green University Press, 1993), http:/mlb.mlb.com/mlb/fan-forum/babyruth/index.jsp?content=history (December 10, 2008); http://www.baseball-almanac.com/prz_qca.shtml (December 11, 2008).
9. Arthur quoted at http://www.baseball-almanac.com/prz_qca.shtml (December 11, 2008). Watterson, *The Games Presidents Play*, 83, indicates that Presidents Andrew Johnson and Ulysses Grant had previously invited baseball teams to the White House, well before the Arthur greeting. President William McKinley would subsequently do the same at the turn of the twentieth century.
10. *Chicago Tribune*, July 7, 1889, 12; Svornost, June 2, 1890; Dziennik Chicagoski, August 10, 1896; both in the Works Progress Administration, Foreign Language Press Survey, 1942. Gems et al., *Sports in American History*, 180, 198.
11. Gems et al., *Sports in American History*, 163–4; Peter Levine, *A.G. Spalding and the Rise of Baseball: The Promise of American Sport* (New York: Oxford University Press, 1989); David Block, *Baseball Before We Knew It: A Search for the Roots of the Game* (Lincoln, NE: University of Nebraska Press, 2005).
12. Gerald R. Gems, *The Athletic Crusade: Sport and American Cultural Imperialism* (Lincoln, NE: University of Nebraska Press, 2006); Beveridge cited in John M. Blum, Edmund S. Morgan, Willie Lee Rose, Arthur Schlesinger, Jr., Kenneth M. Stampp, and C. Vann Woodward, *The National Experience: A History of the United States* (New York: Harcourt, Brace, Jovanovich, 1981), 536.
13. Harold Seymour, *Baseball: The People's Game* (New York: Oxford University Press, 1990), 324–5.
14. Lewis E. Gleeck, Jr., *American Institutions in the Philippines (1898–1941)*, (Manila: Historical Conservation Society, 1976), 39.
15. Gems, *Athletic Crusade*; Gems et al., *Sports in American History*, 192–7.
16. Roosevelt's speech at Harvard University, February 23, 1907, is in the Walter Camp Papers, Yale University Archives, Reel 15. Roosevelt preferred American football over baseball as a more aggressive sport that instilled the martial qualities necessary for American expansion.
17. Mario R. Di Nunzio, ed., *Theodore Roosevelt: An American Mind* (New York: St. Martin's Press, 1994), xiii.
18. Taft quoted at http://www.baseball-almanac.com/prz_qca.shtml (December 11, 2008).
19. Watterson, *The Games Presidents Play*, 93, 98; Sam Weller, 'Murphy Starts Tour Today,' *Chicago Tribune*, November 4, 1913, 14; James E. Elfers, *The Tour to End All Tours: The Story of Major League Baseball's 1913–1914 World Tour* (Lincoln, NE: University of Nebraska Press, 2003).
20. Steven W. Pope, *Patriotic Games: Sporting Traditions in the American Imagination, 1876–1926* (New York: Oxford University Press, 1997), 148.
21. *New York Times*, September 6, 1918, 14.
22. Harvey Frommer, *Shoeless Joe and Ragtime Baseball* (Dallas: Taylor Publishing, 1992); Donald Gropman, *Say It Ain't So, Joe!: The True Story of Shoeless Joe Jackson* (New York: Citadel Press, 1979); Eliot Asinof, *Eight Men Out* (New York: Henry Holt, 1987); Robert W. Creamer, *Babe: The Legend Comes*

to Life (New York: Penguin Books, 1983); Leigh Montville, *The Big Bam: The Life and Times of Babe Ruth* (New York: Doubleday, 2006).
23. Coolidge quoted at http://www.baseball-almanac.com/prz_qca.shtml (December 11, 2008).
24. http://www.baseball-almanac.com/prz_qhh.shtml (December 10, 2008); Mark Dyreson, 'Johnny Weissmuller and the Old Global Capitalism: The Origins of the Federal Blueprint for Selling American Culture to the World' and 'Marketing Weissmuller to the World: Hollywood's Olympics and Federal Schemes for Americanization through Sport,' both in *The International Journal of the History of Sport*, 25:2 (February 15, 2008), 268–83, and 284–306, respectively.
25. http://exhibits.baseballhalloffame.org/baseball-enlists/a01.htm (December 10, 2008).
26. Gems et al., *Sports in American History*, 243.
27. Both quotes appear in Paul Dickson, *Baseball's Greatest Quotations* (New York: Harper Collins, 2008), 166.
28. Watterson, *The Games Presidents Play*, 239–43.
29. Ibid., 282–3, 286, 289, 296–7, 329–32.
30. *People Magazine* interview, November 29, 2008, cited in Jill Zuckman, 'In Bush Presidencies, Similarities Abound,' *Chicago Tribune*, January 11, 2009, 4.
31. Benedict Anderson, *Imagined Communities: Reflections on the Origin and Spread of Nationalism* (New York: Verso, 1991 [1983]).
32. Jacques Barzun, *God's Country and Mine: A Declaration of Love Spiced with a Few Harsh Words* (Boston, MA: Little, Brown, 1954) cited in Dickson, *Baseball's Greatest Quotations*, 44.

6
'Her Dainty Strength': Suzanne Lenglen, Wimbledon and the Coming of Female Sport Celebrity

Stephen Wagg

> In Suzanne Lenglen journalists had at last stumbled upon a subject commensurate with their capacity for hyperbole.[1]

This chapter explores the career and historical significance of Suzanne Lenglen, a French tennis player whose short life spanned roughly the first four decades of the twentieth century: she was born in 1899 and died, of pernicious anaemia, in 1938. Aside from her other trophies (which included four World Hard Court Championships – the first in 1914 – and two French Championships, between 1919 and 1925 Mlle Lenglen won the Wimbledon Women's Singles title six times, having been unable to compete in 1924 through illness. Like many subsequent sportswomen, however, she transcended her own statistical achievements. She was the object of popular fascination and, when in 1926 she withdrew from the Wimbledon tournament circumstances that were widely argued over, the gravity given to the event by the British press was virtually without precedent for a sporting matter.

I first came across Lenglen around 1997 when preparing a series of lectures on the history of sport. One of the lectures was about the early years of women's sport and it drew heavily on a battered, second-hand history of the Wimbledon tennis tournament[2] – the All England Club being, as it happened, a twenty-minute walk from where I was teaching. The book featured a range of photographs of early winners of the women's singles at Wimbledon, virtually all of them attired in heavy ankle-length skirts, bodices and straw hats, secured with hat pins. (The exception was Charlotte 'Lottie' Dod, who first won Wimbledon in 1887 at the age of 15. She was allowed a shorter skirt – around four inches above the ankle – because she was, legally, still a child.) In startling contrast to these apparently statuesque Edwardian figures, Lenglen was pictured hurtling through the air, legs splayed like a hurdler, her shorter, and much lighter, chiffon tennis dresses blowing in the breeze. The 'moment' of Suzanne Lenglen's first participation in a Wimbledon tournament had been captured a year or two earlier by the leading British writer on women's sport, Jennifer Hargreaves. Hargreaves described the women's final of 1919 between a 20-year-old Lenglen and the reigning champion Mrs Dorothea Lambert Chambers, who had first won the title in 1903 and was now 40, as 'a symbolic battle between the old and the new – in terms of styles of play, styles of dress and attitudes to the role of women'. The apparently heavily corseted Mrs Chambers represented the old order, while the glamorous, leaping Mlle Lenglen the new.[3] The eminent sport historian Richard Holt also mentions Lenglen in his history of French sport, published in 1981. Principally, he notes that Lenglen's mother 'was worried in case her daughter became too involved in competitive sport and forgot the real purpose of the ladies' game: to say fit, feminine and to find a man. Suzanne Lenglen grew up in the new world of jolly middle-class adventure, in which young men experimented with cameras, motor-cars and aeroplanes while their sisters practised forehand and backhand returns of serve'.[4]

I want to use these two observations as a starting point for a fuller exploration of the phenomenon of Suzanne Lenglen. As with all the other essays in this book, the primary objective is to provide a fuller context for what are, in effect, historical snapshots. This exploration of Lenglen will consider her as, perhaps, the first female celebrity to emerge from the world of sport, but the purpose here is not to establish *whether* she was indeed the first – so as to clinch some imaginary pub argument – but to show *why*, given the nature of her appeal and of the cultural politics of her time and place, this claim could be made for her. After all, although, like anyone else, Suzanne Lenglen played her own tennis, she did not do so in circumstances of her own choosing. The essay draws on biographies of Mlle Lenglen and on the (copious) coverage she received in British newspapers between 1919 and 1926; nevertheless, a good deal of the argument presented here is, like much history, necessarily speculative.

The Myth of Suzanne Lenglen: *Fabriquée en France*

One thing that can be said with reasonable certainty is that the first female sport celebrity would be drawn from the upper echelons of society. This was because, firstly, the more individualistic sports such as racing, golf and tennis, which were most likely to throw up a celebrated figure, were among those favoured by the upper classes. Secondly, modern sport for women flourished initially among the aristocracy and upper middle classes, notably in the private schools and most prestigious universities.[5] Tennis, in particular, had been a favoured sport among ladies of leisure, although, as Holt notes, female members of tennis clubs were expected to place finding a suitable spouse, perhaps via a mixed-doubles partnership, above the pursuit of victory on court.[6] Wimbledon, indeed, was one of the first arenas in which individual women could, however modestly, display their sporting prowess in public: in the first final in 1884 clergyman's daughter Maud Watson had defeated her sister Lillian.

It was also likely that the first female sport celebrity would be French. For one thing, influential elements in French society and the French state regarded sport as important in the maintaining of national morale and international profile. The principal driving force behind the establishing of the modern Olympics had, after all, been the French nobleman Baron Pierre de Coubertin and France had staged the summer Olympics in 1900 and, again, in 1924. (Tennis, in this period, was an Olympic sport. Lenglen won the gold medal in the women's singles in the Antwerp Olympics of 1920, by which time the Olympics were attracting a good deal more press attention than they had before the First World War.) Moreover, it was in France that the most concerted opposition to the male exclusivity of sport was mounted. In what Bruce Kidd has called a 'breakthrough obscured by time'[7] in 1922 Paris, principally at the instigation of the rower and sport administrator Alice Milliat and in defiance of the International Olympic Committee (IOC), staged the first Women's Olympic Games in 1922.

These two factors – the European aristocracy's love of certain sports and the growing reluctance of women to accept male domination or condescension – circumscribe the life and achievements of Suzanne Lenglen. She was born in Compiegne, a manufacturing town in northern France, in 1899. Her father, now depicted in commentaries on Lenglen[8] as the greatest influence on her career, was a successful businessman and ran a horse-drawn bus company. The family had a tennis court, on which she began to play at the age of around ten or eleven. Lenglen's father moved the family to Nice, where they already had a summer residence, ostensibly for Suzanne's health. While it's true that Lenglen had indifferent health – she suffered from chronic asthma and retired several times from tournaments with colds and coughs – this move also gave M. and Mlle Lenglen easier access to the Riviera tennis circuit, on which Suzanne would make her name, and to the tennis-loving leisured elite of French society. As Holt observes, quoting Simone de Beauvoir, tennis was the only permissible form of exercise for a well-bred young woman in France in the early twentieth century;[9] he adds that, as late as the 1930s in France 'tennis was the only sport in which women played an important part as spectators and of these the majority were well-to-do ladies'.[10] Lenglen established a reputation among these well-to-do ladies (and their menfolk) before the First World War on the aforementioned Riviera tennis circuit, which included such elite venues as the Nice Country Club and the Métropole Hotel in Cannes. She first played on this circuit in 1912, at the age of 13. The following year she won the Italian Championship and, in 1914, she won the annual Nice tournament, beating the formidable Mrs Lambert Chambers, who was by then 36, in the process.

These successes gave her and her family an *entrée* into high society in Europe. In the mid-1920s, for example, Lenglen was the house guest of Count Alberto Bonacossa, alpine skier and Italian member of the IOC; her companion was her friend the English aristocrat Lady Wavertree, at whose garden parties in London's Regent's Park Suzanne played regular exhibition matches.[11] To move in social exalted circles was not unusual for leading tennis players: the Norwegian Anna 'Molla' Bjurstedt (who met Lenglen in the US Championships in 1921 and in the Wimbledon Final the following year) played regularly with the Swedish royal family,[12] as did the Spanish player Lili de Alvarez. There seems little doubt that the already well-off Lenglens, now with access to a higher social realm, were mindful of the codes of this new milieu. For one thing, it was often the mark of an aristocratic sportsperson that he/she did no significant training for a sporting encounter relying instead, as in the wider society, on invocations of 'natural' ability. M. Lenglen, for example, as Engelmann notes, had different accounts of his daughter's success according to who he was speaking to. Although it was well-known that he had studied tennis tactics and coached Suzanne with considerable discipline, even enlisting the help of the leading male players in France to work on her game, he only acknowledged this in certain company – presumably, the business circles in which notions of planning, competition and the importance of winning were taken for granted. Elsewhere he maintained that her prowess on the court was down solely to natural genius.[13] This apparently false, if romantic, rendering of Lenglen was retailed to the public. 'Mlle. Lenglen has played the best men,' wrote an anonymous *Times* correspondent during Wimbledon 1919, 'and, like Ulysses, she is first of all that she has met.

Pedants say that she has acquired her strokes by practice, but we don't believe a word of it; they are nature's response to the aspiration of a good stroke to meet a better. The more testing the ball, the more conspicuous the grace and ease of her execution.'[14]

The latter comment is important because it seeks to claim a naturalness not only for *class* (as manifested by a purportedly uncontrived gift) but also for *womanhood* – as exemplified by equally untutored grace. This myth of Lenglen was already established in France, where the press referred to her as *La Divine* – The Goddess. But young women at this time, however graceful and/or high born, were still expected to marry and this may explain the remark attributed by Holt to Suzanne's mother – that she should stay feminine and find a man. Again this was almost certainly said for public consumption. Lenglen definitely stayed feminine and she also found at least one man – a biographer suggests that she had a long affair with a married American called Baldwin M. Baldwin.[15] But she never married. Reasons for this may include the fact that most of her life was consumed by tennis, usually according to the strict training and tournament regimen dictated by a dominant father, styled in one account as her only love.[16]

A similar double standard attended Suzanne's amateur status. This status, in the time that she played, was, purportedly, conferred on those who played sport for the love of it, forsaking tactical preparation, undue competitiveness and any financial remuneration – be it in the form of expenses (or 'broken time payments') or for playing, coaching or commenting upon their sport. In practice this code worked as a device for excluding sportspeople below a certain social rank from participating in particular sports or events – something acknowledged in several sports such as rowing and athletics whose governing bodies in Britain in the late nineteenth century introduced regulations explicitly barring mechanics or labourers from leading competitions. 'Amateur', as the tennis historian Heiner Gillmeister has argued, was a synonym for 'gentleman'.[17] In 1920, while competing at Wimbledon, a bastion of British upper- and upper middle-class sport and, thus, of exclusive amateurism, Lenglen was contracted to write a column about the tournament in the *Daily Sketch* and in 1925 she published a book of instruction on lawn tennis[18] – either of these transactions giving sufficient ground for excluding her from Wimbledon, had she been from the lower orders. (It should be noted that Lenglen was not unusual in this respect. Lili de Alvarez, daughter of a wealthy Spanish family, and a Wimbledon singles finalist in successive years 1926–8, was signed to cover Wimbledon for the *Daily Mirror* in 1926 and published a book called *Modern Lawn Tennis* the following year.[19])

These, then, were important obstacles to be negotiated by Suzanne Lenglen and her family on the road to tennis success and subsequent stardom. She could not have achieved these things without tacit cultural permission.

La Divine et Wimbledon: Lenglen, celebrity and cultural politics

The task in this section is to establish the nature of Suzanne Lenglen's apparent impact on the Wimbledon tournament and to speculate upon the reasons for it.

In the first week of her first Wimbledon, Lenglen was already inspiring some rhetorical excesses in the press box. 'In defeating her experienced adversary with the loss of but three games,' wrote the *Times* correspondent of her match with the English Mrs. Larcombe, 'Mlle. Lenglen achieved the feat of following Mr Patterson [Gerald Patterson, an Australian who won the men's singles at Wimbledon in 1919] and appearing a hard hitting versatile player – player, be it understood, with no sex allowance. The Australian controlled the volley, the American smash, the French backhand and the English forehand drive –

> 'Take of these elements all that is fusible/Melt them all down in a pipkin' [A quote from *Patience*, an operetta by Gilbert and Sullivan] Clothe them in Paris, put them on centre court and an immense crowd will forget its national preferences in its enjoyment.'[20]

Clearly the attention of the tennis press was drawn not only to Lenglen, but the public enthusiasm that she inspired. The following day *The Times* reported that '...Mlle. Lenglen proved her chieftaincy by drawing almost all the spectators away from the centre court to the overflow "gallery" court where she was to play Miss Craddock...'[21]

This pattern of reportage was sustained the following year. 'A Special Correspondent' wrote that 'men who themselves had played for years on the centre court, scratched their good grey heads in the search for superlatives to describe Mlle. Lenglen – adjectives which seemed colourless and inadequate while she was making her triumphant progress.'[22] Two days later the writer noted that in the middle of a match between 'Mr. Winslow of South Africa' and 'that excellent player Mr. Garland' 'the crowd, which had seemed happy and contented enough, suddenly surged away in waves that were sucked into Court 4. What was seen there no one who fought his way to the front has apparently survived to tell. Experience, however, connects the seismic disturbance with Mlle. Lenglen.'[23] By 1924, the Wimbledon committee could only sensibly schedule her matches on one of their two main courts; hundreds would gather to watch her simply knocking up on an outside court of an evening.[24] Lieutenant Colonel Duncan Macaulay (Secretary of the All England Club 1946–63) recalled coming out of Southfields Underground Station in 1922, with Suzanne due to play Kitty McKane, and finding a queue stretching all the way to the Wimbledon championships (a distance of around 3.5 miles, since the championships were then staged at Worple Road). 'People used to call it the "Leng-len trail a-winding" after the famous war song of those days.'[25] Buoyed by such public enthusiasm, the championships moved to their present (much larger) premises at Church Road the following year.

But what, apart from an extraordinary tennis player, did Wimbledon – the players and spectators – see in Suzanne Lenglen? The players must have regarded her with some ambivalence. In the matters of dress, of the physicality of her play and her philosophy of sport (all clearly connected) Lenglen seemed to kick over the traces that they had been trying merely to loosen. By the mid-1920s the tennis garb that Lenglen and the younger post-war players had pioneered was standard attire. As a writer in the *Daily Mail* observed in 1926, 'The "common-sense fashions which it is the fortunate lot of the modern woman to adopt are nowhere more noticeable than in tennis clothes. The champions of "yesterday", who watched the play at Wimbledon[26] probably marvel that they were able to win their laurels when handicapped by a cloud of petticoats and high starched collar and stiff belt. They probably feel a tinge of regret that the present brief-skirted and sleeveless frocks were not of an earlier day.'[27]

The pre-war generation of female tennis players, their cumbersome outfits notwithstanding, had certainly confronted issues of gender, competitiveness and rational dress. After all, the lives of women from their social stratum had been a certain amount of flux since the turn of the century. There was, of course, the campaign of the suffragist movement, which will have had some support among the women of the metropolitan tennis clubs and there were the emergent ideals of the 'new woman', in search of independence and personal fulfilment. As Constance Rover remarked, many anti-suffragists nevertheless saw themselves as 'new women'.[28] Indeed, in Conservative Party circles – the circles in which most English female Wimbledon contestants moved – women's branches were rapidly supplanting the obedient auxiliaries of the Primrose League.[29] There was increasing promotion of sexual fulfilment and companionship in marriage,[30] although even sexual radicals such as Henry Havelock Ellis and Edward Carpenter believed in separate spheres for men and women.[31]

As early as 1903, Lottie Dod had openly criticized male authority on the question of female tennis attire; she called the editor of *The Field* magazine, the originating organ of the Wimbledon championships, 'an irresponsible despot' for acting as 'the ruler of the game as well as an arbiter of fashion, credited with the ability to regulate not only the weight of a lady's racket, but also the length of her skirt'.[32] Dorothea Lambert Chambers published her thoughts on the women's game in 1910, at the age of 32, and took a cautiously progressive line. Chambers was defending Wimbledon champion in 1919 and lost to Lenglen in a final that for decades afterward was regarded as one of the tournament's greatest matches. She cannot have run the very mobile Mlle Lenglen so close (8–10, 6–4, 9–7) without having considerable agility herself and must have privately resented the extra clothing that custom had obliged her to wear while doing so. In her book she rejected the notion of women as the weaker sex and suggested that the true woman was 'a helpmeet' to man. She urged young women to play tennis, to practise and to learn the strengths and weaknesses of their opponents.[33] She advised them to dress in a 'business-like' way, favouring a skirt 5 inches from the ground, a gymnasium shoe (rather than a shoe or a boot) and no hat.[34] But she doubted the suitability of the overhead service, judging the strain of it 'too severe for the average girl'.[35]

Molla Bjurstedt (later Mallory), a Norwegian who married an American, had published a similar book in 1916, when she too was 32, and, like Chambers advised young female tennis players to wear light clothing and no hat; some English girls, she admonished, dressed as if for afternoon tea. She also stressed the importance of freedom of movement, the necessity to jump dictating that a skirt should be at least 6 inches above the ground.[36] 'Tennis,' she wrote, 'is not for the girl who wants a milk-white face covered with paint and powder; if that is the ideal of female beauty, tennis and every other outdoor game must be avoided.'[37] However, again like Chambers, Bjurstedt insisted that 'complex services' were 'too exhausting' for girls and that a young woman must accept that she 'is not so strong or so enduring as a man and she must acknowledge these limitations when playing tennis'.[38]

By the time Suzanne Lenglen hit her first tennis ball at Wimbledon in 1919, a number of important developments were in train in political and popular culture. The Rational Dress Society, for example, had begun to campaign against cumbersome female attire in 1881. Moreover, feminist campaigns were now starting to have their legislative effect and, in the immediate aftermath of the First World War, the Sex Disqualification (Removal) Act (1919), which gave women greater access to the professions and the Matrimonial Causes Act of 1923, which granted them equality of grounds on which to petition for divorce, passed into the statute book. The chief beneficiaries of these acts were women of the middle and upper-middle classes, many of whom had, like Lenglen,[39] been doing charity work for the war effort, the need for which was now subsiding. Working-class women, many of whom had toiled hard in the war effort[40] had recently been told, in summary fashion, that their services were no longer needed. Indeed, they were now vilified in high places, such as the pages of *The Times*, wherein a correspondent in 1918 sneered at the (mythical) 'expensively-gowned, highly paid munitions worker of whom so much has been heard'.[41] This political impetus to reallocate manual jobs to returning male troops and to persuade women to begin restoring the birth rate also brought a condemnation, and in some instances the curtailment of, the favoured pleasures and sports of working-class women. As the historian Sheila Rowbotham observed: 'The young women workers who formed their own football teams, went bicycling or dancing and flocked to theatres, music halls and cinemas were at once heroines of the war effort and dangerously autonomous. By 1917 the newspapers were calling them "flaunting flappers".'[42] In 1921 the English Football Association, reading the political wind, instructed its members to cease staging women's matches, declaring that 'the game of football is quite unsuitable for females and should not be encouraged'.[43]

To those, principally well-to-do, young women not designated as 'flaunting', the notion of the 'flapper' now flourishing in popular media culture was held out as an alternative source of identity to war work or early marriage: 'emancipated but no feminist', wrote Lesley A. Hall, 'released from chaperonage and the heavy garments of the pre-war era, madly dancing and bent on having a good time, is often seen as epitomising the twenties'.[44] The flapper phenomenon, observed Rowbotham, was 'partly a chimera [...] but behind all the razzmatazz a genuine sense of confusion existed about how to be a modern woman'.[45] It would not require undue powers of association to suggest that Suzanne Lenglen was the flappers' representative on the international tennis courts. But the point about Lenglen is that, before one even comes to consider her likely male following, she had clear potential appeal to all the shades of female opinion to emerge from the social changes of the previous 30 years.

Lenglen was, first and foremost, a tennis player. In that regard, she sought to transcend her gender in a manner, and to an extent, either denied to or simply not contemplated by previous generations of women competitors. Like her predecessors, Lenglen published a book of tennis advice. Called, to give it its full title, *Lawn Tennis: The Game of Nations*, it is a straightforward coaching manual, with a certain amount of perceptible philosophy, but no mention of appropriate court attire. Unlike earlier volumes by Mrs Chambers, Miss Bjurstedt and others, Lenglen's book addressed not merely women but tennis players in general. She began humbly enough: 'In the course of this book, while approaching the subject as a woman, and therefore writing particularly for women, I hope at the same time, as far as lies in my power, to give a general impression of what I believe to be the foundation of the game and its proper theory.'[46] As her instruction progressed, however, Lenglen had stern words for anyone who doubted the worth of the female player. Was tennis 'any the less worthy' she asked in the Preface, 'because a woman can, and many women do, beat some man or men at it?'[47] Tennis women, for their part, should stiffen their resolve: 'Breadth and sound driving are imperative, and it is only by a correct mental attitude, kept sedulously in view, that these will become second nature to most women, because the majority are not "large" in the way in which they look at things. This is nothing in disparagement of my sex, but only the voicing of that barrier which is apt to divide us from men in sport – not all men, but men as a class.'[48] She went on to write a chapter about the volley, a stroke which many in the pre-war tennis world – Molla Bjurstedt, for instance[49] – had thought it beyond a female player to sustain for a whole match. Lenglen, however, declared, on the first page of this chapter, that women will need the volley because: 'Nowadays, women can and do play doubles like men and can join in doubles with the men, say one woman to three men, without spoiling the game in the least'.[50] Men, for their part, were told that they 'should not be obsessed by the idea that a mixed double is a degenerate single in which their partners are merely pickers up of crumbs, or a kind of tail wagging behind them'.[51]

Lenglen was also openly and passionately competitive. 'Without a winner and a loser,' she stated bluntly, 'no game can exist. Neither is it a dishonour to lose nor to desire ardently to win.'[52] According to Engelmann, she found it 'rather amusing' when contesting the US championships at Forest Hills in 1921, 'that Americans feigned shock at her practice of predicting victory before her matches'.[53] The pursuit of these victories, Suzanne knew, involved a politics of the female body hitherto not widely contemplated in the female game, certainly before the First World War. But, she asserted, an 'exercise which calls for the use of all the muscles in the body in continual variety, consistently and constantly, while play lasts, cannot be detrimental, nor can it be feministic in essence, as some assert'.[54] This was a smart disavowal, since many of her readers would not have been feminists, but, for the ones that were, Lenglen's expressed sentiments, and her physical enactment of them on court, would have pleased them greatly. And, for those who were more flapper than feminist and for those women who worried that vigorous sport would rob them of their femininity – a notion with which generations of sportswomen have had to grapple – Lenglen offered huge reassurance. Like young women across the social spectrum she was interested in glamour and wore the latest Paris fashions, on and off the court; she was a living retort to Miss Bjurstedt – a milk-white face covered with paint and powder, who could nevertheless compete with men in practice and mixed doubles and see off most women in straight sets. She would even, when the mood took her, skip momentarily from feminist to flapper: she is reputed, for example, to have wiped the perspiration (something that Wimbledon ladies were not supposed to show – the reason they were required to wear white) on the hem of her skirt.[55] Metaphorically, she came close in her appeal to that of Doris Day's *Calamity Jane* of 1953, who wore buckskin and shot six-guns with the cowboys by day and in the evening went to the ball in a long dress. The *Times* tennis correspondent called it 'her dainty strength'. 'She is not the goddess – nothing so icily regular and insipid,' he wrote, 'she makes perfect strokes often because she tries to make perfect strokes always. So hypnotic is her dainty strength that one is apt to brush aside any errors of hers as if they were grammatical slips in a poem'.[56]

There can be little doubt that Lenglen's exciting play, glamour and stylish, unprecedentedly revealing tennis clothing appealed equally to men, although moralists of either gender may have tut-tutted. Paradoxically, perhaps, one of the few disparaging remarks about Lenglen's appearance to have survived in print was by the American tennis player and three-times Wimbledon singles champion William 'Big Bill' Tilden, who said of her in 1921: 'her costume struck me as a cross between a prima donna's and a streetwalker. She wore a white fur cape over her white tennis costume and around her head a crimson band so flaming that I earnestly hoped no bull was in the neighbourhood.'[57] It might be noted, though, that, as his biographer observes, 'Big Bill didn't care much for women players to start with.'[58] Indeed he was a misogynist: 'Women are a lot of bitches', he once told a young (female) friend, 'When someone is a genius, when they have a great task in life, they cannot afford to be depleted by a woman. Women wear down a man'.[59] He was also an effeminate homosexual with a predilection – albeit usually non-sexual – for young boys and therefore had a vested interest in presenting a bluff, conservative masculinity to the world.[60]

Suzanne Causes a Sensation: Lenglen and the Contradictions of Celebrity

Suzanne's Lenglen's celebrity, founded on the excitement she had engendered in Cannes, Nice and Monte Carlo among the Riviera tennis set and enhanced by her dynamism and lack of inhibition on Wimbledon's Centre Court, had grown steadily from 1919. By then her level of recognition had reached the point where sections of the popular British press felt able to abandon her surname, just as they did for film stars. In 1920 the American actress Mary Pickford visited Wimbledon on honeymoon with Douglas Fairbanks. The press arranged for Lenglen and Pickford to kiss, the *Daily Sketch* rewarding them with the front page headline MARY KISSES SUZANNE. (The *Sketch* was, of course, promoting Lenglen, their columnist. The *Daily Mirror* had the kiss on page 9.)[61] Through the 1920s and early 1930s, Lenglen made the various moves to commodify her popularity that are now routinely associated with sport celebrity. To her book of instruction in 1925 she added a novel and a gramophone record, recorded at the HMV studios in Middlesex, entitled 'Suzanne Lenglen on Lawn Tennis' and, the following year, she wrote a series of articles for the *London Evening News* with a similar theme: 'How to Play Lawn Tennis – and How Not to Play It.'[62] In 1927, having turned professional, she played a series of exhibition matches around Britain, the venues for which included three football grounds: Old Trafford in Manchester, Bloomfield Road in Blackpool and Hampden Park in Glasgow. The latter attracted a crowd of 8000.[63] In 1934, as part of her contract to promote the prestigious London store, she played an exhibition match on the roof of Selfridges in London's Oxford Street against Dan Maskell, then British professional champion.[64] The same year she appeared in a British comedy film called *Things Are Looking Up*, starring Cicely Courtneidge.[65] She marketed a range of clothes and perfumes in her name, and so on.[66]

But Lenglen, in what was to be her final Wimbledon as a competitor, also experienced the contradictions of celebrity. Celebrity is a feature of purportedly meritocratic societies – indeed it is now seen by some writers as a substitute for democracy.[67] Celebrities are celebrities by public affirmation, but they are also, in a sense, an indictment of the people who admire them: after all, the success of the celebrity is, simultaneously, the supposed failure of myriad non-celebrities. Press discourse has, historically, played upon the ambiguous feelings to which this contradiction has given rise: the objective 'She's wonderful', for example, has often readily transmuted into the subjective 'Who does she think she is?' Lenglen experienced this kind of framing of herself during the Wimbledon tournament of 1926. On 23 June she did not show up until over an hour after her appointed playing time. There are several accounts of this incident.[68] Generally speaking, her late arrival has been explained by an indisposition (Lenglen was prone to injury and ill-health) and to a lapse in the normal practice of escorting her to the office of the tournament referee to inform her of her schedule. Press reaction to the incident readily illustrated the ambiguity of her (and all) celebrity.

The correspondent of *The Times* noted, following an announcement that Lenglen had been detained, that the crowd on Court 1, where Lenglen had been due to play a singles against the Ceylon champion Evelyn Dewhurst, had been 'distracted by rumours put about to account for her detention. None so poor but had a tale to tell.' He added that later the same day a ladies' doubles match in which Suzanne and her French partner Diddie Vlasto were to have played Mary Browne and Elizabeth Ryan of the United States on Centre Court 'was one of which the Queen, who was present, would have been a witness'.[69] Lenglen beat Dewhurst the following day, dropping only four games. However, having lost her ladies' doubles match and before she could meet the English Claire Beckingham in the next round of the singles, she withdrew from the tournament, through illness. There had been several Wimbledon withdrawals on health grounds, commented *The Times*, so this year's championships might well have been retitled 'the Microbes' Jubilee Meeting'.

But while *The Times* had added only mild insinuations to their matter-of-fact reporting of the various official Wimbledon statements on the affair, the *Daily Express*, in the person of their Lawn tennis Correspondent S. Powell Blackmore, put Lenglen's difficulties on the front page, rendering the whole matter in some detail and with a plainly more populist inflection. Their readers were regaled with the headlines:

SUZANNE
CAUSES
SENSATION

NON-APPEARANCE IN A MATCH BEFORE THE QUEEN
INDISPOSED
PROTEST AGAINST THE PROGRAMME

Blackmore then began: 'MLLE. SUZANNE LENGLEN held up play at Wimbledon yesterday for an hour and a quarter and disappointed a thousand spectators, among whom was the Queen, by her failure to appear at the time she was expected. It was afterwards announced that she was indisposed.' The article later had her running belatedly up the clubhouse steps and saying, in improbably worded defiance, to Commander Hillyard (until the previous year secretary of the All England Club) 'If the committee is displeased at my action in not being here for the singles match at two o'clock I am indifferent and will scratch from everything.' At six o'clock, continued Blackmore, Mlle Lenglen had left Wimbledon by motor car: 'She was looking hysterical and a portion of the crowd surrounding the car hissed and booed as it moved away.'[70] The following day the front page of the *Express* carried the headline SUZANNE BEATEN IN THE DOUBLES/FAINTING FIT AND TEARS AFTER DEFEAT; on the back was an ironic headline SUZANNE IS PUNCTUAL and a picture of Lenglen and Vlasto, captioned 'TEMPERAMENTAL SUZANNE (in front) was in time yesterday'.[71]

The *Daily Mail* and *Daily Mirror* similarly invited public disapproval for Lenglen, the former printing the headline MLLE. LENGLEN REFUSES TO PLAY on their page 9[72] and the latter referring to her 'sudden indisposition'.[73] Both suggested that Lenglen should no longer be in the tournament. Awaiting personal notification of her matches was no excuse, implied Stanley N. Doust in the *Mail*: 'Technically speaking it is a competitor's own fault if she fails to find out at what time she is required to play as there is a programme for the next day posted in the referee's office at 7 p.m.'[74] The *Mirror* correspondent, beneath the headline SHOULD SUZANNE HAVE BEEN SCRATCHED?, commented that '...Rule 24, rightly or wrongly, gives no grace to a belated player...'[75] Only in the *Daily Sketch*, to which of course Mlle Lenglen was contracted and in which a column bearing her name had appeared throughout the Wimbledon fortnight, did she have a sympathetic rendering of her predicament. Here her headlines were SUZANNE LENGLEN ON HER FAILURE TO PLAY/"Against My Doctor's Advice" and she told *Sketch* readers: 'I wanted to play – wanted so much to play, of course, because Her Majesty the Queen was in her box – but I could not! Tomorrow – I hope so. Anyway, I shall do my best.'[76] The following day the *Sketch* had a photograph of Lenglen 'looking far from well' on its front page and pressed the message home on the inside page with ILLNESS MAY ROB SUZANNE OF HER TITLE/Collapse After Plucky Fight/ 'Every Stroke Was Agony'.[77] Four days later, at her withdrawal from the championships, the *Sketch* carried the valedictory headline SUZANNE GIVES UP THE FIGHT.[78]

In this episode, and its competing discourses, Suzanne Lenglen was recognized as both a *text* and a *commodity* and *news* became indistinguishable from *publicity*. The same woman who had been *La Divine*, doyenne of the international tennis courts and the inspiration for three-mile queues of excited would-be spectators, was now, some readers were asked to believe, an hysteric who had affronted a British queen, let down her loyal subjects and profaned a hallowed sporting institution. Who did she think she was? By citing the presence of the Queen the *Daily Express* and companion newspapers were invoking a traditional authority, rooted in heredity and nation, against a newer, apparently more meritocratic one – celebrity. Nobody – and certainly not someone whose eminence came via the shillings of the multitude – was bigger than the Queen.

And, at another level, the *Daily Sketch* had a scoop – the person at the centre of a news story was contracted to them and could render a first-hand account of it exclusively to them; the *Express*, the *Mirror* and the *Mail* had 'spoilers' – attempting to devalue the copy of competitor papers. Common to all this carry-on was an assertion of the power of the popular commercial press: a 'celebrity', it was implied, was who they said was a celebrity and for as long as they said it.

But very little of the hue and cry was either new or unique to Lenglen. Back in 1921 she had played Molla Bjurstedt Mallory in the second round of the US championships at Forest Hills. Mallory, now an American by adoption and by marriage and a celebrity not unlike Lenglen in the United States, had been winning when Lenglen had begun to complain of a bad cough. The American press had, generally speaking, doubted that Lenglen was genuinely ill, as had the official from the French Tennis Federation who had accompanied her; he had resigned, despite a doctor's confirmation that Lenglen was indeed unwell. Lenglen had beaten Mallory the following year at Wimbledon whereupon, it is claimed, Lenglen said: 'Now Mrs. Mallory, I have proved to you today what I could have done to you in New York last year,' to which Mallory replied: 'Mlle. Lenglen, you have done to me today what I did [to] you in New York last year; you have beaten me.'[79] It seems doubtful that two such laboured remarks could ever have been exchanged. Certainly Mallory sensed that the popular press in the

US wanted to foster the notion of a feud between her and Lenglen and was clearly aghast at the thought of being used as a news item. 'The newspapers are the dirtiest, filthiest things that ever happened,' she said. 'I don't want my name in the papers. I have a better chance on the courts than in the newspapers of my own country.'[80]

Suzanne Lenglen returned to Wimbledon on a number of occasions after 1926; each time she became surrounded by an admiring throng or the recipient of warm applause from the crowd.[81]

Conclusion: Lenglen, Women's Tennis and Posterity

In the early 1960s, Kitty Godfree, the Englishwoman who had won the Wimbledon women's singles title in 1924 and 1926, Lenglen withdrawing in both years, was asked how Lenglen compared to other leading players. 'Oh, I am sure Suzanne Lenglen was the greatest of them all and she also made a far greater impact on the game of Lawn Tennis than anyone else, said Godfree. 'She altered the whole aspect of women's tennis. Few women before her played the all-court game; but Suzanne volleyed like a man and continually played with the best men of her country in practice in doubles. She also entirely altered the style of women's dress, not with the idea of being sensational, but to gain greater mobility. And her lovely one-piece dresses, much shorter than any woman had ever worn before, looked very attractive.'[82]

This is a warm and, for Lenglen, a familiar tribute, but this talented and attractive woman did not reinvent women's tennis all on her own. She was certainly the best female player most tennis people had ever seen; as Mallory said after their first meeting in the World Hard Court Championships in the summer of 1921: 'She is just the steadiest player that ever was. She just sent back at me whatever I sent at her and waited for me to make a fault.'[83] She also had a dress sense that, as Godfree pointed out, was both bold and functional. But, as I argued at the beginning of this essay, she did not – any more than anyone else – play her tennis in circumstances of her own choosing. She lived in changing times. There were other young women like her, pursuing or at least desiring, a greater athleticism and freedom of movement than pre-war players, and a popular culture endorsing their aspirations. In the summer of 1920, for example, the *Daily Mirror* carried a picture of the young English player Evelyn Colyer playing against Kitty McKane (later Godfree) at Wimbledon. She's reaching for a high forehand volley, her right leg virtually horizontal in front of her and her skirt riding up above both knees – a posture more popularly (and often exclusively) associated with Lenglen. Lenglen did not singlehandedly change women's tennis, but, for many, tennis players and watchers, she defined the changes that were in train. Central to this were the burgeoning popular press who showed an increasing interest in both sport and celebrity in their battle for pre-eminence at Britain's breakfast tables. Thus, to flappers, feminists and admiring gentlemen alike – Suzanne Lenglen became one of the first sporting celebrities – the most memorable and exciting representation on the tennis court of the mythic 'new woman'.

Notes

1. Larry Engelmann, *The Goddess and the American Girl: The Story of Suzanne Lenglen and Helen Wills*, Oxford, at the University Press 1988, p. 5.
2. Max Robertson, *Wimbledon: Centre Court of the Game*, London: British Broadcasting Corporation 1981.
3. Jennifer Hargreaves, *Sporting Females: Critical Issues in the History and Sociology of Women's Sports*, London: Routledge 1994, p. 116.
4. Richard Holt, *Sport and Society in Modern France*, London: Macmillan 1981, pp. 178–9.
5. See, for example, Hargreaves, *Sporting Females*, pp. 65–6.
6. Richard Holt, *Sport and the British*, Oxford: The Clarendon Press 1989, p. 127.
7. Bruce Kidd, 'The Women's Olympic Games: Important Breakthrough Obscured by Time' AAAWS (Canadian Association for the Advancement of Women and Sport and Physical Activity) Action Bulletin Spring 1994 Available at http://www.caaws.ca/e/milestones/women_history/olympic_games.cfm (my access: 2 July 2010).
8. Notably Engelmann, *Goddess*.
9. Holt, *Sport and Society in Modern France*, p. 178.
10. Ibid., p. 179.
11. See Alan Little, *Suzanne Lenglen: Tennis Idol of the Twenties*, London: Wimbledon Lawn Tennis Museum 1988, pp. 46, 73.
12. Molla Bjurstedt, with Samuel Crowther, *Tennis for Women*, La Vergne, Tennessee: General Books LLC 2009 (first published New York: Doubleday, Page and Co., 1916).
13. Engelmann, *Goddess*, p. 12.
14. *The Times*, 2 July 1919, p. 5.
15. Little, *Suzanne Lenglen*, p. 82.
16. Engelmann, *Goddess*, p. 57.
17. Heiner Gillmeister, *Tennis: A Cultural History*, London: Leicester University Press 1998, p. 194.
18. Suzanne Lenglen, *Lawn Tennis: The Game of Nations*, New York: Dodd, Mead and Company 1925.
19. Lili de Alvarez, *Modern Lawn Tennis*, London: John Lane 1927.
20. *The Times*, 27 June 1919, p. 5.
21. Ibid., 28 June 1919, p. 6.
22. Ibid., 22 June 1920, p. 7.
23. Ibid., 24 June 1920, p. 8.

24. Little, *Suzanne Lenglen*, p. 55.
25. Lt. Col. A.D.C. Macaulay (as told to Brigadier The Rt. Hon. Sir John Smyth) *Behind the Scenes at Wimbledon*, London: Collins 1965, p. 23.
26. 1926 was the 50th anniversary of the Wimbledon Championships. Many past winners of the Ladies' Singles, including Maud Watson, Lottie Dod and Dorothea Lambert Chambers were presented with medals. Lenglen's drew the loudest cheer. See Macaulay, *Behind the Scenes*, p. 39.
27. 'At the Courts of the Sovereign Summer Game', *Daily Mail*, 25 June 1926, p. 15.
28. Quoted in Beatrix Campbell, *The Iron Ladies*, London: Virago 1987, p. 38.
29. Ibid., p. 48.
30. See Sheila Jeffreys, *The Spinster and Her Enemies: Feminism and Sexuality 1880–1930*, Melbourne, Australia: Spinifex 1997, pp. 166–8; Lesley A. Hall, *Sex, Gender and Social Change in Britain Since 1880*, Basingstoke: Macmillan 2000, p. 108.
31. See Jane Lewis, *Women in England 1870–1950*, Brighton: Wheatsheaf Book 1984, p. 99.
32. Quoted in Gillmeister, *Tennis*, p. 205.
33. Dorothea Lambert Chambers, *Lawn Tennis for Ladies*, Charleston, SC: Biblio Bazaar 2008, pp. 16, 23, 40.
34. Ibid., pp. 53–6.
35. Ibid., p. 45.
36. Bjurstedt, *Tennis for Women*, pp. 59–60.
37. Ibid., p. 6.
38. Ibid., p. 4.
39. Lenglen worked for the Red Cross in France during 1916 and 1917. See Little, *Suzanne Lenglen*, p. 16.
40. See, for example, Arthur Marwick, *Women at War, 1914–18*, London: Fontana 1977.
41. *The Times*, 20 November 1918. Quoted in Fiona A. Montgomery, *Women's Rights: Struggles and Feminism in Britain c 1770–1970*, Manchester, at the University Press 2006, p. 120.
42. Sheila Rowbotham, *A Century of Women: The History of Women in Britain and the United States*, London: Viking 1997, p. 85.
43. Quoted by John Williams and Jackie Woodhouse 'Can play, will play? Women and football in Britain' in John Williams and Stephen Wagg (eds) *British Football and Social Change*, Leicester, at the University Press 1991, p. 93.
44. Hall, *Sex, Gender and Social Change*, p. 99.
45. Rowbotham, *A Century of Women*, pp. 147–8.
46. Lenglen, *Lawn Tennis*, p. 1.
47. Ibid., p. v.
48. Ibid., p. 3.
49. Bjurstedt, *Tennis for Women*, p. 3.
50. Lenglen, *Lawn Tennis*, p. 46.
51. Ibid., p. 111.
52. Ibid., p. 2.
53. Englemann, *Goddess*, p. 32.
54. Lenglen, *Lawn Tennis*, p. vi.

55. Little, *Suzanne Lenglen*, p. 16.
56. *The Times*, 7 July 1919, p. 15.
57. Quoted in Engelmann, *Goddess*, p. 25
58. Frank Deford, *Big Bill Tilden: The Triumphs and the Tragedy*, Wilmington, DE: Sport Media Publishing 2004, p. 112.
59. Ibid., p. 167.
60. Ibid., pp. 33–4.
61. 24 June 1920 for both newspapers.
62. Little, *Suzanne Lenglen*, pp. 60, 74.
63. Ibid., pp. 84–6.
64. Dan Maskell, *From Where I Sit*, London: Willow Books 1988, pp. 58–9.
65. Little, *Suzanne Lenglen*, p. 90.
66. See Maurice Brady, *The Centre Court Story*, London: W. Foulsham and Co. 1957, p. 23.
67. For an overview, see, for example, Chris Rojek, *Celebrity*, London: Reaktion Books 2001.
68. See, for example, Little, *Suzanne Lenglen*, pp. 77–80 and Macaulay *Behind the Scene*, pp. 39–41.
69. *The Times*, 24 June 1926, p. 7.
70. S. Powell Blackmore, 'Suzanne causes a sensation', *Daily Express*, 24 June 1926, p. 1.
71. *Daily Express*, 25 June 1926, pp. 1, 16.
72. *Daily Mail*, 24 June 1926, p. 9.
73. *Daily Mirror*, 24 June 1926, p. 3.
74. Stanley N. Doust 'Mlle. Lenglen refuses to Play', *Daily Mail*, 24 June 1926, p. 9.
75. *Daily Mirror*, 24 June 1926, p. 3.
76. Suzanne Lenglen 'Suzanne Lenglen on her failure to play', *Daily Sketch* 24 June 1926, p. 3.
77. *Daily Sketch*, 25 June 1926, pp. 1, 3.
78. Ibid., 29 June 1926, p. 2.
79. Quoted in Billie Jean King (with Cynthia Starr), *We Have Come a Long Way: The Story of Women's Tennis*, New York: McGraw-Hill 1988, p. 31 and in Engelmann, *Goddess*, p. 41. For an extensive account of this incident see Engelmann, pp. 38–41.
80. Engelmann, *Goddess*, p. 41.
81. Little, *Suzanne Lenglen*, p. 87; Engelmann, *Goddess*, p. 426.
82. In Macaulay, *Behind the Scenes*, p. 44.
83. *New York Times*, 6 June 1921, p. 1.

7
Before and After 1968: Reconsidering the Introduction of Drug Testing in the Olympic Games

Ian Ritchie

Introduction

The 1968 Summer Olympic Games in Mexico City are well-known in Olympic history for several significant events, including the famous black power podium salutes of American athletes John Carlos and Tommie Smith, and the 'Tlatelolco Massacre' of protesters 10 days before the start of the Games. The 1968 Games are also important in terms of Olympic policy history because the International Olympic Committee (IOC) was grappling with three somewhat interrelated issues: (a) altitude training and competition, and specifically the time athletes would be permitted to train at higher than normal altitudes in preparation for the relatively high elevation of Mexico City itself; (b) sex testing, and rumours or suspicions of 'gender ambiguity' of some athletes; and (c) drug testing, with growing concerns that athletes in certain events were using performance-enhancing amphetamines or anabolic steroids.[1] However, in terms of its long-term influence on the Olympic movement, it is likely that the last-named issue above had the greatest impact – the use of performance-enhancing substances and the policies and procedures to catch athletes who 'cheat.' From 1968 on, the use of drugs and the testing and surveillance of athletes' has been at the forefront of the Olympic movement, as it has in high-performance amateur and professional sport in general. Indeed, today the use of performance-enhancing drugs is for many one of the greatest challenges to the perceived integrity of sport.

It is not surprising that the 1968 Summer Olympic Games are seen as a turning point in the 'war against drugs' in sport. Historical accounts commonly cite the 1968 Games as one of the most important 'moments' in modern sport; the year is seen as a 'wake-up call' from a state of naive slumber based on the values of an older era in sport when athletes were amateur and competed for the sheer love of competition, to the brute reality of performance enhancement at all costs. However, was 1968 truly such a 'turning point?'

This chapter does not dispute the accuracy of the basic historical events in the creation of the first Olympic policies against the use of performance-enhancing substances or the first tests that were conducted on athletes. It does, however, dispute some of the underlying assumptions regarding why the first policies were created and the legitimacy of those policies. It is often taken for granted that athletes, coaches, sport administrators, and for that matter the public at large in the 1960s had a common consensus that the use of certain performance-enhancing substances was 'cheating' and that the ethical question regarding drug use was clear and straightforward. It is also typically assumed that the IOC banned drugs out of ethical concerns – to protect the health of athletes and to protect the ideal of the 'level playing field.' This chapter challenges these assumptions and demonstrates that the events leading up to 1968 suggest that the IOC prohibited certain substances for reasons far beyond 'ethics' *per se*. More importantly, it is also suggested that common everyday attitudes regarding athletes who use drugs stem from an important yet often overlooked element of the Olympic Games movement: the creation of Olympic mythology. After considering some basic historical events in the development of the use of drugs in high-performance sport, concentrating on events in the Olympic movement leading up to 1968, this chapter goes on to consider some recent critical historical interpretations of that same history. The latter part of this chapter then examines important components of Olympic Games' mythology, specifically elements of Olympic myths that can be traced back to Pierre de Coubertin's ideals for the Games. The legacy of his creation of certain ideals – to the creation of Olympic mythology – lives on in attitudes towards drug policies today.

The legacy of 1968: historical accounts of drug prohibitions

A short history of drug use and prohibitions

It is important to put the events of 1968 into their proper historical perspective. Virtually all informed accounts of the use of drugs or other performance-enhancers in sport point out that their use is in fact very old and, perhaps surprisingly, quite common in human history.

However, it is a mistake to infer from this observation that the values and attitudes underlying the use of performance enhancers is the same across time and across cultures. As a constantly shifting cultural enterprise, the meanings and values of what today we refer to as 'sport' – what we might refer to more generally as 'physical culture' across time periods and human social systems – shift concomitantly with cultural changes. For example, it is known that athletes in the ancient Olympic Games ingested mushrooms and animal organs, drank wine and brandy, and experimented with various diets in the hope of improving stamina and creating energy, but they did so without any moral misgivings. Understanding the cultural context of ancient sport gives us insight into why that was the case: the 'winner-take-all' attitude of the ancients would, by even the most extreme standards today, be unthinkable.[2]

An important context for the use of drugs in modern times is medical and scientific inquiries in Europe and the United States in the mid- to late nineteenth century, specifically concerns with energy production and the avoidance of fatigue that emerged out of scientific debates regarding thermodynamics and the thesis of the 'conservation of energy.'[3] Some of the substances used as part of 'human experiments' in energy and fatigue were the precursors to the later use of amphetamines and anabolic steroids in high-performance Olympic sport in the twentieth century. After injecting himself with 'testicular extracts,' prominent French physiologist Charles-Edouard Brown-Séquard reported to the Society of Biology in Paris in 1889 that he felt renewed physical energy and mental acumen. Around the same period of time, long-distance runners, walkers, and cyclists used alcohol, coca, kola, oxygen, cocaine, and strychnine to enhance endurance and produce energy. In fact, the first purported death of an athlete came during an endurance cycling race in 1886 when Englishman Arthur Linton supposedly overdosed on 'tri-methyl,' although it is now thought that Linton's death was misreported and that he did not die until 1896, of typhoid fever.[4]

The use of amphetamines to fight fatigue during World War II led, in part, to their use by athletes after the war. The practice should not be surprising given the fact that, as Dimeo reports, a 'pep pill mania' of sorts emerged among the general public, especially in the United States where amphetamines were seen as 'acceptable and legitimate public medicine.'[5] Anabolic steroids were first synthesized in the 1930s and by the post-war period there was a growing interest in their use for therapeutic medical purposes. For more general uses, the 1945 publication of Paul de Kruif's *The Male Hormone* was important because, first, as a scientist who turned to popular writing on topics related to scientific solutions to human problems, De Kruif had a wide following, and second, *The Male Hormone* defended the ability of steroids to enhance energy, build strength, combat fatigue, and even to extend the duration of life.[6] Alongside the first positive experimental evidence for steroids' influence on sport performance published in the *Journal of Clinical Endocrinology* in 1944,[7] it was, as Yesalis and Bahrke suggest, 'a relatively easy extrapolation for some in the physical culture of bodybuilding to expect that additional anabolic-androgenic hormones...would allow development of greater-than-'normal' body size and strength.'[8]

But the real drive to push the boundaries of human physical imitations – both with the aid of performance-enhancing substances and in general with the use of many other means – came with the entry and immediate success of the Union of Soviet Socialist Republics (USSR) into the Olympic movement in 1952. From that point on, the full commitment of the respective politico-bureaucratic apparatus in both the USA and USSR made performance in the Olympic Games a top priority. Anabolic steroids became part of the arsenal of performance-enhancing weaponry both the USSR and USA used to gain medals and, by association, political, and ideological supremacy. As Dimeo summarizes it, for the USSR it 'meant a systematic application of doping medicine and science to the problem of achieving excellence' while, for the USA, 'sports physicians from the 1950s through to the late 1970s (at least) made the connection between politics and doping: defeat in athletic competition to the communists had to be avoided at all costs.'[9] Indeed, the palpable fears in the USA were expressed clearly in the historic first issue of *Sports Illustrated*, published in 1954. Author Gerald Holland reported that 'Russia and her satellites had sent a new breed of athlete out into the free world...a superbly trained, coldly efficient, intensely suspicious fellow...[who] worked full time at sports, although he competed as an amateur, and he swiftly built up a legend of invincibility.'[10]

It is not surprising that the 'origin story' of the use of anabolic steroids has over time been turned into a case of international 'finger pointing' across the (former) Cold War divide, although it is very likely the case that both sides of the Iron Curtain were simultaneously committed to the use of anabolic steroids to improve performance in the increasingly heated atmosphere of Cold War Olympic sport.[11] It is known that at the 1954 World Weightlifting Championships American coach Bob Hoffman alongside team physician John Ziegler were convinced that the Soviet weightlifters were, in Hoffman's words, 'taking the hormone stuff to increase their strength'[12] and, subsequently, Ziegler gave the synthetic steroid methandienone (Dianabol), produced by the Ciba Pharmaceutical Company, to weightlifters at the York Barbell Club in Pennsylvania. From there, the use of anabolic steroids spread quickly; by the 1960s the taking of anabolic steroids had become common in weightlifting circles but also shot-putting, hammer throwing, discus, and several other Olympic, strength-related events.[13]

The IOC's concerns were raised with rumours of accelerated use of amphetamines and anabolic steroids on both sides of the Cold War divide, alongside the deaths of two cyclists – Denmark's Knud Enemark Jensen, who collapsed and died during the road race in the 1960 Rome Summer Games, and British cyclist Tommy Simpson, who died during the 1967 Tour de France, both apparently from amphetamine use.[14] Originally, the IOC discussed the rumours of drug use in its 'Doping Committee' in a fairly *ad hoc* manner. However, those discussions were quickly turned over to the Medical Committee, formed in 1961, and from there the discussions became more numerous and the concerns more serious in nature. At its 1964 meetings in Tokyo, the Medical Committee recommended that the IOC condemn drug use, sanction individuals and national organizations known to encourage substance use, and ask athletes to sign a pledge to the effect they were drug-free. At the Tehran meetings in 1967, the IOC adopted drug and sex testing simultaneously while generating a list of banned substances. Athletes as of 1968 were required to sign a pledge to the effect that they would not use performance-enhancing drugs, female athletes were required to undergo sex tests, and limited random drug tests were conducted at the 1968 Mexico City Games. During those Games, the IOC's Medical Committee selected sports at random each morning of competition, and from those sports ten athletes were selected for tests, again at random. The new Rule 28 of the *Olympic Charter* prohibited 'the use of substances or techniques in any form or quantity alien or unnatural to the body with the exclusive aim of obtaining an artificial or unfair increase of performance in competition.' While there were no tests for anabolic steroids at first, those tests were developed in 1973 and first implemented at the Montreal Games in 1976.[15]

Critical historical interpretations

At face value the history of the creation of the first rules against drugs and the implementation of the first tests seems straightforward enough. Although formal prohibition policies and, even more so, testing procedures have become more nuanced and advanced since 1968, the events leading up to and during the Games in Mexico City are certainly important for the precedent set for the next 50 years, and so what appear to be relatively arcane rules and procedures are important for that reason alone. Also, again at face value, it appears that the IOC was reacting to a growing moral problem based, presumably, on sound judgment and ethical thinking. However, a closer examination suggests otherwise. The creation of the first rules against the use of performance-enhancing substances and the first tests conducted in Mexico in 1968 did not simply evolve out of concerns about the particular cases of cyclists Jensen and Simpson or, for that matter, other athletes. Nor, as it turns out, did prohibitions emerge out of concerns for athletes' health and well-being, at least not this consideration alone. Associations made between drugs – steroids in particular – sport, and totalitarian regime building; accelerated competition and the movement towards full-time, professional training in both the East and the West and the threat many practices – drug use being just one – posed to amateurism as the founding ethos upon which the Olympic movement was based; the perceived virilizing effects of drugs on female athletes, particularly those in Eastern bloc countries; and the specific motivations and world views of individual agents within the IOC during the period of time drugs were banned, are all matters that played important roles in the development of prohibitions and the inception of tests. Each of these warrants more careful attention.

Paul Dimeo's thorough analysis of events leading up to, and the cast of characters that played important roles in the creation of prohibitions and, in turn, the first tests in Mexico City shed light on the motivations of those involved with important decisions that would dramatically come to influence the future of Olympic sport. A relatively small group of medical scientists and sports administrators with conservative views on sport helped to guide public and private discussions about drugs away from the concerns about athletes' health towards a moral crusade against the 'evils' of drugs that, at times, took on a quasi-religious character. Italy's Antonio Venerando, Austria's Ludwig Prokop, and Britain's J.G.P. Williams played particularly important roles, alongside a growing cadre of sport administrators, the most important of whom was long-time IOC president and staunch defender of amateurism Avery Brundage. The motivations and worldviews of these individuals recast the history of anti-doping efforts. As Dimeo says:

> [I]t is clear that the social, cultural and ethical perspectives of scientists were a subtle and implicit – but enormously powerful – force in

setting the framework for anti-doping in the 1960s. Their traditional, paternalistic view of sport accompanied a strong faith in science as a solution to social problems. They also thought the ethics and science of anti-doping could and should be implemented in other countries: they were proselytisers as well as fanatics. It would not be long before they, and their colleagues, were using major international networks to directly influence the sporting cultures in other countries.[16]

An important article authored by Sir Arthur Porritt with the simple title 'Doping' published in *Olympic Review* in 1965 is an important example, because the *Review* was a major forum for the IOC's policy positions; it was published just before the all-important Tehran meetings in 1967 when the IOC formally adopted a drug-testing policy, and finally, Porritt was head of the IOC's Medical Committee. The moral crusade that Dimeo describes is obvious in Porritt's language. 'Doping,' the article begins, 'is an evil – it is morally wrong, physically dangerous, socially degenerate and legally indefensible.' Drug use is described as a 'sinister' and 'pernicious practice,' and the athlete who uses drugs, Porritt tells us, has 'weakness of character,' is expressing 'an inferiority complex,' and is a 'mentally, physically and morally dulled individual.' The article begins with a close-up photograph of a man popping pills into his mouth alongside the caption 'The temptation...' and ends with a second image of a destitute, worn-out face of a second man in sunglasses, frothing at the mouth, alongside the caption '...and the result.'[17]

Porritt's article also defends the prohibition of drugs based on the values of amateurism, and this is relevant to the second point that needs to be understood in terms of thinking objectively about drug prohibitions. Porritt's text reads: 'it behoves every one of us interested in the basic values of amateur sport to keep this matter under the closest surveillance and to remember always that the "dope" in the American sense – the mentally, physically and morally dulled individual – is to some degree at any rate the inevitable corollary of doping.'[18] Debates regarding the 'amateur clause' of the *Olympic Charter* had been raging within the IOC for years. Members were fully aware of the threats to amateurism, including under-the-table payments in sports such as downhill skiing, direct or indirect state support through militaries and universities, and more generally the increasingly professional and full-time approach to training and competition. However, the IOC's formal stance on amateurism remained strong, mainly because of the unyielding position of President Avery Brundage. The IOC was gradually losing control of the other practices that threatened the founding amateur principles of the movement; however it could, in a relatively simple step, create a rule banning certain identifiable substances, which also threatened those founding principles. After years of debate, the IOC finally, irrevocably, removed the amateur clause from the Charter. But, in doing so, Beamish and Ritchie argue that the IOC 'also surrendered the philosophical grounds for justifying the prohibition of particular performance-enhancing substances.'[19] Furthermore, with the removal of amateurism as the central defining principle of the Games, the authors argue that '[t]he IOC accepted...the real social world of high-performance sport that had developed in the post-World War II era. The newly accepted world consisted of state funding, comprehensive, scientifically based, year-round training, an unreserved zeal for victory, an intense, personal commitment to the pursuit of medals, and a resolute drive to push performances to the outer limits of human potential.'[20] The principles of amateurism, and not 'ethics' *per se*, underlay the decision to ban certain substances.

The creation of anti-doping rules must also be considered in light of the post-war associations between steroids and the perceived role of sport as a tool for totalitarian regime building. The following observations of Dr. Nicholas Wade in the prestigious journal *Science* in 1972 are an interesting commentary on these associations:

> The first use of male steroids to improve performance is said to have been in World War II when German troops took them before battle to enhance aggressiveness. After the war steroids were given to the survivors of German concentration camps to rebuild body weight. The first use in athletics seems to have been by the Russians in 1954. John D. Ziegler, a Maryland physician who was the US team physician to the weightlifting championships in Vienna that year, told *Science* that Soviet weightlifters were receiving doses of testosterone, a male sex hormone. The Russians were also using it on some of their women athletes, Ziegler said. Besides its growth-promoting effect, testosterone induces male sexual development such as deepening of the voice and hirsuteness, which might account for the manifestation of such traits in Soviet women athletes during the 1950s.[21]

Here Wade connects Nazi military aggressiveness, concentration camp victims, the Soviets' use of steroids for competition, and the potential masculinization of Eastern bloc women. Anxieties regarding steroids can be traced back to the 1936 Games in Berlin, when Olympic sport was used for overt political and ideological purposes, combined with rumours that the Nazis had used steroids to increase aggressiveness in the troops during World War II.[22] Fears of drugs struck hard in the imaginations of Western sport leaders, especially as rumours spread rapidly of the Soviets using anabolic steroids to enhance the performance of their own athletes. The prohibition of banned substances must be considered in the context of this post-war mindset.[23] Once again, social and political concerns, and not 'ethics' *per se*, played a role in the creation of prohibitions.

Also, several authors have pointed out the connections between the simultaneous developments of drug tests alongside sex tests.[24] Most policy historians regard sex testing to be one of the most misguided policies in Olympic history. Rumours – false ones as it turns out – had been circulating for years about men 'sneaking' into women's events, and as a result various international sport organizations, the IOC included, initiated a battery of tests on female athletes. The British Women's Amateur Athletic Association first required letters of sex verification from physicians in 1948, and during the 1960s various other organizations followed: the International Amateur Athletic Federation (IAAF) requiring a physical inspection by gynecologists at the European Championships in Track and Field in 1966; female athletes at the Commonwealth Games that same year were required to undergo intrusive pelvic examinations; the IAAF added chromosome testing at the European Cup Track and Field events in 1967; and finally, the IOC, after random tests of a few athletes during the 1968 Winter Games in Grenoble, established chromosome testing for all athletes at the Mexico City Games.[25]

The very possibility of sex testing's existence needs to be understood in the context of what family historian Elaine Tyler May refers to as 'domestic containment' – a consolidation of public policy alongside domestic family behaviour that was particularly pronounced during the early days of the Cold War. May's study of American family life demonstrates how 'normal' heterosexual behaviour and traditional nuclear family gender roles became important symbols of nationalism. Those who did not fit the norm were chastized as subversive and even, at times, seen as communist threats.[26] In this climate, female athletes from the Eastern bloc – especially those from the USSR and the German Democratic Republic, two countries (especially the GDR) that had developed high-level competitive athletic training programs for girls and women to take advantage of the male-centered systems of the West – were seen as threats to the hyper-feminized ideals of the West. Robert Kerr, an

American physician who assisted male athletes with steroid regimes, expressed these concerns directly:

> We've been witnessing today, and for the last number of years, how our female athletes are being defeated in certain strength and power sports by Russian and East German women who just seem to have an edge – a masculine edge. Right now we don't want our women to be defeminized in order to win, but in the next Olympics, or the next after that, will we still be willing to feel the same way? I don't know, I hope in this case we don't change.[27]

The 'domestic containment' policies combined with growing Cold War ideological tensions and heightened competition on the increasingly visible Olympic stage explains why, firstly, sex-testing policies were justified for years despite the fact that not one single athlete is known to have attempted to 'sneak' into a male event during the test's entire existence; secondly, why fears of 'hyper-masculinized,' drug-using women struck fear into the hearts of Western sport administrators; and thirdly, why drug testing and sex testing were introduced simultaneously. In a careful historical analysis of IOC policy decisions regarding medical concerns during the Cold War period, Alison Wrynn points out that 'the gender verification of female athletes [was] an artefact of drug use and fear of change as women became larger, stronger, faster, and increasingly more competitive.'[28] Once again, 'ethics' of drug use *per se* took a back seat to other social and political concerns.

Finally, there is an additional point regarding Olympic mythology that is pertinent to the ban on performance-enhancing substances. This point is more subtle, yet its implications are far reaching in terms of understanding the inception of the first drug prohibitions and continued attitudes towards the use of performance-enhancing substances today. A central theme in the present volume is myth, and myth making, as it turns out, is a crucial ingredient of Olympic sport in general throughout its modern history. Olympic myths also underlie the rationale against the use of performance-enhancing substances.

In attempting to explain the power and importance of myth, French social critic Roland Barthes referred to sport, and specifically the Tour de France. Barthes explains that the Tour 'expresses and liberates the French people through a unique fable' in which a utopian ideal of French society becomes intermingled with exaggeration and distortion. The spectacle of the Tour, Barthes continues, appears to provide 'total clarity of relations between man, men, and Nature.' However, the real basis upon which the Tour is run is distorted: 'the economic motives, the ultimate profit of the ordeal' which are the 'material generator of the ideological image' become lost even as the spectacle of the event and the raw physical performances of the athletes are admired by spectators.[29] The problem, for Barthes, is that the sport spectacle's trance evokes a confusion of history and social forces with nature; cultural history becomes confused with something natural, self-evident, clear, and inevitable. Myth, Barthes wrote, 'deprives the object of which it speaks of all history.'[30]

Barthes' description of myth in the Tour de France can equally be applied to Olympic sport. From its very inception the modern Olympic movement has proffered a certain enduring image of sport in its purest, 'transhistorical' form.[31] Pierre de Coubertin, founder of the Modern Olympic Games, realized the importance of public relations, spectacle and ceremony, and propaganda in his attempt to create an idealized image of his Olympic movement to compete against rival sporting interests in late-nineteenth century Europe. Coubertin's decision to link symbolically the Games of ancient Greece to his own modern revival was crucial; indeed, it remains one of the most important, if often overlooked, political legacies of Coubertin's work and writings. Ancient sport, Coubertin wrote, was 'pure and magnificent' and at the site of Olympia 'for a thousand years states and cities met in the person of their young men, who, imbued with a sense of the moral grandeur of the Games, went to them in a spirit of almost religious reverence.' The event, for Coubertin, 'was something grandiose and strong...happily and gloriously influencing the youth of the country, and through them the entire nation.'[32]

It is well-known that Coubertin attempted to elevate the image of his modern Games to that of a religion, but it was also one based on the eternal values of sport he saw emanating from the ancients. In a recorded radio address from Geneva in 1935, only two years before his death, Coubertin told his audience that '[t]he primary, fundamental characteristic of ancient Olympism, and of modern Olympism as well, is that it is a *religion*.' The modern Games would instil 'a religious sentiment transformed and expanded by the internationalism and democracy that are distinguished features of our day... [similar to the] religious sentiment that led the young Hellenes, eager for the victory of their muscles, to the foot of the altars of Zeus.'[33]

Historians now acknowledge that Coubertin's view of ancient sport was both an idealistic one and one based to some degree on inaccurate historical facts.[34] The ancient Olympics were both far more violent than anything that would be considered even remotely acceptable today and they were certainly not amateur in the manner that Coubertin envisioned for his ideal Olympians. Indeed, the athletics of ancient times were indelibly connected to professional military training and athletes hardly had the sense of 'moral grandeur' as Coubertin thought. Nevertheless, the deep associations Coubertin made between the modern movement and the ancient one was, and continues to be, important for three reasons. Firstly, Coubertin was able to counter competing sporting movements, the nationalistic political interests of various sporting authorities, and rising commercial interests in sport, by marketing his Games as 'timeless' and representing sport in its 'purest' form. Secondly, out of self-interest, self-promotion, or perhaps simply ego, Coubertin claimed the idea of regenerating a tradition that was as 'old as the hills' was his own, even though historians now know that the truth was otherwise – Coubertin was hardly the 'originator' of the idea of Olympism. Olympic historian David Young has shown that movements to restart the Olympics were active in Greece and England in the mid- to late nineteenth century, and, contrary to his own claims otherwise, Coubertin very likely used those movements as models for his own. In particular, Coubertin admired the sporting movement inspired by Englishman W.P. Brookes, whose work led to, among other events, the National Olympic Games held in London's Crystal Palace in 1866, many years before the arrival of Coubertin's first Games. Coubertin would later deny Brookes' inspiration for his own Olympic movement. Indeed, as Young expresses it, '[h]istorical evidence clearly demonstrates that Coubertin borrowed the ideas of others for his international festival and knowingly declined to give them appropriate recognition.'[35]

Finally, Coubertin's legacy of mythologizing Olympic sport by drawing direct comparisons between ancient and modern times has always been an integral component of the Olympic Games, and it continues today. A vital part of the Olympic 'brand' has been the notion that Olympic sport is sport in its 'purest' form, unadulterated by imperfections of politics, commerce, and the like. From the earliest amateur ideals inscribed in the movement in the late nineteenth century by Coubertin and his contemporaries, to nationalistic, bureaucratic, and financial challenges during the first few decades of the twentieth century, to the overt use of Olympic sport for ideological purposes during the Cold War and the concomitant challenges of television and rights payments, through to the eventual commercialization of the Games, use of athletes for commercial endorsements, and indeed the recent corporatization of the IOC itself, the myth of Olympic sport as 'pure' and 'old as the hills' continues.³⁶ There was perhaps no IOC president that defended this component of the Olympic brand more stoutly than Avery Brundage, who presided over the movement during the heady first two decades of the Cold War. Amateurism, Brundage decreed, 'coming to us from antiquity, contributed to and strengthened by the noblest aspirations of great men of each generation, embraces the highest moral laws. No philosophy, no religion, preaches loftier sentiments.'³⁷

The specific ideals of amateurism were abandoned by the International Olympic Committee in the 1970s, especially after Brundage stepped down as president in 1972. However, the branding of 'pure' Olympic sport lives on. While at first the relationship between these ideals and the prohibiting of performance-enhancing substances might not be obvious, the connection is in fact crucial, for two reasons. Firstly, as demonstrated earlier, it was the values and ideals of amateurism that played an important role in the banning of drugs. Secondly, the Olympic movement continues to proffer a 'timeless' transhistorical version of sport based on Coubertin's legacy, and this version in fact serves as the central, moral justification for the ban on performance-enhancing substances. In its preamble, the World Anti-Doping Agency's *World Anti-Doping Code* reflects Coubertin's legacy by stating that drug rules 'seek to preserve what is intrinsically valuable about sport. This intrinsic value is often referred to as "the spirit of sport," and it is the essence of Olympism.'³⁸ The implications of the continued effects of this legacy are discussed in the final section.

Implications of 1968

This chapter has attempted to open the historical book on events leading up to and during the first drug tests during the Mexico City Summer Olympic Games in 1968. Scholars are just starting to unpack the significant history of both the development of the systematic use of drugs in the modern Olympic movement, and the creation of anti-doping policies. While a small fraction of that history has been recounted here, its full story is largely unfinished. The full implications of this period for the general approach towards drugs taken in the last half-century must be made clear. Dimeo claims that a 'moral panic' ensued because of the events leading up to 1968: '[the] threat to the patriarchal, middle-class dominance of sports culture and sporting organizations [and the] latent anxiety over the changing nature of female bodies that also threatened this power structure... [led to the] modernistic system of surveillance methods, bureaucratic machinery, and legal power that changed the face of sport.'[39] One of the implications of the events leading up to and including 1968 and the policy decisions made during that period is that open and frank discussions about performance-enhancing drugs have been limited. In their place has been an assumption regarding the 'evils' of drugs; indeed, in many ways public discussions about drugs in sport have not moved significantly beyond the parochial attitude expressed by Arthur Porritt in 1965. The World Anti-doping Agency (WADA)'s *Code* does not engage in a serious discussion about ethics. The 'anti-doping' movement is now committed to advancing detection and surveillance methods, but little else. Largely missing from the history of the fight against drugs in sport is a critical analysis of the reality of high-performance sport as a whole, and this is the first important implication of the events as they occurred and the decisions made in the period leading up to 1968.

A second implication, which flows from the previous point, is that policy discussions must move beyond the 'good versus evil'[40] approach to performance enhancement and drugs if the health of athletes themselves is ever going to be a legitimate concern. Concentrating a vast majority of official efforts on the risks of performance-enhancing substances – some of which are exaggerated, some perhaps not – diverts attention away from greater issues related to the dangers of high-performance sport, especially as it has become practiced in the last half-century or so. While a central justification for the prohibition of substances is the health of athletes, concentrating discussions on banned drugs only serves to obscure the myriad of other openly accepted and encouraged practices that bring physical risk to the lives of athletes. Indeed, in the real world of high-performance Olympic sport, the line between what is 'normal' and 'pathological' is a fine one, and sociologists Robert Hughes and Jay Coakley maintain that athletes 'overconform' to an emerging 'sport ethic' – a set of values and practices that includes accepting pain as part of training and competition, taking physical risks, and refusing to accept limitations, all of which become a 'normal' and unquestioned part of athletes' lives.[41] In the aftermath of a major drug scandal in the 1998 Tour de France, professional cyclist Robert Millar voiced the reality of the ethos:

> The riders reckon that a good Tour takes one year off your life... The pain in your legs is not the kind of pain you get when you cut yourself, it's fatigue, it's self-imposed... You can't describe to a normal person how tired you feel... I can understand guys being tempted to

use drugs in the Tour... I don't think it's an isolated cycling thing, people just expect sport to be cleaner than real life.⁴²

Finally, policy discussions must shift beyond the argument that the ban on certain performance-enhancing substances is justified based on notions such as WADA's 'spirit of sport.' While the authority of WADA as an organization may go largely unquestioned, the justification of drug prohibitions based on any notion of an 'essential' or 'pure' sport is misdirected because these references are sociologically and historically vacuous ones. Also, notions such as the 'spirit of sport' create a false dichotomy between 'real' drug-free sport and 'artificial' drug-enhanced sport, and once again such notions divert attention away from the real historical forces that have shaped Olympic sport – all Olympic sport, not just drug-enhanced Olympic sport in (at least) the last 50 years. So while the Mexico City Summer Games are regarded by many as the moment when the 'war on drugs in sport' began, in reality 1968 should be considered a key moment in the creation of Olympic myths, ones with profound, enduring consequences that are still with us today.

Notes

1. For events in general leading up to and during the Mexico City Games, see Kevin B. Witherspoon, *Before the Eyes of the World: Mexico and the 1968 Olympic Games* (DeKalb, IL: Northern Illinois University Press, 2008) and for a discussion of altitude, sex testing, and drug testing policies, see Alison M. Wrynn, '"A Debt Was Paid Off in Tears": Science, IOC Politics and the Debate about High Altitude in the 1968 Mexico City Olympics,' *The International Journal of the History of Sport*, Vol. 23, No. 7 (2006), 1152–72.
2. Nigel Spivey, *The Ancient Olympics* (Oxford University Press, 2004); David C. Young, *A Brief History of the Olympic Games* (Malden, MA: Blackwell Publishing, 2004); Mark Golden, *Sport and Society in Ancient Greece* (Cambridge: Cambridge University Press, 1998); Bruce Kidd 'The Myth of the Ancient Games,' in Alan Tomlinson and Garry Whannel (eds) *Five Ring Circus: Money, Power and Politics at the Olympic Games* (London and Sydney: Pluto Press, 1984), pp. 71–83.
3. Anson Rabinbach, *The Human Motor: Energy, Fatigue, and the Origins of Modernity* (Berkeley, CA and Los Angeles, CA: University of California Press, 1992).
4. There are several reliable sources for the history of performance-enhancing drug use, many of which repeat the same historical events. Except for individual citations used for very specific information, I have used the following sources in this section (in no particular order): Charles E. Yesalis and Michael S. Bahrke, 'History of Doping in Sport,' *International Sports Studies*, Vol. 24, No. 1 (2002), 42–76; Ray Tricker and David L. Cook, *Athletes at Risk: Drugs and Sport* (Dubuque: Wm. C. Brown Publishers, 1990);

Rob Beamish and Ian Ritchie, *Fastest, Highest, Strongest: A Critique of High-Performance Sport* (London and New York: Routledge, 2006); Paul Dimeo, *A History of Drug Use in Sport 1876–1976: Beyond Good and Evil* (London and New York: Routledge, 2007); Jan Todd and Terry Todd, 'Significant Events in the History of Drug Testing and the Olympic Movement: 1960–1999,' in Wayne Wilson and Edward Derse (eds) *Doping in Elite Sport: The Politics of Drugs in the Olympic Movement* (Champaign, IL: Human Kinetics, 2001), pp. 65–128; Ivan Waddington and Andy Smith, *An Introduction to Drugs in Sport: Addicted to Winning?* (London and New York: Routledge, 2009); John Hoberman, *Mortal Engines: The Science of Performance and the Dehumanization of Sport* (New York: The Free Press, 1992); Tom Donohoe and Neil Johnson, *Foul Play: Drug Abuse in Sports* (Oxford: Basil Blackwell, 1986); Verner Møller, *The Ethics of Doping and Anti-Doping: Redeeming the Soul of Sport?* (London and New York: Routledge, 2010); Robert Voy, *Drugs, Sport, and Politics* (Champaign, IL: Leisure Press, 1991); Terry Todd, 'Anabolic Steroids: The Gremlins of Sport,' *Journal of Sport History*, Vol. 14, No. 1, (1987), 87–107; and Ivan Waddington, *Sport, Health and Drugs: A Critical Sociological Perspective* (London and New York: E&FN Spon, 2000).
5. Dimeo, *A History of Drug Use*, p. 62.
6. Paul de Kruif, *The Male Hormone* (New York: Harcourt, Brace and Company, 1945). See also William C. Summers, 'Microbe Hunters Revisited,' *International Microbiology*, Vol. 1 (1998), pp. 65–8 and Todd, 'Anabolic Steroids,' pp. 92–3.
7. Dimeo, *A History of Drug Use*, p. 72.
8. Yesalis and Bahrke, 'History of Doping,' p. 49.
9. Dimeo, *A History of Drug Use*, p. 75.
10. Gerald Holland, 'The Golden Age is Now,' *Sports Illustrated*, August 16 (1954), p. 48.
11. Dimeo, *A History of Drug Use*, pp. 71–6.
12. Cited in Todd, 'Anabolic Steroids,' p. 93.
13. Dimeo, *A History of Drug Use*, pp. 76–8.
14. See Verner Møller, *The Ethics of Doping and Anti-Doping: Redeeming the Soul of Sport?* (London and New York: Routledge, 2010), pp. 37–42. Møller disputes the historical accuracy of the claim that Jensen died from amphetamine use.
15. Todd and Todd, 'Significant Events,' pp. 67–9; Beamish and Ritchie, *Fastest, Highest, Strongest*, p. 21; and Alison Wrynn, 'The Human Factor: Science, Medicine and the International Olympic Committee, 1900–70,' *Sport in Society*, Vol. 7, No. 2, (2004), 211–31.
16. Dimeo, *A History of Drug Use*, p. 95.
17. Arthur Porritt, 'Doping,' *Olympic Review*, No. 90, May (1965), 47–9.
18. Ibid., p. 48.
19. Beamish and Ritchie, *Fastest, Highest, Strongest*, p. 29.
20. Ibid., p. 29.
21. Nicholas Wade, 'Anabolic Steroids: Doctors Denounce Them, But Athletes Aren't Listening,' *Science*, Vol. 176 (1972), p. 1400.
22. See Beamish and Ritchie, *Fastest, Highest, Strongest*, pp. 38–9 on the rumours regarding the Nazis' use of steroids to increase aggressiveness of the troops.
23. Rob Beamish and Ian Ritchie, 'Totalitarian Regimes and Cold War Sport: Steroid "Übermenschen" and "Ball-bearing Females",' in Stephen Wagg and

David L. Andrews (eds) *East Plays West: Sport and the Cold War* (London and New York: Routledge, 2007), pp. 11–26.
24. See, for example, Cheryl L. Cole, 'Testing for Sex or Drugs?' *Journal of Sport & Social Issues*, Vol. 24, No. 4 (2000), 331–3; Cheryl L. Cole, 'One Chromosome Too Many?' in Kay Schaffer and Sidonie Smith (eds), *The Olympics at the Millennium: Power, Politics, and the Games* (Piscataway, NJ: Rutgers University Press, 2000), pp. 128–46; Beamish and Ritchie, *Fastest, Highest, Strongest*, pp. 40–4; Laurel R. Davis and Linda C. Delano, 'Fixing the Boundaries of Physical Gender: Side Effects of Anti-Drug Campaigns on Athletics,' *Sociology of Sport Journal*, Vol. 9 (1992), 1–19; and Ian Ritchie 'Sex Tested, Gender Verified: Controlling Female Sexuality in the Age of Containment,' *Sport History Review*, Vol. 34, No. 1 (2003), 80–98.
25. M.A. Ferguson-Smith and Elizabeth A. Ferris, 'Gender Verification in Sport: The Need for Change?' *British Journal of Sports Medicine*, Vol. 25, No. 1 (1991), 17; Eduardo Hay, 'Sex Determination in Putative Female Athletes,' *Journal of the American Medical Association (JAMA)*, Vol. 221, No. 9 (1972), 998; Ritchie, 'Sex Tested, Gender Verified.' Interestingly, sex testing continues to this day, only is an altered form. While formal required chromosome testing ceased as of the 2000 Sydney Olympic Games, the IOC Medical Commission's 2003 'Stockholm consensus' statement recommended that athletes who had sex reassignment surgery be accepted as the reassigned sex under certain conditions, and that '[i]n the events that the gender of a competing athlete is questioned, the medical delegate (or equivalent) of the sporting body shall have the authority to take all appropriate measures for the determination of the gender of a competitor.' The Stockholm consensus was adopted by the IOC's Executive Board in 2004 and applied at the 2004 Athens Games for the first time. The Stockholm consensus itself is available online: http://www.olympic.org/Assets/ImportedNews/Documents/en_report_905.pdf, and other information regarding sex reassignment policies can be found on the IOC's website: http://www.olympic.org.
26. Elaine Tyler May, *Homeward Bound: American Families in the Cold War Era* (New York: Basic Books, 1988).
27. Cited in Bob Goldman, *Death in the Locker Room: Steroids & Sports* (South Bend, IN: Icarus Press, 1984), p. 81, emphasis in the original.
28. Wrynn, 'A Debt was Paid Off in Tears,' p. 1164.
29. Roland Barthes, 'The Tour de France as Epic,' in *The Eiffel Tower and Other Mythologies*, trans. Richard Howard (New York: Hill and Wang, 1979), pp. 87–88.
30. Roland Barthes, *Mythologies*, trans. Annette Lavers (New York: Hall and Wang, 1972), p. 151.
31. On the 'transhistoricism' in the Olympic Games, see Beamish and Ritchie, *Fastest, Highest, Strongest*.
32. Pierre de Coubertin, 'Why I Revived the Olympic Games,' [original 1908] in Norbert Müller (ed.) *Olympism: Selected Writings* (Lausanne: International Olympic Committee, 2000), p. 543.
33. Pierre de Coubertin, 'The Philosophic Foundation of Modern Olympism,' [original 1935] in Norbert Müller (ed.) *Olympism: Selected Writings* (Lausanne: International Olympic Committee, 2000), p. 580.

34. See Kidd, 'The Myth of the Ancient Games;' David Young, 'From Olympia 776 BC to Athens 2004: The Origin and Authenticity of the Modern Olympic Games,' in Kevin Young and Kevin B. Wamsley (eds), *Global Olympics: Historical and Sociological Studies of the Modern Games* (Amsterdam, Boston, MA, London: Elsevier JAI, 2005), pp. 3–18.
35. Young, 'From Olympia,' p. 16.
36. On the role of commercial forces in the Olympic Games, see Robert K. Barney, Stephen R. Wenn, and Scott G. Martyn, *Selling the Five Rings: The International Olympic Committee and the Rise of Olympic Commercialism* (Salt Lake City, UT: The University of Utah Press, 2002), and on both political and economic forces in general, see Beamish and Ritchie, *Fastest, Highest, Strongest*.
37. Cited in Allen Guttmann, *The Games Must Go On: Avery Brundage and the Olympic Movement* (New York: Columbia University Press, 1984), p. 116.
38. World Anti-Doping Agency, *World Anti-Doping Code* (Montreal: World Anti-Doping Agency, 2009), www.wada-ama.org, p. 14.
39. Dimeo, *A History of Drug Use*, pp. 134–135.
40. Ibid.
41. Robert Hughes and Jay Coakley, 'Positive Deviance Among Athletes: The Implications of Overconformity to the Sport Ethic,' *Sociology of Sport Journal*, Vol. 8, No. 4 (1991), 307–25. See also Beamish and Ritchie, *Fastest, Highest, Strongest*, pp. 142–3.
42. Robert Millar, 'Tour de France Exhausts Cyclists,' *The Globe and Mail* (Canada), July 31 (1998).

# 8
The 'Revolt of the Black Athlete': Tommie Smith and John Carlos's 1968 Black Power Salute Reconsidered*

Maureen Margaret Smith

Introduction

On Wednesday, October 16 1968, Tommie Smith won the 200-meter race at the 1968 Mexico City Olympics in a world record time of 19.8 seconds, and his American teammate John Carlos finished third. At the awards ceremony Smith wore a black glove on his right hand, a black scarf around his neck, and stood in black socks. Carlos wore the black glove on his left hand, beads around his neck, and stood, similarly, in his black socks. When the national anthem began, in what has become one of the most memorable images in sport history, the two athletes bowed their heads and put their gloved fists into the air. This chapter examines the gesture by Smith and Carlos as a key moment in sport history; by looking at the lead up to the Olympic Games and subsequent reactions to the gesture, as well as how the image has transformed over the last 40 years. Identified by *Life* magazine as one of the '100 photographs that changed the world,' the image of Smith and Carlos has been transformed into a statue on the campus of San José State University in California, and remains an image that generates debate and discussion.[1] This event did not occur during a sport competition or performance, but in the wake of one, on the victory stand; it is an event that used the platform and spectacle of Olympic sport to communicate a statement about civil rights. The continued reinterpretations of the gesture reflect contemporary dialogues of race, sport, and society.[2]

The Olympic Project for Human Rights

In 1968, both Smith and Carlos were students at San Jose State College; Smith had been a member of the university's track team, nicknamed 'Speed City,' and led by famed Coach Bud Winter. 'Speed City' produced a number of world record holders and Olympians. Despite the international success of members of the track team, black athletes, as well as other black students, at San Jose State faced a number of problems on the overwhelmingly white campus.[3]

Harry Edwards, a former athlete at San Jose State, was hired at his alma mater as a lecturer in sociology in 1966 and began documenting the mistreatment of black students on the campus. After the university's administration refused to listen to Edwards' concerns, he threatened to prevent the opening football game of the 1967 season against the University of Texas at El Paso taking place. Faced with the threat of violence, President Robert Clark cancelled the game.[4] Recognizing that sport was a powerful tool for negotiations, Edwards created the Olympic Project for Human Rights (OPHR), an organization designed to advance the cause of black athletes and black Americans.[5] According to Lomax, OPHR viewed African Americans' role in sports as 'intimately interdependent with the overall struggle for human rights in American society.'[6] Both Smith and Carlos were involved with Edwards and, to some extent, Edwards' OPHR.

Edwards and the OPHR campaigned for a boycott of the upcoming Mexico City Games, with Smith initially committed to the boycott.[7] As the Games approached, the proposed boycott lacked support from black athletes. Despite this, the organization continued their campaign and played a critical role in the year leading up to the Games in bringing attention to race issues in sport and society.[8] The main objectives of the organization were the barring of South Africa's participation in the 1968 Games and other athletic events, the restoration of Muhammad Ali's world heavyweight boxing title, and the removal of the American Avery Brundage as President of the International Olympic Committee (IOC). Ultimately it was decided that black athletes who participated in the Games would determine, as individuals, how they would protest.

San Jose State sprinter and 1968 Olympian, Lee Evans, recalled a letter sent to all Olympic athletes before the Games from the United States Olympic Committee (USOC). The letter threatened to send home any athlete who did not 'perform in honor of the US.' Brundage goaded the black athletes, telling them they were 'lucky to be allowed on the team.'[9]

The gesture

Running in Lane 3, Tommie Smith finished first, and teammate John Carlos in Lane 4 finished third in the 200-meter dash finals at the Mexico City Olympic Games. In what has easily become one of the most recognizable moments in American sport, the two teammates raised their black gloved fists in the air in a gesture laden with racial symbolism. Second-place finisher Peter Norman, of Australia, willingly wore a button that read 'Olympic Project for Human Rights,' and did not raise his fist. According to Smith, in an interview with Howard Cosell after the protest, 'My raised right hand stood for the power in black America. Carlos's left hand stood for the unity of black America. Together, they formed an arch of unity and power. The black scarf around my neck stood for black pride. The black socks with no shoes stood for racial poverty in racist America. The totality of our effort was the regaining of black dignity.'[10] Smith stated his pride clearly, 'I represented black America and I am very proud to be a black man and to have a gold medal. I thought in this way I could represent my people by letting them know I am proud to be a black man.'[11] Smith made it clear that his actions were not a singular representation, but his seizing of an opportunity to represent his community. 'When I won that gold medal it's not just mine, the medal is for all black America.'[12] 'We are black,' Smith said, 'and we're proud to be black. White America will only give us credit for an Olympic victory. They'll say I'm an American, but if I did something bad, they'd say [I'm a] a Negro.'[13] His teammate and bronze medalist in the event, John Carlos, also had his views of how white America perceived black athletes. 'After the job is done,' Carlos said, 'we are not supposed to think. We wanted to do something to signify black. We want people to know that we are not animals, not lower animals, not rats and roaches.'[14] Carlos believed that white Americans viewed black athletes as animals used to perform for white audiences, citing these reasons as support for his victory stand actions. 'We want you to print what I say the way I say it or not at all,' said Carlos. 'We want to make it clear that white people seem to think black people are animals doing a job. We want people to understand that we are not animals or rats. We want to tell Americans and all the world that if they do not care what black people do, they should not go to see black people perform.'[15]

The next day the USOC, under pressure from the IOC and Brundage, apologized for the actions of Smith and Carlos and suspended the two athletes from the Olympic Games. The USOC threatened to expel any other black athlete who dared protest and brought in 1936 Olympian

James 'Jesse' Owens to talk with the team. Owens appeared as a moderator between the athletes and the officials, in part because he had been a successful black athlete who believed that the white sports establishment had helped him succeed in life. Many of the younger black athletes viewed Owens as an 'Uncle Tom'; he endorsed the Olympic ideals and credited the movement with bringing about 'tremendous understanding and cooperation in racial matters' and for this reason did not 'think the pride which our black athletes have in themselves and their country will allow them to do anything to embarrass the United States in so conspicuous a world arena.' Before the 1968 Games, Owens had voiced his opposition to any protests at the sporting event, appealing to the American in each athlete, expressing the belief 'that they would not only be hurting themselves, but they might in the end aid our strongest competition, the Russians.'[16]

Despite Owens talk with the team, and the USOC threats, further small acts occurred, though no other athletes were punished. The 4 × 400 meters relay competitors wore black berets and raised their fists, yet stood at attention during the national anthem. Long-jumper Bob Beamon wore black socks on the victory stand.[17] In contrast to Smith and Carlos, boxer George Foreman waved the flag after his victory in the boxing competition.

Smith and Carlos returned to San Jose and a nationwide tour organized by the black Panther party, with the first stop at Howard University. Rap Brown, at the Howard University rally welcoming John Carlos said, 'To be black and proud is not an answer in itself... The man will kill you if you're black and proud or black and ashamed. You must begin to move into a phase of action.'[18] At the same rally, Stokely Carmichael echoed Brown's support of the two trackmen. 'We are letting white America and everybody else know we will pick our own heroes. Our heroes are not those who will bow down to white America, but those who will stand up for our people.'[19] Despite these rousing endorsements from Brown and Carmichael, Smith and Carlos faced death threats upon their return to the United States and an American public and sporting press that was mixed in their reactions to the 'Black Power' gesture.

1968: interpreting the gesture

The victory stand protest by Smith and Carlos at the 1968 Games quickly caused uproar in Mexico City, which extended around the globe and for years after. The image was on the front page of American newspapers and columnists argued both for and against the protest.[20] Many articles published in American newspapers referred to the two athletes using words such as 'defiant', 'martyrs', 'Negro militants', 'ultra-belligerent', and 'divisive,' and described the gesture as a 'Panther salute.'[21] Several themes emerge in the black press and American newspapers: the use of the Olympics as a stage for political protest, the Olympics as apolitical, the status of African American athletes in sport, as well as the significance of African Americans in sport and their potential impact on African American communities. These themes were expressed in various ways by black and white reporters. A majority of columnists disagreed with Smith and Carlos using the Olympic stage as a platform for expressing political ideas. Brad Pye, writing for the black newspaper, the *Los Angeles Sentinel*, wrote that the 'celebrated black glove, black sox, black scarf and black power gestures' by Smith and Carlos 'were not only out of place on the victory stand,' but that 'their display was discourteous and out of place here in Mexico City, period.' Pye thought their 'Hitler-type salute' was 'disrespectful.' He did concede that Smith and Carlos had reason to protest, they had simply done it in the wrong place; 'The problems Smith, Carlos and other black people have should be aired, but not on the Olympic Games victory platform.'[22]

Clint Wilson, one of Pye's co-workers at the *Los Angeles Sentinel*, took an opposing view. Wilson was critical of the white press and their coverage of the event. He felt the USOC and the white press had overreacted to the protest. Wilson noted, sarcastically, that the white press had provided their 'usual "objective"' report of the incident and he then addressed the terminology the *Times* had used. Wilson stated that in the story credited to the Associated Press wire, Smith and Carlos' actions were described as a 'Nazi-like' salute, 'a phrase that wasn't taken kindly in our black community.' Wilson fingered John Hall of the *Los Angeles Times* as a 'white person who can neither comprehend nor empathize with a sincere black gesture.' Hall 'took off into a pathetic and irrelevant sob story of how he loves and appreciates so many wonderful Negro athletes,' but Wilson felt Smith and Carlos' message had eluded his fellow reporter. Wilson then presented the central significance and meaning of the protest: a comprehension of the event that few other reporters were identifying. 'You see, it's the people like Hall who have a 'shallow view of the world; who won't face up to reality; who can't bring themselves to believe that black men have the dignity to show the world that they possess more than world-class ability but also a love for their people that transcends politics and fear for their future careers in a white-dominated society.'[23]

A week later, Wilson addressed the place of protest and the issue of pride. He admitted that many people felt the Olympics were not an appropriate site for protest, but wondered where was such a space? He acknowledged the non-violent nature of the protest, especially in light of recent riots and other demonstrations in the US. He told his readers, 'Smith and Carlos' actions were for YOU; they placed their futures and reputations in jeopardy for YOU, the humble Negro clerks, custodians, gardeners, laborers and unemployed who are 'trying to make it' because YOU can't run 200 meters in 19.8 or dunk a basketball or hit 40 homers a year.'[24]

John Helem, a bowling columnist for the *Chicago Defender*, another black newspaper, addressed African Americans who were critical of Smith and Carlos. 'We sit around and listen to these Negroes criticize every effort of black Americans to carve out an identity of their own...The cries of these Negroes have rung out loud and long, this past week against the action taken by Olympic champions Tommie Smith and John Carlos.' Like Wilson, Helem acknowledged the prominent position of black athletes in American society. 'Can't they realize that only our champions, no matter what their field of endeavor, are our most effective spokesman?' According to Helem, Smith and Carlos's action said to the world, 'Even though we can win international championships and prove to be the best in the world, at home we are not accepted on an equal basis, or judged strictly on how well we perform as human beings!' Helem appealed to the passivity which he felt paralyzed older blacks from seeing the good that might come from the activism of the two athletes and which was shared by many involved in grassroots organizations. 'What they did took more courage than all the do-nothing critical Negroes will do toward the salvation of the black man the rest of their lives. May God give us more Tommie Smiths and John Carloses.'[25]

John Sengstacke, the editor of Helem's *Chicago Defender*, was not in agreement. Sengstacke saw no 'rationale [sic] basis beyond an infantile resolve' for the action, and saw the protest as 'inappropriate...a gesture as if two black baseball players were to perform such a ritual at a World Series Game. The Olympic games are sacrosanct...certainly this is no hippodrome for circus stunts or childish exhibitionism.' The editor examined the treatment of black athletes and subscribed to the mythology of sport as an equal playing field, discounting any reason for protest. Sengstacke concluded, 'Negro athletes at the Olympics are treated with equality and courtesy. What, then, was to be gained by the demonstration of black power?'[26]

Even if most black writers disagreed with the protest or where it took place, they agreed that the punishment of the athletes exceeded the crime. Sengstacke admonished the USOC for its overreaction, owning that the two athletes 'violated basic standards of sportsmanship and good manners,' but arguing that 'banishment from the Olympic Village and subsequent expulsion from Mexico exceeded the nature and extent of the violation.'[27] Booker Griffin, another of Pye's colleagues at the *Los Angeles Sentinel*, highlighted the white media portrayal of the incident. He warned his readers that they were receiving 'shallow and slanted news' of the Olympics, and concluded that the mass media were shirking their 'civic responsibility by virtue of their shallow and subjective approach to informing and entertaining the people of this country.' While Griffin mainly targeted the white media, he recognized that segments of the black press were similarly guilty and that not all black reporters expressed support for the athletes. Griffin clearly supported Smith and Carlos and their efforts to call attention to the conditions of blacks in the country. In a message full of pride and admiration for the two men, he articulated his feeling that 'the incident will probably go down in history as the most profound single act of this Olympics and well it should.' Griffin insisted that the 'gesture on the part of these noble black men is to me one of the greatest moments for the Afro-American in the 400 years of his colonialization in this country,' and he agreed 'with what they did and admire them for their guts and heart-felt belief in the fight for freedom, justice and equality.'[28] Griffin's affirmed the athletes' role in the larger black struggle for equality and presented the matter and the trackmen with dignity.

If the emotions were mixed among black writers, they were just as varied among their white counterparts. White writers, however, wrote for much larger newspapers with higher circulation, while black reporters were writing for black audiences reading black newspapers. Some white reporters criticized Smith and Carlos for similar reasons to the black reporters, believing the Olympics were not meant to be a political forum. Others attempted to defend the actions the IOC took against the athletes, but an equal number of white writers supported Smith and Carlos, sometimes because of the visibility of the Olympics. A *Chicago Tribune* editorial labeled Smith and Carlos as 'renegades' and 'extremists' and compared their 'behavior' to the 'grubby demands' of the politics of the English Labour Party. *New York Times* columnist Arthur Daley criticized Smith and Carlos, suggesting they had brought 'their other world smack into the Olympic Games, where it did not belong, and created a shattering situation that shook this international sports carnival to its very core.' He saw it as a 'very divisive' act.[29]

Shirley Povich, writing for the *Washington Post*, indicated that while he understood the meaning of the action, he did not approve of it. He recognized that the Olympic platform provided Smith and Carlos the opportunity 'to tell the world of their militancy and protests with an impact never before offered a Negro, athlete or otherwise' and he conceded that he, too, felt the punishment exceeded the crime. 'It was not nice that they did not give their full attention to the American flag but their sin otherwise was less than horrible.'[30] Calling the gesture 'unpatriotic and a violation of the Olympic ideal,' Povich pointed out that the uproar was not so much their attire or actions on the victory stand, but 'sullen refusal to respect the American flag.' At the same time that he chastised the two athletes' lack of patriotism, he found it relevant to note that without black athletes on several Olympic teams, especially boxing and basketball, 'there would be no hope. They dominate these teams even more than they do track and field.' He insisted there was a big difference between the athletes in other sports, a point made without explanation, when he suggested 'America's boxing-basketball Negroes appear a different breed than the raging militants on the track team.'[31]

Jim Murray of the *Los Angeles Times* was similar to Povich in his supportive, but sarcastic coverage of the protest, saying he didn't 'care much for the Star Spangled Banner,' but kept his shoes on. He announced to his readers that 'the word is out: we got race problems in our country. This will come as a great astonishment to the reading public of the world, I am sure.'[32] Not only did he mock the 'race problem' in the United States, he attempted to make linkages with other racial incidents of the decade when he wrote, 'American blacks here have mistaken the International Olympic movement for the hierarchy of the state of Mississippi.'[33]

Ron Fimrite of the *San Francisco Chronicle* conceded that politics and the Olympics were irrevocably joined by the very nature of the ceremonies and the Games, noting that national anthems are political. He proclaimed surprise over all the fuss over sprinters Smith and Carlos, since it had long been acknowledged that they were black activists who were sincere in their beliefs. 'In a sense, they sold out to flag and country by even competing in the Games as representatives of what they persistently refer to as "racist America." How then to demonstrate their displeasure with their country? The Olympics, quite naturally, provided them with a stage – that nationalistic victory ceremony ... Political, yes, but no more political than the ceremony itself.'[34]

Fimrite's co-worker, Art Rosenbaum, also appeared to support the athletes, and was not surprised by their action. He had reported on the proposed boycott for over a year, spent time talking with Harry Edwards, and heard the arguments for racial equity. In the end, Rosenbaum thought the display by Smith and Carlos was 'non-violent and less active than anticipated.'[35] The press, both black and white, in large part, helped shape the meanings of the event after the gesture, though many reporters did little to explain the significance of the actions of John Carlos and Tommie Smith.

Among other Olympic athletes, there was a range of reactions to the gesture. Olympic boxing champion Ron Harris believed Smith and Carlos 'had good reasons for their black power salute.' Decathalete Tom Waddell saw the event as somewhat of an equalizer: 'I think they have been discredited more often than they have discredited it. Our image is so bad it can't get any worse. Maybe this will help.' British trackster John Wetton spoke in favor of the gesture: 'We all thought it was a bloody good show. It's bully that these blokes had nerve enough to express their feelings.' Crewman Jacques Fiechter of Harvard was another athlete who agreed with the two athletes: 'By winning their competition, they won the right to do anything they felt proper. It seems to be, in sponsoring an athlete, you don't only sponsor his performance, you sponsor the whole person, the whole consciousness of the athlete.' Tom McKibbon, another American rower, echoed his sentiment: 'It was a strong action to take, throwing them off the team. But they had a strong reason to protest, and this is the right place for it. No nation is free of race problems.'[36] The responses were not limited to male athletes. Wyomia Tyus and the women's 400 meter relay team dedicated their victories to Smith and Carlos.[37] Still, several fellow athletes expressed a belief that the protest was an anti-American sentiment. 'It was kind of cheap of them,' said pole-vaulter Bob Seagren. 'If it wasn't for the United States they wouldn't have been there. I don't think it was very proper. If they don't like the U.S., they can always leave.' Former Olympic champion Bob Richards felt that the protesting athletes had done a 'disservice to black people and to their country.' The flag-waving George Foreman responded, 'That's for college kids. They live in another world.' Barry Weisenberg of the US water polo team thought their action was 'a disgrace. In my opinion, an act like that in the medal ceremony defiles the American flag.'[38]

The architect of the boycott, Harry Edwards, predicted a 1972 Olympic boycott by black athletes and believed that the actions of Smith and Carlos would help increase the support for such a boycott. 'You won't see niggers stepping on each other and fighting to get in line to be used as political propaganda for America's capitalist, racist, imperialist regime anymore.' Edwards felt that black athletes were being used as '20th century gladiators for the white man' and that the domination of black athletes at the 1968 Olympics 'have brought the man to realize he will have to give black people something more than gold medals.'[39]

When Smith and Carlos returned to the San Jose State campus in 1968, they undoubtedly faced repercussions for their protest.[40] But, in contrast to the popular narrative that they received no support, as suggested by Carlos, as well as Harry Edwards, in the days following their return, a campus rally with over 1500 students in attendance celebrated their Olympic accomplishments. President Robert Clark issued a press statement immediately following their Mexico City dismissal honoring their achievements, as well as their gesture.[41] Clark also chastised the USOC and the IOC. A week later, Vice President Hubert Humphrey visited the campus and echoed his support for the campus's Olympic athletes.[42] Smith completed his degree the next year and Carlos helped lead the track team to the 1969 NCAA title.[43]

Remembering the gesture

In the 43 years since the gesture, the image of Smith and Carlos and their raised fists has been used in a variety of ways in popular culture, including posters, t-shirts, artwork, and book covers. Several books and journal articles have been written examining the 1968 Olympic Games, as well as the broader topic of the protest movement by African American athletes in the 1960s. Amy Bass includes a chapter examining the gesture, as well as a chapter looking at the Olympic Project for Human Rights and their pre-Games actions in her book *Not the Triumph But the Struggle*, as does Kevin Witherspoon, who devotes a chapter to the event in *Before The Eyes of the World*, his book on the 1968 Games. Bass, in determining the significance of the 1968 event, suggests that 'Smith and Carlos, as canvases, physically occupied their statement and therefore became the essence of the OPHR movement and the national community it signified in a multinational arena,' providing a useful context from which to consider the event and echoing the newsmen of 1968 in the use of the Olympic Games as a platform for social protest. Bass continues, 'Yet the protest took place *within* the dominant ritual, acknowledged its accompanying symbols, and then proceeded to revolutionize it, subverting the normative presentation of the nation-state with its own tools. Smith and Carlos, then, did not throw the iconography of America out, but rather pushed for a more inclusive politics of citizenship.'[44] Douglas Hartmann's book *Race, Culture and the Revolt of the Black Athlete* is the most comprehensive in examining the event and how the event has been viewed in the decades since. Both Carlos and Smith have published autobiographies. The relationship between Smith and Carlos appears complicated. Linked forever by the gesture, each has their own version of the race, of the subsequent protest, as well as evolving interpretations of the event. Each athlete wrote about the other in their autobiographies, making it clear that while they would always be joined by their moment in history, they were not friends. Between the two, on the issue of the 1968 Games, there is not a version of the events where they are consistently in agreement. Edwards' version was initially published only years after the Games.[45]

Hartmann suggests that interpretations of the image of Smith and Carlos began to change in the 1980s and believes that 'Americans suddenly began to associate a whole new set of memories and meanings with the athletes once described to them as 'racist, black-skinned storm troopers' and the image they had equated with urban violence and rioting not even a quarter of a century earlier.'[46] As evidence of the shift, he notes that Carlos was hired as special consultant on minority affairs for the 1984 Los Angeles Games. In conjunction with those Games, the gesture was featured in an exhibit at the California Afro-American Museum. To Hartmann, this was only the beginning of the revisionist history that began to celebrate the protest. The most revealing version of the rehabilitation of the gesture came in a 1991 two-part article in *Sports Illustrated*.[47] Reflecting the shift in thinking about the protest, Kenny Moore, writing for *Sports Illustrated*, wrote in 1991, 'And now Smith, Carlos and their country have arrived at a stage that seems to allow the good done by their gesture to be weighed against their sacrifice. They, and the civil rights activists of their generation, made the American public understand that the thousand ways – in law and custom and language and stereotype – by which whites oppressed blacks were unconscionable in a society of equals.'[48] Such romanticized readings and recollections soon became part of the norm, and on the 25th anniversary of the gesture in 1993, the image was revisited by newspapers, magazines, and television stations commemorating the occasion with tributes and testimonials. *New York Times* columnist Robert Lipsyte, marking this 25-year anniversary, cites the event as a defining moment in sport history.[49] In 1998, the 1968 Olympic track and field team reunited for the first time in coordination with the US outdoor track and field championships in New Orleans.[50] A year later, HBO produced the documentary, 'Fists of Freedom: The Story of the '68 Summer Games,' which traced 'the political and racial ferment that led to the incident and the fallout that affected' Smith and Carlos post-Olympic lives.[51] San Jose's City Council issued a proclamation for 'Tommie Smith Day' in 1994, a year after granting the same honor to his teammate Lee Evans. By the year 2000, Smith had been inducted into several halls of fame, as well as being named outstanding African American alumnus by San José State.[52] Carlos had also received his share of belated accolades.[53] In the most recent honoring of Smith and Carlos, and the stand they took in 1968, the two former Olympians were named the winners of the ESPY's Arthur Ashe Courage Award in 2008, making them as mainstream within the sport industry as they could be. In one of the more significant ways of remembering and recognizing the two Olympic athletes, San José State belatedly honored the two former students in a number of events over several years, culminating in the unveiling of a statue of the two athletes.

The Smith/Carlos statue was born out of a conversation in a political science class. San José State student Erik Grotz and his political science classmates were challenged by Professor Cobie Harris to be more active in politics, and cited the efforts of Smith and Carlos, while also suggesting that the two former San José State students had not been properly recognized for their actions. While Grotz recognized the image, he knew few details of it and had no idea that Smith and Carlos once attended the university.[54] An active member of the Associated Students, Grotz and his Associated Students peers authored a resolution in December 2002, entitled 'The Celebration of Student Advocacy through the Tommie Smith & John Carlos Commemoration Project.' Citing the 1968 protest as one of the most memorable moments in the American Civil Rights Movement, the resolution acknowledged that Smith and Carlos had been students at San Jose State and that their action protested the treatment of African Americans, empowered the African American community, and 'proved through their courageous act that student advocacy is of utmost importance to bring attention to social issues that affect their community and their nation.' The resolution concluded, 'The student body of San José State University feels the need to celebrate the courageous act of student advocacy by Tommie Smith and John Carlos, and other student advocates from our beloved campus. Therefore, be it resolved, that the Associated Students Board of Directors of San José State University support the Tommie Smith/John Carlos Project to commemorate the courageous acts of our student advocates in the 1968 Olympic Games.'[55] By linking themselves to Smith and Carlos, the Associated Students' discussion also served as a means of promoting student activism, turning the gesture into a tangible reminder of the impact students can have on larger issues.

The Tommie Smith/John Carlos Project served many functions, concomitantly honoring Smith and Carlos while promoting activism, as well as celebrating the school's role in history. Over the next three years, a number of campus-sponsored events honored Smith and Carlos, and worked to raise funds for the statue. The initial overture from the campus was held at 'First Steps,' a Spring 2003 reception honoring the legacy of Smith and Carlos as members of 'Speed City.' Both men were given certificates celebrating them as 'Unsung Heroes.' Grotz, the student who had initiated the project, explained 'It just doesn't make sense why the campus wouldn't promote student activists like that. It was a story that needed to be told.' He thought it would serve as an inspiration to other students and proved that they could make an impact in their communities. Alfonso de Alba, the Executive Director of Associated Students, said the two sprinters were not given their due respect despite the significance of their role in the civil rights movement. 'Thirty five years ago they were chastised and shunned by the community. Years later, we want to say, "Welcome back." This is the way it should have been.'[56] Soon after the 'First Steps' reception, Smith and Carlos began to make appearances at the school for various fundraisers for the project, including 'Raise your voice' week and the Literacy Classic.[57] By the start of the Fall 2003 semester, Associated Students worked with Faculty Senate to craft a resolution from campus faculty. In October 2003, a daylong festival, 'Welcome Back Tommie Smith and John Carlos,' was held commemorating the 35-year anniversary of the Olympic gesture. A panel discussion, a barbecue, and a fund-raising dinner were held (with tickets at $100 per person), as well as the announcement of the selection of Rigo 23 as the artist to create the statue.[58]

In Fall 2004, Smith and Carlos appeared at a number of events, including the Read 2 Lead Rally and a celebration of the 36th anniversary of the protest.[59] In May 2005, Smith and Carlos were awarded honorary doctorates at the spring commencement ceremonies, and the groundbreaking ceremony was held days later.[60] Smith was especially pleased to be honored in such a way and remarked that he still felt very close to the SJSU campus.[61] In Fall 2005, flags and banners were hung across campus and the statue of Tommie Smith was already on site. Rigo 23 and his team worked into the nights applying the ceramic tiles in the weeks leading up to the unveiling. On the day of the unveiling, there were multiple viewings of HBO's 'Fists of Freedom' and a panel discussion on 'SJSU Activism During the 60s,' with the unveiling ceremony planned for 4:30 p.m.[62] In the *Spartan Daily*, the campus newspaper, Associated Students President Alberto Gutierrez reminded students that they had made the biggest contributions to the project (now over $240,000 in student funds!) and encouraged their attendance at the ceremonies.

Executive Director Alfonso De Alba commented, 'The whole purpose of this celebration is not to build a sculpture. By placing a sculpture in the middle of an academic institution, we're saying it is ok to stand up; it is ok to be an act; it is an appropriate method of change.'[63]

On October 17, 2005, 37 years and one day after their 200-meter race and subsequent protest, the university unveiled the 20-foot statue of the two former San José State students on the victory platform, made of fiberglass, covered with ceramic tiles, and faces and fists of bronze. With a crowd in excess of one thousand, the campus finally paid permanent tribute to the former students. After the event, Smith said 'he was intimidated by the size of the monuments but appreciated the message with which future generations are left.' Carlos thought the statue stood for diversity, vision, strength, and the belief in right things. Both athletes agreed that the tribute almost makes up for being banned from the Olympics and being ostracized at home.[64] Second-place finisher Australian Peter Norman, whose second-place platform was left empty, attended the ceremonies and reflected on his role in the event. As for his noticeable absence on the victory stand, Norman said, 'As I am told, anyone can stand in and get a picture taken and be a part of the event...I am honored to be commemorated in part of the celebrations.'[65,66] Ironically, almost 40 years later, Edwards reflected, echoing the assertions of Lowenthal, Rosenfeld, Norkunas, Dupré, and others, 'History is funny. It's one of the realities of life that offers you more clarity the further you get away from it. Everything else gets clearer the closer you get to it.'[67]

The contemporary depictions of the athletes' gesture are uniquely situated within a framework that acknowledges the past failures of San José State, the USOC, and even the United States, to properly recognize and celebrate the two athletes for their performances, both on and off the track, but also for being unable to discuss racism and civil rights. Sydnor, citing Lowenthal, explains 'the past is a world into which time travelers may pry without embarrassment or fear of rebuff. The "remoteness" of the past enables people to engage with it creatively, to frame it however they want.'[68] It is this ability of objects, such as statues and monuments, to engage with the historical imagination of the viewer that makes the multiple readings of said objects so critical to the ways we attempt to reconstruct the past in the present through the medium of permanent objects. According to Rosenfeld, 'the past is never permanently fixed, but rather shifts in contour and meaning with the changing shapes of symbolization and interpretation.'[69] Simply put, Dupré tells us, 'Monuments are history made visible. They are shrines that celebrate the ideals, achievements, and heroes that existed in one moment in time... They reflect the politics of remembering... The best of them are redemptive, allowing us to understand the past in a way that is meaningful in the present.'[70]

The statue of Tommie Smith and John Carlos is both a gesture of reparation while also honoring the two athletes. Reparation and commemoration are not mutually exclusive, but rather serve as a reminder that monuments serve multiple purposes as well as produce multiple meanings. At some level, even Tommie Smith considered the San Jose statue as a means of reparation when he wrote in his autobiography, 'Why not write a check to us for $200,000 and say, "This is for reparations, we know you've suffered?"'[71] One indication that there is more than commemoration with the Smith–Carlos statue is the time that elapsed between their achievement and the construction of the statue.[72] The statue was built over 35 years after the controversial gesture, indicating that it took a considerable amount of time for the university to recognize the value or need to remember the former student athletes on campus. Additionally, as the image of the two athletes changed over time, the university may have been more cognizant of the ways they might benefit from their affiliation with the civil rights icons. According to Dupré, 'The very process of deciding how an event should be remembered allows reconciliation with the event itself, and in doing so frees history to move forward.'[73] Phillips et al. tell us that monuments both construct and disseminate myths, privileging selected narratives while marginalizing others.[74]

Hartmann explains that the 'dramatic transformation' of the image of Smith and Carlos 'goes back to the dynamics of cultural remembering and rehabilitation... the cultural processes by which "radical" images, objects, and practices such as those associated with the 1960s are appropriated and transformed into commodities available for mass-market consumption in ways that dilute or subvert their original meanings and intentions,' as well as racial reforms and transformations in sport in the 1970s. In remembering the 1968 gesture, there is little discussion of the social and racial context of the civil rights movement. Such shifts allowed for the 'radical impulses and controversial ideals' to be 'absorbed and insulated, thus relegated to the sports world's past and rendered impotent with respect to its future.'[75] Perhaps the moment represented by the image becomes more palatable in its three-dimensional frozen form, although to radical sports columnist Dave Zirin, the statue of Smith and Carlos 'cheapens' the original event and in his view detracts from the 'significance of the struggle' both then and now.[76] Urla Hill, in writing about the statue, wonders how 'such a vilified and...controversial moment find[s] rejuvenation if not outright rehabilitation under the guise of an entirely different context?'[77] The Smith/Carlos statue, which is a tangible representation of the salute, embodies the image and multiple readings of the image over the last 40 years.

According to Hartmann, and as evidenced by the narrative of Erik Grotz in his efforts to recognize Smith and Carlos, 'This is not a movement that most Americans know much about. In fact, to the extent that they 'know' about it at all, they are likely to only recognize it in the form of a single and singularly powerful image,' that of Smith and Carlos.[78] The accompanying plaque does little to rectify this lack of information. For three years, without an explanatory plaque, the statue was reliant on the passerby's recognition of the image, and relieved the statue and the university of re-telling the story and the subsequent apology. Even now, with the accompanying text, which reads, 'At the Mexico City 1968 Olympic Games, San José State University student athletes Tommie Smith and John Carlos stood for Justice, Dignity, Equality, and Peace. Hereby the University and Associated Students Commemorate Their Legacy,' much of the story is missing. For instance, what legacy is the school commemorating? The use of the word 'commemorate' indicates the statue is being presented as such. It does not indicate the general lack of support from the university following the event; it does not mention the racism on the campus leading up to the Olympic Games or what followed the Games. Instead, it celebrates the former student athletes as part of the university community. Malveaux suggests that statues can be used as 'cultural leverage, as ways of telling a story.'[79] So, we must ask what story this statue of Smith and Carlos tells the viewer. Even Smith, in considering the statue as a means of reparation and remembrance, emphasizes that he 'can't *not* accept the graciousness of those who now are thanking us for what we did 35 years ago. The people who are doing it now weren't even there; for them, it's a historical search and recovery.' He does not feel the same about the individuals who were there in 1968 and did what he perceives as nothing. Smith concludes, '35 years is a long time to stay silent. Thirty-five years later is a hell of a time to stand up and recognize me.'[80]

Conclusions

Jack Olsen, in the late 1960s, commented that 'Every morning the world of sports wakes up and congratulates itself on its contributions to race relations. The litany has been repeated so often that it is believed almost universally. It goes: 'look what sports has done for the Negro.'[81] The civil rights activism of African American athletes during the late 1960s and early 1970s was notable in part because it refuted such claims of peaceful race relations. Over 40 years later, we return to this 1968 iconic event to remember and forget the activism of Smith and Carlos.

Hartmann cautions that rehabilitation comes at a cost, and suggests that with the rehabilitation of the image, and subsequently I would suggest the construction of a statue, the 'actual experiences and grievances and radical intent that prompted their demonstration have been neglected or ignored in favor of their individual courage and an abstracted commitment to equality, dignity, and justice.'[82] Smith, in his autobiography, tells his readers they can 'take the victory stand in a number of ways besides the one way it usually is portrayed.'[83] Harry Edwards, talking about the event 40 years later, says the two athletes are 'trying to figure out what happened 40 years ago. They had no idea, 40 years after the fact, there'd be a statue of them on San José State's campus. But now people ask them for explanations, so they go back and try to figure it out. But at the end of the day, what you have is two old dudes sitting at the end of the bar, an hour before closing time, telling war stories. And every night the stories change. The only thing that really matters is that they became the iconic emblems of an era that changed how we look at, and how we deal with, developments at the intersection of race, sports and society.'[84] Over the passage of time, the ways scholars and citizens have interpreted, remembered, and assigned meaning to the protest has shifted with every re-telling of the story. Even the narratives as retold by Smith and Carlos change details of the original event, and do not tell a singular story, revealing the power and flaws of memory. Moreover, racial attitudes in the US have experienced significant shifts in the last 40 years that contribute to the reconsideration of the gesture's significance. Other universities have made conciliatory gestures to black athletes who were previously scorned for their civil rights activism and use of college sport as a platform to change their local campuses. For example, Syracuse University presented eight former football players who were removed from the team in the late 1960s with letterman jackets. In addition to the statue of Smith and Carlos as San José State, the University of Wyoming and the University of Washington have erected monuments honoring the activism of black athletes on their campuses in the 1960s.

The once controversial image of Smith and Carlos has evolved into a moment that is celebrated and honored, and yet cannot be separated from the historical baggage of racism at the university and in the United States. The Olympic gesture served and continues to be emblematic of the revolt of the black athlete in the 1960s. The competing narratives of the 'Black Power Salute' over the last 40 years are emblematic of our own attempts to explicate the complicated narratives embodied in the image 'that changed the world.'

Notes

*Parts of this chapter were previously published and are reprinted here with the permission of the *Journal of Sport History*. For the original article, see M.M. Smith, 'Frozen Fists in Speed City: The Statue as Twenty-First-Century Reparations,' *Journal of Sport History*, 36(3), 2009, 401–20

1. Robert Sullivan, '100 Photographs that Changed the World,' *Life* (New York: Time Warner, 2003).
2. For more on this gesture see Amy Bass, *Not the Triumph but the Struggle: The 1968 Olympics and the Making of the Black Athlete* (Minneapolis, MN: University of Minnesota Press, 2002); Harry Edwards, *Revolt of the Black Athlete* (New York: Free Press, 1969); Douglas Hartmann, *Race, Culture, and the Revolt of the Black Athlete: The 1968 Olympic Protests and Their Aftermath* (Chicago, IL: University of Chicago Press, 2003); Kevin Witherspoon, *Before the Eyes of the World: Mexico and the 1968 Olympics* (Dekalb, IL: Northern Illinois University Press, 2008); Urla Hill, 'Racing After Smith and Carlos: Revisiting Those Fists Some Forty Years Hence, in David C. Ogden and Joel Nathan Rosen (eds.),' *Reconstructing Fame: Sport, Race, and Evolving Reputations* (Jackson, MS: University Press of Mississippi, 2008); Smith, 'Frozen Fists in Speed City: The Statue as Twenty-First-Century Reparations,' 401–20; Gary Osmond, 'Photographs, Materiality and Sport History: Peter Norman and the 1968 Mexico City Black Power Salute,' *Journal of Sport History*, 37(1), 2010, 119–37. For an excellent article detailing protests of black athletes during 1968, see David K. Wiggins, '"The Year of Awakening,": Black Athletes, Racial Unrest and the Civil Rights Movement of 1968,' *International Journal of the History of Sport*, 9 (1992), 188–208. For an overview of college athletics and the integration movement in sports in the 1960s, see Adolph H. Grundman, 'The Image of Intercollegiate Athletics and the Civil Rights Movement: A Historian's View,' in Richard E. Lapchick (ed.), *Fractured Focus: Sport as a Reflection of Society* (Lexington, MA: Heath, 1986): 77–85; Donald Spivey, 'Black Consciousness and Olympic Protest Movement, 1964–1980,' *Sport in America: New Historical Perspectives* (Westport, CT: Greenwood Press, 1985): 239–62; David K. Wiggins, '"The Future of College Athletics is at Stake:" Black Athletes and Racial Turmoil on Three Predominantly White University Campuses, 1968–1972,' *Journal of Sport History*, 15 (1988), 304–32.
3. For more on Speed City, see History San Jose, 'Exhibits & Collections,' *Speed City: From Civil Rights to Black Power*, retrieved http://www.historysanJosé.org/exhibits_collections/current_upcoming_exhibits/speedcity.html. Accessed 22 July 2008. Also see 'Sports Distortion of SJS,' *Spartan Daily*, 10 April 1969, 2; Ann Killion, 'An Accomplishment Most Rare-SJS Track Title was

Beginning of the End,' *San Jose Mercury News*, 4 June 1989, 1D; Mark Purdy, 'Preserving Track's Past Isn't Enough,' *San Jose Mercury News*, 5 December 1996, 1D. For a sample of press coverage of Speed City's 1969 season, see footnote 44. John Carlos with C.D. Jackson, *Why? The Biography of John Carlos* (Los Angeles, CA: Milligan Books, Inc., 2000).

4. This event has been cited as the impetus for black student protests on campuses around the country. See Edwards, *Revolt of the Black Athlete*, pp. 42–7 for conditions and details of San Jose State campus issues. For another version of the events, see Themis Chronopoulos, 'Racial Turmoil at San Jose State: The Incident of the 1967 University of Texas at El Paso vs. San Jose State Football Game,' Paper presented at the Annual Meeting of the Popular Culture Association/American Culture Association, Philadelphia, PA, April 12–15, 1995. For examples of protests following the San Jose State protest, see Edwards, *Revolt of the Black Athlete*, pp. 80–8.
5. For more on Harry Edwards, his tenure at San Jose State, and his role in the OPHR, see Michael E. Lomax, 'Bedazzle Them with Brilliance, Bamboozle Them with Bull: Harry Edwards, Black Power, and the Revolt of the Black Athlete Revisited,' in *Sports and the Racial Divide: African American and Latino Experience in an Era of Change* (Jackson, MI: University of Mississippi Press, 2008), pp. 55–89; also see Ron Briley, "The Black Panther Party and the Revolt of the Black Athlete: Sport and Revolutionary Consciousness," pp. 90–104, in the same collection.
6. Lomax, 'Bedazzle Them With Brilliance,' p. 80.
7. Ibid., pp. 71, 73.
8. For more on the OPHR and the lead up to the 1968 Olympic Games, see Bass, *Not the Triumph but the Struggle*; Edwards, *Revolt of the Black Athlete*; Hartmann, *Race, Culture, and the Revolt of the Black Athlete*.
9. Moore, 'A Courageous Stand,' 71; Harry Edwards, *The Revolt of the Black Athlete* (New York: Free Press, 1969); For an account of Brundage's recollections of the incidents, see Allen Guttman, *The Games Must Go On: Avery Brundage and the Olympic Movement* (New York: Columbia University Press, 1984).
10. Tommie Smith with David Steele, *Silent Gesture: The Autobiography of Tommie Smith* (Philadelphia, PA: Temple University Press, 2007), p. 173.
11. 'Opinions Vary on Black Protestors,' *San Francisco Chronicle*, 18 October, 1968, 57.
12. 'Carlos, Smith Feel Beautiful,' *Chicago Defender*, 24 October 1968, 38.
13. '2 Accept Medals Wearing Black Gloves,' *New York Times*, 17 October 1968, 59.
14. 'Carlos Airs Black Stars Bias Protest,' *Chicago Defender*, 19–25 October 1968, 18.
15. Shirley Povich, 'Black Power on Victory Stand,' *Los Angeles Times*, 17 October 1968, Part III, 1,4.
16. 'Olympic Stars Should Evoke Pride – Ownes,' *Los Angeles Sentinel*, 17 October 1968, B1. Also see, Milton Richman, 'Pride, Prejudice Affect Owens Anew,' *Washington Post*, 20 October 1968, C4; 'Ouster of Carlos, Smith 'just',' *San Jose Mercury*, 30 October 1968, 106. For recollections of the event, read Jesse Owens, *Blackthink: My Life as Black Man and White Man* (New York: William Morrow and Company, 1970), pp. 75–6. For another account of

Owens' involvement in the Smith–Carlos affair, see William Baker, *Jesse Owens: An American Life* (New York: Free Press, 1988), pp. 206–17.
17. 'Nonmilitant Boston Joins Beamon 'Act',' *Washington Post*, 19 October 1968, C3, A12 (photo); *New York Times*, 19 October 1968, photo, 45; *Amsterdam News*, 26 October 1968, photo, 1.
18. Adrienne Mann, 'Olympic Stars Get Rousing Welcome,' *Washington Afro-American*, 26 October 1968, 31.
19. Ibid., 31.
20. For a sampling on the press reaction, see Maureen Margaret Smith, 'Identity and Citizenship: African American athletes, sport, and the freedom struggles of the 1960s,' Ph.D. dissertation, The Ohio State University, 1999, 'Chapter 7: Tommie Smith and John Carlos Salute Black America at the 1968 Mexico City Olympics,' pp. 233–88; Bass, *Not the Triumph but the Struggle*, pp. 233–89.
21. *San Francisco Chronicle*, 24 October 1968, 50; *Los Angeles Times*, 17 October 1968, III, 1; *New York Times*, 19 October 1968, 1; 17 October 1968, 59; *San Francisco Chronicle*, 17 October 1968, 51; *Washington Post*, 17 October 1968, C1; 18 October 1968, D1; 19 October 1968, C1; *New York Times*, 20 October 1968, V, 2. These are just some of the quotes. Similar quotes could be found on almost every page that an article appeared.
22. Brad Pye, Jr, 'Olympics No Platform for Problems,' *Los Angeles Sentinel*, B3; for another Pye article, see 'Prying Pye by Brad Pye, Jr,' *Los Angeles Sentinel*, 14 November 1968, B1.
23. Clint Wilson, Jr, 'Olympic Games' Events Most Disturbing,' *Los Angeles Sentinel*, 24 October 1968, B4; for Hall's original article, see John Hall, 'It Takes All Kinds,' *Los Angeles Times*, 18 October 1968, Section 3, p. 3.
24. Clint Wilson, Jr, *Los Angeles Sentinel*, 31 October 1968, B4.
25. 'Take Ten by John A. Helem,' *Chicago Defender*, 26 October–1 November 1968, 17.
26. John H. Sengstacke, 'Olympic Black Power,' *Chicago Defender*, 21 October 1968, 13.
27. Ibid., 21 October 1968, 13. For a similar editorial, see *Amsterdam News*, 26 October 1968, 18.
28. Booker Griffin, 'Some Untold Tales of Mexico City,' *Los Angeles Sentinel*, 24 October 1968, B5, D4. For another example of an editorial supportive of Smith and Carlos, see Editorial, *Los Angeles Sentinel*, 24 October 1968, B3.
29. W.D. Maxwell, 'Editorial: The Natural of Being a Slob,' *Chicago Tribune*, 19 October 1968, 10; Arthur Daley, 'Sports of The Times,' *New York Times*, 20 October 1968, V, 2.
30. Shirley Povich, 'This Morning,' *Washington Post*, 19 October 1968, C1.
31. Ibid., 24 October 1968, K1. While Povich offers no explanation for the differences in racial militancy between black boxers and basketball players and their track and field counterparts, one explanation could be that boxing and basketball offered professional careers and protests could jeopardize those professional opportunities. Track and field offered little opportunity for professional careers or money-making opportunities.
32. Jim Murray, 'Excuse My Glove,' *Los Angeles Times*, 18 October 1968, III, 1.
33. Jim Murray, 'The Olympic Games – No Place for a Sportswriter,' *Los Angeles Times*, 20 October 1968, D1, 3.

34. Ron Fimrite, 'Do Away With the Anthems,' *San Francisco Chronicle*, 25 October 1968, 51.
35. Art Rosenbaum, 'Reaction to the Protest,' *San Francisco Chronicle*, 18 October 1968, 55; Art Rosenbaum, ' "That Salute" Lifted the 200,' *San Francisco Chronicle*, 24 October 1968, 50.
36. *Chicago Defender*, 23 October 1968, 28; 29 October 1968, 24; *Washington Post*, 18 October 1968, D1; *Los Angeles Times*, 18 October 1968, III, 3; 20 October 1968, D3; *Washington Post*, 19 October 1968, C1.
37. The citation of the article quoted concerning the Black Power of black female athletes is from *New York Times*, 21 October 1968, 60.
38. *Chicago Defender*, 22 October 1968, 26; *Chicago Defender*, 24 October 1968, 39; Arthur Daley, 'The Incident,' *New York Times*, 20 October 1968, V, 2; 'Some Negro Athletes Threaten to "Go Home",' *New York Times*, 19 October 1968, 45.
39. Mann, 'Olympic Stars Get Rousing Welcome,' 31.
40. 'Smith Claims 200,' *Spartan Daily*, 17 October 1968, 3; Louis Duino, 'Tommie in record 200 win, then 'salutes' black Power,' *San Jose Mercury*, 17 October 1968, pp. 73–75; 'Yanks Apologize for Race Protest,' *San Jose Mercury*, 18 October 1968, 58; Louis Duino, 'Americans Boo Smith, Carlos,' *San Jose Mercury*, 18 October 1968, 58; 'Ousted Olympic Stars to File Suit,' *San Jose Mercury*, 20 October 1968, 1; 'San José received world recognition,' *San Jose Mercury*, 20 October 1968, 3F; Louis Duino, 'Aftermath in Mexico,' *San Jose Mercury*, 20 October 1968, 76; Arthur Daley, 'Far-reaching percussions,' *San Jose Mercury*, 20 October 1968, 79; Bill Hurschman, 'Smith, Carlos Ousted from Olympic Games,' *Spartan Daily*, 21 October 1968, 1; Scott Moore and Wes Mathis, 'Newsmen outrun Smith, Carlos,' *San Jose Mercury*, pp. 1, 2; 'Editorial: Two wrongs don't – and all that,' *San Jose Mercury*, 22 October 1968, 16; Sue Amon, 'Smith, Carlos back in San José after 'too exciting' time,' *Spartan Daily*, 22 October 1968, 1; Leigh Weiners, 'The Lee Side,' *San Jose Mercury*, 23 October 1968, 22; Sue Amon, ' "We'd do it again tomorrow," John Carlos tells SJS crowd,' *Spartan Daily*, 23 October 1968, 1; Mike Elvitsky, "Sport Shorts," *Spartan Daily*, 25 October 1968; Rick Rodgers, 'Carlos differentiates on human rights,' *Spartan Daily*, 8 November 1968; Jeff Mullens, 'Evans discredits Bay Area stories,' *Spartan Daily*, 22 November 1968, 2. For campus reactions to the gesture, see *Spartan Daily*, 21 October 1968, 2, which includes two letters to the editor in support of the athletes as well as a guest editorial by Hobert Burns, PhD, Academic Vice President, who chastised IOC President Avery Brundage. For an editorial cartoon that addresses Brundage, see *Spartan Daily*, 28 October 1968, 2. Also see the editorial page of the *Spartan Daily* for 22 October 1968, 2, and 23 October 1968, 2 for additional mixed reactions. As these events unfolded, campus strife within athletics continued. See 'Athletic Director asked to resign,' *Spartan Daily*, 22 October 1968, 1; Susy Lydle, 'ASB Probes Athletics,' *Spartan Daily*, 22 October 1968, 1; 'BYU game target: blacks to boycott?' *Spartan Daily*, 19 November 1968, 1; John Robert Muir and Jim Paxton, 'Blacks to lose scholarship aids if boycott BYU,' *Spartan Daily*, 22 November 1968, 1; 'Sports editor, black student, in brief scuffle,' *Spartan Daily*, 22 November 1968, pp. 1–2; Mike Elvitsky, 'Basketball boycott by black athletes at Fresno game,' *Spartan Daily*, 4 December 1968, 1. For a retrospective look at the events, see George

Hostetter, 'He Sent Message to World Athlete Still Paying Price for Taking Stand at '68 Olympics,' *Fresno Bee*, 25 August 1988, D1; Steve Dilbeck, 'When Raised Fists Raised Nation's Ire,' *Daily News of Los Angeles*, 16 October 2003, S1.

41. In the 24 October 1968 edition of the *Spartan Daily*, p. 2, President Clark authored an editorial calling the two athletes 'honorable men' and noted that the university was proud of the students, as should all of America. Clark went on to apologize for the treatment of black athletes that prompted the gesture. He closed with 'They do not return home in disgrace, but as the honorable young men they are.' Also see Scott Moore, 'Dr. Clark Praises Smith and Carlos,' *San Jose Mercury*, 19 October 1969, pp. 1, 2; 'Editorial: Clark Leaves SJS,' *Spartan Daily*, 5 May 1969, 2; Mark Lundstrom and Sandra Gonzales, 'R. Clark, SJS chief in '60s tumult dies,' *San Jose Mercury News*, 20 June 2005, 3A; Nanette Asimov, 'Robert Clark – former San Jose State president,' *San Francisco Chronicle*, 3 July 2005, A25; Lydia Sarraille, 'Old library has new purpose,' *Spartan Daily*, 23 August 2005.
42. 'Vice President Humphrey will visit SJS Friday,' *Spartan Daily*, 23 October 1968, 1; Harry Farrell, ' 'HH' Backs Peace Students,' *San Jose Mercury*, 26 October 1968, 1, 2.
43. See Jackson, *Why? The Biography of John Carlos*, pp. 226–9. For a sampling of *Spartan Daily* press coverage of Carlos and the track team following his return from the 1968 Games and their winning the 1969 NCAA title, see Don Hansen, 'SJS Unleashes Power,' 4 March 1969, 3; 'Spikers Face Stiff Challenge,' 7 March 1969, 5; 'SJS Spikers 3rd in NCAA,' 19 March 1969, 4; Don Hansen, 'Relay Squad Ready to Roll,' 21 March 1969, 6; 'Spartans hose Indian Spikers,' 27 March 1969, 6; Don Hansen, 'Carlos Eyes Sprint Record in Invitational,' 30 April 1969, 4; Don Hansen, 'Carlos Sprints World's First Nine Flat,' 5 May 1969, 5; Lane Wallace, 'John Carlos lightning strikes,' 7 May 1969, 4; 'Spartans Seek Relay Title,' 8 May 1969, 4; Don Hansen, ' "Watch" Out – Here Comes Big John,' 18 May 1969, 8; Don Hansen, 'Carlos' Defeat an Omen of World Mark?' 20 May 1969, 8; Don Hansen, 'Spartan Mile Quartet Seeks NCAA Berth,' 28 May 1969, 5; Lane Wallace, 'Lee's Triumphs Not Over – Yet,' 28 May 1969, 5; Don Hansen, 'SJS Trackmen Eye First NCAA Title,' 4 June 1969, 4. These articles do not remind the reader of Carlos' Olympic gesture, instead focusing on his performance during the 1969 season.
44. Bass, *Not the Triumph but the Struggle*, p. 241.
45. For example, see Bass, *Not the Triumph but the Struggle*; Witherspoon, *Before the Eyes of the World*; Hartmann, *Race, Culture, and the Revolt of the Black Athlete*; Smith with Steele, *Silent Gesture*; Carlos, *Why*; Edwards, *The Revolt of the Black Athlete*.
46. Hartmann, *Race, Culture, and the Revolt of the Black Athlete*, p. 265. Also see William Rhoden, 'Sports of the *Times*: Vilified to Glorified: Olympic Redux,' *New York Times*, 17 October 2005; Mike Cassidy, '1968 Protest Has Become 2005 Symbol,' *San Jose Mercury News*, 25 October 2005, 1B; George Hostetter, 'Picture This: Smith–Carlos Photo Most Memorable,' *Fresno Bee*, 9 June 1991, C9; Robert Lipsyte, 'Silent Salute, Ringing Impact,' *New York Times*, 17 October 1993; William C. Rhoden, 'They Punched the Sky, and Ran into a Nation's Consciousness,' *New York Times*, 17 October 1993; Andy Boogaard,

'Image of the Future Thirty-Two Years After His Message Was Broadcast Around the World, Tommie Smith Is Finally Seeing it Being Received,' *Fresno Bee*, 1 October 2000, D1.
47. See 5 August and 12 August, 1991 issues of *Sports Illustrated*.
48. Kenny Moore, 'Black Athletes Revisited: The Eye of the Storm,' *Sports Illustrated*, 73. Also see Moore, 'The Black Athlete Revisited: A Courageous Stand,' *Sports Illustrated*, 5 August 1991, 62–77; 'The Black Athlete Revisited: The Eye of the Storm,' 12 August 1991, 62–73.
49. Robert Lipsyte, 'Silent Salute, Ringing Impact,' *New York Times*, 17 October 1993, pp. 1,11.
50. Steve Popper, '1968 Team to Hold Reunion,' *New York Times*, 7 May 1998; Neil Amdur, 'Memories of 1968, With No Regrets,' *New York Times*, 14 June 1998.
51. Richard Sandomir, 'The Medals, and Then the Uproar,' *New York Times*, 8 August 1999.
52. Chauncey Bailey, 'Gold Medalist Helps Kids Shape Up – African-American Group Holds Free Track Meet Targeting Obesity,' *Oakland Tribune*, 21 May 2004; Loretta Green, 'Track Legend Hasn't Run Out of Grace, Fans,' *San Jose Mercury News*, 31 May 1994, 1B; Beth Harris, '68 Medalist Who Shocked World Joins Torch Relay,' *Daily News of Los Angeles*, 28 April 1996, N8; Bruce Farris, 'Courage and Convictions – Lemoore's Tommie Smith Stood Up for His Beliefs During the 1968 Olympics and Lives by Them Now,' *Fresno Bee*, 19 April 1997, D1; Steve Popper, '1968 Olympic Team to Hold Reunion,' *New York Times*, 7 May 1998; Neil Amdur, 'Memories of 1968, With No Regret,' *New York Times*, 14 June 1998; Jody Meacham, 'Maybe it's About Time to Embrace Tommie Smith, Finally Will be Honored in San José,' *San Jose Mercury News*, 26 May 1994, 1F; Bob Burns, 'Devers, Cason and Effiong Burn Up the Track,' *San Jose Mercury News*, 29 May 1994, C12; 'Lemoore Honors Track Star, Gold-Medalist Smith,' *Fresno Bee*, 17 April 1997, D4; Sheldon Spencer, 'S.J. Sports Fall to Induct 6,' *San Jose Mercury News*, 4 July 1997, 3D; Pat Sullivan, 'Bay Area Sports Hall of Fame,' *San Francisco Chronicle*, 4 March 1999, E8; David Steele, 'Smith's Crusade Still on Track,' *San Francisco Chronicle*, 12 November 1999, E1. Smith, in his autobiography, recalls other times he had been honored by his alma mater; see Smith with Steele, *Silent Gesture*, p. 3.
53. 'Cubs Acquire Lee from Marlins – ex-SJSU Sprinter Entering Track Hall,' *San Jose Mercury News*, 26 November 2003, 2D.
54. 'Art and Political Activism,' Jean Damu. http://www.sfbayview.com/102605/theraising102605.shtml. Retrieved 1 November 2005.
55. Associated Students Board Minutes, 11 December 2002. All Associated Board minutes can be retrieved from http://www.as.sjsu.edu/asgov/docs. Also see David Steele, 'Historic Act to be Honored,' *San Francisco Chronicle*, 15 October 2003, C1.
56. Juliana Barbassa, 'Campaign Launched at San Jose State to Honor '68 Olympians,' *San Diego Union-Tribune*, A4; Elliott Almond, 'SJSU Students Honor a Historic Stand – Statue Would Commemorate Spartans Sprinters' Olympic Protest,' *San Jose Mercury News*, 15 May 2003, 1A. De Alba, despite not being a student, was critical to the project. See his letter to the editor, co-written with associate professor Scott Myers-Lipton, *Spartan Daily*,

20 October 2003. However, De Alba was terminated in February 2006 for providing alcohol to minors at an Associated Students retreat in August 2005. See John Myers, 'De Alba Terminated,' *Spartan Daily*, 9 February 2006; John Myers, 'Investigative Report Details Drinking at A.S. Retreat,' *Spartan Daily*, 13 February 2006; John Myers, 'New A.S. Board, Expect Same Stiffness,' *Spartan Daily*, 4 April 2006. Myers usually made connections from De Alba to the statue project in his articles on De Alba's termination. At least one person connected De Alba's involvement with the statue project as a reason for his termination; see letter from Rigo 23, 'Finally Campus Offers Something Positive,' *Spartan Daily*, 1 December 2005.

57. Associated Students Board Minutes, 12 February 2003; Associated Students Board Minutes, 27 August 2003; Associated Students Board Minutes, 26 February 2003.

58. Associated Students Board Minutes, 10 September 2003; Chris Giovannetti, 'A Story of Courage, Bravery and Civil Rights,' *Spartan Daily*, 16 October 2003; Associated Students Board Minutes, 8 October 2003; JaShong King, 'A.S. to Name Statue Artist Today,' *Spartan Daily*, 8 October 2003; Janet Pak, 'A.S. Chooses Memorial Sculptor,' *Spartan Daily*, 9 October 2003; 'Activist Athletes Set for Anniversary Events,' *San Jose Mercury News*, 14 October 2003, 2B; Becky Bartindale, 'Olympians Remembered – San Jose State Honors Athlete's Protest,' *San Jose Mercury News*, 17 October 2003, 1C; 'Those Fists in the Air Were Acts of Courage,' *San Jose Mercury News*, 17 October 2003, 8C. This was not the pair's first return to San Jose to be remembered for their gesture. In April 1987, they spoke about their experiences to a social sciences seminar. See Colin Seymour, 'Smith, Carlos Says Racism Has Not Been Conquered,' *San Jose Mercury News*, 10 April 1987, 4E; Rigo 23 is a political artist who lives in San Francisco. Born in 1966, he is known for several murals in the San Francisco area. For examples of these works, including 'One Way', 'Truth', and 'Innercity', see http://www.mistersf.com/new/index.html?newrigo.htm. For other examples of his artwork, see http://www.gallerypauleanglim.com/rigo_23.html.

59. Associated Students Board Minutes, 25 August 2004; Janet Pak, 'Marching Bands Rally Support for Weekend Game,' *Spartan Daily*, 17 September 2004. Pak reported on Smith's appearance a rally for the football team, where he said it was nice to be home; Associated Students Board Minutes, 22 September 2004; Smith and Carlos signed posters and shirts at one event raising $1500. Kevin Yuen, 'Carlos and Smith visit King Library, Discuss SJSU Athletics, '68 Olympics,' *Spartan Daily*, 18 October 2004. For more on the 36th anniversary events, see 10 November 2002, Associated Students Board Minutes.

60. Associated Students Board Minutes, 27 April 2005. Also see Associated Students Board Minutes, 11 May 2005. For more on the degree granting, see Traci Newell, 'Fillmore to Speak at Commencement Ceremony,' *Spartan Daily*, 8 May 2005; John Ryan, 'Chatter Box,' *San Jose Mercury News*, 22 May 2005, 2C; 'An Image for the Ages,' *San Francisco Chronicle*, 26 May 2005, B8; Glenn Dickey, 'Overdue Honor: SJS Pays Tribute to both Smith, Carlos,' *San Francisco Chronicle*, 27 May 2005, D1; Becky Bartindale, 'SJSU Graduation Promotes Dreams – School's Commencement Ceremony Marked by Spirit of Activism,' *San Jose Mercury News*, 29 May 2005, 1B.

61. Joe Shreve, 'Famous Alumni to be Honored,' *Spartan Daily*, 15 May 2005. Add something from Smith's autobiography; John Branch, 'Proper Accord Was on a Slow Track,' *Fresno Bee*, 29 May 2005, C1; Thaai Walker, 'Remembering a Monumental Moment in '68 – SJSU Statue to be Erected to Mark Athletes' Olympic black Power Salute,' *San Jose Mercury News*, 1B.
62. Associated Students Board Minutes, 28 September 2005. See 'Fists of Freedom: The Story of the '68 Summer Games,' HBO/Black Canyon Productions, 1999; also see 'Fields of Fire: Sports in the 60s,' HBO/Black Canyon Productions, 1995. Becky Bartindale, 'SJSU Homecoming Celebrations Aim to Reconnect Alums,' *San Jose Mercury News*, 15 October 2005, 1B.
63. Cheeto Barrera, 'Statue Set to be Unveiled Today,' *Spartan Daily*, 16 October 2005.
64. http://www.nbc11.com/news/5118518/detail.html. Retrieved 1 November 2006; John Crumpacker, 'Olympic Protest: Smith and Carlos Statue Captures Sprinters' Moment, San Jose State Honors Protest of Oppression,' *San Francisco Chronicle*, 18 October 2005, C2; Becky Bartindale, 'Honoring Activism – SJSU Unveils Statue Marking Athletes' black Power Salute at 1968 Olympics,' *San Jose Mercury News*, 18 October 2005, 1B; 'SJSU Statue is a Fitting Tribute – Medalists Showed Power of Courage,' San Jose Mercury News, 18 October 2005, 16A.
65. 2005, ABC7/KGO-TV/DT. http://abclocal.go.com/kgo/story?section=local&id=3544925&ft=print. Retrieved 1 November 2005. Mark Purdy, 'He's Still Standing – Aussie Athletes Also Made Statement for Human Rights,' *San Jose Mercury News*, 16 October 2005, 1D; Mike Wise, 'The Third Man in the Middle,' *New York Times*, 17 September 2000. For an excellent analysis of Norman's absence in photographs of the event, as well as his absence from Rigo 23's statue of the gesture, see Osmond, 'Photographs, Materiality and Sport History: Peter Norman and the 1968 Mexico City Black Power Salute,' pp. 119–37.
66. Cheeto Barrera, 'Recipients, Audience Pleased with Statue Unveiling,' *Spartan Daily*, 17 October 2005; Ilbra Beitpolous, '1968 a Time of Social Change,' *Spartan Daily*, 17 October 2005; Christina Young, 'Olympic Medalists Discuss the School's Protest History,' *Spartan Daily*, 17 October 2005. Smith writes extensively in his autobiography about the events at San Jose State, and specifically the statue, on pp. 7–19, 238–43; see Smith with Steele, *Silent Gesture*.
67. John Branch, *Fresno Bee*, 29 May 2005.
68. Synthia Sydnor, 'Sport, Celebrity and Liminality,' in Noel Dyck (ed.), *Games, Sports and Culture* (New York: Berg), p. 231.
69. A. Rosenfeld, 'Popularisation and Memory: The Case of Anne Frank,' in P. Hayes (ed.), *Lessons and Legacies: The Meaning of the Holocaust in a Changing World* (Evanston, IL: Northwestern University Press, 1991), p. 277.
70. Judith Dupré, *Monuments: America's History in Art and Memory* (New York: Random House, 2007), p. 7.
71. Smith with Steele, *Silent Gesture*, pp. 252–253.
72. Martha K. Norkunas, *Monuments and Memory: History and Representation in Lowell, Massachusetts* (Washington, DC: Smithsonian Institution Press, 2002), p. 160.

73. Dupré, *Monuments*, p. x.
74. Murray G. Phillips, Mark E. O'Neill, and Gary Osmond, 'Broadening Horizons in Sport History: Films, Photographs and Monuments,' *Journal of Sport History*, 34 (1), Spring 2007, 283–7.
75. Hartmann, *Race, Culture, and the Revolt of the Black Athlete*, p. 267.
76. Dave Zirin, 'When Fists Are Frozen: The Statue of Tommie Smith and John Carlos,' *Common Dreams News Center*, 20 October 2005, http://www.commondreams.org.
77. Hill, 'Racing After Smith and Carlos: Revisiting Those Fists Some Forty Years Hence,' p. 119.
78. Hartmann, *Race, Culture, and the Revolt of the Black Athlete*, pp. xiv, xv.
79. Julienne Malveaux, 'Fall Follies, Myths and Statues,' *Black Issues in Higher Education*, 16 (18), 28 October 1999, 45.
80. Smith with Steele, *Silent Gesture*, p. 252.
81. Jack Olsen as cited in Rosen, *Reconstructing Fame: Sport, Race, and Evolving Reputations*, p. 10.
82. Hartmann, *Race, Culture, and the Revolt of the Black Athlete*, p. 269.
83. Smith with Steele, *Silent Gesture*, p. 41.
84. Austin Murphy, 'Where Are They Now? John Carlos: Forever the Fighter,' *Sports Illustrated*, 14–21 July 2008, 84–6.

9
The D'Oliveira Affair: Cricket, 'Race' and Politics

Rob Steen

In 1968, there occurred one of the greatest controversies in the history of cricket. The England team were due to tour South Africa, a country that held fast to the policy of state racism known as apartheid. There was a clear possibility that Basil D'Oliveira might be picked in the English touring party. Now qualified by residence to play for England, D'Oliveira had been born in South Africa where the colour of his skin had placed him in the administrative category of 'Cape Coloured', meaning that he could not play first-class cricket – the exclusive province of 'whites'. Would the MCC, English cricket's governing body, who were adamant that politics should never influence sport, defer to a racist government? Equally, would the South African state refuse to admit a citizen of a country with whom it had founded the Imperial Cricket Conference in 1909?

D'Oliveira's original omission from the England party led to an outcry in the UK. His inclusion, following the withdrawal of another player, brought cancellation of the tour. Arguments over why this player was originally excluded, and then selected, have raged for 40 years. It has become a case study in the now discredited, but then conventional, doctrine that politics should not intrude upon sport and remains a landmark in the struggle against racism in sport. In 2004, the journalist Peter Oborne published an angry vindication of D'Oliveira (*Basil D'Oliveira: Cricket and Controversy*, London: Time Warner). Oborne is identified with the political right – an index of how established anti-racism in sport has become.

The D'Oliveira Affair remains an important and still widely interrogated moment in the early post colonial politics of a colonial sport. This chapter contends that the political undercurrents that dominated the cricket season of 1968 were such that the England selectors were prepared to lose a Test series against Australia if it meant maintaining sporting relations with apartheid South Africa.

> I come down on the side of honesty, a good honest piece of bungling by good honest men.[1]

Thus did Ted Dexter, sometime England captain and one-time prospective Conservative MP, famously characterize the most important selection meeting in cricket and, perhaps, sporting history. More recently, in the *Sunday Telegraph*, the political columnist Kevin Myers delivered much the same verdict, except that he described the original omission of Basil D'Oliveira from the MCC party to tour South Africa in the winter of 1968–69 as 'cretinous'.[2] And not simply because D'Oliveira's century and priceless final-day wicket had just helped England win the final Test to square the Ashes series. In 2003, *Observer Sport Monthly* named his non-selection among its 'Ten Worst Sporting Decisions'. But were they all too generous?

History tells us D'Oliveira was summoned as a replacement for the supposedly injured Tom Cartwright three weeks after that selection meeting, whereupon South Africa Prime Minister John Vorster denounced the party as 'the team of the Anti-Apartheid Movement' and MCC cancelled the tour, fuelling the sports boycott that ultimately did so much to bring down the most despicable regime of modern times. Not for nothing would Nelson Mandela convey his heartfelt thanks to 'Dolly'.

It is remarkable that no film producer has yet sought to bring this classic political espionage thriller to the screen. Even more than Bodyline, this is assuredly the cricketing tale that demands to be filmed. It had everything: a battle to beat seemingly insurmountable odds, 'race', class, Empire and Third World, spies and bribes, a *deus ex machina* to warm the coldest cockles and a stoical hero to match Gary Cooper in *High Noon*. That said, Sam Mendes, Hollywood's best-known cricket aficionado, could well be casting right now – Denzel Washington in the lead...Michael Gambon as Vorster...Kevin Spacey as Colin Cowdrey...Sir Anthony Hopkins as Cartwright. The problem, of course, is that, 40 years on, the jigsaw still lies incomplete. Over the past few years, while speaking to some of the major figures, my research has thrown up more questions than answers. Most notably: was D'Oliveira's initial non-selection politically motivated? Indeed, could the same be said of his demotion to 12th man for the Lord's Test two months earlier, a pivotal chapter all too often ignored by historians? The evidence is such that the reply in both instances should have a strictly rhetorical, distinctly Jewish bent: 'How could it not?'

At bottom, it was all about power and white supremacy. Cricket in 1968 was still a game dominated by the white elite. England, Australia and South Africa, the founders of the original Imperial Cricket Conference in 1909, had enjoyed double voting rights on international cricket's governing body until 1958, and the first two would retain their hegemony until India's improbable 1983 World Cup triumph paved the way for the game's biggest constituency to assert itself. When the newly formed Republic of South Africa left the Commonwealth in 1961, it continued blithely, with the support of England and the Australasians, to wave away any protests about apartheid by India, Pakistan and the West Indies, none of whom had ever played Test matches against the exclusively white sons of Transvaal and Durban.

The central figure, the noble Basil D'Oliveira, may be viewed, and has been depicted, as the ultimate political pawn, a courageous outsider tossed around by a pair of spiders weaving a complex web of intrigue. Indeed, his autobiography, with no little pathos, begins thus:

> For more years now than I care to remember, one question keeps cropping up. 'If you had the choice', I'm asked, 'where would you like to have been born'? My honest answer is always 'England'. I'm proud of my colour, of what I've achieved for myself and non-whites all over the world and I dearly love my own people in Cape Town – but I can't deny that I would have been a better person and cricketer if I'd been born a coloured Englishman.[3]

A determined Cape Coloured who 'never had a hatred for the white man', the young D'Oliveira excelled with bat and ball, captaining the first tour by a team of non-European South Africans, to Kenya in 1958. Cricket, he believed, would be his path to betterment. The apartheid laws, however, prevented him from being considered for the South African Test XI so he sought a fresh start in England. Enlisting the aid of the BBC cricket commentator John Arlott and favoured by the late withdrawal of the great West Indies fast bowler Wes Hall, he found employment with the Central Lancashire League club Middleton, and brought his young family to England in 1960, soon after the Sharpeville massacre.[4] Acclimatization was far from easy, but by 1964 he was playing in the County Championship for Worcestershire. Subtracting three years from his age to make himself more marketable, he made his Test debut at Lord's two summers later, against the West Indies, whose fielders applauded him after he was run out in freakish circumstances for 27. A number of defiant innings in that series led to regular selection for what proved to be one of the most successful of all England teams. In all, he won 44 Test caps, hitting five centuries and helping his adopted country regain the Ashes in the winter of 1970–71. By the time he retired from the professional game in 1979, he was nothing less than a folk hero, a symbol of possibility and stoical resistance.

The start of the 1968 season, though, found D'Oliveira's Test career in the balance: a poor tour of the Caribbean had seen his focus and form affected by the mounting controversy over the following year's tour of South Africa. In view of the possible repercussions, would he be selected? Finding consolation in alcohol, his tour report was far from blemish-free. Had he written himself out of the script? It would have been enormously convenient for a great many people had he done so.

In the spring and summer of 1968, rebellion was in the air. The civil rights movement in the United States was gaining unprecedented momentum. Martin Luther King was assassinated in Memphis, sending a wave of race riots rippling through the nation; student unrest erupted into violent clashes across Europe, including the worst street fights Paris had witnessed since Liberation in 1944. Muhammad Ali was stripped of his world heavyweight boxing crown after stating, having happily flunked his Army exam, that he had no quarrel with the Vietcong, with whom the United States were at war. Come autumn, in Mexico City, Tommie Smith and John Carlos would hoist their Black Power salutes on the Olympic podium. The growth of the anti-apartheid movement was profoundly in keeping with this climate.

As Thunderclap Newman's No. 1 hit had it in the summer of 1969, there was indeed *Something in the Air*. The spirit of disenchantment, dissent and anarchy was captured and bottled by Lindsay Anderson's film *If . . .* a surreal diatribe against public schools, the class system and pretty much everything about England that the director despised. '[It] took a knife and shoved it right through the heart of the Establishment', recalled its young Yorkshire-born star, Malcolm McDowell.[5] 'This was empire and gentlemanly behaviour and deference and privilege! This is what this whole fucking country is built on! And we went for them.' And if you weren't One Of Us, you could only be One Of Them.

Reviewing Bruce Murray and Christopher Merrett's *Caught Behind: Race and Politics in Springbok Cricket*, Goolam Vahed from the University of KwaZulu-Natal's School of Anthropology supplied the South African context: 'The Sharpeville massacre of March 1960 increased international criticism of South Africa. The leaders of the ANC and

Pan-Africanist Congress (PAC) in exile were buoyed by support from newly independent Third World countries, which pressed for South Africa's exclusion from international sports.' Sport, the authors argue, 'became the soft underbelly of the apartheid regime'. It was easier to target, reasoned Vahed, 'than the might of international capital or military alliances'.[6] Besides, white South Africans were fanatical about it. Yet while the new republic was suspended from international soccer in 1961 and the Olympic Games in 1964, primarily as a consequence of pressure from Communist and Third World countries, England, Australia and New Zealand continued to play in and against South Africa at cricket and rugby union. The latter, according to the sports historian Huw Richards, was 'the cherished game of the National Party's core Afrikaner voters',[7] which may explain why it was first to crack: New Zealand Maoris were permitted to tour as All Blacks in 1970. The home nation's selection policies did not waver, however, prompting Ken Gray, New Zealand's best prop forward, to retire. Cricket appealed to those of Anglo-Saxon rather than Dutch stock, and was hence less integral to the pursuit of apartheid (apartheid having been established by the ruling – and Dutch-descended – Afrikaner Nationalist Party), but was still run along strictly separatist lines. In 1970, the same year it was banished from the Davis Cup tennis competition and the IOC, South Africa embarked on a 21-year Test cricket exile; the following year, the United Nations backed a general sports boycott.

The teenaged Peter Hain, whose liberal parents had fled South Africa for England in 1966, was already *au fait* with some of this political terrain. During his campaign for Labour's deputy leadership in May 2007, the then Secretary of State for Northern Ireland recalled being 'outraged' by D'Oliveira's non-selection. So much so, it would lead him to form the successful 'Stop the 70 Tour' campaign that would keep the South African cricket team from British shores. 'Most Anti-Apartheid activists didn't care about sport,' Hain believes. 'By [August 1968] I was 18 and a rank-and-file activist. I'd already seen D'Oliveira bat for England at Lord's and The Oval: his story touched me very closely. So when he was excluded I was outraged. All I was aware of was John Arlott writing an article in the *Guardian* for which the headline read something like 'Nobody will believe D'Oliveira was omitted for cricketing reasons. *Everyone* knew there was more to it.'[8]

'FAR MORE IS KNOWN about the cabinet meetings of Harold Wilson, or the activities of the secret service in Moscow, or the details of the Poseidon nuclear missile programme, than what the England selectors said and did that night.'[9] So reckoned D'Oliveira's biographer, the Conservative political commentator and *Daily Mail* columnist Peter Oborne, referring to the original selection meeting on August 28 that excluded D'Oliveira. Curiously, the minutes, never made public, have reportedly disappeared, though Donald Carr, the man who says he 'probably wrote them', assured one interviewer that they never went missing at all. What is certain is that, if they were *ever* written, this crucial piece of evidence has been expertly kept from the public domain.

Oborne also contends that there was 'at least one spy' in the room, 'feeding information straight back to the South African Cricket Association (SACA), whence it was instantly passed back on to [South African Prime Minister John] Vorster.'[10] The 'clinching' evidence? A private letter sent by the SACA convenor of selectors Arthur Coy, a policeman by profession, to Vorster a week after the party was chosen, promising the 'inside story' of the MCC meetings and stating that D'Oliveira was still a candidate. For all his remarkably philosophical reflections down the years, and his kindly, if *naïve*, refusal to believe that his captain, the famously indecisive Colin Cowdrey, who loathed bearing bad tidings, did not back his selection as promised (all the evidence, even Cowdrey's own, is to the contrary), D'Oliveira's immediate thoughts were of racism and political footballs. 'I was like a zombie,' he would attest. 'The stomach had been kicked out of me. I remember thinking, "You just can't beat the white South Africans"'.[11]

There were at least ten men in that committee room that long night of 27–28 August, in addition to any spy. Or spies. The four Test selectors, Doug Insole (chairman of the panel since 1965), Alec Bedser, Don Kenyon and Peter May; tour manager Les Ames; captain Cowdrey; Billy Griffith and Donald Carr, respectively MCC secretary and assistant secretary; MCC president Arthur Gilligan, a former member of the British Union of Fascists; and the treasurer Gubby Allen, Insole's predecessor as chairman of selectors, a former England captain and long the most powerful figure in English cricket, whose objections to D'Oliveira, he insisted, were on purely cricketing grounds. Bedser would co-found the right-wing Freedom Association, part-funded by the Pretorian government (though his artlessness and naivety were both confirmed in 1977 when, after the Commonwealth prime ministers announced the Gleneagles Declaration imposing a sporting ban on South Africa, he wondered: 'What's a golf course got to do with it?'[12]); May's wife's uncle was Arthur Gilligan; Insole's commitment to the game was such that he spent the next four decades as a quasi-, if benign, Henry Kissinger figure, a shuttle diplomat determined that cricket should always defeat politics, that the show should always go on. In a 41-page chapter about MCC's

1956–57 tour of South Africa[13] in a book wherein the author thought nothing of devoting another chapter exclusively to the idiosyncrasies and sins of the press, Insole contented himself with precisely one sentence about the political climate: 'The maintenance of interest in the game is vital to the Board of Control, which is handicapped by the fact that because of the colour problem South Africa has infrequent visits from touring sides, who do most to keep interest alive.' Of those present, only Kenyon – the former captain of Worcestershire, D'Oliveira's county club, and hence perhaps slightly biased in his favour – could not be considered a member of the establishment.

Allen remains the key figure. Not only did he have business interests in South Africa, but his diary of the 1936–37 Ashes tour revealed him to be something of a racist. After various sightings of aboriginals at railway stations along the Nullarbor Plain, he had noted: 'They really are a ghastly sight and the sooner they die out the better.'[14]

Some in that committee room, if not all, were privy to the fact that, five months earlier, Vorster had informed Lord Cobham, England's senior Viscount, that there would be no tour should D'Oliveira be chosen (their meeting did not become public knowledge until the following year). As a snapshot of Olde Tory England, under threat from women in trouser suits and boardrooms, long-haired pop stars, the erosion of deference to alleged elders and betters, a Yorkshire accent at No. 10 and a Labour government with a couple of socialist policies, it was perfect. The greatest irony was that Vorster evidently regarded MCC as Harold Wilson's loony-lefty poodle.

But back to Allen. On 5 January 1968, relates Professor Murray, whose tireless research at the National Archives in Pretoria informed Oborne's book, 'the MCC had written to the [South African Cricket Association] requesting assurances, and Sir Alec Douglas-Home, the shadow home secretary and recent MCC President, was briefed to assess the situation concerning D'Oliveira during his discussions in February with Vorster and with SACA officials. Hitherto it has always been asserted, including by the MCC, that the MCC never received a reply from SACA to its inquiry. This is not correct. A reply dated 1 March 1968 was taken personally to Lord's by Jack Cheetham, vice-chairman of the SACA. On 6 March a copy was also handed to Vorster by Arthur Coy'.[15] It was what the letter didn't say that reveals most. There was no assurance that any MCC team would be permitted to tour; no mention of the attitude of the Vorster Government, or whether it had been consulted. And it was on the advice of Gubby Allen that the letter was never submitted to the MCC Committee, in case its contents were 'twisted and leaked to the press'.[16] Instead, Cheetham was advised by Allen and Billy Griffith that SACA 'need not answer their letter and it has been agreed to continue with the normal preparations and negotiations that are necessary when a tour is due to take place'. The South African Tour subcommittee, chaired by Insole, was instructed to proceed but not discuss '(a) Rhodesia [another former British territory in Africa governed by a white minority], or (b) D'Oliveira', and instead await 'direction.'[17]

Jon Gemmell has highlighted the mutual interests of Whitehall and Pretoria, Lord's and The Wanderers. 'The two countries had been traditionally tied in the Cold War alliance by the twines of trade, political interest, culture, blood and a sense of sacrifice through war. It was considered with contempt that politics within the arena of the cricket field could potentially damage this relationship.'[18]

Viewing sport as 'one of the most effective bridges in linking people',[19] and for all his antipathy towards apartheid, Cowdrey had had little hesitation in accepting the England captaincy for the tour of South Africa albeit only, he would subsequently reveal, after requesting assurances that there would be no political interference in selection. Yet he would later write: 'Whatever we might think about apartheid, at least it seems to work in their country; it is none of our business.'[20] Indeed, come 1976, he was forgiveness personified: 'They have had enough of the admonishing finger.'

Cowdrey's role and influence should not be underestimated. When Vorster decreed that his tour party was unwelcome, he wanted to hop straight on a plane to the Republic and talk the PM round. 'I had been at the heart of things throughout,' he would write, 'and could answer every question.'[21] One of the era's most influential, complex and contradictory cricketers, Cowdrey was the son of a tea plantation manager, perceived as a gentleman amateur but in essence a pro – or, as Oborne prefers, 'a member of the deracinated imperial middle-class'.[22] He wanted the tour to go ahead, just as he would urge that the projected visit by South Africa two summers hence should proceed. 'I cannot reconcile an isolation policy and boycott with the Christian ethic,' he would tell the *Daily Mail* in 1970.[23]

One who begged to differ was Cowdrey's one-time England colleague and captaincy rival, the Reverend David Sheppard, who was about to be anointed Bishop of Woolwich and had refused to play against South Africa in 1960 on grounds of conscience. Not that there was any unanimity in the Church of England on this issue. When the *Sunday Times* polled the diocesan Bishops in February 1970 about that summer's abortive South African tour, 13 of the 20 who commented thought it should go ahead yet 16 favoured anti-apartheid demonstrations. The Bishop of Southwell, the Rt Rev Gordon Savage, proffered a bright idea: 'Let the South Africans tour Britain as "The Apartheid Team".'[24]

Donald Carr insists that, contrary to all previous assertions, D'Oliveira's candidacy dominated the selection meeting. Other than that Kenyon spoke up for D'Oliveira and Cowdrey, contrary to his personal assurances to Basil, against, nobody knows definitively who voted which way, much less why, though Carr's experience was probably a common one. 'I was genuinely talked around,' he says.[25]

The most neglected aspect of this story, one that Oborne conceded he should have pursued further, is D'Oliveira's other non-selection, earlier in the summer, for the England side for the second Ashes Test at Lord's. Although he had just returned from a poor tour of the Caribbean, his first for England, he had been picked for the opening Test at Old Trafford. In a surprise and heavy defeat against opponents England were expected to beat with ease, he was one of only two home players to emerge with credit, making an unbeaten 87 in the second innings; no other England batsman reached 50 in the entire match. Come Lord's, he was 12th man.

On cricketing grounds, only hindsight justifies this. Rain scotched England's hopes of a series-levelling win at Lord's but D'Oliveira's replacement, Barry Knight, took three cheap wickets as Australia were hustled out for 78, their lowest Ashes total for 30 years. So far as most were concerned, the selection had been vindicated. D'Oliveira would remain in the cold until the late withdrawal of Roger Prideaux, a batsman, on the eve of the final Test at The Oval. It was there that Dolly promised his wife a century and duly delivered it, which in turn led to a public outcry when he was excluded from the South African party.

Wary that England had been fatally cautious in Manchester and desperate to make amends in the 200th Anglo-Australian Test, captain Colin Cowdrey wanted a seam bowler such as Tom Cartwright (who was injured) or Knight for Lord's, not a swing bowler like D'Oliveira. But what on earth were the selectors doing going into an Ashes series – a contest England hadn't won for a dozen years – with D'Oliveira as first-change? D'Oliveira was a gentle medium-pace bowler, a partnership-breaker not an initiative-taker.

No fewer than five changes were made for the Lord's Test, as Doug Insole reminded me somewhat defensively in 2007, even then smarting from what he remembers as the 'massacre at Manchester'.[26] And no, he insisted, D'Oliveira was not dropped on anything other than cricketing grounds. Yet this remains every bit as worthy of scrutiny as his overlooking in August, maybe more so. After all, it was made under similarly pressurized circumstances, carried no more cricketing justification and was even more politically expedient.

Stoking D'Oliveira's suspicions was a 'curious' incident at the eve-of-Test dinner. 'A top cricket official,' he would write, said the only way the tour could be saved would be if he announced he was unavailable for *England* but would like to play for *South Africa*. 'I was staggered,' related D'Oliveira, and angrily said: 'Either you respect me as an England player or you don't. The next day an eminent cricket writer put the same proposition to me.'[27] He was too discreet to say so, but the 'official' was Billy Griffith, the 'eminent cricket writer' EW Swanton of the *Daily Telegraph*, Gubby Allen's confidante and biographer. Swanton was the same correspondent who, curiously, would lament D'Oliveira's initial omission from the winter tour party.

One of the tour's archest proponents was Charles Lyttleton, the 10th Viscount Cobham, whose previous offices included Lord Steward, Governor of New Zealand, captain of Worcestershire and, just like his father and grandfather before him, MCC president. He had been targeted as a receptive conduit by Coy. Thus it was that Cobham, whose mother hailed from South Africa and who had extensive business interests there, was summoned, while visiting in March, to meet John Vorster, who told him the tour would be scrapped were D'Oliveira chosen. Which rather belied an assertion by Sir Alec Douglas-Home to MCC three weeks earlier that no answer could be given to 'a hypothetical question'.[28]

Advised by Gubby Allen, Cobham relayed the information on a need-to-know basis. Had he simply written to Griffith, as he might normally have done, Griffith would have been obliged to pass the news on to the club, whose official position, encouraged by the ruling Labour Party, was that no interference in selection would be tolerated. Had Cobham acted thus, the tour would almost certainly have been called off then and there. In 1998, the former England captain and Bishop of Liverpool, David Sheppard, recalled to me how he had cut short a visit to Belgium when he heard of D'Oliveira's non-selection for the tour. He decided to call Cobham to see whether anyone, as he put it, 'might want to take up the cudgels on Dolly's behalf'. When the pair met, recalled Sheppard, '[Cobham] was wildly indiscreet'.[29] Thus did he learn of Cobham's audience with Vorster. Was it purely coincidental, then, that several South African grandees were due in London for the Lord's Test, including Coy? It was to Lord Cobham's box that Coy repaired.

It should be stressed that D'Oliveira was not informed of his exclusion from England's Lord's XI until the opening morning, that is after Griffith and Swanton's proposals. Was this his punishment for spurning their advances? The backlash was strong, even vicious. The 'cynics', noted Cowdrey, 'refused to believe that D'Oliveira's exit was not some sort of fascist plot'. Letters 'rolled in'.[30] It is hard to avoid the conclusion that picking D'Oliveira to play in front of Coy and other South Africans would have sent a provocative and contradictory message when the aim of MCC – as further evidenced by Griffith and Swanton's attempts to dissuade D'Oliveira from touring – was so plainly conciliation.

By way of emphasizing fate's conspicuous role in the saga, it is worth mentioning that, had Barry Knight not injured an ankle at Leyton a few days earlier, he, and not D'Oliveira, would have played at The Oval. While still officially a secret, says Knight,[31] rumours about Vorster's stance had reached the county dressing rooms. 'We'd heard, certainly by then, that he'd said the team wouldn't be welcome there if Dolly was included. We thought the MCC didn't have the guts to pick him. When the tour party was first announced, I thought "They're as weak as gnat's piss. They're kow-towing to Vorster." The pros were revulsed. It was always them and us. We thought [the former chairman of selectors] Walter Robins was mad and Gubby Allen was a bleedin' snob. He was a bit of an idiot, a bit up himself. And Basil was one of us'.[32]

When I showed my findings to Professor Murray, he had one major reservation. Did I really want to publicly accuse the England selectors of risking losing to Australia to keep the South Africans sweet?[33] I admitted that I hadn't considered it that way but yes, I am prepared to make that inference.

Enter Geoffrey Howard. Shortly after D'Oliveira was finally dismissed at The Oval, the Surrey secretary's phone rang. 'The caller was on the line from Prime Minister Vorster's office in Pretoria,' recalled Howard. 'A fellow called Tiene Oosthuizen...a director of Rothmans, based in South Africa, and he'd been trying to contact [Billy] Griffith..."I can't get hold of him [Oosthuizen said], so will you take a message to the selectors. Tell them that, if today's centurion is picked, the tour will be off".'[34] That same afternoon, a well-informed prediction was filed to *The Guardian* by Louis Duffus, South Africa's pre-eminent cricket writer, whose history of cricket in the Republic, published by the SACA, would, tellingly, eschew any mention of black players. To him, D'Oliveira was 'politically motivated and an opportunist with an axe to grind'. 'If D'Oliveira is selected,' he wrote from The Oval, 'South Africa are unlikely to host the MCC tour...'

Tiene Oosthuizen had delivered another message from Pretoria after the Lord's Test, offering the confused and troubled D'Oliveira a long-term coaching job in the Republic, at a salary that would probably secure his family's financial future, if he declared himself unavailable, and duly courted him until late August. D'Oliveira, though, had declined. As he told the *Sunday Mirror* nearly 30 years later, he wanted 'to prove that I could bat and that people from the black and coloured community, whatever you like to call it, know how to conduct themselves'.[35]

'No way I'm saying that Geoffrey [Howard] didn't tell me of Pretoria's telephone warning', replied Insole after *The Guardian*'s Frank Keating had brought Howard's recollection to his attention in 2001, 'but, frankly, I don't recall it specifically because at that time every Tom, Dick and Harry was saying what would happen if we didn't pick a certain someone. All I remember is opening a very long meeting by saying "Gentlemen, forget South Africa, let's just choose the best MCC cricket team..."'[36]

'I think I believed in, or was talked into believing, that it was all on cricketing grounds,' concedes Donald Carr. 'There had been so much chatter about it. I think there were people high up in the cricketing hierarchy in England who were talking a lot about it and knew what the possibilities could be.'[37]

The latest substantial piece of the jigsaw only emerged with the publication in May 2007 of Stephen Chalke's biography of Tom Cartwright, for whom D'Oliveira was a late replacement in the party for South Africa, and who died shortly after the book was published. I had interviewed him by phone a few months earlier, ostensibly on another topic. I had been utterly unable, that said, to resist congratulating him on what I had long suspected to have been his conscience-driven withdrawal from the 1968–69 South African tour party, a suspicion reinforced by our mutual friend, the *Guardian* journalist David Foot, who had written a discreetly revealing chapter about Cartwright in his book *Fragments of Idolatry*. At the time, Cartwright sounded sheepish, parrying my interpretation and insisting that, in discussing his replacement with Cowdrey, D'Oliveira had never been mentioned. A few months later we were due to talk about Chalke's book, at Cartwright's request. Apparently, for all his evasiveness during that pre-Christmas conversation, now the book was due to be published he wanted to be more expansive. It remains my biggest regret as a journalist that I did not make that call more speedily. Happily, I did receive confirmation of this twist from another source.

The long-stated cause of Cartwright's withdrawal from the South Africa tour party was a shoulder injury, but there were more extenuating causes. For one, his young son was fed up seeing him spend winters overseas. What seems to have most affected Cartwright, though, was 'a little news item' in the *Daily Express*, which reported that, when the party was announced on August 28, National Party members at a congress in Bloemfontein stood and cheered. 'When I read that,' he recalled, 'I went cold. And I started to wonder whether I wanted to be part of it.'[38]

Murray and Merrett elaborate: 'As J H P Serfontein, political correspondent of the *Sunday Times*, reported "Mr Vorster received the most frenzied and enthusiastic ovations a Nationalist Prime Minister has received in many years". He added: "I regard this reaction of the audience as evidence of the relief felt by rank-and-file Nationalists who have been worried over stories that Mr Vorster was a 'liberal' and that his outward policy would affect apartheid". It was Serfontein who revealed, in the *Sunday Times* of 22 September, the government's decision not to allow D'Oliveira to tour with the MCC even if he had been selected in the first instance. He had, he wrote, been told this by Nationalists "very close to the Party leadership". Serfontein represented the decision as a strategic political victory for Vorster, making his position as National Party leader "impregnable"... For all that, the D'Oliveira affair was a significant, if temporary, setback for Vorster's new sports policy. His first attempt at "liberalization" had failed, and it was a failure that helped ensure South Africa's cricketing isolation. What enabled Vorster to disguise his retreat was the MCC's mishandling of D'Oliveira's selection. Had D'Oliveira been selected in the first instance, Vorster's new sports policy [to relax the regulations governing segregated sports] would have been exposed as hollow. [South African Sport Minister] Frank Waring had already prepared a statement to announce the cancellation of the tour in the event of D'Oliveira's selection. The statement largely reflected Nationalist paranoia. Its thrust was that "it would be naïve... on anybody's part to maintain that there had been no political intervention, not only in this MCC team but also in cricket generally".'[39]

Cartwright, who had toured South Africa four winters earlier, was an unusual cricketer: politically aware, a proud and vocal Labourite. The flight to the Republic coincided with Polling Day during the 1964 General Election; when he saw the Tory MP Quintin Hogg drive up Baker Street campaigning with a loudhailer, he shook his fist and 'shouted something'. In South Africa he and the team had had tea with Henrik Verwoerd, the father of apartheid, but what lingered longer was seeing the conditions under which Joe, his driver and a Cape Coloured, lived. When he took his mother to her brother's hotel in Paarl, Cartwright related, he had to drop her at the front and go round the rear entrance himself. 'That was mind-boggling to me, how people could be so inhuman. It was a country without any human dignity at all.'[40]

Peter Hain confirmed this fresh angle. 'Ironically, Tom Cartwright became a constituent of mine in Neath, where he'd moved to and married a local girl. In 1991, my son Drake was training with Glamorgan youth, whom he was coaching, and we became friends. He told me that his "injury" was not the reason he pulled out. Basically, he told the selectors he wouldn't be fit, but the point was, he didn't want to go'.[41]

By any standards, the switch to D'Oliveira after Cartwright's withdrawal was a leap and a half. Substituting a batsman who bowled a bit (D'Oliveira) for a bowler who batted a bit (Cartwright) made little sense – unless one interprets the decision as an attempt to curry public favour and/or correct the perceived error of 28 August, when his exclusion was explained away on the ground that he offered little as a bowler. What made his eventual selection even more curious was a conversation Cartwright had with Cowdrey while the captain was trying to persuade him to tour. Even if he did fail to regain fitness in South Africa, Cowdrey said, there would be adequate replacements on hand from the ranks of English coaching in the Republic, notably Yorkshire's Don Wilson, a spinner.[42]

'I think some people [at the original selection meeting] put a lot of onus on Dolly's poorish tour of the Caribbean, maybe unfairly,' says Donald Carr. '[When Cartwright pulled out] we decided that Dolly was the best bet, but it all looked so fearful. I felt that it had not been very well handled. I don't think anyone supported apartheid. A lot of people believed in cricket.'[43] While unsure how well his memory serves him, Carr hints at yet more subterfuge: 'I think the MCC committee decided we should take this line, to leave or not to include Dolly as a political challenge to South Africa.'[44] For which one interpretation, arguably the only one, is: the original decision to exclude him was done to placate South Africa.

That the MCC and the SACA colluded seems eminently possible, attested the then South Africa-based journalist and author Trevor Chesterfield.[45] 'Especially,' he wrote, 'if private papers are to be believed. The papers support the document shown to [me] by Ben Schoeman, a member of the Vorster cabinet which made the decision to ban D'Oliveira.' That decision was taken on 27 August, just hours before the MCC selection meeting. 'Not all were in favour,' reported Chesterfield. 'Had it not been for a growing right wing revolt there could have been several dissenters. If what Schoeman said could be taken at face value... [Jack Cheetham] was deliberately leaked a report citing reasons for the banning should it be necessary. Not only would Dolly's selection cut across a variety of apartheid laws; it would lead also to an intolerable situation and the anti-apartheid movement would capitalise on Basil's presence.'

Chesterfield suspects that the 'spy' in the committee room was EW Swanton, a friend and later biographer of Gubby Allen. 'My own feeling, and I had this suspicion grow because of the affiliation between E W Swanton and Gubby Allen, is that it was Swanton, fed by Allen. The background to this was the link between Swanton and Coy and the man who Coy fed all his SACA information to, Louis Duffus, a white ant in the woodpile. I first met Duffus in 1960 during the South African tour of England and again in 1963–64 when on tour of Australia as an extra hand needed to do reports for AAP. It was while in Sydney 1963 that I realised to an extent Duffus was a racist when he refused to share a lift with a couple of African types (West Indians I think) who stepped in two floors from the ground and decided to take the stairs for reason of exercise. Earlier in that tour, I recall Garry Sobers scoring a nifty century [for South Australia] against South Africa and Eddie Barlow and Peter Pollock were full of admiration – Duffus dismissed it, and from memory, as "an innings quantified by moments of fortune and several fielding errors and he fed on missed chances. It isn't one to remember and of no genuine significance. Certainly Australia have more masterful batsmen in their ranks than this West Indian." He was chided at dinner that night for his comments by Jack Fingleton.'[46]

It is hard not to conclude that the key decisions that summer – the Lord's XI and the tour party – were taken in part by men with vested interests in keeping D'Oliveira out of his homeland, notably Gubby Allen. Or that others who were party to the tour selection thought they were acting honourably, and wholly in cricket's interests, when in reality their deliberations, whether consciously or not, were inevitably compromised, by knowledge of the likely repercussions. It would have been unnatural had it been otherwise. Even so, Ted Dexter's talk of 'honest bungling' seems *naïve* at best. When, in response to D'Oliveira's original non-selection, David Sheppard called for a Special General Meeting of the MCC, the committee, led by Aidan Crawley (a television executive and former MP) and Dennis Silk (a public school headmaster and ex-captain of Somerset), responded that South Africa's domestic policies were no concern of the club, stressing once more the primacy of the game. 'This,' argues Gemmell, 'was a firm endorsement of the doctrine that politics should not mix with sport in any situation,' which 'by definition, was a political position.'⁴⁷ Crawley, in fact, had been an MP for both major parties, while Silk revelled in the third name of 'Whitehall'. The 'Lord's-centred elite' were not, argued Murray and Merrett, 'the helpless victim of the political intervention of the apartheid regime but a willing collaborator with the government in enforcing segregation on the cricket field. White cricket generally showed no interest in promoting black cricket or in pursuing the notion of non-racial cricket.'⁴⁸

The bottom line seems plain: when moral fibre was called for, the lords of English cricket, and their friends in high places – often one and the same – offered a masterclass in self-preservation. Griffith and Swanton's overtures and D'Oliveira's exclusion from the Lord's Test XI were early indications of how far those lords were prepared to go, and what was to come when the party to South Africa was picked. It is worth recalling, too, that 1968 was the year the MCC ceded its traditional power over English cricket to the Test and County Cricket Board: was all this a final flexing of muscles?

Lest we forget, however, there was a happy ending. That Oval victory marked the fourth in England's record unbeaten sequence of 26 Tests, the triumphant Ashes tour of 1970–71 the centrepiece; D'Oliveira, once recalled, was an ever-present and vital cog, scoring four centuries, most notably a match-saving 114 against Pakistan in Dacca, in addition to breaking many a stubborn partnership. Wherever he played, however he fared, the affection, of crowds, teammates and opponents, was unmistakeable. The 1972 Ashes series proved his international farewell but he continued serving Worcestershire until the end of the decade. A stand at the club's home ground, New Road, would be named after him. At the opening of the 2003 World Cup in Cape Town, he was included in a parade honouring South Africa's 50 greatest sportspeople: considerable recognition for someone who had only ever represented his country in the symbolic sense. His tale, warranted John Arlott in 1980, 'is the ultimate success story. It provides comfort and hope for non-white-skinned people of many races in South Africa; offering them evidence that no government can completely cut off their right to prove themselves. This is not simply a matter of sport. There have been few comparable achievements in any field.'⁴⁹

Let us give thanks, then, to misguided men in old school ties, Barry Knight's dodgy ankle, the *Daily Express* – and Tom Cartwright's conscience. The unexpurgated truth, however, may take another 40 years to emerge. And that may be a conservative estimate. Roll those cameras.

Notes

1. Peter Ball and David Hopps, *The Book of Cricket Quotations*, Stanley Paul.
2. Kevin Myers, 'The African anarch v the anoraks of cricket', *Sunday Telegraph* 28 November, 2004.
3. Basil D'Oliveira, *Time to Declare*, JM Dent, 1980.
4. On 21 March, 1960, 69 black South Africans were killed and 180 wounded by police (some shot while trying to flee) in what came to be known as The Sharpeville Massacre. Organized by the Pan-Africanist Congress and Nelson Mandela's African National Congress, between 5000 and 7000 people had gathered at the police station in the township of Sharpeville to stage a purportedly 'peaceful' protest against the pass laws that constrained their movement in white areas. The police were highly apprehensive, not knowing what to expect. When the crowd began pelting them with stones, retaliation was extreme. Eyewitnesses said men, women and children fled 'like rabbits' as up to 300 officers began randomly shooting. Three days later, the government banned all public meetings in 24 magisterial districts and on 8 April the PAC and the ANC were banned and a state of emergency declared. The following September, 224 people lodged civil claims but the government responded by introducing the Indemnity Act that relieved all officials of any responsibility for the Sharpeville atrocities. No police officer was ever convicted.
5. *The Word* magazine, August 2007.
6. Goolam Vahed, 'More than a Pastime: Cricket, Culture, and Society in South Africa'(http://www.h-net.msu.edu/reviews/showpdf.php?id=10533).
7. Huw Richards, *A Game for Hooligans*, Mainstream, 2006.
8. Interview with author, May 2007.
9. Peter Oborne, *Basil D'Oliveira – Cricket and Conspiracy: The Untold Story*, Little, Brown, 2004.
10. Ibid.
11. D'Oliveira (1980).
12. Frank Keating, 'Arlott's imperishable voice will never be forgotten', *The Guardian*, 10 December, 2001.
13. Douglas Insole, *Cricket From the Middle*, Heinemann, 1960.
14. Brian Rendell, *Gubby Under Pressure: Letters From Australia, New Zealand and Hollywood*, ACS Publications, 2008.
15. Bruce Murray and Christopher Merrett, *Caught Behind: Race and Politics in Springbok Cricket*, Wits University Press, 2004.
16. Ibid.
17. Ibid.
18. Jon Gemmell, *The Politics of South African Cricket*, Routledge, 2004.
19. Colin Cowdrey, *MCC: The Autobiography of a Cricketer*, Hodder & Stoughton, 1976.
20. Ibid.
21. Ibid.
22. Oborne (2004).
23. Ibid.
24. John Lovesey, Nicholas Mason and Edwin Taylor (eds), *The Sunday Times Sports Book*, World's Work, 1979.

25. Interviewed by Richard Evans, March 2007.
26. Letter to author, March 2007.
27. D'Oliveira (1980).
28. Oborne (2004).
29. Interview with author, 1998, quoted in *This Sporting Life – Cricket*, David & Charles, 1999.
30. Cowdrey (1976).
31. Interview with author, March 2007.
32. Ibid.
33. Email to author, November 2007.
34. Stephen Chalke, *At the Heart of English Cricket: The Life and Memories of Geoffrey Howard*, Fairfield Books, 2001.
35. Mike Langley, 'Hello Dolly...', *Sunday Mirror*, July 7, 1996.
36. Frank Keating, 'Arlott's imperishable voice will never be forgotten', *The Guardian*, 10 December, 2001.
37. Interviewed by Richard Evans, www.overtimeonline.co.uk, March 2007
38. Stephen Chalke, *Tom Cartwright – The Flame Still Burns*, Fairfield Books, 2007.
39. Murray and Merrett (2004).
40. Chalke (2007).
41. Interview with author, May 2007.
42. Interview with author, December 2006.
43. Interviewed by Richard Evans, March 2007.
44. Ibid.
45. Trevor Chesterfield, *Cricket Captains of South Africa* (2003, Zebra Press – unedited manuscript).
46. Email to author, November 2007.
47. Gemmell (2004).
48. Murray and Merrett (2004).
49. D'Oliveira (1980).

10
The Physical Activism of Billie Jean King
Jaime Schultz

Even the most cursory glance at the accolades awarded to Billie Jean King over the years demonstrates that this is a woman who deserves a prominent place in the pantheon of sporting greats. In a tennis career spanning four decades, she amassed 39 Grand Slam titles, including 20 Wimbledon and 13 US Open crowns. Yet, her legacy transcends the sports world. 'Very likely,' mused venerated sportswriter Frank Deford in 1975, she 'will go down in history as the most significant athlete of this century. That is not said lightly. But then few athletes ever reach beyond their games to exert any dominion over the rest of society.'[1] Indeed, a recent spate of tributes indicates the depth and breadth of her influence. Of the 100 Most Important Americans of the Twentieth Century, for instance, *Life* magazine included just four athletes: Babe Ruth, Jackie Robinson, Muhammad Ali, and King. In 2006, the United States Tennis Association rededicated its National Tennis facility as the Billie Jean King National Tennis Centre. Host to the US Open, the New York site is the largest and most eminent sports venue named for a woman. Three years later, President Obama decorated King with the Medal of Freedom, 'America's highest civilian honor... awarded to individuals who make an especially meritorious contribution to the security or national interests of the United States, world peace, cultural or other significant public or private endeavors.'[2]

As such, Billie Jean King does not constitute a 'milestone' in sport. Instead, her biography is made up of more significant milestones than almost any other athlete in history. To trace from one episode to the next is to sketch a constellation worthy of astronomical study. I have therefore limited the scope of this chapter to focus on a series of events that took place from 1970 to 1973. The story of women's tennis during these years, suggests historian Angela Lumpkin, 'could almost be described as the history of Billy Jean King.'[3] And, as King writes, 'Women's tennis players made greater gains in the three years between 1970 and 1973 than in the thirty previous years combined.'[4] These dates mark a definitive era that began with the formation of the separatist Virginia Slims tour and ended with a powerful triumvirate: the formation of the Women's Tennis Association (WTA), equal prize money for men and women at the U.S. Open, and King's 'Battle of the Sexes' match against Bobby Riggs.

This delimitation unfortunately omits many important aspects of King's *résumé* including her roles in establishing *womenSports* magazine, the Women's Sports Foundation, and World Team Tennis. The temporal focus of this essay also crops out much discussion of King's sexuality. Though it was during the early 1970s that King shared a now infamous relationship with Marilyn Barnett, it was not until 1981, when Barnett sued her for what the press labeled 'galimony,' that she was outed publicly. While she has since become a staunch supporter of gay rights, King first denied the affair with Barnett before conceding that it had been a 'mistake.' Her autobiography, co-written with Deford and released the year after the trial, was a transparent attempt at damage control, which, one could argue, was somewhat understandable considering the number of product endorsements she lost after Barnett's disclosure, not to mention the rampant sexual prejudice in both sport and the wider society. King protested the lesbian 'label' (e.g., 'Marilyn and I were only having an isolated homosexual experience, and...not participating in a full homosexual life-style'; 'Obviously I must be bisexual.'), while asserting affection for her husband and attraction to other men.[5] The book, writes journalist Selena Roberts, 'was a candid lie.'[6]

In spite of the political machinations that may have motivated the authorship of *Billie Jean*, I rely on the manuscript as an important source for this project. In the same way, the 'Billie Jean King party line' on certain topics undoubtedly dominated many interviews she granted the press, masking contentious, unfiltered, or possibly disruptive opinions for the good of the game, as well as for the good of herself.[7] The task here is not to debunk these sources or debate their veracity, but rather to read them for dominance.[8] Taken together, they offer readers a largely cohesive, populist narrative in which a girl from humble beginnings realizes her latent potential to change the game and, in turn, the world.

To this end, I consulted biographies and autobiographies about King, along with books about the history of women's tennis, and sport more generally, that feature her prominently.[9] I also considered several films authorized by King and available to a general viewing public: *When*

Billie Beat Bobby, an ABC-produced account of the 1973 match against Riggs, along with the HBO documentaries *Dare to Compete: The Struggle of Women in Sports* and *Billie Jean King: Portrait of a Champion*.[10] Finally, for an understanding of King's representation during the early 1970s, I surveyed major print media outlets including the *New York Times*, *Washington Post*, *Time*, *Life*, *Newsweek*, and *Sports Illustrated* magazines.

After a brief account of the recurring elements in the pre-1970 Billie Jean King saga, the crux of this essay concerns her articulation with second-wave feminism. I refer to her work during this time as *physical activism*, or the melding of physical activity and political activism. Though sport was not the only way she expressed her insistence on equitable treatment, it provided a powerful technology for affecting social change. Other leaders within the women's movement worked for equality through legal, political, and other cultural streams; however, by demonstrating her physical capabilities and asserting those capabilities worthy of respect, King became an athletic celebrity feminist, reaching segments of the populace that others could not.

The rumblings of greatness

The story of Billie Jean King (*née* Moffitt) typically unfurls in classic rags-to-riches style, though the rags were the hand-sewn shorts in which her mother outfitted her; with riches came one-of-a-kind tennis frocks designed by the legendary Ted Tinling. It began in a Long Beach, California tract home. Billie Jean Moffitt's was a solidly middle-class, conservative upbringing in which her firefighting father and homemaking mother raised their daughter and her younger brother Randy with equal measures of discipline and affection. Ever the 'tomboy,' Billie Jean took to sports. At four years old, 'Dad said he couldn't afford a baseball bat, but he got a piece of wood and carved one for me and I thought it was the greatest thing in the world.'[11] Years later, it was Randy who would actualize a successful career in Major League Baseball. His sister was encouraged to pick a sport more 'appropriate' for girls: golf, swimming, or tennis. 'I didn't swim well and I considered golf an old man's game. But I always liked to run a lot so I chose tennis,' she recalled.[12] Soliciting odd jobs around her neighbourhood, she earned $8 and bought her first racket. The initiation phase of her journey into tennis usually goes something like this: 'The first ball Billie smacked went over the net. She was hooked.'[13]

While her more affluent peers learned the intricacies of the game within the members-only enclave of the country club circuit, Moffitt's inauguration took place via free group lessons on public courts. The prevailing Billie Jean King history regularly pivots on a scene, either apocryphal or prescient, in which she tells her mother that she will someday be the 'Number One tennis player in the world.'[14] She repeats the declaration often – to her minister, her succeeding coach Alice Marble (who took the proclamation as a personal affront), and eventually 'To all who asked.'[15] In later years, King has imbued this compulsion with strategic significance. As she recollected in an HBO documentary, 'I had an epiphany that I was going to change things. I was very clear that unless I was number one, no one was going to listen to me... If god gave me this gift, I was going to do everything in my power to make this world a better place.'[16] This retrospective estimation brings together the various puzzle pieces to form a more coherent image – her future greatness stood on the shoulders of gritty determination and an incontrovertible sense of purpose.

In addition to her modest roots and audacious predictions, there are a number of examples that illustrate Moffitt's sense of 'otherness' in the elite world of tennis. Unable to afford the two-dollar entry fee at her first tournament or to buy her lunch at the clubhouse like the other girls, neither she nor her parents ever quite fit in with 'the stuffy, country club atmosphere that was such a big part of tennis in those days.'[17] One oft-invoked anecdote involves her lack of understanding, and thereby savvy, about appropriate athletic attire. Alternatively framed as 'her first lesson in class discrimination' and a swift schooling in gender bias, she arrived at her initial tournament at the Los Angeles Tennis club in a pair of shorts sewn by her mother.[18] Girls were, apparently, expected to play in tennis skirts and for her transgression she was not permitted in the group photograph.

The story usually ends there, as if to suggest that she bucked convention from the very start of her career and set out to transform tennis: 'Ever since that day when I was eleven years old I wanted to change it. I thought it was just for the rich and just for the white. Ever since that day when I was eleven years old and I wasn't allowed in a photo because I wasn't wearing a tennis skirt, I knew I wanted to change the sport.'[19] Over time, this affirmation has become even stronger, though as Roberts contends, the incident did not ignite an activist fuse, but rather induced adherence to tennis norms. She allegedly 'loved the look' of dresses and, from that day forward, 'Billie was never underdressed again.'[20] Elsewhere, King writes that she encouraged women on the Virginia Slims tour, 'to be as attractive and as feminine as possible... We urge all our members to wear tennis dresses and skirts.'[21] These counter-narratives appear infrequently. Instead, the Billie Jean King mythology is such that her first collision with discrimination sent her down an inevitable and irreversible activist path.

There are other examples these accounts proffer as evidence of her 'misfit status.'[22] While the tennis establishment emphasized decorum and propriety, Moffitt was described as 'brash' and 'plucky.' Against tacit norms, she emoted her exuberance and frustration through her words, facial expressions, and gestures, which grated the sensibilities of the starchier tennis aficionados. She was also hampered by physical limitations. Short in stature, she constantly battled her weight, poor eyesight, and damaged knees, yet the tenacious athlete ploughed her way through shortcomings that might fell a lesser competitor. She was 12 when she won her first tournament. In 1961, at just 17 years old, she and her doubles partner, Karen Hantze, became the youngest team to win a Wimbledon title. That fall, she began classes at Los Angeles State College. Though she continued to play tennis, there was little reward or recognition for women athletes.

At L.A. State, she met Larry King, a blond, handsome, tennis playing, biochemistry major. The man who would become her husband is the individual most often credited with raising her feminist consciousness. He reportedly enlightened her as they strolled through campus in the early 1960s: 'I'm the seventh man on a six-man team, but why do I get the grant and you don't? I'm a boy. You're the biggest name at the school, and you can't get anything because you're a girl.'[23] She often reflects that this is the moment that began to sharpen her acuity towards gender biases.

Moffitt dropped out of college in 1964 and spent several months in Australia honing her skills and revamping her game. The following year, she married Larry. The year after that, she won her first Wimbledon title and accomplished her goal of becoming the top player in women's tennis.

In the late 1960s, the International Lawn Tennis Federation (ILTF) insisted that players retain their amateur status to compete in Grand Slam events, the Davis, Wightman, and Federation Cups, and other notable competitions. 'The system,' wrote King, 'was infuriating and riddled with hypocrisy. The same officials who made the rules about amateurism literally bribed us to play in their tournaments.'[24] She, like the others, collected under-the-table payments to support herself, all the while stridently decrying the practice of 'shamateurism,' much to the chagrin of the United States Lawn Tennis Association (USLTA).[25] Incited by fears that the top players would turn professional and deplete the amateur ranks, the ILTF voted for open tennis in 1968.

Described as an 'unabashed antielitist,' King's keen awareness of social injustices became the hallmark of her career. As sportswriter Robert Lipsyte characterized, 'Her reputation for being "controversial," however, did not come from an early feminist position but from an unselfconscious populism that was so exotic in tennis.'[26] Her efforts to usher in tennis' Open Era, in addition to other activist and community-based projects, helped to popularize and democratize the game from which she often felt ostracized. And whether or not she initially exhibited an 'early feminist position,' once athletes earnings were no longer paid clandestinely, no one could fail to notice the imbalance between the prizes awarded to men and women. It was on this point that King most vehemently confronted the establishment.

Women's movement, 1970–73

With her budding awareness of gendered inequalities, King was both ahead of her time and, simultaneously, perfectly situated in the early 1970s. The civil rights movements of the 1960s matured the following decade as women expressed their discontent with the dominant social order. The years between 1970 and 1973 were riddled with demands for access to male-dominated sectors of society, railings against cultural constraints with regard to gender and sexuality, concerns related to reproductive freedom, and the right to work – as well as to do so in positions outside the 'pink ghetto' and to earn equitable pay for it.

These blossomed into significant legislative efforts, including the Equal Rights Amendment, the Equal Employment Opportunity Act, the Education Amendments of 1972, and the legalization of abortion. Women marked historic firsts in the traditionally male preserves of politics, religion, the military, and in sports ranging from horseracing to marathon running to surfing. Even 'America's pastime' was not immune to wider societal shifts. In 1973, New Jersey's branch of Little League Baseball reluctantly lifted its ban on girls' participation. Protests were vociferous, as were those regarding Bernice Gera, who fought for the chance to umpire in the professional leagues. Faced with intolerable abuse and discrimination from her male colleagues, Gera quit after officiating her first game.

Women's athletic participation also changed at the scholastic level during this time. In 1971, the Division of Girls and Women's Sports

(DGWS) of the American Association for Health, Physical Education and Recreation (AAHPER) established the Association of Intercollegiate Athletics for Women (AIAW) to govern post-secondary sports and sponsor national championships, creating tremendous opportunities. The following year, Congress passed the Educational Amendments Act with its Title IX provision barring sex discrimination at any institution receiving federal financial assistance. Initially, the law made no mention of sport but, in the following years, it would become synonymous with the sweeping changes in athletics.

Even with these transformations, as *Sports Illustrated* declared in its May 28, 1973 cover story, 'Women are getting a raw deal.' The first in a three-part series began

> There may be worse (more socially serious) forms of prejudice in the United States, but there is no sharper example of discrimination today than that which operates against girls and women who take part in competitive sports, wish to take part, or might wish to if society did not scorn such endeavors. No matter what her age, education, race, talent, residence or riches, the female's right to play is severely restricted. The funds, facilities, coaching, rewards and honors allotted women are grossly inferior to those granted men. In many places absolutely no support is given to women's athletics, and females are barred by law, regulation, tradition or the hostility of males from sharing athletic resources and pleasures.[27]

The essays went on to detail the myriad ways in which the sports world excluded, discouraged, and disadvantaged girls and women. That such an influential publication addressed women's sports, and in such a high-profile way, provides clear evidence that, notwithstanding the persistent inequities, women's sport was on the move in the early 1970s.

Just one year earlier, *Sports Illustrated* named King its first Sportswoman of the Year. She shared the cover with the Sportsman of the Year (UCLA men's basketball coach John Wooden), an honour bestowed on males since the publication's 1954 inception. It was a milestone and, as King wrote in her 1974 autobiography, 'I felt it was a step in the right direction because it meant that maybe the most prestigious sports magazine in the world had finally accepted women as a legitimate part of the sports world. And it meant that it had accepted the women's pro tour. My selection was a three-way triumph: for me, for women's tennis, and for women everywhere.'[28] This would become the secular trinity of King's vocation in the coming years, as well as the central plotline in her enduring narrative.

Slim chances

Athletes hoped that tennis' Open Era would usher in greater financial opportunities. It did. For men. Women, on the other hand, found themselves gradually phased out of the professional tour and disappointed by males who expressed little concern for their athletic sisters. There were few competitions for women and their prize money was woefully out of balance with what the men collected. At national tournaments, males typically garnered purses that were 2.5 times greater than the females' and, at less prestigious competitions, the discrepancies widened considerably: 5–1, 8–1, and sometimes even as high as 12–1. The players learned that the men's first place prize at the 1970 Pacific Southwest tournament in Los Angeles amounted to $12,500, while the winning woman would take home just $1500. In fact, promoter Jack Kramer determined that the total prize money, to be divided among at least 16 women, tallied only $7500. Unable to convince Kramer to soften the glaring incongruity, several women decided it was time to take action.

They initially took their grievances to Gladys Heldman, a former player and the founder, publisher, and editor of *World Tennis* magazine. Heldman tried to reason with Kramer, but he would not budge on the prize money. As Heldman would later reflect, 'When people ask me who founded the [women's] tour, I always say Jack Kramer.'[29] As an alternative to the USLTA's Pacific Southwest tournament, Heldman organized a competing event for the women sponsored by Virginia Slims cigarettes. And so, the 'Original Nine,' as they came to be called (King, Rosie Casals, Nancy Richey, Val Ziegenfuss, Kristy Pigeon, Peaches Bartkowicz, Kerry Melville, Judy Tegart Dalton, and Julie Heldman) boycotted Kramer's competition.

The USLTA reacted first by refusing to sanction the Virginia Slims Invitational. To play in an unauthorized tournament was to risk suspension, which would affect their rankings, their chances to play in the Wightman and Federation Cups, and jeopardize their participation in the U.S. Open. The USLTA then conceded to endorse it as an amateur tournament – that meant no prize money. To sidestep this latest roadblock, the nine women agreed to become contract professionals with *World Tennis* magazine, signing $1 treaties with Heldman that could have easily spelled 'career suicide.'[30] They were summarily dismissed by the USLTA. The next week, Virginia Slims and *World Tennis* joined forces to announce the eight-tournament women's professional tennis circuit that would begin in January 1971. As Lichtenstein wrote, after the first Invitational, 'The New Feminism in tennis was born.'[31] To break away from the patriarchal organization and form an entirely new, self-governing association was nothing short of revolutionary.

The first year, 16 women signed on for the Virginia Slims circuit. Others joined the ranks after learning that the tour offered a minimum of $10,000 per tournament. But some of the biggest draws in the sport – Chris Evert, Virginia Wade, Evonne Goolagong, and Margaret Court – elected to stay with the USLTA. Those aligned with Gladys Heldman, whose contributions have been woefully unsung, played a gruelling schedule. Their unrelenting commitment to promote their sport exacerbated their exhaustion. 'When I think about what I did during those two years,' King remembered, 'the only thing I come up with is "Tennis, interviews, promotion; tennis, interviews, promotion," and I can't get beyond that.'[32] They attended cocktail parties thrown by their sponsors, showed up for personal appearances, staged clinics, gave tickets away at traffic intersections, and even went into the stands between matches to meet their fans. They frequently stayed up until two o'clock in the morning doing interviews after a match, only to wake up at six the next morning to appear on local talk shows. They were building a brand – one established on shaky ground.

In perhaps the most important match she played during this time, King faced Chris Evert, the young phenom and media darling, in the 1971 Forest Hills semi-finals. Because of Evert's continued alliance with the USLTA, the match 'meant far more to me than any other, including the Riggs extravaganza,' King reflected. 'If I had lost to Chrissie at Forest Hills, so much more would have been affected.'[33] It would provide confirmation for those who suspected that the USLTA's was the better circuit and, quite possibly, spell the end of the incipient group. Fortunately, King boosted her own legitimacy and that of her tour by winning in straight sets.

The year 1971 marked several historic milestones for King, two of which were particularly ensconced in the bustle and swirl the contemporaneous women's movement. First, she became the first woman athlete to win $100,000 in prize money in a single year. It was a terrific breakthrough for a woman athlete, despite the fact that the men's top earner, Rod Laver, took home three times that amount playing in one-third the number of tournaments.

Secondly, it was in 1971 that King quietly terminated a pregnancy. A year later, this became public knowledge – fodder for those supporting the abortion ban as well as those who fought against it. She had not intended for anyone to find out, but in a complicated and sometimes contradictory story, her name appeared, along with 52 others, on a *Ms.* Magazine petition that ran under the headline 'We Have Had Abortions.' Either her husband signed her name or she had confused the wording, thinking it said that 'we signees were only in favor of legalized abortion, *not* that we'd had abortions ourselves.'[34] Whatever the case, the *Washington Post* picked the story with the sensational headline, 'Abortion Made Possible Mrs. King's Top Year.'[35] She became a lightning rod for the larger controversy, receiving hate mail from opponents and adulation from allies. Selena Roberts maintains that, 'She may have arrived at activism by accident, but she was determined to wear the cause well.'[36] As she did with several issues, King became an initially reluctant advocate before embracing her role as celebrity feminist.

In the meantime, the Virginia Slims tour soldiered on. By 1972, 60 women had joined in and additional sponsors backed their play. King took a 'militantly commercial stance' to tennis.[37] Her argument had never been that men and women deserved equal money because of comparable athletic abilities. Instead, it was that men and women provided equivalent *entertainment* value. 'The best men players were better than the best women, and I'd never said they weren't (although I do wonder what would happen if we played against men on equal terms right from birth; it might be interesting). But from a show-biz standpoint I felt we put on as good a performance as the men – sometimes better – and that that's what people paid to see.'[38]

The philosophy behind the circuit was to offer fans 'sportainment', generating interest not just through tennis, but by turning tennis into a spectacle. Players were asked to drum up excitement by way of media appearances, personal interactions with the public, and through fashionable attire, for which the tour hired Ted Tinling to ensure the players were dressed to impress.

'The new feminism in Tennis'

Women's tennis reached a tipping point in 1973. The prize money and popularity of the Virginia Slims line-up convinced Margaret Court to join and the tour stopped in 22 cities, offering a total of $775,000 in prize money. At the Wimbledon tournament, King unionized her cohort, inviting 63 women to meet in the conference room at the Gloucester Hotel. As the story goes, King instructed Betty Stove to stand in front of the door and not allow anyone to leave until they reached an agreement. Larry had drawn up the bylaws and, after hours of discussion, the group established the Women's Tennis Association (WTA). A few days later, King won her fifth Wimbledon singles title.

After a series of legal battles and debates, the two competing women's tours merged to form, as King described the setup in her 1974 autobiography, 'The Virginia Slims–United States Lawn Tennis Association–Women's Tennis Association pro tour.' She went on to explain the arrangement: 'Simply put, Philip Morris – that's Virginia Slims – underwrites most of our tournaments; the WTA (of which I am the very reluctant president) supplies most of the players; and the USLTA agrees to go along with the whole deal.'[39] Part of the negotiations included the stipulation of a minimum of $50,000 prize money for each tournament, compared with the 1972 Slims Tour's $25,000. The USLTA's old-boy network countered that the women must remove Gladys Heldman as the director of their tour. Said Heldman, 'I was out, but the war was over and that was the most important thing... it ended absolutely wonderfully in that the women players still had the support of Virginia Slims, and for the first time the USLTA was working with them instead of fighting them.'[40] Her graciousness should not detract from her indispensable contributions. 'Without Gladys,' King commented in Heldman's 2003 obituary, 'there wouldn't be women's professional tennis.'[41]

The year 1973 also marked the first time that men and women won equal prize money at a Grand Slam tournament. In 1972, King set the wheels in motion after winning $10,000 at the U.S. Open while the men's champion, Ilie Nastase, took home $25,000. She offered an ultimatum to U.S. Open chairman Bill Talbert and threatened that if the purses were unequal following year, she and a number of other top women players would boycott.[42] Talbert subsequently secured a new sponsor, acquiesced to her demand, and equalized the monies. The 1973 U.S. Open awarded both champions, Margaret Court and John Newcombe, $25,000 each, thus initiating a new era in tennis.

The battle of the sexes

Arguably, King's foremost event of 1973, or at least the one that drew the most publicity, was her match against Bobby Riggs. As she later commented, 'The truth is – and I am sad to say it – my showdown with Riggs was the biggest match in the history of tennis. No match since has received as much exposure.'[43] She had worked hard to get women equitable pay, to create a successful tour, and to unionize the players, but the 'Battle of the Sexes' persists as perhaps the defining moment of her career: 'Everybody I meet has a compulsion to tell me where exactly they were when I beat Bobby... When I die, at my funeral, nobody's going to talk about me. They're all just going to stand up and tell each other where they were the night I beat Bobby Riggs.'[44]

Riggs, then 55 years old, had been the number one amateur player in the world in the late 1930s and early 1940s. He had then turned professional and, following military service during the Second World War, again become a top player. He was also the consummate hustler, though he writes that the word 'bettor' is a more accurate descriptor.[45] He gave big odds and big handicaps in countless contests and he usually won. He loved the spotlight but also felt that the men on the USLTA's Senior tour, of which he was a part in the early 1970s, deserved more pay. Certainly, he believed, they were a bigger draw than the women's circuit.

By 1971 'he was already into his Male Chauvinist Pig thing. He claimed *any* man could beat *any* woman, that the women's game was dull compared to the men's, and that there was no reason for us to get equal prize money.' He challenged King, whom he called 'the sex leader of the revolutionary pack,' goading, 'If she can't beat a tired old man, she doesn't deserve half her dough.' She initially refused, remembering, 'we didn't need him, we were making it on our own merits.' But Margaret Court, lured by the lucrative payday, consented to a match against Riggs scheduled for Mother's Day, 1973.[46]

Court was a disappointment in the role of protagonist. In her words, 'I am not carrying the banner for women's lib. I've never said we deserve prize money equal to the men. I'm playing this match for me. A woman is not supposed to be a man, so I've nothing to lose.' The historic moment nonetheless precluded her efforts to depoliticize the contest.

> The match, played during the height of the women's movement and promoted by Rigg's endless chauvinistic blather, took on political overtones that made it bigger than any women's match had ever been. Margaret, who hated women's liberation and embraced everything gracious and traditional in tennis, had unwittingly walked into a circus carrying the banner of women's rights.[47]

Court's performance was also crucial for the women's tour's continued viability. King recalled, 'Our circuit was struggling then, and if Bobby had won, just enough people might have believed his spiel to send our whole tour down the drain. It was that touchy.'[48] Court, rattled by the carnival atmosphere Riggs incited, lost 6-2, 6-1 in what was dubbed the 'Mother's Day Massacre,' but it set the stage for the drama's true heroine to enter.

By every account, King felt she had no choice but to play Riggs. They agreed to a best-of-five (as opposed to three sets women traditionally played), $100,000, winner-take-all contract, though the champion was expected to gross twice that amount after endorsements and television rights. In a deal brokered by Jerry Perenchio, promoter of the 1971 'Fight of the Century' between Muhammad Ali and Joe Frazier, ABC paid $750,000 for exclusive rights to broadcast the event. Odds makers favored Riggs at 8–5. Courtside seats sold for $100. Both contenders knew the value and power of the press, for promoting themselves and the causes with which they affiliated, and did their parts to ballyhoo the match.

Riggs exaggerated his boorish, misogynist character to such a degree that *Time* magazine described him as 'a male of supernaturally loathsome porcinity...a garrulous, demonic elf, a street-shrewd promoter who has finally found a way to satisfy his gargantuan appetite for both action and attention.'[49] He hammed up his performance as the quintessential male chauvinist pig with remarks like 'I plan to bomb Billie Jean King in the match and set back the Women's Lib movement about another 20 years.'[50] He spewed sound bites such as 'a woman's place is in the bedroom and the kitchen, in that order,' 'Women who can, do. Those who don't, become feminists,' 'The best way to handle women is to keep them pregnant and barefoot,' and 'If a woman wants to get in the headlines, she should have quintuplets.' He showed up for a press conference in a shirt with holes cut out at the nipples: 'I was gonna give this to Billie Jean King – she might look better in it than I would.'[51] The degree to which he believed his own drivel is debatable, but it certainly made for good copy.

Riggs, 'Came along at the confluence of two phenomena: the rise of Women's Lib and the country's need, more desperate than ever to be entertained. Watergate, inflation, shortages – the catalogue of ills is dispiriting to contemplate.'[52] He provided a steady stream of comic, albeit offensive, relief and proved the perfect foil for King, who 'personifie[d] the professional female athlete that Riggs loves to taunt.'[53] While he mocked and jeered, King took the match very seriously, recalling 'This is about history. The tour could go away, Title IX could be damaged. Everything is so tenuous.'[54] In time, King became a strong proponent for Title IX and, since 1973, has articulated the importance of the Battle of the Sexes with the then nascent legislation: 'My job in the match, and I remember this being very clear, was to change the hearts and minds of people to match the legislation of Title IX and what we were trying to do with the women's movement. It was to validate it, to celebrate it, and to get going toward changing a world where we had equality for both genders.'[55] There is some room to question whether, in 1973, King really made the connection between the match and Title IX, but the two elements have dovetailed nicely in subsequent years, situated within the athletic feminist moment of the early 1970s.

The match was scheduled for 8:00 p.m., Thursday September 20 in the Houston Astrodome. In the weeks leading up to it, King 'had been behaving like a paranoid bitch,' isolating herself from the press, fans, dropping out of three major tournaments, and sequestering herself in a Hilton Head Island villa where she prepared without distraction.[56] Though she has become the *grande dame* of women's tennis, history should not slip into hagiography. No pioneer is universally loved and King inspired a good deal of animosity, even amongst her fellow players. Some resented her 'open pursuit of money and fame.' She once confessed that critics 'don't like me because I talk about money all the time. I'm mercenary. I'm a rebel.'[57] Others begrudged her celebrity status; Tinling nicknamed her, 'Madam Superstar,' a moniker that was not entirely complimentary.[58] Then there were those represented by the outrageous figure Riggs had cast for himself – those who felt women undeserving of equality that demands for change should be silenced.

Over 30,000 people attended what Lichtenstein called 'Astrotennis': 'a space-age Hollywood version of the Christians versus the Lions.'[59] It was a surreal, absurd environment, replete with celebrities, men dressed mockingly in aprons, and couples getting married in the stands. As a line of majorettes and someone in a pig costume danced on the sidelines to the swells of the University of Houston marching band, commentator Howard Cosell likened the milieu to that of a college football game. There was an almost political component as well, as constituents rallied for their respective candidates with campaign-sized buttons and placards reading, 'Libber v. Lobber,' 'Go Bobby Go,' 'I love Billie Jean,' 'I love Bobby Riggs,' 'Whiskey, Women, and Riggs,' 'Bobby Riggs, Bleagh!' and 'King wears jockey shorts.'

Perenchio had carefully orchestrated the occasion for maximum schlock value. Six toga-clad members of the Rice University men's track team carried King onto the court atop a litter decorated with gold lame and huge plumes of feathers. Perenchio had expected her to refuse the procession but, as she explained, 'a feminist can understand show business.'[60] Riggs arrived on a red rickshaw with gilded wheels, surrounded by Bobby's Bosom Buddies, a group of women whose title requires little explanation. Riggs presented King with a two-foot Sugar Daddy lollipop; King responded in kind, bestowing her rival with a squealing baby pig.

On television, 90 million viewers in over 40 different countries tuned in to see King wallop Riggs in three straight sets: 6-4, 6-3, 6-4. The lopsided scores actually made the match sound closer than it really was. Riggs had not stood a chance.

Though it was not the best tennis of her career, King 'hit 64 percent outright winners, balls placed so well Bobby never got his racquet on them.'[61] *Sports Illustrated* described it as 'a brilliant rising to an occasion; a clutch performance under the most trying of circumstances. Seldom has there been a more classic example of a skilled athlete performing at peak efficiency in the most important moment of her life.'[62] But as King has repeatedly reminded the public in the decades since that momentous occasion, it was about more than sport: 'it was about social change.'[63] In the end, it 'legitimized women's tennis. It was the culmination of an era, the noisy conclusion to the noisiest three years in the history of the women's game.'[64] The match also brought the traditionally elite pastime to the masses. Moreover, its significance extended beyond the sportscape to wind its way around and through contemporary gender politics.

The overriding symbolism spun out from the 'Battle of the Sexes' is that of women's empowerment. On the Senate floor, one politician remarked that through her victory King 'ratified the 26th Amendment' (i.e., the Equal Rights Amendment).[65] There were stories of women who asked their bosses for raises the day after Riggs' defeat. *When Billie Beat Bobby* exaggerates this point, informing viewers about the future of several women, and one man, who witnessed the momentous event: one browbeaten woman will leave her husband and go to law school, a younger woman will go on to coach in the WNBA. Women will be CEOs of major corporations, superior court justices, politicians, astronauts, surgeons, and professional athletes. Men will one day give women top positions in their companies – all because, viewers are led to assume, of a tennis match.

The physical is political

Until the spectacle of the Battle of the Sexes, few members of the women's movement recognized the gravity that sport could give their cause. They saw athletics as 'frivolous' and 'unhealthy' – a 'male construct' easily 'dismissed as a "fascist" domain,' and 'a product of a capitalistic, patriarchal society.' Feminists coined the term '*jockocracy* to describe the social power of a certain male obsession with athletes and victory.' In the eyes of the larger movement, sociologist Jan Felsin explains, 'sport achievement is always singularly related to excellence and, therefore, of limited usefulness as a source of expanding opportunities for women.'[66] Yet King was fighting the same battles in sport for which the larger movement lobbied in society: equal opportunity, equal pay, equal recognition, corporeal autonomy, and legitimacy. Her actions, both on and off the court, relied on and fostered solidarity with other women, even while they competed against one another. She showed that sisterhood was powerful and that women did not have to capitulate to the oppressive *status quo*.

Some disregarded King's efforts, arguing that they were more commercially driven than they were motivated by a feminist consciousness. Lichtenstein, for instance, wrote that, 'feminism had been forced on her; she used it as a tool to win the superstar acceptance she craved.'[67] Before the match with Riggs, writer Nora Ephron commented, 'Billie Jean's not the feminist she says she is.'[68] Detractors compiled evidence against her: as president of the WTA, King hired a man to run the organization; her alliance with Virginia Slims' was also an issue. The brand espoused women's liberation as the freedom to choose a 'feminine' cigarette and boasted the infantilizing slogan, 'You've Come a Long Way, Baby.' But, as King described it, 'When it comes to Women's Lib, I'm pretty much a pragmatist,' and 'if backing from Virginia Slims paved the way for equality, then it was worth it'.[69] This notion of 'Women's Lib,' a term so prevalent within the discourse of women's tennis in the early 1970s (though Heldman declared it 'Women's Lob'[70]), was another problem. Gloria Steinem wrote that, '*Women's Libber* was a trivializing term that feminists tried to argue against,' as was the use of the phrase 'male chauvinist pig,' a dehumanizing misnomer.[71]

Then there have been moments in King's life when she has backed away from the feminist label. As reported in a 1972 article in the *Washington Post*, she wanted 'to make one thing clear. She is not a raving maniac for Women's Lib. She does not carry banners. Nor does she demonstrate.'[72] Her 1984 autobiography, published on the heels of her legal battle with Marilyn Barnett, also disassociated her efforts from 'the more outspoken feminists [who] really had so little in common with me...Often I disliked the feminists because they were so doctrinaire.' She goes on to state 'I am generally a conservative' and 'I still carry some outright biases based on sex, and not all of them pro-female.'[73] Then again, one might reject the entire work as propaganda – an attempt to re-ingratiate her with the public following the 'galimony' suit that so thoroughly damaged her image. In truth, segments of the American public conflate 'feminist' with 'lesbian' and so, to rehabilitate her image, she distanced herself from both categories. In that case, to take the book as evidence of her dismissal of feminism is misguided.

Ultimately, any discussion of whether or not she is a feminist or 'feminist enough,' is wildly off beam. Moreover, as sport sociologist Nancy Spencer writes, 'Whatever the reality, Billie Jean King will no doubt be remembered through narratives that portray her in the symbolic role of liberator for women.'[74] King spoke frankly about issues that may not seem radical by today's standards, but in the context of the early 1970s, she struck audiences as defiant. In just one of countless examples, she unapologetically defended her right to play professional tennis: 'Almost every day for the last four years, someone comes up to me and says, 'Hey when are you going to have children. I say "I'm not ready yet." They say, "Why aren't you at home?" I say, "Why don't you go ask Rod Laver why he isn't at home." '[75] Still, for all her efforts off the court, we should not lose sight of what she did in the context of her sport and the ways her athleticism challenged people to rethink their gendered assumptions.

When a *Seventeen* magazine reader poll determined that King was the most admired woman in the world, the managing editor explained 'This was a tremendous departure from past surveys... It seems to be important to the girls that Billie Jean did it all on her own, just her and that damn tennis racket.'[76] That 'damn tennis racket' demonstrates the ways in which sport can be a powerful conduit for social change and that the *uses* of sport are too often disregarded. To Congresswoman Bella Abzug King lamented, 'You know, the real shame is that women's sports could be so visible. It is such an obvious tool. But you've never used it. No one has.'[77] To Gloria Steinem she implored, 'You should use us more,' to which Steinem responded, '"Billie, this is about politics." "Gloria," King replied, "We are politics." '[78] She is right. While the phrase 'the personal is political' became an important rallying cry for second-wave feminists, we would do well to consider the ways in which the *physical* is political.

This was something that Grace Lichtenstein, in her coverage of women's tennis during the 1970s, found to be the case with many athletes. She writes that in the beginning she was 'keenly disappointed that the players' feminist consciousness was not higher than it was... Before long, however, I realized that the astonishing point about these players was that they were jocks first, women second.' It was, she recognized, a 'jock sisterhood.' Lichtenstein continued, 'They didn't know much about feminism on an intellectual level, but in their gut they had the rest of us beat two sets to love.'[79] Together, they shattered the myths of female frailty and, by necessity, cultivated and performed their tenacity, competitiveness, cooperation, independence, stamina, sweat, power, weaknesses, successes, and failures for all who cared to watch. And as women entered sport in increasing numbers throughout the 1970s, studies found that their athletic experiences augmented their self-confidence, self-actualization, and leadership abilities. They determined 'sports are a training ground for female assertiveness and defiance of sex-role restrictions' and that 'competition brings about a sense of mastery and accomplishment that has a profound impact on the rest of their lives.'[80] Athletic participation is not an isolated, apolitical, or trivial realm, but a field rife with potential for both the individual and society.

Sport, writes Jan Graydon in the *Feminist Review*, 'maybe considered somewhat irrelevant, or at best peripheral, to the interests of women and to the furtherance of feminist perspectives on society.' She goes on to counter that this line of thinking is 'erroneous.'[81] Physical culture, in all its myriad forms, offers a great deal to larger political issues. With regard to what she calls the 'athletic feminism of the seventies,' Stephanie Twin contends that, 'Sport is part of a larger movement for female physical autonomy, a movement in which efforts to gain control over pregnancy, birth, family size, and individual safety figure prominently. As this movement proceeds, athletics may well form its backbone.'[82] While issues of embodiment are paramount to feminist concerns, athletics continue to be marginalized. This is a mistake, for as Elspeth Probyn insists, 'In an obvious manner, sport highlights that bodies *do* something.'[83]

Billie Jean King's advocacy comes in many configurations. For the purpose of this essay, though, I am interested in her physical activism – the ways that she brings together physical activity and political activism – to change how people regard and treat one another in sport and society. As she told Lichtenstein, 'I'm interested in the women's movement, but from an action point of view, not an intellectual one. Tennis helps the women's movement just by *doing*... If people see us out there every day, that changes people's minds, not *talking* about it.'[84] By making the physical political, her feminist legacy is indelibly scripted onto the parchment of the past, thoroughly soaked into its pulpy fibres.

Notes

1. Frank Deford, 'Mrs. Billie Jean King!' *Sports Illustrated*, May 19, 1975. Retrieved April 2, 2010 from http://sportsillustrated.cnn.com/vault.
2. The White House, Office of the Press Secretary, 'President Obama Names Medal of Freedom Recipients.' Retrieved April 30, 2010 from http://www.

whitehouse.gov/the_press_office/president-obama-names-medal-of-freedom-recipients/.
3. Angela Lumpkin, *Women's Tennis: A Historical Documentary of the Players and Their Game* (Troy, NY: The Whitson Publishing Company, 1981), 93–4.
4. Billie Jean King with Cynthia Starr, *We Have Come a Long Way: The Story of Women's Tennis* (New York: Regina Ryan, 1988), 120.
5. Billie Jean King with Frank Deford, *Billie Jean* (New York: Viking Press, 1982), 26–7.
6. Selena Roberts, *A Necessary Spectacle: Billie Jean King, Bobby Riggs, and the Tennis Match that Leveled the Game* (New York: Crown Publishers, 2005), 180.
7. Grace Lichtenstein, *A Long Way, Baby: The Inside Story of the Women in Pro Tennis* (Greenwich, CT: Fawcett, 1974), 54.
8. Richard Johnson, Deborah Chambers, Parvati Raghuram, and Estella Tincknell, *The Practice of Cultural Studies* (London: Sage, 2004).
9. Billie Jean King with Kim Chapin, *Billie Jean* (New York: Harper & Row, 1974); King with Deford, *Billie Jean*; King with Starr, *We Have Come a Long Way*; Billie Jean King with Christine Brennan, *Pressure Is a Privilege: Lessons I've Learned from Life and the Battle of the Sexes* (New York: LifeTime Media, 2008); Roberts, *A Necessary Spectacle*; Lichtenstein, *A Long Way, Baby*; Lumpkin, *Women's Tennis*; Francene Sabin, *Women Who Win* (New York: Dell, 1975); Bobby Riggs with George McGann, *Court Hustler* (New York: Signet, 1974); Ted Tinling, *Tinling: Sixty Years in Tennis* (London: Sidgwick and Jackson, 1983); Bud Collins and Zander Hollander, eds., *Bud Collins' Tennis Encyclopedia* (Detroit: Visible Ink, 1997). For an account of King's rankings, records, and honors see Dennis J. Phillips, *Women Tennis Stars: Biographies and Records of Champions, 1800s to Today* (Jefferson, NC: McFarland and Company, 2009).
10. *When Billy Beat Bobby* (American Broadcast Company, 2001); *Billie Jean King: Portrait of a Pioneer* (Home Box Office, 2006); *Dare to Compete: The Struggle of Women in Sports* (Home Box Office, 1999).
11. King with Chapin, *Billie Jean*, 24.
12. Sabin, *Women Who Win*, 22.
13. Roberts, *A Necessary Spectacle*, 54.
14. King with Chapin, *Billie Jean*, 27.
15. Kim Chapin, 'Center Court Is Her Domain,' *Sports Illustrated*, June 24, 1968. Retrieved April 2, 2010 from http://sportsillustrated.cnn.com/vault.
16. *Billie Jean King: Portrait of a Pioneer*.
17. King with Chapin, *Billie Jean*, 31.
18. Roberts, *A Necessary Spectacle*, 56.
19. Lichtenstein, *A Long Way, Baby*, 54.
20. Roberts, *A Necessary Spectacle*, 56.
21. King with Deford, *Billie Jean*, 148.
22. Roberts, *A Necessary Spectacle*, 54.
23. Ibid., 62.
24. King with Starr, *We Have Come a Long Way*, 115.
25. In 1975, the USLTA (United States Lawn Tennis Association) became the USTA. For the sake of historical accuracy, I will use the titles appropriate to the time period discussed.
26. Robert Lipsyte, *SportsWorld: An American Dreamland* (New York: Quadrangle Books, 1975), 223–4.

27. Bil Gilbert and Nancy Williamson, 'Sport Is Unfair to Women', *Sports Illustrated*. Retrieved May 28, 1973 from http://sportsillustrated.cnn.com/vault/article/magazine/MAG1087396/index.htm.
28. King with Chapin, *Billie Jean*, 147.
29. King with Starr, *We Have Come a Long Way*, 127.
30. Dare to Compete.
31. Lichtenstein, *A Long Way, Baby*, 26.
32. King with Chapin, *Billie Jean*, 125.
33. King with Deford, *Billie Jean*, 179.
34. King with Chapin, *Billie Jean*, 157; Roberts, *A Necessary Spectacle*, 87.
35. Mark Asher, 'Abortion Made Possible Mrs. King's Top Year,' *Washington Post*, February 22, 1973, D1.
36. Roberts, *A Necessary Spectacle*, 88.
37. Lichtenstein, *A Long Way, Baby*, 54.
38. King with Chapin, *Billie Jean*, 101.
39. Ibid., 2.
40. King with Starr, *We Have Come a Long Way*, 142.
41. Lena Williams, 'Gladys Heldman, 81, a Leader in Promoting Women's Tennis,' *New York Times*, June 25, 2003, B8.
42. King with Starr, *We Have Come a Long Way*, 142.
43. Ibid., 145.
44. King with Deford, *Billie Jean*, 82.
45. Riggs with McGann, *Court Hustler*, 30.
46. King with Chapin, *Billie Jean*, 165; Roberts, *A Necessary Spectacle*, 15–16.
47. King with Starr, *We Have Come a Long Way*, 143.
48. King with Chapin, *Billie Jean*, 166.
49. 'How Bobby Runs and Talks, Talks, Talks,' *Time*, September 10, 1973. Retrieved April 24, 2010 from www.time.com.
50. Joe Jares, 'Riggs to Riches – Take Two,' *Sports Illustrated*, September 10, 1973. Retrieved April 2, 2010 from http://sportsillustrated.cnn.com/vault.
51. Quoted in Roberts, *A Necessary Spectacle*, 19; William Gildea, 'Riggs-King Promotion: Heavy on the Gross,' *Washington Post*, September 16, 1973, D11; Lichtenstein, *A Long Way, Baby*, 29.
52. 'How Bobby Runs and Talks, Talks, Talks.'
53. 'Billie Jean King: I'll Kill Him!' *Time*, September 10, 1973. Retrieved April 24, 2010 from www.time.com.
54. Quoted in Roberts, *A Necessary Spectacle*, 93.
55. Ibid., 99.
56. Lichtenstein, *A Long Way, Baby*, 21.
57. In Robin Herman, 'Court Queen and Women's Lib Symbol,' *New York Times*, September 10, 1974, 47.
58. *Tinling: Sixty Years in Tennis*, 177.
59. Lichtenstein, *A Long Way, Baby*, 22.
60. *Billie Jean King: Portrait of a Pioneer*.
61. Lichtenstein, *A Long Way, Baby*, 240.
62. Curry Kirkpatrick, 'There She Is, Ms. America,' *Sports Illustrated*, October 1, 1973. Retrieved April 2, 2010 from http://sportsillustrated.cnn.com/vault.
63. Dare to Compete.
64. King with Starr, *We Have Come a Long Way*, 146.

65. Pennsylvania Senator Hugh Scott, quoted in 'Leaders in Senate Acclaim Mrs. King,' *New York Times*, September 22, 1973, 25.
66. Hollis Elkins, 'Time for a Change: Women's Athletics and the Women's Movement,' *Frontiers: A Journal of Women Studies* 3 (1978): 23–4; Roberts, *A Necessary Spectacle*, 159; Gloria Steinem, 'Introduction,' in *The Decade of Women: A Ms. History of the Seventies in Words and Pictures*, ed. Susanne Levine and Harriet Lyons (New York: Paragon, 1980), 19; Jan Felshin, 'The Social Anomaly of Women in Sports,' *The Physical Educator*, 30 (October 1973), 124.
67. Lichtenstein, *A Long Way, Baby*, 150.
68. Ibid., 231.
69. King with Chapin, *Billie Jean*, 142.
70. King with Starr, *We Have Come a Long Way*, 120.
71. Steinem, 'Introduction,' 19, 23.
72. Asher, 'Abortion Made Possible.'
73. King with Deford, *Billie Jean*, 160, 139.
74. Nancy E. Spencer, 'Reading Between the Lines: A Discursive Analysis of the Billie Jean King vs. Bobby Riggs "Battle of the Sexes," ' *Sociology of Sport Journal*, 17 (2000): 399. See also Spencer, 'Once Upon a Subculture: Professional Women's Tennis and the Meaning of Style, 1970–1974,' *Journal of Sport & Social Issues*, 21 (1997): 363–78
75. Quoted in Robert Lipsyte, 'Sports of the Times,' *New York Times*, August 27, 1970, 59.
76. Quoted in Deford, 'Mrs. Billie Jean King!'
77. King with Deford, *Billie Jean*, 82.
78. Quoted in Sally Jenkins, 'Title IX Opponents a Bunch of Sad Sacks,' *Washington Post*, June 24, 2002, D1.
79. Lichtenstein, *A Long Way, Baby*, 16–17.
80. Joanna Bunker Rohrbaugh, 'Femininity on the Line,' *Psychology Today* (August 1979): 30–42.
81. Jan Graydon, ' "But It's More than a Game. It's an Institution." Feminist Perspectives on Sport,' *Feminist Review*, 13 (1983): 5.
82. Stephanie L. Twin, *Out of the Bleachers: Writings on Women and Sport* (Old Westbury, NY: The Feminist Press, 1979), xxxvi, xxxix.
83. Elspeth Probyn, 'Sporting Bodies: Dynamics of Shame and Pride,' *Body & Society*, 6 (2000): 13–14.
84. Quoted in Lichtenstein, *A Long Way, Baby*, 150.

11
John L. Sullivan: The Champion of All Champions

Elliott J. Gorn

> *His colors are the Stars and Stripes,*
> *He also wears the green,*
> *And he's the grandest slugger that*
> *The ring has ever seen,*
> *No fighter in the world can beat*
> *Our true American,*
> *The champion of all champions*
> *Is John L. Sullivan!*
> – Popular Vaudeville Song

John Lawrence Sullivan's total mastery, his complete domination of the ring, captivated men's imaginations. But Sullivan was equally imposing outside the ropes; everything about him was larger than life. As champion of the world, he occupied center stage for a full decade, longer than any previous fighter. 'Excepting General Grant,' one newspaper reported, 'no American has received such ovations as Sullivan.' By the end of the 19th century, he was certainly America's best-known sports celebrity and probably the nation's most famous citizen.

No one would have guessed that such fame was possible as the 1880s dawned. Born in Roxbury, MA, in 1858, Sullivan reached adulthood carrying the equivalent of an eighth grade education, a checkered work record, and a burden of anti-Irish prejudice. His aggressive temperament, however, combined with his unusual strength and agility, pointed him toward sports. Like many young working-class Irish-Americans, Sullivan loved the free and easy life of saloons, where athletic prowess as well as hard drinking and physical toughness were esteemed. It was not an unusual step to try earning a few extra dollars in semiprofessional athletics. A gifted baseball player, Sullivan joined a variety of local teams and even was offered a professional contract to play in Cincinnati. But his talents led him in a different direction.

'At the age of nineteen,' he recalled in his autobiography, 'I drifted into the occupation of a boxer.' Drifted was precisely the word. After winning a number of street fights, Sullivan strolled on stage at a vaudeville house one night to accept a professional boxer's challenge to all comers. Such 'scientific exhibitions of skill' were technically legal since the combatants wore gloves and allegedly refrained from any hard hitting. The lad stripped off his coat, put on the gloves, and knocked his opponent around at will. Encouraged by this initial success, Sullivan began sparring throughout Boston.

Since midcentury, bare-knuckle prize fighting had been the pet sport of 'the fancy' – the urban underworld that included gamblers, keepers of working-class saloons, drifters, street brawlers, fops and dandies, cock breeders, and especially young laborers who rejected the bourgeois ethic of steady habits and domesticity. From its earliest appearance in America, prize fighting was a taboo sport. The gambling and drinking, the profanity and violence associated with boxing caused magistrates to prosecute fighters, their seconds, referees, even spectators under the laws against riot and mayhem. The *New York Tribune* spoke for all in polite society when it described the crowd at an 1858 fight: 'Probably no human eye will ever look upon so much rowdyism, villainy, scoundrelism, and boiled-down viciousness, concentrated upon so small a space...Scoundrels of every imaginable genus, every variety of every species, were there assembled; the characteristic rascalities of each were developed and displayed in all their devilish perfection.'

Sports like boxing violated the ideals of hard work, sober self-control, and social reform in which evangelical and bourgeois citizens placed their faith. During the antebellum years, several states passed anti-prize fight statutes, testimony to Victorian intolerance for all displays of revelry but also evidence of the ring's growing popularity with the working class. A series of spectacular matches held in out-of-the-way places reached by railroads or steamships attracted tens of thousands of men to ringside and millions more to the sporting press. Ministers, reformers, and editors of respectable journals might rail against the ring, but working-class males found in prize fighting symbolic confirmation of their values: prowess, virility, and violent defense of honor. Boxers were heroes of urban street culture, men whose fame and muscle made them leaders in gangs, saloons, and similar institutions.

But during the decade or so preceding Sullivan's entrance into the sport, boxing became too corrupt for even this rough constituency. A descending spiral of fixed fights, violence among spectators, and police interference almost destroyed prize fighting. By 1868, *Wilkes' Spirit of the Times* began a report by referring to 'the ring, or rather what is left of it,' while the *New York Clipper*, long a defender of pugilism, declared, 'exponents of the manly art can no longer find the influential backers and patrons who formerly took an interest in this sport, for they have become disgusted with mob rule...'

There were countertrends, however, less visible but ultimately more powerful. As Sullivan began to spar on urban stages in the late 1870s, a leisure revolution was just beginning. Despite uneven distribution and chronic recessions, per capita income rose slightly over the coming decades, while the length of the average work week declined a bit. Brash entrepreneurs began to glimpse the potential new market for commercialized leisure. Some experimented with advertising and mail-order sales, others promoted spectacles like circuses and cabaret shows, still others sought to fill the growing demand for sporting goods and athletic events. Not only working-class and ethnic peoples – who never fully accepted the Victorian ethos of piety, steady habits, and social progress anyway – but also members of 'respectable' society including white-collar workers, managers, and professionals, as well as the old elite 'Brahmin' caste, began to pursue leisure-time activities as never before.

Historian John Higham has described this trend as a 'reorientation of American culture.' Time clocks, rigid moral codes, factories, corporations, stuffy manners, all made Americans hunger, in Higham's words, 'to break out of the frustrations, the routine, the sheer dullness of an urban industrial culture. It was everywhere an urge to be young, masculine and adventurous.' In a world where frontiers were closing, businesses built, and fortunes made – in a world of mature capitalism – the old work ethic grew less compelling. Masses of men labored for salaries in large bureaucracies or for wages in enormous factories. Immense concentrations of corporate wealth and highly specialized labor obviated the transcendent republican goal of autonomy, of owning productive property and receiving the fruits of one's efforts. Feeling cut off from 'real life,' many men turned to vigorous sports as one way to fill the void.

Boxing, football, and other violent contests invaded colleges and athletic clubs. The drama of two men in the ring especially fascinated the middle and upper classes, now grown weary of Victorian demands for tight self-control. Thus the psychologist G. Stanley Hall confessed in his memoirs to being captivated by 'the raw side of life,' and he ventured into urban backstreets whenever he got the chance. Hall's slumming led him to the fancy's pet sport: 'I have never missed an opportunity to attend a prize fight if I could do so unknown and away from home, so that I have seen most of the noted pugilists of my generation in action and felt the unique thrill at these encounters.'

The problem, however, was that professional fighting under the old bare-knuckle rules was not only illegal, it was also associated with the dregs of society. The solution, according to men who wished to see boxing reformed, was to assimilate the professional ring to amateur rules, which had originated in Britain and were named for the Marquis of Queensberry. Under the old code, a round lasted until a man was knocked, pushed, or wrestled down, and a fight ended when either combatant could no longer continue. In the new order, punching was the sole legal means of offense, rounds were timed at three minutes each with one minute of rest in between, and the ten-second knockout rule made pounding one's opponent into temporary unconsciousness the most spectacular way to win a fight. Gloves did not make prize-fighting any less corrupt or brutal; they protected fighters' hands rather than their heads, rendering the sport more not less dangerous. But the Marquis of Queensberry rules gave the ring a fresh start by bringing boxing into the open, and thereby allowing a greater degree of crowd control.

Sullivan began his ring career when championships were still decided with bare knuckles, when oldtimers considered glove-fighting a pale reflection of real prize combat. The youth was so talented that within a few short years and after a handful of easy victories, he challenged champion Paddy Ryan for the title. Ryan accepted, and they fought bare-fisted in Mississippi City near New Orleans on February 2, 1882, for $2500 a side. The fight, of course, was illegal, yet thousands of men crowded around a ring pitched in front of a local hotel. 'When Sullivan struck me,' Ryan said after the bout, 'I thought that a telegraph pole had been shoved against me endways.' The battle lasted only nine rounds of about a half-minute each. From first to last Sullivan dominated his opponent. The pace exhausted both men, and neither escaped unharmed, but the challenger was always in control. 'Among the sporting men and old ring goers that witnessed the mill,' the *New Orleans Times-Democrat* concluded, 'it is generally conceded that the Boston Boy is a wonder. His hitting powers are terrific, and against his sledge-hammer fists the naked arms of a man are but poor defense. He forced the fighting from the start and knocked his opponent about as though he were a football.'

At age 23, previously unable to keep a job, John Lawrence Sullivan was heavyweight champion.

A surge of enthusiasm greeted Sullivan's victory. When the *National Police Gazette* issued an illustrated extra edition with complete coverage, public demand proved insatiable and the presses rolled for weeks. Crowds mobbed every railroad station to catch a glimpse of the new champion as he made his way back north. Appearing in leading saloons or sparring in local sporting houses, he was heralded in Chicago, Detroit, Cleveland, Pittsburgh, Philadelphia, and New York. Back home in Boston, he received a thunderous reception at the Dudley Street Opera House, where just three years before he had sparred in his first exhibition. But the adulation was just beginning. Over the next decade, Sullivan became one of the best-known public figures in the world and the most idolized athlete of the era.

For ten years he reigned as the unquestioned master of pugilism and the 'physical superior of all men.' Yet he entered the regular prize ring only twice. Although we remember Sullivan as the last great bare-knuckle champion, his reputation was based largely on his prowess with the gloves. He quickly discovered that short Queensberry fights were a gold mine. Sullivan would enter an arena, challenge the house for 50, 100, or eventually 1000 dollars, and then knock out some hapless local hero inside four three-minute rounds. If no one dared meet the champion, then another professional, whose services were retained for such emergencies, would spar a few rounds with him. Sullivan also insisted that before he would give them title fights, serious challengers must first prove their mettle in glove battles, lucrative affairs that packed stadiums like Madison Square Garden and yielded thousands of dollars. The champion was so adept with the gloves that most seasoned professionals fell before a few rounds were over, obviating bare-knuckle fights.

Sullivan and his managers – mostly former fighters, buccaneers by genteel Victorian standards, but all in the mainstream of Gilded Age hucksterism – quickly found a way to tap the new potential market for recreation. Taking their cue from traveling circuses and vaudeville shows, they organized troupes of fighters along with assorted other variety acts, and put them on the road. The grand tour of 1883–84 was the prototype. For eight months they traveled all over the country, usually spending only one night in each town, boarding a train after a performance, and heading for the next stop. These tours required careful planning to assure that arenas were prepared, publicity arranged, accommodations made, and schedules kept. During the 1883–84 road campaign, Sullivan alone cleared $80,000, and he earned nearly one million dollars before his career ended.

In addition to these 'knocking-out tours,' as Sullivan called them, the champion coined money by lending his name to a variety of commercial endeavors. He made personal appearances at baseball games, endorsed products ranging from boxing gloves to beef broth, and acted in a series of stage shows. Sullivan's career exemplified the growing commercialization of leisure late in the 19th century. A New York wax museum presented his likeness to the public; a circus advertised a boxing elephant named for the champion; and sheet music vendors hawked the popular song, 'Let Me Shake the Hand That Shook the Hand of Sullivan.' He earned more each year than presidents or business executives, and unlike the old bare-knucklers who lived in the shadows of urban vice and criminality, Sullivan basked in the public spotlight. In a word, the champion was a professional entertainer whose livelihood depended on constant adulation.

It was Sullivan the celebrity as much as Sullivan the fighter who electrified men. His raw, spontaneous personality drew endless comment in the press. He knew how to accumulate money, but he knew even better how to spend it. The champion's legendary conviviality, his embrace of the easy camaraderie of saloons and sporting houses, were central to his public image. John L. loved the good life, including elegant clothes, expensive jewelry, the finest foods, the best cigars, and free-flowing champagne. Everyone knew of his drinking binges and his extramarital affairs. Everyone also knew of the gorgeous barroom he opened in Boston to treat and toast his friends. He embodied Gilded Age fascination with rich living and gaudy displays of wealth. In his reigning decade he strode into countless saloons, slapped a hundred-dollar bill on the counter, and treated the house. Like a padrone or public benefactor, Sullivan met an endless stream of down-and-out men asking for handouts, widows without means, and religious missionaries in need of support. He always turned to his current manager – he changed them often – and barked a gruff demand for a 5, or a 10, or a 50 to help the supplicant. The champion's extravagance and his lack of bourgeois prudence were an ingratiating part of his public persona in an age grown weary of stern self-control.

Emblematic of an emerging national mass culture that partially transcended the divisions of class and gender, of religion and ethnicity, Sullivan represented sensual fulfillment and consumption of leisure, previously seen as working-class vices but now becoming hegemonic norms. The champion's monikers, 'the Boston Strong Boy,' 'the Boston

Boy,' or simply 'the Boy,' indicate that the public Sullivan was very much a child in a man's body. Above all, he seemed a creature of impulse. Editor Charles Dana of the *New York Sun* commented on Sullivan's enormous appetites; he dined like Gargantua, drank like Gambrinus, had the strength of Samson and the ferocity of Achilles; he moved with a child's ease but hit like a giant.

Stories circulated about Sullivan protecting newsboys against bullies, aiding women in distress, and giving up liquor at his dying mother's request. More stories circulated that Sullivan kicked newsboys and chased waitresses, that he beat his wife and kept mistresses, and that he broke up saloons in drunken rages. Inebriated one night in Philadelphia, he tore up his hotel room, went outside to harass passers-by, returned at dawn for a breakfast of six dozen clams and whiskey, and then had to be carried to bed. When awakened, Sullivan calmed his belligerence with another pint. Police avoided him during such drunken sprees, while newspapers editorialized that the immunity of the 'hulking ruffian' only encouraged his brutality.

Both images of Sullivan – the generous, good-natured boy and the brooding, destructive boy – contained much truth; both were united by themes of adolescent impulsiveness. He was a hero and a brute, a *bon vivant* and a drunk, and a lover of life and a reckless barbarian. In the public mind, Sullivan the man and Sullivan the fighter were one. He cut through all restraints, acted rather than contemplated, and paid little regard to the morality or immorality of his behavior. He was totally self-indulgent, even in acts of generosity, totally a hedonist consuming the good things around him and beckoning others to do the same. For individuals deeply ambivalent about the transition from middle-class Protestant virtues of productivity to new values of consumption, he was a transcendent symbol. And for bourgeois men terrified of losing vital 'nerve force,' the key ingredient to success, Sullivan seemed a glorious example of abundant human energy. He epitomized action in an age that feared inertia.

Perhaps Sullivan's most important fight was the epic 1889 struggle against Jake Kilrain. Weary after years of touring, Sullivan's exhibitions grew spiritless. He engaged in only one bare-knuckle battle after winning the title, an embarrassing draw with the English champion Charlie Mitchell, fought in Chantilly, France in 1888. Years of excess had eroded his physique, and shortly after he returned to America, his health broke down completely. He claimed to suffer from typhoid fever, gastric fever, inflammation of the bowels, heart trouble, liver complaint, and incipient paralysis. Acute alcoholism was a more plausible diagnosis. He lay bedridden for weeks, finally rising on his 30th birthday against the advice of his doctors. His claim to the title shaken by Mitchell, his health and age betraying him, his fans clamoring for vindication, and his enemies out for blood, Sullivan staked his career on a single desperate battle. He signed articles to fight Kilrain, whom the *National Police Gazette* had declared champion at the depths of Sullivan's fall.

John L.'s backers remanded him to the custody of William Muldoon, a champion wrestler, celebrity strongman, and health fetishist. Sullivan shed years of dissipation and regained much of his lost vitality. Once again, New Orleans with its cosmopolitan atmosphere and libertine ways was chosen as the battle's staging ground. Exclusive men's athletic clubs lent their facilities to the fighters, fans poured into the Crescent City, and newspapers covered the story with gallons of ink. Declared the *New Orleans Picayune,* 'The city is fighting mad... Everybody has the fever and is talking Sullivan and Kilrain, Ladies discussed it in street cars, men talked and argued about it in places which had never heard pugilism mentioned before.' On the morning of July 8, 1889, special trains rolled into Richburg, Mississippi, and 5000 fans crowded the ring as the temperature soared past 100 degrees.

Sullivan appeared to be in excellent shape, and his performance matched his appearance. Kilrain wrestled, backpedaled, and counter-punched, but he only succeeded in angering the champion, who growled and cursed throughout the fight. Sullivan controlled the pace, stalking Kilrain, pressing, keeping him always off balance. 'His old time ferocity seemed to come back,' *Police Gazette* reporter William Edgar Harding wrote; 'he rushed at Kilrain like a tiger at its prey. His eyes flashed, his lips were set and he seemed to become larger and more massive than he was.' The battle lasted 2 hours and 15 minutes. The July sun blistered Kilrain's pale back, while Sullivan cut up his face, smashed his ribs, and verbally abused him: 'Stand up and fight like a man'; 'I'm no sprinter, I'm a fighter'; 'You're a champion eh? A champion of what?' The only doubt about the outcome came in the 44th round. A drink of cold tea spiked with whiskey made Sullivan vomit. Word quickly went round the ring that his stomach was retaining the whiskey but rejecting the tea, a bit of humor that barely masked his partisans' alarm. But when Kilrain offered a draw, the champion barked 'No, you loafer,' and punched him down again. The final 30 rounds were more lopsided than the first 45. The 55th time they toed the scratch, Kilrain barely could defend himself. Ten rounds later gamblers offered 500 dollars to 50 on Sullivan with no takers. After 75 rounds, fearing for their man's life, Kilrain's seconds threw up the sponge. No one knew it then, but the world had witnessed the last bare-knuckle championship fight.

After the Kilrain bout, the good life beckoned again and Sullivan followed. For three years he did very little fighting. Much of his time was spent on the stage in a melodrama called *Honest Hearts and Willing Hands*. Playing a blacksmith, Sullivan took off his shirt, pounded an anvil, beat a bully, and mutilated his lines. Critics hated it; the American people loved it. More than ever, Sullivan was the consummate celebrity, one on whom the public spotlight shone so brightly that person and persona merged. Besides fighting *per se*, John L.'s greatest talents lay in the show business arts of self-advertisement and self-promotion. His troupe toured North America in the second half of 1890, then went to Australia in 1891.

The overseas tour was not a success. Worse, while the champion was away, hungry young boxers mocked his abilities, and when he returned to America fans clamored to know whether he dared renew his claim as the world's greatest fighter. Hurt by his supporters' loss of confidence and angered at the petty pretenders, he answered in his own distinctive way:

> I hereby challenge any and all the bluffers who have been trying to make capital at my expense to fight me, either the last week in August or the first week in September, this year, at the Olympic Club, in the city of New Orleans, La., for a purse of $25,000 and an outside bet of $10,000, the winner of the fight to take the entire purse...The Marquis of Queensberry rules must govern this contest, as I want fight, not foot-racing, as I intend keeping the championship of the world.

There it was: the next heavyweight title fight would be settled with gloves. Young James J. Corbett immediately picked up the gauntlet. Part of the challenger's stake money came from the usual bookmakers and sporting men, but his trainer, former middleweight champion Mike Donovan, also garnered a large portion of Corbett's cash from wealthy socialites at the New York Athletic Club. While depositing the stakes in New York, Corbett's manager, William Brady, allegedly remarked, 'there are men, members of high standing clubs right in this city, who will put up almost any amount on Corbett.' Significantly, Brady was not an oldtime boxer or ring man but a show business entrepreneur, soon to become a motion picture promoter, who saw prize fighting as an extension of the entertainment field. Indeed, he viewed the championship as a way to cash in on the real money afforded by the stage. Accordingly, Brady wrote the play, *Gentleman Jack*, expressly for Corbett to star in after he won the title.

Although the usual sporting men and pugs gathered for the signing of articles of agreement, they met not at the *Police Gazette* offices but in the *New York World* building. Such respectable journals as E. L. Godkin's *The Nation* bemoaned the decline of newspaper editors' moral stewardship. Godkin railed that the press pandered to the 'offscourings of human society – gamblers, thieves, drunkards and bullies...persons whose manners and morals are a disgrace to our civilization.' But *World* editor Joseph Pulitzer and other new moguls of the print media understood the power of spectacles, and they wanted to capture the *Police Gazette's* readership for their dailies. Indeed, to compete for the *Gazette*'s clientele, they established separate sports sections and carried feature stories on muscular heroes.

Corbett's public image also added a unique dimension to the ring. After attending college, he held a respectable job as a bank clerk; heavy labor for Corbett meant training, not putting bread on the table. He learned boxing in a sparring club rather than on the streets, and his reputation rested totally on glove fighting under the Queensberry rules. The newspapers called him 'Handsome Jim,' 'Pompadour Jim,' and eventually 'Gentleman Jim.' Clean-cut, intelligent, and highly skilled, Corbett denied the old equation of boxers with bruisers.

But the most striking thing of all about the upcoming fight was its business arrangements. Late in 1889 New Orleans' silk-stocking athletic clubs began sponsoring professional bouts, expanding old arenas and building new ones, all the while hiding behind the thin padding of five-ounce gloves. As one newspaper put it, 'steady businessmen, society bloods, and in fact, all classes of citizens are eager and anxious to spend their wealth to see a glove contest.' On March 14, 1890, the New Orleans city council authorized Queensberry fights, with the proviso that no liquor be served, that no bouts be staged on Sundays, and that promoters contribute 50 dollars to charity. The final obstacle fell when the Olympic Club defeated the old anti-prize fight statutes in court.

All of this testifies to the ring's transformation. During the 1880s, many socially prominent men had surreptitiously attended Sullivan's bare-knuckle fights in Mississippi. Lawyers, doctors, school board members, police commissioners, civic officials, even one college president later acknowledged their presence in Richburg for the Kilrain match. With glove fights legal, these men would *openly* attend the upcoming bout.

Sensing the large potential audience for the sanitized sport, new clubs now competed to sign up prominent contenders, and they offered handsome purses in the belief that gate receipts would exceed expenses. Boxing failed to become as rationalized and bureaucratically regulated as baseball or football; the corrupt underworld scent always lingered. Still, promotional techniques shifted control away from gamblers to entrepreneurs. The *de facto* legalization of prize fighting in New Orleans and the transformation of the ring into something approaching a business gave unprecedented opportunities to promising young fighters such as Robert Fitzsimmons, Arthur Upham, Billy Myer, Jimmy Carroll, Peter Mahar, Andy Bowen, and Frank Slavin.

New Orleans athletic clubs did more than simply attract new talent; they helped systematize boxing. Six weight classifications that *Police Gazette* editor Richard Kyle Fox had informally recognized with championship belts were standardized. Referees, now club employees, were empowered to stop bouts and award decisions if a fighter's life became endangered. Some clubs sponsored contests with a limited number of rounds and authorized the referee to declare a winner if the battle went the distance. All the old pugilistic categories – prize fights, sparring exhibitions, Queensberry contests – began to merge under the new order. Especially important, the challenge system, derived from dueling's code of honor, was eliminated. Club owners selected contenders, hired agents to negotiate their contracts, rented or built indoor arenas, and made all the local arrangements for matches. These changes ratified the fact that control of the ring had moved out of the old, honor-bound neighborhoods. Boxing was becoming commercial entertainment, more accessible than ever before to all classes.

As the first heavyweight championship bout under the new rules promoted by an athletic club and held in an urban arena, the Sullivan–Corbett fight put a seal of approval on these changes. Sullivan was the key player in this transition because he was by far the most prestigious figure in the boxing world. But while the champion had done so much to encourage the ring's transformation, he would always be remembered better as the last great bare-knuckler than as the bringer of the modern era. Declared the *New Orleans Picayune*, 'It was the old generation against the new. It was the gladiator against the boxer.'

'Handsome Jim' Corbett had already bested Jake Kilrain, beaten the fine Jewish fighter Joe Choynski, and fought to a draw against the masterful Australian black, Peter Jackson. The challenger worked out in California with Mike Donovan and, by the time he left for New Orleans, felt sure that Sullivan would also fall. Meanwhile the champion packed the house for a few more performances of *Honest Hearts and Willing Hands*, trained lightly for the coming bout, and enjoyed a triumphal round of benefits all the way South.

As both men arrived, the Crescent City was in an uproar. The Olympic Club not only built another new arena and put up the twenty-five-thousand-dollar purse for the heavyweight bout on September 7, 1892; it also arranged a lightweight title fight between Jack McAuliffe and Billy Myer on September 5 and a featherweight championship contest between Jack Skelly and George 'Little Chocolate' Dixon for September 6. *The New York Herald* marveled that 'the odium which rested upon the prize ring and the majority of its exponents a decade or two ago, because of the disgraceful occurrences connected with it, have in a measure been removed, until now the events on hand are of national and international importance.' The *Chicago Daily Tribune*, recalling the old bare-knuckle days, concurred: 'Now men travel to great boxing contests in vestibule limited trains; they sleep at the best hotels... and when the time for the contest arrives, they find themselves in a grand, brilliantly lighted arena.'

The great pugilistic carnival sent a surge of excitement through the country. Grover Cleveland's and Benjamin Harrison's presidential campaigns simmered on the back burner as boxing coverage boiled over onto front pages. McAuliffe retained his lightweight title by knocking out Myer in the 15th round. The following night, despite the controversy over a black fighting a white, Dixon thrashed Skelly in eight rounds. The bout may have demoralized Southern whites in this dawning age of Jim Crow, and many resolved that a black man must never strike a white one again in the ring, but 'Little Chocolate' retained his crown for seven more years.

By September 7, fans from across the country swelled New Orleans to bursting, and the festive crowds in the French Quarter evoked Mardi Gras. Colorfully dressed sportsmen, solid planters, ragged black roustabouts, and Italian street vendors paraded the teeming thoroughfares. Merchants' windows were filled with pictures of the pugilists and replicas of their fighting colors. Until fight day betting had been light at three or four to one on Sullivan, as fans expected a repetition of 1882 and 1889. Ominously, however, a surge of last-minute money for Corbett brought the odds close to even.

That night at ringside, former New Orleans Mayor Joseph Guillotte announced the fighters' weights to 10,000 fans in the Olympic Club arena. Sullivan scaled in at 212 pounds, close to his size against Kilrain. But the champion's flabby body showed none of the tautness of three years earlier. Corbett, his hair as always in an impeccable pompadour, entered the ring in splendid condition, 25 pounds lighter and 8 years younger than the champion. Urbane clubmen, respected professionals, and businessmen in formal evening attire sat nervously at ringside until the introductions ended. But it was not only men – and a few elegant women – in the Crescent City who waited anxiously. In every metropolis excited fans gathered in theaters and newspaper offices to learn the results. On top of the Pulitzer Building in New York, a red beacon was poised to signal when the fight went Sullivan's way, a white one for Corbett. Small towns were also caught up in the information network. Miners in Blocton, Alabama gathered at the local Odd Fellows lodge where, for 50 cents each, they heard the round-by-round telegraphic reports read aloud and shared for a moment in an instantaneous national culture. With hundreds of thousands on the edges of their seats, then, the bout began.

The fight was no contest. Young Corbett circled, danced, jabbed, and countered, while Sullivan rushed his fleeting form and slugged the air. At first the crowd hissed the challenger's running tactics but soon applauded his strategy. By the fifth round, having measured Sullivan's slow reactions, the Californian landed consistently. Fans grew ever more excited, sensing what was coming. Corbett probably could have ended the fight any time after the 12th round, but he waited until the champion staggered with exhaustion. Then in the 21st, the *Police Gazette* reported:

> he rushed in and planted blow after blow on Sullivan's face and neck. The champion, so soon to lose his coveted title, backed away, trying to save himself. He lowered his guard from sheer exhaustion, and catching a fearful smash on the jaw, reached to the ropes, and the blood poured down his face in torrents and made a crimson river across his broad chest. His eyes were glassy, and it was a mournful act when the young Californian shot his right across the jaw and Sullivan fell like an ox.

Youth, skill, and science, the newspapers said, overage, dissipation, and brute strength.

The day after the fight, William Lyon Phelps, professor of English at Yale, read the daily newspaper to his elderly father, a Baptist minister. 'I had never heard him mention a prize fight and did not suppose he knew anything on the subject, or cared anything about it. So when

I came to the headline CORBETT DEFEATS SULLIVAN, I read that aloud and turned the page. My father leaned forward and said earnestly, "Read it by rounds."' A few commentators welcomed Sullivan's defeat as the fitting end for a swaggering rowdy. Pontificated *The New York Times*, 'The dethronement of a mean and cowardly bully as the idol of the barrooms is a public good that is a fit subject for public congratulations.'

But more sensitive observers saw larger significance in Sullivan's career. A young journalist named Theodore Dreiser remembered meeting the great man shortly after his last fight:

> And then John L. Sullivan, raw, red-faced, big-fisted, broad shouldered, drunken, with gaudy waistcoat and tie, and rings and pins set with enormous diamonds and rubies – what an impression he made! Surrounded by local sports and politicians of the most rubicund and degraded character... Cigar boxes, champagne buckets, decanters, beer bottles, overcoats, collars and shirts littered the floor, and lolling back in the midst of it all in ease and splendor his very great self, a sort of prize-fighting J. P. Morgan... I adored him.

Here was Sullivan the hedonist, garish in every detail, flattered by hangers-on, luxuriating in the good life. With his own masculine prowess unquestioned, he gloried in pleasure and excess. Crude, boisterous, gargantuan in his powers and his appetites, Sullivan was the perfect symbol for an expansive age.

Within ten years of losing his title, having gained a hundred pounds and pawned his championship belt, he filed for bankruptcy. For a while his fortunes revived as he gave theater tours and temperance lectures and even collaborated on fight stories under his own by-line. Sullivan became a sort of elder statesman, brusque yet comical, always on hand for a championship bout. According to popular legend, his last years were painful ones, as heart disease, cirrhosis of the liver, and poverty debilitated his body and spirit. He died on February 2, 1918 and was buried in Roxbury.

Yet it was Sullivan in his full powers that men remembered, the raw, bare-knuckled giant who challenged the world and beat all comers. At the turn of the century, Ernest Thompson Seton, founder of the Boy Scouts of America, worried aloud that mothers coddled American youths and made them flabby. But Seton was reassured by the thought that he never met a boy who would not rather be John L. Sullivan than Leo Tolstoy.

Looking back on his own boyhood, Vachel Lindsay also recognized the champion as the central symbol of the era:

> When I was nine years old, in 1889,
> I sent my love a lacy Valentine.
> Suffering boys were dressed like Fauntleroys,
> While Judge and Puck in giant humor vied.
> The Gibson Girl came shining like a bride
> To spoil the cult of Tennyson's Elaine.
> Louisa Alcott was my gentle guide...
> Then...
> I heard a battle trumpet sound.
> Nigh New Orleans
> Upon an emerald plain
> John L. Sullivan
> The strong boy
> Of Boston
> Fought seventy-five rounds with Jake Kilrain.

Heroic strife broke through the sentimental clutter of lace and ruffles and curls. Sullivan rejected the routine world of work and family to live by his fists and his wits. If one may think of culture in terms of gender, then John L. Sullivan, the greatest American hero of the late 19th century, represented a remasculinization of America. To Lindsay, writing in the shadow of World War I, the Strong Boy of Boston embodied a lost era of genuine heroism, betrayed now by the complexity of modern life. To turn-of-the-century American men, Sullivan symbolized the growing urge to smash through the fluff of bourgeois routine and the ensnarements of corporate dependencies to the throbbing heart of life.

12
The 'Packer Affair' and the Early Marriage of Television and Sport
David L. Andrews and Andrew D. Grainger

> His father once advised him to join any club he wanted to before he was thirty-five: after that too many people wouldn't like him. Now he was thirty-eight, he might have to think about founding his own.[1]

The Centenary test match between Australia and England was played at the storied Melbourne Cricket Ground in March 1977, to mark the 100th anniversary of the first test match (played in 1877 in Melbourne, between Australia and England). As in the first test played between these fiercest of sporting rivals, so in the Centenary Test, Australia proved victorious. However, the 1977 rendering of this classic contest proved to be – in the truest sense of the cliché – a fantastic advert for test match cricket. Dominated by the penetrative and intimidatory bowling of the Australian Dennis Lillee, and the cavalier batting of Englishman Derek Randall, the fortunes of the sides ebbed and flowed throughout the game. Finally, on day five of the test – and having set England an improbable 463 runs for victory – Australia prevailed, winning by 45 runs having extinguished England's ultimately futile, but nonetheless stirring, run chase. As is so infrequent within the unpredictable sporting domain, here was a contest whose epic, and at times exhilarating, performance provided an appropriate spectacle for the celebratory context in which it was played. In the prevailing congratulatory aftermath of the Centenary Test, the majority of those interested and invested in the celebrated Ashes rivalry saw the future set fair for another 100 years; presumably marked by long periods of Australian dominance, punctuated by the occasional flicker of English resistance. Such prognostications of cricketing continuity proved dramatically short lived.

The cricket establishment's Centenary Test-induced complacency was rapidly torn asunder by the radical vision, and furthermore the resolute ambition, of the larger-than-life Australian media oligarch, one Kerry Francis Bullmore Packer, whose ubiquitously described cricket 'circus'[2] provides the focus for this chapter. Since the death of his father in 1974, Kerry Packer had been the head of his family's media corporation Consolidated Press Holdings, whose national television network, Channel Nine, had long struggled for ratings. To revive the fortunes of the floundering network, Packer turned to cricket, and looked to capitalize upon Australians' seemingly insatiable appetite for the game. Despite offering the Australian Cricket Board (ACB) AU$1.5 million – more than eight times the value of the previous arrangement – for a three-year contract to broadcast home test matches in Australia beginning with the 1976–77 season, the ACB chose to remain with the publicly funded Australian Broadcasting Corporation (ABC). Such a choice would have been unsurprising – after all, the ACB had a broadcasting relationship of over 20 years with ABC – were it not for the paltry sum of AU$210,000 it took to secure the contract.[3] Clearly, the denizens of the ACB were sending out a message to Channel Nine's fiscally brash upstart.

Having been so patently spurned by the conservative Australian cricket authorities, Packer summarily adopted more aggressive and unconventional means of forcing his way into the culturally significant – and thereby both strategically and financially rewarding – realm of cricket broadcasting. Indeed, even as the Centenary Test was being played, Packer had already covertly planted the seeds of cricket revolution, by securing the future services of many of those involved in the game for his secessionist World Series Cricket (WSC) venture. From the vantage point of more than three decades of informed *post facto* rationalization, it is difficult to express the degree to which the revelation of Packer's stealthy manoeuvrings shocked the cricket establishment. As Christopher Martin-Jenkins, the renowned cricket journalist and putative mouthpiece of cricket traditionalists, noted: 'For those of us who admittedly take the game (which is or was, just a game) too seriously, it was like learning that a wife whom one loved and trusted had been secretly, and for some time, making love to another man'.[4] The Packer affair (the secretive expropriation of cricket's leading talent away from the sport's traditional governing bodies) subsequently led to the Packer *war* (a costly struggle between the forces and products of the cricket establishment and those of Packer's alternative WSC vision), the outcome of which was the Packer revolution (the incorporation into the cricketing mainstream of the rationalities and innovations used to secure victory in the Packer *war*).

Far from being an expression of sporting continuity, in retrospect the 1977 Centenary Test proved to be a cricketing watershed. The very nature of the event as presented to the general public contrasted starkly with the emergent[5] form of the game soon championed by Packer and Channel Nine. Here was a cricket revolution in the making, agitated by the contrived production of entertainment-driven, highly commercialized and inveterately populist forms of the game that disrupted the perceptibly archaic amalgam of amateur and colonial sensibilities that (not always successfully) had governed the manner in which cricket was structured, understood, and experienced up until that moment in time. And, disrupt the cricketing world it did, prompting headlines such as that which ran in the *Daily Mirror*, on 9 May 9 1977, 'TEST PIRATES: Aussie TV tycoon's bid could shatter world of cricket'.

To many, the conjoined worlds of cricket and Australian broadcasting may well appear rather parochial preoccupations. However, and as is hopefully demonstrated in this chapter, the strategies, structures, and sensibilities advanced by Packer through the WSC initiative have permeated the sporting, and media, boundaries of both cricket, and Australia, respectively. Indeed, while rarely acknowledged or even recognized as such, the widespread adoption of Packer*esque* initiatives have profoundly impacted the workings of the global sport media industry, and thereby the very nature and experience of the global sport landscape more generally. The period of Packer's WSC (1977–79) can hence be viewed as a generative rupture, or radical discontinuity, out of which the game of cricket dialectically evolved and, as a result of which, the global sport media complex continues dialectically to evolve. For this reason, the motives and machinations of this 'ogre who smashed up a cosy, amateur-run game in the interests of television ratings'[6] remain highly relevant. Hence, this chapter critically examines the form, articulations and influences of the WSC moment.

Form

> It is the pervading law of all things organic and inorganic
> Of all things physical and metaphysical
> Of all things human and all things super-human
> Of all true manifestations of the head
> Of the heart, of the soul
> That the life is recognizable in its expression
> That form ever follows function. This is the law.[7]

The core tenet of modern architect Louis Sullivan's famous dictum – subsequently contracted into the more readily accessible *form follows function* – lies in its recognition of nature's ability to craft 'things' whose material expression provided an organically harmonious vehicle for the very essence of its being. Thus, in architectural terms, according to this mantra, the form of a space should be inextricably linked to its intended function. Although it's doubtful whether Kerry Packer was a knowing advocate of this proto-modernist aesthetic, there is nonetheless a palpable sense of utilitarian pragmatism evident within his design for an alternative version of cricket. For, if nothing else, Packer recognized the commercial potential of a strategically choreographed version of cricket presented as 'prime-time entertainment'.[8]

In all likelihood, however, the establishment of WSC was a last resort for Packer; something only brought forth once all negotiations with the ACB had failed. Nevertheless, having been set in motion, the WSC machinery moved swiftly to secure agreements with the top cricketing talent from teams around the world, and not simply Australia. For, while understandably Australia-based and oriented (Channel Nine was, after all, a national network), WSC was envisioned as an international tournament, involving elite players from England, the West Indies, Pakistan and South Africa, in addition to the cream of the current Australian team. As such, it was direct competition for international test match cricket, and not simply a regional cricketing sideshow. Beginning in early 1977, WSC began the process of forging agreements with key playing personnel. By the time of the Centenary Test, it has been estimated that more than two dozen cricketers had secretly signed. This number was to rise to more than 50 for the inaugural WSC season, with virtually all the luminaries of world cricket involved (including ten of the Australians involved in the Centenary Test; West Indians Vivian Richards, Gordon Greenidge, Michael Holding and Andy Roberts; Englishmen Tony Greig, Alan Knott and Derek Underwood; Pakistanis Imran Khan, Zaheer Abbas and Javed Miandad; and, hitherto banned from the international sporting stage, South Africans Barry Richards, Mike Proctor and Clive Rice).

That Packer should have been so successful in enticing the international cricketing elite away from the game's establishment, to what was a potentially career-damaging renegade venture, can be explained by the peculiar economics of the game at that particular time. While many other sports had already embraced professionalism and commercialism as an unavoidable, and indeed necessary, part of their continued existence, cricket remained uncomfortable in its engagements with mammon.⁹ The cricket authorities, both internationally and the within the individual national boards, seemingly preferred an understated (or, in more entrepreneurial terms, underexploited) relationship with commercial capital. This was certainly evident in Australia, where the legendary Don Bradman, as with other members of the ACB at the time, 'largely missed the secular shift towards the professionalisation of sport in the late '60s and early '70s, which finally found expression in Kerry Packer's World Series Cricket'.¹⁰ This failure, or perhaps unwillingness, to accede fully to the commercial demands of the time resulted in an inability, and equal unwillingness, to adequately address the issue of player payment.

Well into the 1970s, many of the elite Australian cricketers were sufficiently poorly paid that they had to secure off-season employment. Packer and WSC were thus able to exploit this situation, by offering player's contracts that dwarfed the ones they had previously received. According to evidence given in a subsequent restraint of trade trial in the High Court (which three Packer-backed players won against the Test and County Cricket Board's attempts to ban them from test matches and first-class cricket), WSC contracts paid between AU$20,000 and AU$35,000 for an annual commitment of 55 days. These were astronomical salaries, particularly since the fee for participation in an overseas tour with the England team was only £3,000 (approximately AU$5,000), and that for a home test match a paltry £210.¹¹ The iconic Dennis Lillee once calculated that, after taxes and expenses, he was paid AU$30 per day for playing test match cricket in the pre-Packer era.¹² The West Indian captain, Clive Lloyd, graphically captured the sentiment of many players at the time:

> The principal thing which operates in my mind was the financial security offered by my World Series Cricket contract. Here it was; a few months after leading the West Indies to a creditable performance against England, I was being offered three times what I had been paid for that series. Many of us never imagined such sums of money were possible in cricket.¹³

Clearly, given the meagre player compensation to which cricketers were accustomed, the game's authorities had made themselves vulnerable to Packer's open and expansive chequebook. As he later noted, it was 'the easiest sport in the world to take over. Nobody bothered to pay the players what they were worth'.¹⁴

In early May 1977 – and once the Australian team had already reached England in preparation for the forthcoming Ashes series, rendering sackings or team recalls unlikely – details of the 'Packer project' were released, with a predictably scaremongering response from both the cricket establishment and media telling of threats to the future of the game.[15] Despite last-ditch attempts to incorporate Packer back into the cricket fold, beginning in December 1977 – and incorporating a series of five-day 'Supertests' and one-day matches between the WSC Australian XI, a West Indies XI and a World XI – WSC began its quest to usurp traditional test match cricket's place within the hearts, minds and wallets of the Australian cricket-viewing public. What followed were two years of organizational conflict, financial struggle and sporting evolution.

At this point, it is perhaps appropriate to remind ourselves of the motives for Packer's involvement in cricket, and particularly the reasons for his single-minded desire to secure the broadcast rights to Australian test cricket. Unlike his rival Australian media mogul, Rupert Murdoch – who was acknowledged to be indifferent at best in his feelings toward sport *qua* sport[16] – Packer was certainly someone with a great personal interest in a wide range of sports, including cricket, golf and polo.[17] However, as a calculated media corporation executive – someone Westfield described as an 'instinctive opportunist'[18] – such personal preoccupations did not influence his thinking. Nor was his rationale for effectively reinventing the cricket industry motivated by an ethical yearning to see players receive increased remuneration packages: his later description of his involvement in WSC as being 'half-philanthropic', surely attested to a wry sense of humour, as opposed to any sincere commitment to player welfare. Rather, the motivating force driving Packer's involvement in cricket was quite simply the need to make Channel Nine profitable. The considerable ratings success of the recently launched drama series, *The Sullivans* and *The Young Doctors*, meant that Channel Nine was on the rise. However, such marquee productions were expensive to produce, costing as much as AU$70,000 per hour.[19] To accommodate such expenditure, Packer required ready access to more affordable sources of popular programming, hence his rebuffed tender for the ACB contract and the ensuing WSC enterprise. Packer's actions and intentions empirically confirmed Sage's insightful notation that 'The media have no inherent interest in sport' rather, its entrenched popularity, ability to generate mass viewership and relative affordability rendered it an efficient and attractive 'means for profit making'.[20] Or, within the context of the

ACB–WSC schism, Packer had no ambitions 'to run world cricket. He wanted to exploit it through television'.[21]

Returning, then, to Louis Sullivan's dictum: the form of WSC spectacle proved – through innovation and evolution – indivisible from its primary function, that of profit generation. During its two years of existence (1977–79), WSC was always a media product in process, in that it was constantly being reworked according to the demands of gaining the largest possible television audience, and therefore generating the maximum possible advertising revenue. Packer's preoccupation with WSC was not solely about engaging the traditional Australian cricket supporter, assuming, perhaps, that *he* would be effectively compelled to watch due to the level of cricketing talent on display. Rather, in fashioning WSC as a form of popular programming with potentially broad-based appeal, Channel Nine sought to embrace the non-traditional cricket audience – specifically, women and recent immigrants or new Australians – who had long been both formally and informally excluded from the patriarchal and white ethnocentric domain of modern Australian cricket.[22] To this end, WSC was produced as a mainstream, television-driven entertainment phenomenon. As Marqusee pointed out:

> In World Series Cricket, broadcasting called the tune; the matches were staged entirely for its benefit. Spectators were admitted free to the early WSC matches in order to provide 'atmosphere' for the television cameras. Through promotion and commentary, the WSC machine manufactured cricket drama for instant sale over the airwaves. There were Lillee and Thomson bashing Amiss and Greig, Viv Richards pulling Max Walker, Holding and Roberts bouncing the Chappells. It had all happened before – in official cricket. This was an all-action replay with the colours heightened and the boring bits edited out. It was 'virtual cricket', a contrived experience.[23]

Channel Nine also developed a number of innovations designed to enhance the entertainment quotient of the televised WSC spectacle. Packer may not have invented one-day professional cricket, however, he clearly recognized its value in maximizing the action, drama and excitement of the WSC spectacle. In Appadurai's terms, 'One-day cricket encourages risk taking, aggressiveness, and bravado while suiting perfectly the intense attention appropriate to high-powered television advertising and a higher turnover of events and settings'.[24] As a consequence, more emphasis was placed on one-day contests within the WSC schedule. Day/night fixtures, much of which were played under lights and against the atmosphere-enhancing backdrop of the evening sky, also came to the fore, doubtless propelled by their incursion into the potentially lucrative primetime viewing schedules. Restrictions on the positioning of outfielders were also introduced, designed to encourage batsmen to play more expansive and exhilarating shots. Most notoriously perhaps – prompting the widespread condemnation of WSC as 'pyjama cricket'[25] – an attempt was made to increase the visual appeal of the WSC product through the adoption of coloured uniforms for each of the teams. The adoption of a white ball and dark sightscreens, and more frequent and intrusive on-screen graphics, also sought to enhance the telegenic nature of the coverage. Any excitement or interest generated on the field of play was further enhanced through advances made in the number and usage of television cameras and instant replays, providing viewers with the best angle for live play and the obligatory televisual repetition of any notable action.[26]

Despite these and other on- and off-field WSC innovations, in monetary terms it would be true to say that it was by no means an unqualified success. While viewing and attendance figures improved in the WSC's second season, the significant capital outlay required for establishing the venture meant that Packer's financial losses were considerable, with no sign of their abating. The ACB was in an even more parlous state, saddled as it was with a sub-par national team, widespread public indifference and an attendant decline in revenues generated. So, in early 1979, the fiscal problems that threatened the future of both versions of the game, brought Packer and the ACB together to hammer out what has been described as a 'historic compromise'.[27] If it was, indeed, a compromise, the 'Packer risorgimento'[28] has to be considered an extremely inequitable one, for there is little doubt that Packer came away with the overwhelming share of the spoils. In return for ceasing and desisting with the WSC competition, Channel Nine was awarded the exclusive contract to televise Australian home test matches (the prize that launched the entire conflict, and a right the network has yet to relinquish). In addition, the ACB proffered Packer the authority to modify the cricket schedule according to his and, more pertinently, Channel Nine's needs. Even more astoundingly, the ACB also handed PBL Marketing, a newly established Packer company, a 10-year contract to promote and market the game in Australia. The fruits of this historic compromise resulted in many of the WSC initiatives and sensibilities soon becoming routine aspects of the establishment game, much to the chagrin of cricket traditionalists. In two short years, Packer had created and exploited a sporting schism whose repercussions are still being felt. However, before we consider further the reverberations associated with the 'pyjama game that woke the world',[29] both cricketing and beyond, it is first necessary to analyse the intersection of social forces and institutions out of which the WSC emerged.

Articulations

> Cultural studies often tends to operate in what looks like an eccentric way, starting with the particular, the detail, the scrap of ordinary or banal existence, and then working to unpack the density of relations and of intersecting social domains that inform it.[30]

Up to this point in the discussion, one might consider that the analysis has engaged in little more than a *reductive anthropomorphization* and *abstracted fetishization* of the WSC phenomenon. In terms of the former, this refers to the substitution of the structures and workings of complex corporations (in this case, Channel Nine) for its most recognizable mortal embodiment, usually its organizational principal (in this case, Kerry Packer). Of course this substitution – hopefully understandable in discussions of abstract institutional entities – is merely a rhetorical device rather than a statement of actuality. Packer may have been a highly visible executive figure, known for his broad-ranging involvement in many aspects of the corporate enterprise, yet it would be foolhardy not to acknowledge the legion of largely anonymous business, legal, marketing, media and cricket executives and consultants responsible for developing and implementing Channel Nine's 'private television circus'.[31] The opening section was also, and purposely, a largely descriptive account of WSC, which did not discuss the complex network of constitutive relations with which it is dialectically articulated.[32]

Pace the understanding of cultural studies as a theory and practice preoccupied with the critical reading and writing of contexts,[33] this section looks to begin to connect the WSC event – a 'practice that crystallizes diverse temporal and social trajectories'[34] – to the multiple material, institutional and discursive determinations with which it is articulated; remembering also, that as a noun as opposed to a verb, an historical process as opposed to an interpretive method, an articulation refers to the 'form of the connection that can make a unity of two different elements, under certain conditions. It is the linkage which is not necessary, determined, absolute and essential for all time'.[35] Of course, within the constraints of a single chapter, it would be impossible to carry out a comprehensive inventory of the multidimensional and multidirectional network of relationships and determinations that sutured WSC into the conjuncture of which it became, simultaneously, a constituting element.[36] Rather, our aim is to discuss what we consider to be the most significant and generative articulations pertaining to the constitution of the WSC moment. Identifying what are the ascendant determinations, directions, and effects at any given conjuncture is important, since this elucidates the control and operation of power and, thereby, the 'state of play in cultural relations'.[37]

Perhaps invoking Althusser, Bateman described Australian cricket as a 'relatively autonomous field' in which Packer intervened, leading to its increased commodification.[38] However, even in the immediate pre-Packer environment, Australian cricket's autonomy from broader social forces was, at best, relative, and relative only to the rapid and intensive commercialization of Australian society more generally, which occurred in the period from the 1960s onwards.[39] For, although haphazard and frequently ill-conceived, the commercialization of Australian sport, and cricket specifically, clearly pre-dated 1977.[40] Packer was responsible for ushering in cricket's 'hyper-commercialization',[41] which arose from his ability – as a powerful figure within the media industry – to reinvent the game first and foremost as a commercial media spectacle. Packer was thus able to connect (or articulate) a cultural form (cricket) to an expanding and avaricious media sector, which had itself become seamlessly incorporated into the workings of the broader economy. In doing so, he realized a phenomenon that was a quintessential example of the 'institutional alignment of sports and media in the context of late capitalism'.[42] Of course, the momentum of late capitalist forces and determinations was sufficiently vigorous that the conjoined spectacularization and commodification of an Australian popular practice, such as cricket, was an inevitability, if one accelerated by a combination of corporate exigency and individual tenacity.

Returning to the assumptions of dialectic cultural studies, WSC was both a product and simultaneously a producer of Australia's actualizing late capitalist moment.[43] Jameson's Mandel-informed notion of late capitalism refers to a stage in the evolution of capital accumulation wherein the maturing, and potentially stagnating, economic order has compelled a search for new sources of surplus value that have moved beyond the customary preoccupations of the traditional industrial manufacturing complex, to previously un(der)exploited domains.[44] Under this compulsion, 'economics has come to overlap with culture' resulting in the latter becoming ever more 'economic or commodity oriented'.[45] The collapsing of the boundaries between culture, commerce and the media were clearly at the heart of the WSC initiative, which could thus be considered an example of 'Disneyized' sport.[46] According to Bryman,[47] the concept of Disneyization refers to the multifaceted process (somewhat complementary to Ritzer's neo-Weberian concept of McDonaldization)[48] wherein the 'principles of the Disney theme parks are coming to dominate more and more sectors of American society as well as the rest of the world'.[49] Crucially, Bryman's spatial preoccupation with theme parks disregards that which occupies Disney's cultural and economic core; he overlooks the role and function of the mass-mediated products (the branded spectacles delivered via film, video, television, magazine and web platforms) that constitute the integrative and generative heart of Disney's media entertainment complex, stimulating the consumption of a bewildering array of Disney products and experiences.[50]

As within Disney's global media entertainment empire, so within the narrower confines of WSC: it deliberately produced mass-mediated entertainment spectacles that represented the cultural and commercial epicentre of the venture. Indeed, WSC could be considered an 'integrated' spectacle that coalesced both its monumental (mediated event) and vernacular (ancilliary and corroborative texts, products and services) elements in looking to secure the complete 'colonization of social life' by the spectacle.[51] The creation of the monumental WSC spectacle was touched upon in the previous section, and refers to the structural, technological and televisual manufacture of the event as a mass entertainment experience. Importantly, Packer recognized that – unlike Disney spectacles created at the hands or computers of animation artists – a large part of the WSC spectacle keyed on the on-field performance of its cast of assembled characters. For this reason, and after a series of sub-par showings, in the second WSC season Channel Nine introduced a series of individually specific targets, 'weight reduction, mobility, stamina, wind and speed',[52] designed to professionalize player's images and hopefully improve performance, all with the aim of enhancing the quality of the broadcast product.

Away from the live staging and broadcast coverage of games, WSC introduced a series of vernacular initiatives,[53] through which the brand was propelled into the everyday lives of the Australian populace. Most notably, these included a series of marketing and promotional measures designed to heighten, and indeed broaden, Australian interest in, and emotional attachment to, the game. WSC – and particularly the WSC Australian XI – were relentlessly marketed to the Australian public through the cloying yet infectious *C'Mon Aussie C'Mon* promotions, whose anthemic lyrics included the following nationalistic call to cricketing arms:

> You've been training all the winter
> And there's not a team that's fitter
> And that's the way it got to be
> 'Cause you're up against the best you know
> This is Supertest you know
> And you've go to beat the best the world has seen

The seeming intent of this refrain was to galvanize the Australian nation against a mighty cricketing foe (the metonymic personification of which was the superlative West Indian batsman, Vivian Richards, whose image accompanied the 'Cause you're up against the best you know' line). Through these and other promotions, WSC created a sense of public enthusiasm for and affinity – real or otherwise – with the rebel Australian collective (the WSC Australian XI). *C'Mon Aussie C'Mon* thus helped constitute and stimulate the audience for WSC programming, by normalizing the Australian consumer's elevated emotive attachment toward the WSC product. It also pre-emptively assisted in the narrativizing of the actual WSC contests. Such were the dictates of recasting, or perhaps more accurately 'Disneyizing',[54] cricket as primetime televisual entertainment.

A related element of WSC marketing and promotion was the concerted process of nurturing individual players as highly visible public figures (or celebritization). The cricket media coverage had long been preoccupied with celebrating, and constituting the mythos of, key figures within the game.[55] This process was taken to an entirely new level within WSC, which could not wait for its heroes and villains to evolve organically on the field of play. By humanizing and embellishing the public persona of individuals within the teams, so games became represented as dramas played out between casts of ever more familiar characters, as much as they were battles between superlative athletes. For instance, the second verse of the original *C'Mon Aussie C'Mon* offering focused on lionizing various Australian players as a means of inspiring popular adulation:

> Lillee's pounding down like a machine
> Pascoe's making divots in the green
> Marshy's taking wickets
> Hooksey's clearing pickets

> And the Chappells' eyes have got that killer gleam
> Mr Walker's playing havoc with the bats
> Redpath, it's good to see you back
> Lairdie's making runs
> Dougie's chewing gum
> and Gilmour's wielding willow like an axe

In this way, WSC mobilized another of Bryman's Disneyizing principles: the operationalizing of the emotional labour of its workforce in the presentation of the appropriate self to the consuming public.[56] WSC players may not have been as emotionally consistent and controlled as Disney staff during the course of their time at work (specifically on the playing field), as there were a number of regrettable incidents that marred WSC contests.[57] Nevertheless, considerable time and effort was focused, through marketing and promotional campaigns, on constituting these pivotal WSC subjects.

Within the conclusive convergence of economic and cultural spheres, so redolent of the late capitalist epoch, Channel Nine was clearly no longer in a position to operate purely as a media corporation, in the traditional sense of the term. As a consequence, and corroborating its Disneyized credentials, it sought to mobilize the trend toward the commercialization of Australian sport more generally[58] through 'welcoming any business innovation that could increase the potential for commercial revenues' within WSC.[59] This process was initiated through the very establishment of WSC as a themed spectacle imbued with 'excitement, glamour, aggression, superstars and non-stop entertainment'.[60] The WSC spectacle, and these associated themes, were subsequently extended through: 'promotion strategies [that] were implemented – at the ground, on television, on radio, in newspapers and magazines, and in department stores and supermarkets across the country – which resulted in multiple layers of cricket consumption. World Series Cricket sold books, fruits, paint and even lunchboxes, as well as cricket apparel'.[61] Predictably, WSC proved of considerable interest to a number of corporations interested in aligning their brand to the anticipated consumer interest – particularly in the youth and young adult markets – in this new sporting format prefigured on the generation of excitement and entertainment. This is perhaps exemplified in the sponsorship relationship between WSC and the fast-food behemoth, McDonald's, a relationship graphically expressed in a promotional poster circulated at the launch of the WSC's inaugural season in December 1977. The poster presents all the WSC playing personnel, dressed in WSC-branded cricket apparel, with a World Series Cricket 1977/78 banner above them, which was flanked on either side by the Channel Nine and McDonald's corporate logos. There appears nothing too remarkable about this scene, until one discerns the shocking red hair, clown-like visage and multicoloured clothing of a Ronald McDonald, sitting in the immediate proximity of Australian cricket luminaries Rodney Marsh, Doug Walters and Greg Chappell. Here in embodied, if awkward and slightly ridiculous, form was the conjoining of two – one established, one aspirant – manifestations of late capitalist consumer culture, each looking to benefit from the symbolic, and hence market, value of the other.

To sport marketers the aforementioned WSC initiatives are merely examples of the workings of the sport–promotion mix. However, to the cultural sociologist, they are more viewed as exemplars of the de-differentiation of consumption – or, the 'general trend whereby the forms of consumption associated with different institutional spheres become interlocked with each other and increasingly difficult to distinguish'[62] – whereby the values and materials of consumer capitalism insidiously encroach into ever more aspects of social life. Such are the workings of the vernacular sporting spectacle.

Influences

You won't spend half of today looking at a batsman's bum. Thank Kerry Packer for that.
When a wicket falls, you'll see it in slow motion. Thank Kerry Packer for that.
If a catch is dropped, you'll see replays from three different angles. Thank Kerry Packer for that.
Day/night internationals. The triangular summer series. Coloured clothing and white balls. Field restrictions. Full-time professionals.
Thank Kerry Packer for them.[63]

Kerry Packer was arguably the first person to concertedly expose and exploit the 'fruits of a marriage between cricket and television',[64] and there is a plausible case to be made that in doing so he successfully instigated and administered a cricket revolution, the effects of which are still being felt today. However, as has been noted elsewhere,[65] sufficient time has yet to elapse for us to be able to make conclusive statements about Packer's, and indeed WSC's, influence on Australian cricket, and specifically, the broader sporting landscape. Yet, in this concluding section, it is possible to offer some observations in this regard, however preliminary and contingent.

Within the Australian context, following the WSC–ACB compromise, Packer, Channel Nine – and particularly PBL Marketing – commandeered many of the functions, roles and profits that had previously been the province of the ACB. This led to a putatively amateur cricket ethos and officialdom being replaced by a new, unapologetically professional and corporate order, resulting in a situation where Australian cricket was 'taken over by agents with strong media and business interests, and for its administration to be given over to individuals and groups whose cultural capital derived from the economic, media and legal fields, rather than that of sport'.[66]

In the post-WSC cricket environment, the game became rapidly professionalized, commercialized and spectacularized, with many of the on- and off-field WSC innovations soon becoming incorporated into the establishment delivery of the game. This was particularly evident in the cricket scheduling, which placed more and more emphasis on the one-day version of the game and dramatically increased the number of games making up the international cricket calendar.[67] So, while players undoubtedly benefited from the increases in salaries resulting from the professionalization of the game, their bodies doubtless strained under the increased demands placed upon them. Off the field, Packer had developed a prototypical model of a 'Disneyized' sport,[68] wherein televisual spectacle provided the fulcrum for the evolution of the sport into an expansive and diverse cultural industry, whose products became manifest and hence could be consumed in a variety of different forms.

The Packer revolution was certainly not restricted to Australia. Despite periodic backlashes from the cricket establishment, within a remarkably short space of time throughout the world the game witnessed the erosion of its 'Victorian moral integument' and its replacement by 'aggressive, spectacular, and frequently unsporting' sensibilities, with no obscuring the fact that players and promoters alike are "out for the buck"'.[69] While broader changes relating to the hegemony of the late capitalist order[70] meant that the professionalization, commercialization and spectacularization of world cricket was an inevitability, it was one that came to fruition much more quickly due to the machinations and preoccupations of WSC. Virtually all major nations within the international cricket community (the ten members of the International Cricket Council) – the one exception being England – have been transformed by the spreading influence of WSC initiatives into cricket cultures where the one-day version of the international game has taken commercial, and oftentimes cultural, precedence over the test match version. Once viewed as cricket's apotheosis, for many the test match is now considered a cricketing anachronism. As Harriss noted more than two decades ago:

> The shift to one-day cricket marks the emergence of an era in which the game is no longer based on the rational, calculating bourgeois individual. Indeed, the essence of or 'depth' of Test cricket has given away to the glittering surface and spectacle of the highly commercialised commodity that is One-Day Cricket.[71]

If Packer was responsible for dragging cricket into the commerce and culture of the late twentieth century through the popularization of one-day cricket, in doing so he set in motion a process that, through the recent advent of the Twenty20 version of the game, has updated it for the new millennium. Ironically perhaps, the idea for Twenty20 cricket was generated by research commissioned in 2000 in the once staid corridors of the England and Wales Cricket Board (ECB), which had identified steep declines in match attendance and participation.[72] In an attempt to counter these declines, and in true Packer fashion, the marketing manager of the ECB, Stuart Robinson, developed and proposed a radically shortened version of even the one-day game played over one inning per team of 20 overs each, which subsequently became known as Twenty20.

The first Twenty20 games were played in English domestic cricket in 2003, with the first international match played between Australia and New Zealand in 2005. In the intervening period, and largely as a result of the implementation and success of the World Twenty20 tournament, and particularly the Indian Premier League,[73] Twenty20 has become a lucrative format for domestic and international cricket schedulers. By condensing the game into a highly televisual 3-hour window, and by even more aggressively accenting exhilarating and entertaining performances, Twenty20 represents the 'manifest destiny'[74] of Packer's cricket revolution. As cricketer Ed Smith suggested, Twenty20 would have been 'unimaginable without Packer'.[75] Furthermore, and in a dialectic sense, it is the cricketing response to ever-encroaching social and economic determinations, with regard to both the sport's producers and consumers. It is a celebrity-nurturing, entertainment-driven form of the game designed to engage the time-poor, instant gratification-demanding and brand spectacle-driven sensibilities of 21st global metropolitans, wherever they may reside. As such, it is a potentially fruitful catalyst for corporate advertisers and sponsors looking to penetrate the brand-cluttered landscape and experiences of the contemporary metropolis. This is warp speed WSC; it is the 'next generation of Packer cricket'.[76]

Of course Packer's influence is not reserved to cricket. Although the structure, promotion and delivery of WSC was heavily informed by American influences, Packer realized a protypical model of Disneyized sport that proved both confirmative and generative to the global sport industry. Additionally, in a broader strategic sense, his tactic of establishing a rival sport league – and/or focusing on the production of mainstream sport entertainment – as means of securing media broadcast rights, proved influential both in Australia and abroad. Most notably, this self-same approach was utilized by Packer's primary rival within the Australian media complex, Rupert Murdoch, who actually adopted this strategy in a direct struggle with Packer for the rights to Australian rugby league,[77] and who clearly incorporated many of the strategies and techniques honed within WSC in his forays into British rugby league, English Premier League football and, more recently, English test match cricket.[78] However, the Packer influence can also be discerned in sport media manoeuvres in North America, Europe and Asia. Of the utmost irony, given their enduring rivalry, *Murdochization* is the term that has been used to describe media corporations' commandeering of sporting assets as a means of furthering their commercial interests,[79] when the provenance of the strategy surely renders *Packerization* the more appropriate term.

Notes

1. G. Haigh, *The Cricket War: The Inside Story of Kerry Packer's World Series Cricket*, 30th anniversary edition edn (Melbourne: Melbourne University Press, 2007), p. 34.
2. L. Allison, ed., *The Politics of Sport* (Manchester: Manchester University Press, 1986), P. Barry, *The Rise and Rise of Kerry Packer Uncut* (Sydney: Bantam/ABC Books, 2007), A. Bateman, *Cricket, Literature and Culture: Symbolising the Nation, Destabilising Empire* (Farnham: Ashgate, 2009), R.J. Holt, *Sport and the British: A Modern History* (Oxford: Clarendon Press, 1989), M. Westfield, *The Gatekeepers: The Global Media Battle to Control Australia's Pay TV* (Annandale: Pluto Press, 2001).
3. Haigh, *The Cricket War*.
4. Quoted in W. Buckland, *Pommies: England Cricket through and Australian Lens* (Matador: Leicester, 2008), p. 65.
5. R. Williams, *Marxism and Literature* (Oxford: Oxford University Press, 1977).
6. Anon, 'Kerry Packer: The Times Obituary', *The Times Online* 27 December, 2005.

7. L. Sullivan, 'The Tall Office Building Artistically Considered', *Lippincott's Magazine* March (1896).
8. M. Marqusee, *Anyone but England: An Outsider Looks at English Cricket* (London: Aurum Press, 2005), p. 122.
9. A.J. Walsh and R. Giulianotti, 'This Sporting Mammon: A Normative Critique of the Commodification of Sport', *Journal of the Philosophy of Sport* XXVIII (2001).
10. G. Haigh, *Game for Anything: Writings on Cricket* (Melbourne: Black Inc., 2004), p. 46.
11. R. Sissons, *The Players: A Social History of the Professional Cricketer* (Leichhardt, NSW: Pluto Press, 1988).
12. Newman, P. 'Packer the Pioneer with Enduring Legacy of Pyjama Game that Woke the World'. *The Independent* 28 December, 2005.
13. Quoted in Beckles, p. 73
14. Buckland, *Pommies*, p. 65.
15. Haigh, *The Cricket War*, p. 55.
16. W. Shawcross, *Murdoch: The Making of a Media Empire* (New York: Touchstone Books, 1997).
17. J. Shaw, 'Kerry Packer, 68, Australia's Media Magnate, Is Dead', *The New York Times* 27 December 2005.
18. Westfield, *The Gatekeepers: The Global Media Battle to Control Australia's Pay TV*, p. 121.
19. Haig, *The Cricket War*.
20. G.H. Sage, *Power and Ideology in American Sport: A Critical Perspective* (Champaign: Human Kinetics, 1990), p. 123.
21. Marqusee, *Anyone but England*, p. 127.
22. W. Vamplew, 'It's Not Cricket and Perhaps It Never Was: An Historical Look at Australian Crowd and Player Behaviour', *Sport in History* 14.1 (1994).
23. Marqusee, *Anyone but England*, p. 127.
24. A. Appadurai, *Modernity at Large: Cultural Dimensions of Globalization* (Minnesota: University of Minnesota Press, 1996), pp. 107–8.
25. Bateman, *Cricket, Literature and Culture: Symbolising the Nation, Destabilising Empire*, p. 202.
26. D. Rowe, 'Sport: The Genre That Runs and Runs', *The Australian TV Book*, eds G. Turner and S. Cunningham (Sydney: Allen & Unwin, 2000).
27. Marqusee, *Anyone but England*, p. 127.
28. G. Haigh, 'A Price for Everything: A Look Back at the Packer Revolution, Three Decades On', *ESPN Cric Info* 3 December, 2007.
29. P. Newman, 'Packer the Pioneer with Enduring Legacy of Pyjama Game That Woke the World'.
30. J. Frow and M. Morris, 'Cultural Studies', *Handbook of Qualitative Research*, eds N.K. Denzin and Y.S. Lincoln, Second edn (Thousand Oaks, CA: Sage, 2000), p. 327.
31. Holt, *Sport and the British*, p. 321.
32. S. Hall, 'The Problem of Ideology: Marxism without Guarantees', Hall, 'On Postmodernism and Articulation: An Interview with Stuart Hall (Edited by Lawrence Grossberg)', *Stuart Hall: Critical Dialogues in Cultural Studies*, eds D. Morley and K.H. Chen (London: Routledge, 1996).

33. L. Grossberg, *Bringing It All Back Home: Essays on Cultural Studies* (Durham: Duke University Press, 1997).
34. Frow and Morris, 'Cultural Studies'.
35. Hall, 'On Postmodernism and Articulation: An Interview with Stuart Hall (Edited by Lawrence Grossberg)', p. 141.
36. Frow and Morris, 'Cultural Studies'.
37. S. Hall, 'Notes on Deconstructing "the Popular"', *People's History and Socialist Theory*, ed. R. Samuel (London: Routledge & Kegan Paul, 1981), p. 235.
38. Bateman, *Cricket, Literature and Culture*, p. 202.
39. P. Bell and R. Bell, *Americanization and Australia* (Sydney: University of South Wales Press, 1998).
40. R. Cashman and A. Hughes, 'Sport,' *Americanization and Australia*, eds P. Bell and R. Bell (Sydney: University of South Wales Press, 1998), J. McKay and T. Miller, 'From Old Boys to Men and Women of the Corporation: The Americanization and Commodification of Australian Sport,' *Sociology of Sport Journal* 8.1 (1991).
41. B. Stewart and A. Smith, 'Australian Sport in a Postmodern Age', *International Journal of the History of Sport* 17.2 (2000), p. 288.
42. M.R. Real, 'Mediasport: Technology and the Commodification of Postmodern Sport', *Mediasport*, ed. L.A. Wenner (London: Routledge, 1998), p. 15.
43. F. Jameson, *Postmodernism, or, the Cultural Logic of Late Capitalism* (Durham: Duke University Press, 1991), F. Jameson, *The Cultural Turn: Selected Writings on the Postmodern 1983–1998* (London & New York: Verso, 1998).
44. D.L. Andrews, 'Sport, Culture, and Late Capitalism', *Marxism, Cultural Studies and Sport*, eds B. Carrington and I. McDonald (London: Routledge, 2009).
45. Jameson, *The Cultural Turn*, p. 73.
46. D.L. Andrews, 'Disneyization, Debord, and the Integrated NBA Spectacle', *Social Semiotics* 16.1 (2006).
47. A. Bryman, 'Theme Parks and McDonaldization' *Resisting McDonaldization*, ed. B. Smart (London: Sage, 1999).
48. G. Ritzer, *The McDonaldization of Society: An Investigation into the Changing Character of Contemporary Social Life* (Thousand Oaks, CA: Pine Forge Press, 1993), G. Ritzer, *The McDonaldization Thesis: Explorations and Extensions* (London: Sage, 1998), G. Ritzer, *The McDonaldization of Society*, Revised New Century Edition edn (London: Sage, 2004).
49. Bryman, 'Theme Parks and McDonaldization', p. 26.
50. Andrews, 'Disneyization, Debord, and the Integrated Nba Spectacle'.
51. G. Debord, p. 20.
52. H. Beckles, ed., *A Spirit of Dominance: Cricket and Nationalism in the West Indies – Essay in Honour of 'Viv'* (Mona: Canoe Press – University of the West Indies, 1998), p. 80.
53. G. Debord, *The Society of the Spectacle*, trans. D. Nicholson-Smith (New York: Zone Books, 1994 [1967]).
54. Bryman, 'Theme Parks and McDonaldization'.
55. B. Hutchins, *Bradman: Challenging the Myth* (Cambridge: Cambridge University Press, 2002).
56. Bryman, 'Theme Parks and Mcdonaldization'.
57. Haigh, *The Cricket War: The Inside Story of Kerry Packer's World Series Cricket*.

58. Cashman and Hughes, 'Sport', McKay and Miller, 'From Old Boys to Men and Women of the Corporation: The Americanization and Commodification of Australian Sport'.
59. P. Kitchin, 'Twenty-20 and English Domestic Cricket', *International Cases in the Business of Sport*, eds S. Chadwick and D. Arthur (Oxford: Butterworth-Heinemann, 2007), p. 103.
60. D. Shilbury, H. Westerbeek, S. Quick and D. Funk, *Strategic Sport Marketing* (Crows Nest, NSW: Allen & Unwin, 2009), p. 155.
61. Shilbury, Westerbeek, Quick and Funk, *Strategic Sport Marketing*, p. 155.
62. A. Bryman, 'The Disneyization of Society', *The Sociological Review* 47.1 (1999), p. 33.
63. D. Hughes, 'Obituary: Kerry Packer', *The Western Australian* 28 December, 2005, p. 7.
64. Beckles, ed., *A Spirit of Dominance: Cricket and Nationalism in the West Indies – Essay in Honour of 'Viv'*, p. 80.
65. Haigh, *The Cricket War: The Inside Story of Kerry Packer's World Series Cricket*.
66. Bateman, *Cricket, Literature and Culture: Symbolising the Nation, Destabilising Empire*, p. 202.
67. Horne, J. 'Cricket in Consumer Culture: Notes on the 2007 Cricket World Cup'.
68. Andrews, 'Disneyization, Debord, and the Integrated NBA Spectacle'.
69. A. Appadurai, p. 107.
70. Andrews, 'Sport, Culture, and Late Capitalism'.
71. I. Harriss, 'Packer, Cricket and Postmodernism', *Sport and Leisure: Trends in Australian Popular Culture*, eds D. Rowe and G. Lawrence (Sydney, Australia: Harcourt Brace Jovanovich, 1990), p. 117.
72. Kitchin, 'Twenty-20 and English Domestic Cricket', p. 104.
73. A. Gupta, 'India and the IPL: Cricket's Globalized Empire', *The Round Table: The Commonwealth Journal of International Affairs* 98.401 (2009), D. Rowe and C. Gilmour, 'Global Sport: Where Wembley Way Meets Bollywood Boulevard', *Continuum: Journal of Media & Cultural Studies* 23.2 (2009), 171–82.
74. Haigh, 'A Price for Everything: A Look Back at the Packer Revolution, Three Decades On'.
75. E. Smith, *What Sport Tells Us About Life* (London: Penguin Books, 2008), p. 95.
76. A. Lee, 'It's Just Good Old Twenty20, with Money', *The Times* 21 April, 2008.
77. S.L. McGaughey and P.W. Liesch, 'The Global Sports-Media Nexus: Reflections on the 'Super League Saga' in Australia', *Journal of Management Studies* 39.3 (2002), J. McKay and D. Rowe, 'Field of Soaps: Rupert V. Kerry as Masculine Melodrama', *Social Text* 50 (1997), D. Rowe, 'Rugby League in Australia: The Super League Saga', *Journal of Sport & Social Issues* 21.2 (1997).
78. D.L. Andrews, *Sport-Commerce-Culture: Essays on Sport in Late Capitalist America* (New York: Peter Lang, 2006), D. Denham, 'Modernism and Postmodernism in the Professional Rugby League in England', *Sociology of Sport Journal* 17.3 (2000).
79. E. Cashmore, *Sports Culture: An A–Z Guide* (London: Routledge, 2000).

References

Allison, L., ed., *The Politics of Sport*. Manchester: Manchester University Press, 1986.
Andrews, D.L. 'Disneyization, Debord, and the Integrated Nba Spectacle'. *Social Semiotics* 16.1 (2006): 89–102.
Andrews, D.L. *Sport-Commerce-Culture: Essays on Sport in Late Capitalist America*. New York: Peter Lang, 2006.
Andrews, D.L. 'Sport, Culture, and Late Capitalism'. *Marxism, Cultural Studies and Sport*. Eds. Carrington, B. and I. McDonald. London: Routledge, 2009. 213–31.
Anon. 'Kerry Packer: The Times Obituary'. *The Times Online* 27 December 2005.
Appadurai, A. *Modernity at Large: Cultural Dimensions of Globalization*. Minnesota: University of Minnesota Press, 1996.
Barry, P. *The Rise and Rise of Kerry Packer Uncut*. Sydney: Bantam/ABC Books, 2007.
Bateman, A. *Cricket, Literature and Culture: Symbolising the Nation, Destabilising Empire*. Farnham: Ashgate, 2009.
Beckles, H., ed. *A Spirit of Dominance: Cricket and Nationalism in the West Indies – Essay in Honour of 'Viv'*. Mona: Canoe Press – University of the West Indies, 1998.
Bell, P. and R. Bell. *Americanization and Australia*. Sydney: University of South Wales Press, 1998.
Bryman, A. 'The Disneyization of Society'. *The Sociological Review* 47.1 (1999): 25–47.
Bryman, A. 'Theme Parks and McDonaldization'. *Resisting McDonaldization*. Ed. Smart, B. London: Sage, 1999. 101–15.
Buckland, W. *Pommies: England Cricket through an Australian Lens*. Leicester: Matador, 2008.
Cashman, R. and A. Hughes. 'Sport'. *Americanization and Australia*. Eds Bell, P. and R. Bell. Sydney: University of South Wales Press, 1998. 179–92.
Cashmore, E. *Sports Culture: An A-Z Guide*. London: Routledge, 2000.
Debord, G. *The Society of the Spectacle*. Trans. Nicholson-Smith, D. New York: Zone Books, 1994 [1967].
Denham, D. 'Modernism and Postmodernism in the Professional Rugby League in England'. *Sociology of Sport Journal* 17.3 (2000): 275–94.
Frow, J., and M. Morris. 'Cultural Studies'. *Handbook of Qualitative Research*. Eds Denzin, N.K. and Y.S. Lincoln. Second edn, Thousand Oaks, CA: Sage, 2000. 315–46.
Grossberg, L. *Bringing It All Back Home: Essays on Cultural Studies*. Durham: Duke University Press, 1997.
Gupta, A. 'India and the IPL: Cricket's Globalized Empire'. *The Round Table: The Commonwealth Journal of International Affairs* 98.401 (2009): 201–11.
Haigh, G. *Game for Anything: Writings on Cricket*. Melbourne: Black Inc., 2004.
Haigh, G. *The Cricket War: The Inside Story of Kerry Packer's World Series Cricket*. 30th anniversary edn, Melbourne: Melbourne University Press, 2007.
Haigh, G. 'A Price for Everything: A Look Back at the Packer Revolution, Three Decades On'. *ESPN Cric Info* December 3, 2007.
Hall, S. 'Notes on Deconstructing "the Popular"'. *People's History and Socialist Theory*. Ed. Samuel, R. London: Routledge & Kegan Paul, 1981. 227–40.

Hall, S. 'On Postmodernism and Articulation: An Interview with Stuart Hall (Edited by Lawrence Grossberg)'. *Stuart Hall: Critical Dialogues in Cultural Studies*. Eds Morley, D. and K.H. Chen. London: Routledge, 1996. 131–50.

Hall, S. 'The Problem of Ideology: Marxism Without Guarantees'. *Stuart Hall: Critical Dialogues in Cultural Studies*. Eds Morley, D. and K.H. Chen. London: Routledge, 1996. 25–46.

Harriss, I. 'Packer, Cricket and Postmodernism'. *Sport and Leisure: Trends in Australian Popular Culture*. Eds Rowe, D. and G. Lawrence. Sydney, Australia: Harcourt Brace Jovanovich, 1990. 109–21.

Holt, R.J. *Sport and the British: A Modern History*. Oxford: Clarendon Press, 1989.

Horne, J. 'Cricket in Consumer Culture: Notes on the 2007 Cricket World Cup'. *American Behavioral Scientist* 53.10 (2010): 1549–68.

Hughes, D. 'Obituary: Kerry Packer'. *The Western Australian* 28 December, 2005: 7.

Hutchins, B. *Bradman: Challenging the Myth*. Cambridge: Cambridge University Press, 2002.

Jameson, F. *Postmodernism, or, the Cultural Logic of Late Capitalism*. Durham: Duke University Press, 1991.

Jameson, F. *The Cultural Turn: Selected Writings on the Postmodern 1983–1998*. London & New York: Verso, 1998.

Kitchin, P. 'Twenty-20 and English Domestic Cricket'. *International Cases in the Business of Sport*. Eds Chadwick, S. and D. Arthur. Oxford: Butterworth-Heinemann, 2007. 101–13.

Lee, A. 'It's Just Good Old Twenty20, with Money'. *The Times* 21 April 2008.

Marqusee, M. *Anyone but England: An Outsider Looks at English Cricket*. London: Aurum Press, 2005.

McGaughey, S.L., and P.W. Liesch. 'The Global Sports-Media Nexus: Reflections on the "Super League Saga2 in Australia"'. *Journal of Management Studies* 39.3 (2002): 383–416.

McKay, J. and T. Miller. 'From Old Boys to Men and Women of the Corporation: The Americanization and Commodification of Australian Sport'. *Sociology of Sport Journal*, 8.1 (1991): 86–94.

McKay, J. and D. Rowe. 'Field of Soaps: Rupert V. Kerry as Masculine Melodrama'. *Social Text*. 50 (1997): 69–86.

Newman, P. 'Packer the Pioneer with Enduring Legacy of Pyjama Game that Woke the World'. *The Independent* 28 December, 2005.

Real, M.R. 'Mediasport: Technology and the Commodification of Postmodern Sport'. *Mediasport*. Ed. Wenner, L.A. London: Routledge, 1998. 14–26.

Ritzer, G. *The McDonaldization of Society*. Revised New Century Edition edn, London: Sage, 2004.

Ritzer, G. *The McDonaldization of Society: An Investigation into the Changing Character of Contemporary Social Life*. Thousand Oaks, CA: Pine Forge Press, 1993.

Ritzer, G. *The McDonaldization Thesis: Explorations and Extensions*. London: Sage, 1998.

Rowe, D. 'Rugby League in Australia: The Super League Saga'. *Journal of Sport & Social Issues* 21.2 (1997): 221–6.

Rowe, D. 'Sport: The Genre That Runs and Runs'. *The Australian TV Book*. Eds Turner, G. and S. Cunningham. Sydney: Allen & Unwin, 2000. 130–41.

Rowe, D. and C. Gilmour. 'Global Sport: Where Wembley Way Meets Bollywood Boulevard'. *Continuum: Journal of Media & Cultural Studies* 23.2 (2009): 171–82.

Sage, G.H. *Power and Ideology in American Sport: A Critical Perspective*. Champaign: Human Kinetics, 1990.

Shaw, J. 'Kerry Packer, 68, Australia's Media Magnate, Is Dead'. *The New York Times* 27 December, 2005.

Shawcross, W. *Murdoch: The Making of a Media Empire*. New York: Touchstone Books, 1997.

Shilbury, D. et al. *Strategic Sport Marketing*. Crows Nest, NSW: Allen & Unwin, 2009.

Sissons, R. *The Players: A Social History of the Professional Cricketer*. Leichhardt, NSW: Pluto Press, 1988.

Smith, E. *What Sport Tells Us About Life*. London: Penguin Books, 2008.

Stewart, B. and A. Smith. 'Australian Sport in a Postmodern Age'. *International Journal of the History of Sport* 17.2 (2000): 278–304.

Sullivan, L. 'The Tall Office Building Artistically Considered'. *Lippincott's Magazine* March (1896).

Vamplew, W. 'It's Not Cricket and Perhaps It Never Was: An Historical Look at Australian Crowd and Player Behaviour'. *Sport in History* 14.1 (1994): 3–12.

Walsh, A.J. and Richard Giulianotti. 'This Sporting Mammon: A Normative Critique of the Commodification of Sport'. *Journal of the Philosophy of Sport* XXVIII (2001): 53–77.

Westfield, M. *The Gatekeepers: The Global Media Battle to Control Australia's Pay TV*. Annandale: Pluto Press, 2001.

Williams, R. *Marxism and Literature*. Oxford: Oxford University Press, 1977.

13
All these Years of Hurt: Culture, Pedagogy and '1966' as a Site of National Myths

Michael L. Silk and Jessica Francombe

The twentieth century witnessed a strengthening of the bond between the discursive (re)production – literally, the perpetuation through language (writing, conversation...) – of specific national cultures and select sporting practices. This bond is such that sport has become arguably the most emotive – peacetime – vehicle for harnessing and expressing bonds of national cultural affiliation. These sporting discourses often reflect and reproduce social hierarchies,[1] are often highly gendered and offer particular constructions of *the* character, culture and the historical trajectory of a people – constructions that by their very nature are acts simultaneously both of inclusion and exclusion.[2] In this sense, sporting discourses often serve as a means by which particular dominant groups further (re)define the parameters of *the* 'sanctioned' national identity and these discourses are often mobilized and appropriated with regard to the organization and discipline of daily life. Thus, they play a key part in the shaping and 'education' of citizens and in the service of particular corporate-political agendas.[3]

In this chapter, we examine the way these cultural discourses operate within the material and institutional contexts of everyday life.[4] Understanding sport as a particularly 'lustrous' and affective cultural form which constitutes part of what Stuart Hall termed the 'narratives of nation', we address the very public, and highly educative, potentialities of sporting discourse as one of a number of powerful public pedagogies that frame the cultural present. These profound and often misconceived cultural pedagogies 'contribute to *educating* us how to behave and what to think, feel, believe, fear and desire – and what not to'.[5] Our specific focus is the seemingly ubiquitous sporting moment of 1966 (ubiquitous because it is the only time England has ever won the World Cup) in the English-based promotional discourses prior to the 2010 World Cup in South Africa. As such, we are interested in how, more than ever, as 'cultural citizens', we are seduced, inducted and incorporated into discursive systems and materialisms dictated by both state and transnational capital.[6] While 'internal' political forces previously responsible for harnessing and contouring national cultural identity have not been rendered obsolete, their position of influence is being eroded by external, commercially driven forces. In this sense, following Kellner and Kim,[7] we suggest that people are increasingly prone to be educated by the commercial media's popular pedagogies; education is a lifetime process increasingly controlled by dominant economic institutions.[8] The *context* then and the *processes* through which national cultures are produced and reproduced are being transformed.[9] In this scenario, the locus of control in influencing the manner in which the nation and national identity are represented becomes exteriorized through, and internalized within, the promotional strategies of (trans)national corporations. Simply put, and prefigured on the operations and machinations of corporate entities, the politico-cultural nation of the nineteenth century has been replaced by the 'corporate-cultural nation' of the twenty-first century.[10] As such, in the balance of the chapter, we point to a dialectic of collective remembering and forgetting, excavating 1966 as a powerful mnemonic – a cultural and corporatized pedagogy – that educates us in our present.[11]

'All those years of hurt': the presence of the past in the present

Two world wars, and one world cup

Screamed by the desperate divided crutch.

Used to have an Empire then we grew up.

Lost everything, who gives a fuck (Jamie T – 'Chaka Demus')

What does it mean to take seriously, in our present conjuncture, the thought that cultural politics and questions of culture, of discourse, and of metaphor are absolutely deadly political questions? ... I want to persuade you that is so.[12]

1966

There is a relative perversity in writing about 1966 as a key moment in sport history. For, at the time, unlike say the terrorist activity in Munich

1972, the 'clenched fist salute' (see Smith, this volume) of 1968, or, perhaps the dying American baseball player Lou Gehrig's 'luckiest man' farewell in 1939, 1966 was relatively unremarkable. For sure, the English FA wanted the 1966 World Cup to be a festival of football, and the tournament was lauded for its breadth and sophistication of television coverage, yet, it was an event of modest commercialism, unsegregated crowds, insignificant tourism, restrained patriotism and modest (as opposed to triumphant) celebration.[13] In short, while England won the final against West Germany, courtesy perhaps of a generous Russian official, the political, social and economic significance of this was quite unremarkable.[14] As Jimmy Greaves, a member of the 1966 England squad suggested in 2003, it was quite a low-key affair: 'If we won it now, the country would come to a stop for a week, and every player would become an immediate superstar: when we won it in '66 everybody cheered, a few thousand came out to say well done, and within a week everybody had disappeared, we'd all gone on our way, and we'd started playing the next season. That was the end of it. Now you get all this aura surrounding '66, but it was never quite like that'.[15] Yet, as Mason indicates, the World Cup Finals of 1966, and particularly the final match itself, have become part of the collective memory of the English; our critical excavation then of 1966 is with regard to its ideological and pedagogical significance in our contemporary moment.

Located within our cultural present, but entirely predicated upon a memory of a distant, rose-tinted past, 1966 as a date, a temporal marker, has been permitted to speak unequivocally for itself.[16] Drawing on Redfield's analysis of 9/11 as a name-date,[17] 1966 serves to both inscribe and efface, such that it speaks to a singular imposition of knowledge (remembering) and amnesia in what Anderson[18] (borrowing from Benjamin) termed the homogenous empty time of the nation-state. Connoting more than football, it is a historically situated toponym, or 'place name', that, in our current moment, conjures up the supremacy of Britain on the international stage and an acceptance and enactment of mythical English 'values'. The recourse to these invented, 'suitable' and palatable versions of the past[19] is juxtaposed with a present in which Britain's international standing – in transition from 'a global power to one European nation among many'[20] – is as ambiguous as England's centralized position within Great Britain in the face of Scottish and Welsh devolution.[21] The 1966 name-date is a powerful evocation of the collective exertion of men, personal and familial cognizance and the national narratives of post-war Britain; it calls up 'a myth of national superiority based on the projection of past glories into the present, a gentlemanly brand of masculinity and a submerged reference to class that reflects the roots of the game in the British working class'.[22] 1966 is, in effect, a powerful, self-sustaining myth that has been wired into the nation's collective consciousness.[23] With Hall[24] we seek here to 'unpack' 1966 to gain critical insight and understanding of our contemporary 'corporate nation'.[25] We suggest that the popular mythology, the corporatized 'beautiful game' of 1966, is being continuously (re)played out, (re)constituted, displayed and embodied as part of a national mnemonic – the jogger, so to speak, of a national memory. This has brought a 'commodified' response to the widespread yearning in a more complex era for something simpler, a mythical past or a sense of belonging to a time when 'England was great'.[26]

The memory of the English is continuously being nudged and ignited by reminders of the match that took place at Wembley Stadium on 30 July 1966,[27] a match that is as renowned for its resultant 'sound bites' and imagery as its sporting merit. Coverage, at least in public discourse, of the 'real' event in 1966 was far from xenophobic or militaristic, and in the public sphere through the early 1970s the game remained a largely unpoliticized event.[28] Yet, by the early 1980s, as the Falklands war anointed Margaret Thatcher as *the* embodiment of an age of national decline[29] amid reasserted suspicion of former enemies and notions of a reinvigorated 'glorious past', discourses of 1966 began to take on decidedly jingoistic overtones.[30] This perhaps reached its epitome in media discourse surrounding the 1996 European Championships, where coverage exhumed past hostilities between England and Germany and recollected national glories from a bygone era in a wilfully nostalgic fashion.[31]

1996

Penned to celebrate England hosting the 1996 European Championships, the (for many) now infamous *Three Lions* football anthem composed by Ian Broudie of the Lightning Seeds, with words by comedians David Baddiel and Frank Skinner, offers the most popular invocation of 1966. The lyrics, somewhat playfully, and as part of the 'new laddism' of the 1990s,[32] evoke the nostalgia of 1966, as well as England's failures (as a football team/nation) since that date. Collapsing distinct temporal moments, and disrupting the linear chronology of the past, the song harks back to the 'halcyon' date in which England lifted the Jules Rimet trophy and the hurt that has ensued:

> ...So many jokes, so many sneers, but all those oh-so-nears
> Wear you down, through the years
> But I still see that tackle by Moore

> And when Lineker scored
> Bobby belting the ball and Nobby dancing
> Three Lions on shirt, Jules Rimet still gleaming
> Thirty years of hurt, never stopped me dreaming
> I know that was then but it could be again
> It's coming home, it's coming home, it's coming, football's coming home

Carrington read the 'Three Lions' discourse as part of a wider reassertion of a narrow and closed white male 'new-lad' identity[33]. For Carrington, the song is part of a colonial and ethnocentric political discourse, an attempt to reconstruct an imperial Britain, that posits that England lost its way and its world position and that now, after '30 years of hurt', football, as a metaphor for the nation, is returning to its 'rightful' place. The video accompanying the song reconstructs the great moments of the 1966 World Cup, yet, as Carrington points out, depicts both a past and a present England (in terms of players, supporters, children emulating the past) as completely homogenous in its whiteness and maleness; black faces are 'completely absent'.[34] It is perhaps of little surprise that the song has surfaced again as part of the pre-2010 cultural discourse – in various permeations the song has formed part of every major football tournament in which England has been present since 1996. In its current format, and titled *3 Lions 2010*, the song features soprano Olivia Safe, ex-Take That solo artist and English 'icon' Robbie Williams and 'outrageous comedian' Russell Brand; the '30 years of hurt' lyric has simply been replaced with 'All these years of hurt'.

Although far from teleological fault lines, 1966 and 1996 appear as two instructive dates. For if 1966 is mythologized as a time of unabashed national glory and confidence, 1996 acted as the catalyst for the popularized consumption of football. For sure, such processes were well under way, and were in part based on the increased regulation and commodification of the game as a result of the Taylor report of 1990, the subsequent creation of the Premier League and the impact of satellite television coverage by Rupert Murdoch's BSkyB. Perhaps more poignantly, the European Championships in 1996 can, in the sense deployed by the French theorist Guy Debord, be read as part of both the monumental and vernacular architecture of a spectacular society. Following Debord, this consists of the upper-case spectacle (the actual mediated mega-event) and the lower-case spectacle (relentless outpourings of the corroborating and/or parasitic culture industries) that accompany the mega-event.[35] Football, at least in its present form in England, as capitalist product and process, epitomizes a situation in which the 'commodity completes its colonization of social life'.[36] Importantly, in this new heightened stage of the spectacle, which sees the 'autocratic reign of the market', the 'spectacle has never before put its mark to such a degree on almost the full range of socially produced behavior and objects'.[37] In this sense, such corporate sporting discourse is part of wider and inherently contradictory (given the supposed rolling back of government under neoliberal policy regimes) governance of the marketplace in which social practices and subjectivities are increasingly commercially directed.

2010

In the 14 years between the original *Three Lions* and the current *3 Lions 2010* we have witnessed the further entrenchment of what Bourdieu and Wacquant term a 'new planetary vulgate'[38]: a neoliberalism centred on bolstering the logics of the market, socializing individual subjects and disciplining the non-compliant.[39] Replacing politically organized and state-directed assemblages (schools, asylums, reformatories, work houses, washhouses, museums, homes [for the young, old or damaged], unified regimes of public service broadcasting, housing projects) are an array of other practices for shaping identities and forms of life – advertising and marketing discourses, the proliferation of goods, the multiple stylizations of the act of purchasing, cinemas, videos, pop music, lifestyle magazines, television soap operas, advice programmes and talk shows.[40] In other words, moral, sober, responsible and obedient individuals are now consumers; consumption itself is a 'civilizing project very different from the 19th-century attempts to form moral, sober, responsible, and obedient individuals, and from 20th century projects for the shaping of civility, social solidarity, and social responsibility'.[41] In this regard, an array of corporatized practices and technologies exist (e.g. the stylized display of clothing obtained through acts of consumption) for the assemblage, or indeed display, of the normalized, regulated, corporo-national subject. As such, popular cultural discourses act as very normalizing public pedagogies, educating us about belonging, being, other, us, them; the remnants and rampant mythologizing of 1966 in our present is a powerful *cultural pedagogy* that can shape, mould and educate citizens in our present conjunctural moment.

For Hobsbawm,[42] sport acts as an important 'badge of membership' – one that seems all the more tangible or 'real' when embodied by the 11 men selected to represent the imagined English nation. Following

Young,[43] the current vogue for donning football jerseys, waving flags and watching international tournaments in pubs or open-air venues seems commercially dictated and directed; corporations provide the framework for temporally distinct phases of national adulation. However, such 'moments of national hysteria are based on the rhythms of individual consumption. The frame might be national and communal, but the practice today is personal'.[44] Appearing as hollowed out, empty signifiers, detached and distant from their original moorings within a neoliberal conjuncture centred on consumptive practice, our literal and metaphorical 'badges of membership'[45] are, in our present, emblazoned on goods and products that fill our high streets. Sport, football – and 1966 specifically – has emerged again, albeit in many different forms, as part of the popular, everyday imaginary. At the time of writing, in the build-up to the 2010 South Africa World Cup Finals and as England delivers its bid to host the 2018 World Cup Finals, 1966 is an inescapable past that is ubiquitous in the present. Embodied, waved, worn, displayed and performed, watched, heard and sung, signifiers of 1966 form part of the ethopolitics[46] of the past-present: informed, fashion-conscious consumers proudly displaying the symbolic and iconic.

The politicization and corporatization of 1966 entails the production and distribution of cultural goods and representations that deploy power to shape identities and subjectivities.[47] On a given day the public (re)appropriation, (re)telling and (re)constructing of the 1966 popular mythology can take multiple forms and allude to multiple stylizations of the self. In this World Cup year, the ideologies of consumption have propelled 1966 onto the bodies of the national team (England's 2010 World Cup kit is modelled on the '66 attire) and onto the bodies of the general population (the high street offers a plethora of fashion garments, namely New Look, Sainsbury's and Umbro's '66 clothing ranges, French Connection's 66 series (FCUK 66), Next's Ecru Bobby Moore t-shirts; in fact, you do not have to look far to see the Three Lions logo adorned on torsos up and down the country). The year has been thrust into our bodies (both Carlsberg, 'Men of England, it's time to join the immortals' featuring players from 1966, and McDonalds offer up 1966 for consumption in the form of the perfect pint and twisty fries); into our leisure time (in the form of Paul Weiland's 2006 film *Sixty Six* and former England coach Terry Venables' fronting of *The Sun* newspaper's World Cup coverage with his rendition of Elvis Presley's *If I Can Dream*: a country dreaming of two stars [world cup wins] when all could be like before); into our practices of charitable giving (Cancer Research's number 6 Bobby Moore: World Cup campaign); and, perhaps less tastefully, although more playfully, into our bedrooms (Ann Summers invites it's (fe)male consumers to 'get into the spirit of the summer season of football' and support their country by wearing their exclusive England outfit. The parodic intent of the '69' (with the second six turned upside down to signify the erotic act) insignia on the shorts, over the knee socks and back of the t-shirt is not lost as Ann Summers equates to being patriotic and looking drop-dead sexy).

Normalized everyday life is seemingly cluttered by such commercial paraphernalia; alongside the allusions to '66 sit an array of products based on the St George's cross,[48] a subject of intense contestation, given its symbolic associations. The cross has contemporary associations with racism and far-right groups and it carries historical allusions to both Empire and anti-Islamic sensibilities: it was the banner under which the Crusades embarked on a holy war with Muslim-controlled Jerusalem, and further controversy was caused in 2000 when the English FA chose the song Jerusalem by Fat Les as its official song for the European Championships. Similarly, amid debates over devolution, the flag of St. George has been reappropriated by England football supporters, replacing the Union Jack as their favoured motif.[49] No visit to the petrol station, the supermarket, the vet, the doctor, the garden centre, the bank or the local village Bank Holiday festival is seemingly complete without the 'opportunity' to purchase a teddy bear, flag, car-set, sticker, pencil case, packet of condoms, hat, ball, towel, mug, frisbee, confectionary, bottle opener, 'bopper' head gear, lighters, flip-flops, pillow, wig, tea towel, oven glove, bunting, pens, wallets, commemorative medal, notepads, a four-year football bond (offered by national team sponsor, Nationwide) or an inflatable hand (a far from exhaustive list) that depicts the St George's cross.[50] Of course, these products, these (un)waved flags, do not constitute an innocent discourse; rather the omnipresent utilization of the St George's cross works, in Billig's parlance, to 'flag' the nationhood 'unflaggingly'.[51] Yet, what does this signify? What is being remembered? Who is being re-*membered*?

The Foci Imaginarii of the 1966 mythscape: corporatism, atavism and invocations of nation

> [Englishness] is continuous, it stretches into the future and the past, there is something in it that persists, as in a living creature.[52]

We should perhaps not be surprised that corporate-inspired inf(l)ections of nation are often – although are not preordained to be – superficial, depthless and draw on selective and depoliticized representation of *the* national history to 'elide social injustices of the past and patterns of institutionalized inequality'[53] in the present. Over 100 years ago, Ernest Renan claimed that forgetting was a 'crucial element in the creation of nations'.[54] For Renan, once a nation is established, it depends upon its collective amnesia for its continued existence. However, and crucially, forgetting is not a result of absent-mindedness; it is rather a result of the carefully contoured discursive reconstitution of the past by powerful groups at particular points in time. In this way, history, or social memory, is a construction, actively invented and reinvented, a site of struggle and contestation over the reconstitution of an 'authorized', collectively held, past.[55] In this sense, the process of forgetting, as Billig[56] points out, is juxtaposed with the process of remembering: remembering is simultaneously a collective forgetting: the nation, which celebrates its antiquity, celebrates its historical recency. Such corporatized discursive constructions then build upon common histories and memories, no matter how exclusionary and fabricated, which, through particular reconstructions of the history, link the present to the past.[57] This process points to questions regarding which 'national histories' are told, by whom, and what, and how, do they recollect?[58] Indeed, these promotional cultural discourses are highly pedagogic; as Healey has proposed, the acting out of the past in contemporary spectacles is a space in which powerful groups can retell history to suit the present. Such discourses become the very public educative 'arenas in which social memory is acted out, performed, or demonstrated; in between moments when we cease to live in time and space in order to reflect on, or be trained in, or entertained by something of our historicity, our being-in-history'.[59]

However, crucial questions remain to be asked with regard to such corporate-cultural discourses when the past becomes *manipulated in the interests of capital*, especially with respect to the political and pedagogic dimensions of myth: whose/which version of the past forms the essence of such discourse, whose past is silenced or marginalized, what is 'authentic' and to whose past does it bear resemblance.[60] As Bell proposed, such discourses raise the question of how particular stories are shaped and circulated[61] and who has the relative power to control historical knowledge and disseminate such knowledge; the key question then becomes 'how national identities emerge in specific instances and are then translated over time...how is history, indeed time, represented?'[62] The mythological discourses of 1996 certainly provide consumers with the 'presence of the past within the present'[63] and offer a 'preferred' sense of place[64] that links the past and the present, yet the past is not retrieved; rather it is reconfigured and colonized 'by obliging it to conform to present configurations'.[65] In this regard, the atavistic presence of 1966 in the present – as *mere commodity* – speaks more to the corporate appropriation of history than with the conveyance of historical veracity. Indeed, in a present characterized by the contradictory dissolution/blurring *and* reassertion of national borders, the birth of a culture of fear surrounding the figurative 'other' living next door and a capitalist consumer market (in crisis) that effeminizes the phallus,[66] the past is reordered from the perspective of today: in the process of looking back, the past is explored, mourned and exorcized to enable consumers/citizens to come to terms with the present. As such, the discursive constitutions of 66 mythology in the present act as *foci imaginarii*[67] that centre on a nation at ease with itself, an implicitly white, simple, stable, safe and purified 'eternal England' – no matter that 1966 for many, especially black Britons, was a period of struggle for recognition, public persecution, discriminatory immigration laws and racial violence.

How then, does such 'knowledge' of the past aid us in 'coming to terms' with the present? Fortier proposes that assertions of a 'multiculturalist nationalism' work to assuage ongoing anxieties about national legitimacy. In a 'neo-ethnic version of national identity that has emerged in Britain'[68] 'minority groups' may not only be 'let in', but redefined as integral to the nation; standing as exemplary embodiments of multicultural Britain, the perfect rejoinder to assertions of ethnic essentialism, racism and intolerance – these narratives certainly formed the essence of the London 2012 Olympic Bid and have been part of the strategizing of English football authorities, especially the Football Association's efforts to 'sanitize' English football fandom.[69] Yet, following the 7/7 bombings in London in 2005 (again, far from a teleological fault line), diversity was once again redefined as disruptive;[70] threat lies with division, as such, the appeal remains to a foundational unity, a nationalist narrative that asks us to recover a lost moment of harmony.[71] In this regard, the rampant mythologizing of 1966 and the reappropriation of the St George's cross offer a purportedly *authentic* national (English, not British) culture that others (however defined) have little to do with; there is no need to focus for example on *inadequate integration*[72] to the British way of life by British Muslims (as per the media coverage of the 7/7 bombings), of insipient far-right politics, intensified hostility towards British Muslims since the commencement of the 'war on terror'; feelings of disillusionment and resentment; 'Islamophobia'; urban segregation; disproportionate levels of unemployment, health and poverty;

and differential immigration statuses and the concomitant restrictions of rights.[73] Evoking Gilroy's terminology, the myth of 66 is:

> an imaginary definition of the nation as a unified *cultural* community. It constructs and defends an image of national culture – homogenous in its whiteness yet precarious and perpetually vulnerable to attack from enemies within and without... This is a racism that answers the social and political turbulence of crisis and crisis management by the recovery of national greatness *in the imagination*.[74]

Subsequently, and following Carrington as with the 1996 European Championships, what is promoted in such discourse is not the cultural diversity of contemporary Britain; rather a fixed, closed and racially homogenous sense of national cultural identity that excludes Black, Asian and 'other' representations from the national imaginary. As with the discursive reconstitution of the Blitz (the bombing of London by the German Luftwaffe between autumn 1940 and the spring of 1941), again, an enduring and omnipresent name-date, 1966 serves as a 'nationally defining' moment evoking resilience, unity, spirit and whiteness,[75] with history 'lessons' deployed as the metaphor through which the current world is viewed.[76] As Gilroy notes, the Blitz narrative has endured as a model of commonality, of Britishness at its best, to which people should aspire: the dominant trope through which to understand contemporary national 'struggle'.[77] Following Stephens' discussion of the ways in which the Blitz was evoked in media discourse post-7/7,[78] the mythologizing of 1966 offers a similar, albeit commodified, point of origin (no matter how arbitrary) and the idea that we are a unified community, travelling through history together. In so doing, whiteness disappears, becoming normalized as Englishness,[79] the past acting as an important cultural pedagogy of the present in the legitimation of social structures and inequalities.

The Blitz discourse also evokes a number of distinctive parallels to sporting discourse, a set of interrelated narratives of war, masculinity, heroism and, unity in beating a 'common enemy'.[80] Again, as with the Blitz, the mythologizing of 1966 centres on 'ordinary' men (Ball, Hurst, the Charltons, Law, Moore...),[81] who display a work ethic and a willingness to push the male body to almost unimaginable extremes in the defeat of West Germany. Unlike the 'pampered' (feminized) stars of contemporary hypercommerical trite hagiographic sporting structures (from which we are increasingly disconnected), stories prevail of the 'ordinariness' of 66 world cup 'heroes'; eating egg and chips with family and friends at a service station or catching the bus home the day following World Cup victory.[82] Furthermore, given the supposition that sport forms a warrior mentality, promotes traditional, hyper-masculine stereotypes, puts 'real men' in touch with primal instincts for competition and violence, lets men connect with each other through the overcoming of fear, pain and fatigue,[83] 'ordinary men' are those who are hard-bodied, tough and probably perform such an identity through playing football – just like the 'boys of 66'. Yet, this definition of masculinity with its hard-boiled, white, tough image of manliness has been disturbed; a rampant culture of consumption, coupled with a loss of manufacturing and middle-management jobs, presents white males with an identity crisis of unparralleled proportions – the male body has been transformed from an agent of production to a receptacle for consumption. The neoliberal everyman exists as an emasculated, repressed corporate drone whose life is simply an extension of a reified and commodified culture.[84] In this regard, 'all these years of hurt' speaks as much to the loss of the 'right to be a man' as it does to a relative lack of success on the football pitch – the mythology then of 1966 in the present providing a safe sanctuary for the reassertion of 'real white men' (and this is certainly the case in sporting/advertising discourse; Snickers, e.g. sponsors the Saturday morning football programme *Soccer AM* with the slogan, Not for Girls, and has a World Cup advertising strategy centred around the tagline 'get some nuts'). The irony here however, is that corporatized cultural discourse becomes the sanctioned space for being a man – it invites, interpellates, supporters to embody a masculinity that refuses the seductions of consumerism when it is in the very crisis of consumption in which men are allegedly domesticated, rendered passive, soft and emasculated.[85] Furthermore, and albeit anecdotal (although played out through the pages of tabloid newspapers such as the *Sun* and the *Daily Mail*), it seems that those who are perhaps most disenfranchised from neoliberalism's competitive individualism – those positioned in what Giroux termed the degraded borderlands of late capitalism[86], the English lower class – are most enfranchised by such corporatized cultural pedagogic discourse. For it seems that those on the lower fringes of a normalized middle-class England are precisely those who embody, display, wave and perform these corporatized renditions of nation; *pace* the overwhelming presence of such signifiers in lower-class (council-house) neighbourhoods, on builders' lorries, 'white-van' drivers' windscreens and lower-end cars.[87] In this sense, it is the white-lower classes, those who have perhaps 'hurt' the most – mourning the loss of masculinity, the lower-class origins of football, of nation, of Empire – who perhaps are searching most for, and are perhaps most susceptible to, a corporatized sense of belonging. What goes unquestioned here, however, when such 'belonging', however ephemeral, comes in the form of corporatized cultural pedagogies, are the important concerns over exactly 'whose nation' is normalized and which bodies 'belong'. In this regard, the distinctive celebration of a past Englishness in the present does little more than act as a powerful, and extremely public, exclusionary discursive device that associates 'authentic' Englishness – and provides opportunity for display, performance and embodiment – with a historically grounded, white, working class primordial nationalism.[88]

Concluding comments

> ...politics cannot be separated from the pedagogical force of culture. Pedagogy should provide the theoretical tools and resources necessary for understanding how culture works as an educational force, how public education connects to other sites of pedagogy, and how identity, citizenship, and agency are organized through pedagogical relations and practices. Rather than viewed as a technical method, pedagogy must be understood as a moral and political practice that always presupposes particular renditions of what represents legitimate knowledge, values, citizenship, modes of understanding, and views of the future.[89]

In an expanded conceptualization of education, which, following Giroux and Kellner involves seeing the mediated advertising discourses as forms of cultural pedagogy[90] as means of education that convey values, knowledges and power relations, corporatized sport discourse provides a cultural tool *par excellence* for negotiating ideas of nation, class and race 'after Empire'.[91] With Giroux, our boundaries for comprehending the pedagogic and political significance of popular discourse, in this case the presence of 1966 in the present, have shifted – the result of the organizing force of a neoliberal ideology – and the mechanisms by which we come to engage and understand particular mythologies are now, perhaps more than ever, formulated upon the capability and ubiquity of certain (consumptive) discourses to construct 'knowledge, values, and identities'.[92] The mythologizing of 1966 in the present suggests that nation, at least in a cultural sense and *despite*, if not *because* of, a global age, is a crucible of our lived daily experiences that can 'anchor people in particular experiences, practices, identities, meanings and pleasures'.[93] 1966 as a key moment in sport history then has a life, as a name-date, far beyond the conjunctural/temporal moment in which it is located. In this regard, corporatized discourses of 1966 in the present are as much about social reproduction, cultural production and moral and political regulation, about the culture of politics and how that culture of politics is, in part, educating us towards a particular future,[94] as they are about a football match all those years ago. Through recalling *the* past, *the* sanitized nation becomes sanctioned; a series of promotional discourses that assert sport as an affectively charged, and highly pedagogic, sphere of mediated popular culture. Through remembering the existential values, meanings and 'authorized, collectively held past' and simultaneously forgetting and essentializing difference and diversity, the discourse offers a synthetic and seductive version of national in which difference – or perhaps more accurately, contestations over difference – has been banished or erased.[95]

Following Billig, we are writing in a moment of hot nationalism[96] – as with the seemingly ubiquitous array of discourse, product and image of 1966. Yet, commercial imperatives seem to bastardize, or cannibalize this hotness; pointing to the banalization and normalization of such discourses. The cooling off, or banalization of hotness, is precisely the reason why such discourses are such powerful forms of cultural pedagogy – for it is here, in normalized, contemporary and corporatized popular culture where such discourses operate at their most insidious level, slipping coolly under the radar of popular and indeed academic consciousness and critique. Our role is surely to illuminate and expose such cultural pedagogies responsible for normalization, processes that are clearly anchored in power relations that serve particular ends, and thereby perpetuate structural inequalities. The atavistic presence of 1966 then is significant far more than in a sporting sense: it speaks of the very ways in which sanctioned corporate and exclusionary inf(l)ected national discourses circulate, educate and, shape the present.

Notes

1. cf. David Andrews and C.L. Cole. 'The nation reconsidered', *Journal of Sport and Social Issues* 26, 2 (2002); Rudolph De Cillia, Martin Reisgel and Ruth Wodak. 'The discursive construction of national identities', *Discourse and Society*, 10, 2 (1999); Joanna De Groot. 'The dialectics of gender: Women, men and political discourses in Iran c. 1890–1930', *Gender & History*, 5 (1993); Jackie Hogan, 'Staging the nation: Gendered and ethnicized discourses of national identity in olympic opening ceremonies,' *Journal of Sport and Social Issues*, 27, 2 (2003); Michael L. Silk and Mark Falcous. 'One

day in September/one week in February: mobilizing American (sporting) nationalisms', *Sociology of Sport Journal*, 22, 4 (2005); Michael L. Silk and Mark Falcous. 'Sporting spectacle and the post 9–11 patriarchial body politic' in *The Day that Changed Everything: The Impact of 9/11 on the Media, Arts and Entertainment*, ed. Matt. Morgan (New York: Palgrave MacMillan).
2. Hogan, 'Staging the nation'; see also Eric Hobsbawm. *Nations and Nationalism since 1870: Programme, Myth, Reality* (Cambridge: Cambridge University Press, 1990); Maurice Roche. *Mega-Events and Modernity: Olympics and Expos in the Growth of Global Culture* (London and New York: Routledge, 2000); Alan Tomlinson. 'Olympic spectacle: Opening ceremonies and some paradoxes of globalization', M*edia, Culture and Society*, 18 (1996).
3. David Andrews. 'Excavating Michael Jordan: notes on a critical pedagogy of sporting representation,' in *Sport and Postmodern Times: Culture, Gender, Sexuality, the Body and Sport*, ed. Genevieve Rail and John Harvey (Albany, NY: State University of New York Press, 1995); Henry Giroux. 'Cultural studies as performative politics', *Cultural Studies ↔ Critical Methodologies*, 1, 1 (2001); Lawrence Grossberg. *We Gotta Get Out of this Place: Popular Conservatism and Postmodern Culture* (London: Routledge, 1992); Lawrence Grossberg. *Bringing it all Back Home: Essays on Cultural Studies.* (Durham, NC: Duke University Press, 1997).
4. Giroux, 'Cultural studies'.
5. Douglas Kellner. *Media Culture: Cultural Studies, Identity and Politics between the Modern and the Postmodern* (London and New York: Routledge, 1995): 2 (emphasis added).
6. Michael Giardina. *Sporting Pedagogies: Performing Culture and Identity in the Global Arena* (New York: Peter Lang, 2005); Cameron McCarthy, Michael Giardina, Jin-Kyung Park and Susan Harewood. 'Cultural inter/connections', *Cultural Studies ↔ Critical Methodologies*, 5 (2005).
7. Douglas Kellner and Gooyong Kim, G. 'You tube, critical pedagogy, and media activism', *Review of Education, Pedagogy, and Cultural Studies*, 31, 3 (2010).
8. cf. Henry Giroux. *Disturbing Pleasures: Learning Popular Culture* (New York: Routledge, 1994); Christopher Robbins. 'Searching for politics with Henry Giroux: Through cultural studies, public pedagogy and the 'terror of neoliberalism', *Review of Education, Pedagogy, and Cultural Studies*, 31, 5 (2009).
9. David Held, Anthony McGrew, David Goldblatt and Jonathon Peraton. *Global Transformations: Politics, Economics and Culture* (Stanford, CA: Stanford University Press, 1999).
10. Michael L. Silk and David Andrews. 'Beyond a boundary: Sport, transnational advertising, and the reiminaging of national culture', *Journal of Sport and Social Issues*, 25, 2 (2001); Michael L. Silk, David Andrews and C.L. Cole (eds). *Corporate Nationalisms: Sport, Cultural Identity and Transnational Marketing* (Oxford, UK: Berg, 2005).
11. This chapter is a revised, condensed and reworked version of an article by the authors currently under review in *Nations and Nationalism*.
12. Stuart Hall. 'Subjects in history: making diasporic identities', in *The House that Race Built*, ed. Wahneema Lubiano (New York: Pantheon, 1997).

13. Tony Mason. 'England 1966: traditional and modern?' in *National Identity and Global Sports events: Culture, Politics and Spectacle in the Olympics and Football World Cup*, eds Alan Tomlinson and Christopher Young (New York: SUNY Press, 2006).
14. see also Christopher Young. 'Two world wars and one world cup: Humour, trauma and the asymmetric relationship in Anglo-German football', *Sport in History*, 27, 1 (2007).
15. Mason, 'England 1966'.
16. Dominic Malcolm, Alan Bairner and Graham Curry. '"Woolmergate": Cricket and the representation of Islam and Muslims in the British press', *Journal of Sport and Social Issues*, 34, 2 (2010).
17. Marc Redfield. 'What's in a name-date? reflections on 9/11', *Review of Education, Pedagogy, and Cultural Studies*, 30, 3 (2008).
18. Benedict Anderson. *Imagined Communities* (London: Verso, 1991).
19. Ben Carrington. ' "Football's coming home" but whose home? and do we want it? nation, football and the politics of exclusion', in *Fanatics! Power, Identity & Fandom in Football*, ed. Adam Brown (London: Routledge, 1998); Jon Garland. 'The same old story? Englishness, the tabloid press and the 2002 football world cup', *Leisure Studies*, 23, 1 (2004).
20. Jon Garland and Mike Rowe. 'War minus the shooting? Jingoism, the English press, and Euro 96', *Journal of Sport and Social Issues*, 23, 1 (1999): 89.
21. Garland and Rowe, 'War minus the shooting'; Susanne Reichl. 'Flying the flag: the intricate semiotics of national identity', *European Journal of English Studies*, 8, 2 (2004).
22. Young, 'Two world wars, 3–4; although compare with Chas Critcher, 'England and the world cup: world cup Willis, English football and the myth of 1966', in *Hosts and Champions: Soccer Cultures, National Identities and the USA World Cup*, eds John Sugden and Alan Tomlinson. Aldershot, UK: Ashgate, 1994.
23. Dilwyn Porter. 'Egg and chips with the Connellys: remembering 1966', *Sport in History*, 29, 3 (2009).
24. Hall, 'Subjects in history'.
25. Silk, Andrews and Cole. *Corporate Nationalisms*.
26. Garland and Rowe, 'War minus the shooting'; Joseph Maguire, Emma Poulton and Catherine Possamai. 'Weltkrieg III? media coverage of England versus Germany in Euro 96', *Journal of Sport and Social Issues*, 23, 4 (1999); Porter, 'Egg and Chips'.
27. Porter, 'Egg and Chips'.
28. Young, 'Two world wars'.
29. see Cannadine, 2002, in Young, 'Two world wars'.
30. Young, 'Two world wars'.
31. cf. Carrington, 'Football's coming home'; Maguire, Poulton and Possamai, 'Weltkrieg III'.
32. Ibid.
33. Carrington, 'Football's Coming Home'.
34. Ibid., 113.
35. see David Andrews. 'Disneyization, Debord, and the integrated NBA spectacle', *Social Semiotics*, 16, 1 (2006).

36. Guy Debord. *The Society of the Spectacle*. Translated by D. Nicholson-Smith (New York: Zone Books, 1994 [1967]), 29.
37. Guy Debord. *Comments on the Society of the Spectacle*. Translated by M. Imrie (London: Verso, 1990 [1988]), 2, 9.
38. Pierre Bourdieu and Lois Wacquant. 'Neoliberal speak: notes on the new planetary vulgate', *Radical Philosophy*, 105 (2002), 2.
39. Jamie Peck and Adam Tickell. 'Neoliberalizing space', *Antipode*, 34, 3 (2002).
40. Rose, Nikolas. 'Community, citizenship, and the third way', *American Behavioral Scientist*, 43, 9 (1999).
41. Ibid., 1399.
42. Eric Hobsbawm. 'Introduction: inventing traditions', in *The Invention of Tradition*, eds Eric Hobsbawm and Terence Ranger (Cambridge: Cambridge University Press, 1983), 11.
43. Young. 'Two world wars'.
44. Ibid., 7.
45. Hobsbawm, 'Inventing traditions'.
46. Nikolas Rose, 'Government and control', *British Journal of Criminology*, 40 (2000).
47. Henry Giroux. 'Public pedagogy as cultural politics: Stuart Hall and the 'crisis' of culture', *Cultural Studies*, 14, 2 (2000); Hall, 'Subjects in History'.
48. see also Jessica Robinson, 'Tackling the anxieties of the English: Searching for the nation through football', *Soccer in Society*, 9, 2 (2008).
49. see e.g. BBC Online, 'St George comes under fire'; Julie Burchill. 'Sorry, but I can't wait for England to get knocked out of the World Cup', *Mail Online* 11 June, 2010; Adam Edwards and Judith Woods. 'By George, it's time to raise the flag', *Telegraph Online*, 21 April, 2007; Susanne Reichl. 'Flying the flag: the intricate semiotics of national identity', *European Journal of English Studies*, 8, 2 (2004); Sarah Sands. 'England flags: Patriotic or plain chav?' *Mail Online*, 1 June, 2006; David Wooding. 'Kid flag ban by PC teachers', *The Sun Online*, 29 February, 2008.
50. The ephemerality of such corporatized discourses became most evident as the 2010 World Cup unfolded. As England disappointed and were knocked out of the competition, so the prices fell, the merchandise finding its way into bargain buckets, the flags were quickly packed away, and the air of expectancy quickly disappeared, the nation free again to think about financial deficits and public-service cuts.
51. Michael Billlig. *Banal Nationalism* (London: Sage, 1995), 41.
52. George Orwell. 'The Unicorn and the Lion' in Reichl, 'Flying the flag', 209.
53. Hogan, 'Staging the nation', 120.
54. in Billig, 'Banal nationalism', 36.
55. Roger Bromley. *Lost Narratives: Popular Fictions, Politics and Recent History* (London: Routledge, 1988); James Brow. 'Tendentious revisions of the past in the construction of community', *Anthropology Quarterly*, 64, 1 (1990); Robert Foster. 'Making national cultures in the global ecumene', *Annual Review of Anthropology*, 20 (1991).
56. Billig, 'Banal Nationalism', 37.
57. Hall, 1994 in De Cillia, Reisgel and Wodak, 'The discursive construction'.
58. De Cillia, Reisgel and Wodak, 'The discursive construction'.

59. Chris Healey. *From the Ruins of Colonialism: History as Social Memory* (Cambridge: Cambridge University Press, 1997).
60. cf. Alexandros Apostolakis. 'The convergence process in heritage tourism', *Annals of Tourism Research*, 30 (2002); Deepak Chhabra, Robert Healey and Erin Sills. 'Staged authenticity and heritage tourism', *Annals of Tourism Research*, 30, 3 (2003); Gary Edson. 'Heritage: pride or passion, product or service?' *International Journal of Heritage Studies*, 10, 4 (2004); Tazim Jamal and Hyounggon Kim. 'Bridging the interdisciplinary divide: towards an integrated framework for heritage tourism research', *Tourist Studies*, 5, 1 (2005); Kevin Markwell, Deborah Stevenson and David Rowe. 'Footsteps and memories: interpreting an Australian urban landscape through thematic walking tours', *International Journal of Heritage Studies*, 10, 5 (2004); Gordon Waitt. 'Playing games with Sydney: marketing Sydney for the 2000 Olympics', *Urban Studies*, 36, 7 (2000).
61. Duncan Bell. 'Mythscapes: memory, mythology, and national identity', *British Journal of Sociology*, 54, 1 (2003): 69; see also Fiona McLean. 'A marketing revolution in museums?' *Journal of Marketing Management*, 11 (1995).
62. Bell, 'Mythscapes', 69.
63. Pierre Nora. 'Between memory and history: Les lieux de mémoire', *Representations*, 26 (1989), 20.
64. Lawrence Grossberg. 'History, politics and postmodernism: Stuart Hall and cultural studies', in *Stuart Hall: Critical Dialogues in Cultural Studies*, eds Stuart Hall, David Morley and Kuang Hsing Chen (London: Routledge, 1996).
65. Patrick Hutton. 'Collective memory and collective mentalities: Halbwachs-Ariès connection', *Historical Reflections*, 15 (1988), 311.
66. cf. Susan Faludi. *The Terror Dream: What 9/11 Revealed about American Culture* (London: Atlantic Books, 2008); Malcolm, Bairner and Curry, 'Woolmergate'; Nasar Meer and Tariq Madood. 'The multicultural state we're in: "Multiculture" and the "civic rebranding" of British multiculturalism', *Political Studies*, 57 (2007); Silk and Falcous, 'Sporting spectacle'.
67. Zygmunt Bauman. *Modernity and Ambivalence* (Cambridge, MA: Polity Press, 1991).
68. Anne-Marie Fortier. 'Pride politics and multiculturalist citizenship', *Ethnic and Racial Studies*, 28, 3 (2005), 561
69. cf. Tim Crabbe. '*englandfans* – A new club for a new England? Social inclusion, authenticity and the performance of Englishness at "home" and "away"'. *Leisure Studies*, 23, 1 (2003); Mark Falcous and Michael L. Silk. 'Olympic bidding, multiculturalist nationalism, terror and the epistemological violence of "making Britain proud"', *Studies in Ethnicity and Nationalism* (2010); John Hughson and Emma Poulton. 'This is England: Sanitized fandom and the national soccer team', *Soccer & Society*, 9, 4 (2008); Jessica Robinson. 'Tackling the anxieties of the English: Searching for the nation through football', *Soccer in Society*, 9, 2 (2008).
70. cf. Arun Kundnani. 'Integrationism: the politics of anti-Muslim racism', *Race & Class*, 48, 4 (2007); Angharad Stephens. ' "Seven million Londoners, one London:" National and urban ideas of community in the aftermath of the 7 July 2005 bombings in London', *Alternatives*, 32 (2007); Steven Vertovec. 'Super-diversity and its implications', *Ethnic and Racial Studies*, 30, 6 (2007).

71. Stephens, 'Seven million Londoners'.
72. Shane Brighton. 'British Muslims, multiculturalism and UK foreign policy: "Integration" and "cohesion" in and beyond the state', *International Affairs*, 83, 1 (2007).
73. Vertovec, 'Super Diversity' uses the term 'super-diversity' to move the discussion of diversity beyond the parameters of ethnicity. He suggests that additional variables, such as differential immigration statuses, and their concomitant entitlements and restriction of rights, divergent labour experiences, discrete gender and age profiles and patterns of spatial distribution provide a more complex picture of the conjunctions and interactions that have arisen through patterns of immigration to the UK over the last decade. His argument suggests that the outcomes of these patterns – in public discourse, policy debate and academic literature – provide a more complex understanding of the interplay, assemblages and juxtapositions of diversity in Britain than consideration of diversity in purely ethnic composition. See also Meer and Modood, 'The multicultural state'; Javaid Rehman, 'Islam, "war on terror" and the future of Muslim minorities in the United Kingdom: Dilemmas of multiculturalism in the aftermath of the London bombings', *Human Rights Quarterly*, 29 (2007).
74. Paul Gilroy. 'The end of anti-racism', in *Race, Culture and Difference* eds James Donald and Ali Rattansi (London: Sage, 1992), 53.
75. see Ben Pitcher, *The Politics of Multiculturalism: Race and Racism in Contemporary Britain* (New York: Palgrave Macmillan, 2009).
76. see Betty Winfield, Barbara Friedman and Vivara Trisnardi. 'History as the metaphor through which the current world is viewed: British and American newspapers' uses of history following the 11 September 2001 terrorist attacks', *Journalism Studies*, 3, 2 (2002).
77. Paul Gilroy. *After Empire* (London: Routledge, 2004). See also Angus Calder *The Myth of the Blitz* (London: Jonathan Cape, 1990).
78. Stephens, 'Seven million Londoners'.
79. Richard Dyer. *The Matter of Images: Essays on Representations*. (London: Routledge, 1993); Carrington, 'Football's coming home'.
80. cf. George Orwell. *The Sporting Spirit* (London: Tribune, 1945); Silk and Falcous, 'Sporting spectacle'; Stephens, 'Seven million Londoners'.
81. see e.g. Porter, 'Egg and chips'.
82. Ibid.
83. Giroux, Henry. 'Private satisfactions and public disorders: "Fight Club", patriarchy, and the politics of masculine violence', *JAC: A Journal of Composition Theory*, 21, 1 (2001); cf. Michael Messner, *Taking the Field: Women, Men, and Sports*. (Minneapolis, MN: University of Minnesota Press, 2002).
84. cf., Homi Bhaba. 'Are you a man or a mouse?' in *Constructing Masculinity*, eds Maurice Berger, Brian Wallis and Simon Watson (New York: Routledge, 1995); Giroux, 'Private satisfactions'; Kyle Kusz, ' "I want to be the minority": The politics of youthful white masculinities in sport and popular culture in 1990s America', *Journal of Sport & Social Issues*, 25, 4 (2001).
85. Giroux, 'Private satisfactions'.
86. Henry Giroux, *The Terror of Neoliberalism: Authoritarianism and the Eclipse of Democracy* (Boulder, CO: Paradigm Publishers, 2004).
87. cf. Burchill, 'Sorry, I can't wait'; Sands, 'England Flags'.

88. Les Back, Tim Crabbe and John Solomos. *The Changing Face of Football: Racism, Identity and Multiculture in the English Game* (Oxford, UK: Berg, 2006); Carrington, 'Football's coming home'; Crabbe, 'englandfans'.
89. Henry Giroux and Susan Searls-Giroux. 'Challenging neoliberalisms new world order: the promise of critical pedagogy', *Cultural Studies ↔ Critical Methodologies*, 6, 1 (2006), 28.
90. Giroux, 'Disturbing pleasures'; Kellner, 'Media culture'; Kellner, 'Reading culture critically'.
91. Robinson, 'Tackling anxieties'.
92. Giroux, 'Disturbing pleasures', 497.
93. Grossberg, 'We gotta get out'. 82.
94. Robbins, 'Searching for politics'.
95. Paul Gilroy. 'Diaspora and the detours of identity', in *Identity and Difference*, ed. Kath Woodward (London: Sage, 1997).
96. Billig, 'Banal nationalism'.

Bibliography

Adam, Barbara. 'Radiated identities: In pursuit of the temporal complexity of conceptual cultural practices' in *Spaces of Culture: City-Nation-World*, edited by Mike Featherstone and Scott Lash, 138–58. London and Thousand Oaks, CA: Sage, 1999.

Anderson, Benedict. *Imagined Communities*. London: Verso, 1991.

Andrews, David. 'Excavating Michael Jordan: Notes on a critical pedagogy of sporting representation' in *Sport and Postmodern Times: Culture, Gender, Sexuality, the Body and Sport*, edited by Genevieve Rail and John Harvey, 185–221. Albany, NY: State University of New York Press, 1995.

Andrews, David. 'Disneyization, Debord, and the integrated NBA spectacle', *Social Semiotics* 16, 1 (2006): 89–102.

Andrews, David and Cole, C.L. 'The nation reconsidered', *Journal of Sport and Social Issues* 26, 2 (2002): 123–4.

Apostolakis, Alexandros. 'The convergence process in heritage tourism', *Annals of Tourism Research* 30 (2002): 795–812.

BBC Online 'St George comes under fire' Last modified April 24, 2006. http://newswww.bbc.net.uk/1/hi/england/1937546.stm.

Back, Les, Crabbe, Tim and Solomos, John. *The Changing Face of Football: Racism, Identity and Multiculture in the English Game*. Oxford, UK: Berg, 2006.

Bauman, Zygmunt. *Modernity and Ambivalence*. Cambridge, MA: Polity Press, 1991.

Bell, Duncan. 'Mythscapes: Memory, mythology, and national identity', *British Journal of Sociology* 54, 1 (2003): 63–81.

Bhaba, Homi. 'Are you a man or a mouse?' in *Constructing Masculinity*, edited by Maurice Berger, Brian Wallis and Simon Watson, 57–65. New York: Routledge, 1995.

Billlig, Michael. *Banal Nationalism*. London: Sage, 1995.

Bourdieu, Pierre. *Distinction: A Social Critique of the Judgment of Taste*. Cambridge, MA: Harvard University Press, 1984.

Bourdieu, Pierre and Wacquant, Lois. 'NeoliberalSpeak: Notes on the new planetary vulgate', *Radical Philosophy* 105 (2002): 2–5.

Brighton, Shane. 'British Muslims, multiculturalism and UK foreign Policy: "Integration" and "cohesion" in and beyond the state', *International Affairs* 83, 1 (2007): 1–17.

Bromley, Roger. *Lost Narratives: Popular Fictions, Politics and Recent History*. London: Routledge, 1988.

Brow, James. 'Tendentious revisions of the past in the construction of community', *Anthropology Quarterly* 64, 1 (1990): 7–17.

Burchill, Julie. 'Sorry, but I can't wait for England to get knocked out of the World Cup'. *Mail Online*, 11 June, 2010. Accessed 7 September, 2010. http://www.dailymail.co.uk/debate/article-1285739/WORLD-CUP-2010!-Sorry-I-wait-England-knocked-out.html.

Carrington, Ben. 'Football's coming home' but whose home? And do we want it? Nation, football and the politics of exclusion' in *Fanatics! Power, Identity & Fandom in Football*, edited by Adam Brown, 101–23. London: Routledge, 1998.

Chhabra, Deepak, Healey, Robert and Sills, Erin. 'Staged authenticity and heritage tourism'. *Annals of Tourism Research* 30, 3 (2003): 702–19.

Cook, Pam. *Screening the Past: Memory and Nostalgia in Cinema*. New York: Taylor and Francis, 2005.

Crabbe, Tim. '*englandfans* – A new club for a new England? social inclusion, authenticity and the performance of Englishness at "home" and "away"', *Leisure Studies* 23, 1 (2003): 63–78.

Critcher, Chas. 'England and the world cup: World cup Willis, English football and the myth of 1966' in *Hosts and Champions: Soccer cultures, National Identities and the USA World Cup*, edited by John Sugden and Alan Tomlinson. Aldershot, UK: Ashgate, 1994.

De Cillia, Rudolf, Reisgel, Martin and Wodak, Ruth. 'The discursive construction of national identities', *Discourse and Society* 10, 2 (1999): 19–173.

De Groot, Joanna. 'The dialectics of gender: Women, men and political discourses in Iran c. 1890–1930', *Gender & History* 5 (1993): 256–68.

Debord, Guy. *Comments on the Society of the Spectacle*. Translated by M. Imrie. London: Verso, 1990 [1988].

Debord, Guy. *The Society of the Spectacle*. Translated by D. Nicholson-Smith. New York: Zone Books, 1994 [1967].

Dyer, Richard. *The Matter of Images: Essays on Representations*. London: Routledge, 1993.

Edson, Gary. 'Heritage: Pride or passion, product or service?' *International Journal of Heritage Studies* 10, 4 (2004): 333–48.

Edwards, Adam and Woods, Judith. 'By George, it's time to raise the flag'. *Telegraph Online*, 21 April, 2007. Accessed 7 September, 2010. http://www.telegraph.co.uk/news/features/3632216/By-George-its-time-to-raise-the-flag.html.

Falcous, Mark and Silk, Michael. 'Olympic bidding, multiculturalist nationalism, terror and the epistemological violence of "making Britain proud"'. *Studies in Ethnicity and Nationalism*, 10, 2 (2010): 167–186.

Faludi, Susan. *The Terror Dream: What 9/11 Revealed about American Culture*. London: Atlantic Books, 2008.

Featherstone, Mike. *Consumer Culture and Postmodernism*. London: Sage, 1991.

Fortier, Anne-Marie. 'Pride politics and multiculturalist citizenship', *Ethnic and Racial Studies* 28, 3 (2005): 559–78.
Foster, Robert. 'Making national cultures in the global ecumene', *Annual Review of Anthropology* 20 (1991): 235–60.
Garland, Jon. 'The same old story? Englishness, the tabloid press and the 2002 football world cup', *Leisure Studies* 23, 1 (2004): 79–92.
Garland, Jon and Rowe, Mike. 'War minus the shooting? Jingoism, the English press, and Euro 96', *Journal of Sport and Social Issues* 23, 1 (1999): 80–95.
Giardina, Michael. *Sporting Pedagogies: Performing Culture and Identity in the Global Arena*. New York: Peter Lang, 2005.
Gilroy, Paul. 'The end of anti-racism' in *Race, Culture and Difference*, edited by James Donald and Ali Rattansi, London: Sage, 1992.
Gilroy, Paul. 'Diaspora and the detours of identity' in *Identity and Difference*, edited by Kath Woodward, 299–347. London: Sage, 1997.
Gilroy, Paul. *After Empire*. London: Routledge, 2004.
Giroux, Henry. *Disturbing Pleasures: Learning Popular Culture*. New York: Routledge, 1994.
Giroux, Henry. *Impure Acts: The Practical Politics of Cultural Studies*. New York and London: Routledge, 2000.
Giroux, Henry. 'Public pedagogy as cultural politics: Stuart Hall and the 'crisis' of culture', *Cultural Studies* 14, 2 (2000): 341–60.
Giroux, Henry. 'Cultural studies as performative politics" *Cultural Studies ↔ Critical Methodologies* 1, 1 (2001): 5–23.
Giroux, Henry. 'Private satisfactions and public disorders: "Fight Club", patriarchy, and the politics of masculine violence', *JAC: A Journal of Composition Theory* 21, 1 (2001): 1–31.
Giroux, Henry. *The Terror of Neoliberalism: Authoritarianism and the Eclipse of Democracy*. Boulder, CO: Paradigm Publishers, 2004.
Giroux, Henry. 'Cultural studies, public pedagogy, and the responsibility of intellectuals', *Communication and Critical/Cultural Studies* 1, 1 (2004): 59–79.
Giroux, Henry and Searls-Giroux, Susan. 'Challenging neoliberalisms new world order: The promise of critical pedagogy', *Cultural Studies ↔ Critical Methodologies* 6, 1 (2006): 21–32.
Graham, Brian. 'Heritage as knowledge: Capital or culture?' *Urban Studies* 39, 5–6 (2002): 1003–17.
Grossberg, Lawrence. *We Gotta Get Out of this Place: Popular Conservatism and Postmodern Culture*. London: Routledge, 1992.
Grossberg, Lawrence. 'History, politics and postmodernism: Stuart Hall and cultural studies' in *Stuart Hall: Critical Dialogues in Cultural Studies*, edited by Stuart Hall, David Morley and Kuang Hsing Chen, 151–73. London: Routledge, 1996.
Grossberg, Lawrence. *Bringing it all Back Home: Essays on Cultural Studies*. Durham, NC: Duke University Press, 1997.
Hall, Stuart. 'Subjects in history: Making diasporic identities' in *The House that Race Built*, edited by Wahneema Lubiano, 289–99. New York: Pantheon, 1997.
Healey, Chris. *From the Ruins of Colonialism: History as Social Memory*. Cambridge: Cambridge University Press, 1997.
Held, David, McGrew, Anthony, Goldblatt, David and Peraton, Jonathon. *Global Transformations: Politics, Economics and Culture*. Stanford, CA: Stanford University Press, 1999.

Hobsbawm, Eric. 'Introduction: Inventing traditions' in *The Invention of Tradition*, edited by Eric. Hobsbawm and Terence Ranger. Cambridge: Cambridge University Press, 1983.
Hobsbawm, Eric. *Nations and Nationalism since 1870: Programme, Myth, Reality*. Cambridge: Cambridge University Press, 1990.
Hogan, Jackie. 'Staging the nation: Gendered and ethnicized discourses of national identity in olympic opening ceremonies', *Journal of Sport and Social Issues* 27, 2 (2003): 100–23.
Hutton, Patrick. 'Collective memory and collective mentalities: Halbwachs-Ariès connection', *Historical Reflections* 15 (1988): 311–22.
Hughson, John and Poulton, Emma. 'This is England: Sanitized fandom and the national soccer team', *Soccer & Society* 9, 4 (2008): 509–19.
Tazim, Jamal and Hyounggon, Kim. 'Bridging the interdisciplinary divide: Towards an integrated framework for heritage tourism research', *Tourist Studies* 5, 1 (2005): 55–83.
Kearns, Gary and Chris Philo (eds). *Selling Places: The City as Cultural Capital, Past and Present*. Oxford, UK: Pergamon, 1993.
Kellner, Douglas. *Media Culture: Cultural Studies, Identity and Politics between the Modern and the Postmodern*. London and New York: Routledge, 1995.
Kellner, Douglas. 'Reading culture critically', *Review of Education, Pedagogy, and Cultural Studies* 20, 5 (1998): 428–78.
Kellner, Douglas and Gooyong Kim, G. 'You tube, critical pedagogy, and media activism', *Review of Education, Pedagogy, and Cultural Studies* 31, 3 (2010): 281–90.
Kundnani, Arun. 'Integrationism: The politics of anti-Muslim racism', *Race & Class* 48, 4 (2007): 24–44.
Kusz, Kyle. '"I want to be the minority": The politics of youthful white masculinities in sport and popular culture in 1990s America', *Journal of Sport & Social Issues* 25, 4 (2001): 390–416.
Leonard, David. 'Young, black (& brown) and don't give a fuck: Virtual ganstas in the era of state violence', *Cultural Studies ↔ Critical Methodologies* 9, 2 (2008): 248–72.
Lofgren, Orvar. 'The nationalization of culture', *Ethnologies Europeaea* 19 (1989): 5–24.
Lugo-Lugo, Carmen and Bloodsworth-Lugo, Mary. ' "Look out new world, here we come" '? Race, racialization, and sexuality in four children's animated films by Disney, Pixar, and Dreamworks', *Cultural Studies ↔ Critical Methodologies* 9, 2 (2009): 166–78.
McCarthy, Cameron, Giardina, Michael, Park, Jin-Kyung and Harewood, Susan. 'Cultural inter/connections', *Cultural Studies ↔ Critical Methodologies* 5 (2005): 135–44.
McIntosh, Alison and Richard Prentice. 'Affirming authenticity: Consuming cultural heritage', *Annals of Tourism Research* 26, 3 (1999): 589–612.
McLean, Fiona. 'A marketing revolution in museums?' *Journal of Marketing Management* 11 (1995): 601–16.
Maguire, Joseph, Poulton, Emma and Possamai, Catherine. 'Weltkrieg III? Media coverage of England versus Germany in Euro 96', *Journal of Sport and Social Issues* 23, 4 (1999): 439–54.

Malcolm, Dominic, Bairner, Alan and Curry, Graham. ' "Woolmergate": Cricket and the representation of Islam and Muslims in the British press', *Journal of Sport and Social Issues* 34, 2 (2010): 215–35.

Markwell, Kevin, Stevenson, Deborah and Rowe, David. 'Footsteps and memories: Interpreting an Australian urban landscape through thematic walking tours', *International Journal of Heritage Studies* 10, 5 (2004): 457–73.

Mason, Tony. 'England 1966: Traditional and modern?' in *National Identity and Global Sports Events: Culture, Politics and Spectacle in the Olympics and Football World Cup*, edited by Alan Tomlinson and Christopher Young, New York: SUNY Press, 2006.

Meer, Nasar and Tariq Madood. 'The multicultural state we're in: 'Multiculture' and the 'civic rebranding' of British multiculturalism,' *Political Studies* 57 (2007): 473–497.

Messner, Michael. *Taking the Field: Women, Men, and Sports*. Minneapolis, MN: University of Minnesota Press, 2002.

Nora, Pierre. 'Between memory and history: Les lieux de mémoire', *Representations* 26 (1989): 7–25.

O'Riordan, Kate. 'Technologized bodies: Virtual women and transformations in understandings of the body as natural' in *Physical Culture, Power, and the Body*, edited by Jennifer Hargreaves and Patricia Vertinsky, 232–53. London: Routledge, 2007.

Orwell, George. *The Sporting Spirit*. London: Tribune, 1945.

Peck, Jamie and Tickell, Adam. 'Neoliberalizing space', *Antipode* 34, 3 (2002): 380–403.

Pitcher, Ben. *The Politics of Multiculturalism: Race and Racism in Contemporary Britain*. New York: Palgrave Macmillan, 2009.

Porter, Dilwyn. 'Egg and chips with the Connellys: Remembering 1966', *Sport in History* 29, 3 (2009): 519–39.

Redfield, Marc. 'What's in a name-date? Reflections on 9/11', *Review of Education, Pedagogy, and Cultural Studies* 30, 3 (2008): 220–31.

Reichl, Susanne. 'Flying the flag: The intricate semiotics of national identity', *European Journal of English Studies* 8, 2 (2004): 205–17.

Rehman, Javaid. 'Islam, "war on terror" and the future of Muslim minorities in the United Kingdom: Dilemmas of multiculturalism in the aftermath of the London bombings' *Human Rights Quarterly* 29 (2007): 831–78.

Robbins, Christopher. 'Searching for politics with Henry Giroux: Through cultural studies, public pedagogy and the "terror of neoliberalism"', *Review of Education, Pedagogy, and Cultural Studies* 31, 5 (2009): 428–78.

Robinson, Jessica 'Tackling the anxieties of the English: Searching for the nation through football', *Soccer in Society* 9, 2 (2008): 215–30.

Roche, Maurice. *Mega-Events and Modernity: Olympics and Expos in the Growth of Global Culture*. London and New York: Routledge, 2000.

Rose, Nikolas. 'Community, citizenship, and the third way', *American Behavioral Scientist* 43, 9 (1999): 1395–411.

Rose, Nikolas. 'Government and control', *British Journal of Criminology* 40 (2000): 321–39.

Sands, Sarah. 'England flags: Patriotic or plain chav?' *Mail Online*, 1 June, 2006. Accessed 7 September, 2010. http://www.dailymail.co.uk/news/article-388597/England-flags-patriotic-plain-chav.html.

Silk, Michael and Andrews, David. 'Beyond a boundary: Sport, transnational advertising, and the reimaging of national culture', *Journal of Sport and Social Issues* 25, 2 (2001): 180–202.

Silk, Michael, Andrews, David and Cole, C.L. (eds). *Corporate Nationalisms: Sport, Cultural Identity and Transnational Marketing*. Oxford, UK: Berg, 2005.

Silk, Michael and Falcous, Mark. 'One day in September/one week in February: Mobilizing American (sporting) nationalisms', *Sociology of Sport Journal* 22, 4 (2005): 447–71.

Silk, Michael and Falcous, Mark. 'Sporting spectacle and the post 9–11 patriarchial body politic' in *The Day that Changed Everything: The Impact of 9/11 on the Media, Arts and Entertainment*, edited by Matt Morgan, 221–35. New York: Palgrave MacMillan, 2010.

Stephens, Angharad. ' "Seven million Londoners, one London:" National and urban ideas of community in the aftermath of the 7 July 2005 bombings in London', *Alternatives* 32 (2007): 155–76.

Thomas, Paul. 'The impact of community cohesion on youth work: A case study from Oldham', *Youth and Policy* 93 (2006): 41–60.

Tomlinson, Alan. 'Olympic spectacle: Opening ceremonies and some paradoxes of globalization', *Media, Culture and Society* 18 (1996): 583–602.

Vertovec, Steven. 'Super-diversity and its implications', *Ethnic and Racial Studies* 30, 6 (2007): 1024–54.

Waitt, Gordon. 'Playing games with Sydney: Marketing Sydney for the 2000 Olympics', *Urban Studies* 36, 7 (2000): 1062–73.

Wooding, David. 'Kid flag ban by PC teachers', *The Sun Online*, 29 February, 2008. Accessed 7 September, 2010. http://www.thesun.co.uk/sol/homepage/news/article859734.ece

Winfield, Betty, Friedman, Barbara and Trisnardi, Vivara. 'History as the metaphor through which the current world is viewed: British and American newspapers' uses of history following the 11 September 2001 terrorist attacks', *Journalism Studies* 3, 2 (2002): 289–300.

Young, Christopher. 'Two world wars and one world cup: Humour, trauma and the asymmetric relationship in Anglo-German football', *Sport in History* 27, 1 (2007): 1–23.

14
The 1960 Rome Summer Olympics: Birth of a New World?

Barbara Keys

'The Olympics that changed the world': such is author and journalist David Maraniss's audacious, myth-making subtitle to his 2008 book on the 1960 Rome Summer Olympic Games. It is a statement that is true of most Olympic Games, for all of them change the world of sport in some way and many of them make a mark on the larger world, but Maraniss claims more for the 1960 Summer Olympics. They were, he says, the moment when one era died and another was born, a watershed when the modern world was 'coming into view.'[1] What made these Games so seminal? As Maraniss summarized his case in *Newsweek*, 'politics, commercialism, doping, nonstop TV coverage – it all started in 1960.'[2]

Like most myths, this one contains a small core of substance surrounded by a large dose of hyperbole and sheer fiction.[3] Politics, commercialism, doping, and nonstop television coverage did not begin in 1960. With the exception of television coverage, none of these elements saw dramatic change in 1960. There have been transformative Olympic Games such as the 1932 and 1984 Los Angeles Games, both of which recast the Games as a new kind of entertainment, raised commercialism to unprecedented levels, introduced lasting innovations, and truly reshaped international sport.[4] Rome had no such impact. The 1960 Games have been largely forgotten for good reason: they did not break sharply with the past or leave a lasting imprint. What occurred at the Rome Olympics was but a step in a decades-long progression; it was evolution, not revolution.

What makes the Rome Olympics illuminating is their sheer ordinariness. They provide an excellent lens for viewing the key issues the Olympic Games confronted in the early Cold War years, as the International Olympic Committee (IOC) grappled again and again with the same suite of sporting and political dilemmas. Thorny debates over racism, the representation of new states, and the commercialization and professionalization tugging at the heels of Olympic sport provided recurring refrains for 'the Olympic movement' for years after the end of the Second World War. The early postwar decades featured growing pains as the Soviet bloc and then the newly decolonized nations clamoured for entry and pressed for organizational changes at the IOC to reflect new political realities. The pressures exerted by new technologies, television, the scientization of training, and consumerism were acutely felt at the Olympic Games in the 1950s and 1960s.

For the most part, however, what was notable about the 1960 Games was not the visible emergence of new forms but the tenacity with which sports administrators sought to hold on to old, familiar ways. The IOC presidency was held in these years (1952–1972) by Avery Brundage, a millionaire construction magnate from Chicago and a former Olympic decathlete who was once described by *Sports Illustrated* as 'a man with a discus where his heart should be,' a reputation he earned largely from his harsh application of amateur rules.[5] Writer David Margolick aptly characterized him as a 'bigoted, self-important pooh-bah.'[6] Sports journalist Robert Creamer overstated the power of the IOC president when he wrote that the position 'has no counterpart in the world but would be roughly analogous to that of president of the United Nations, if there were such a powerful office in the U.N., and if the U.N. exercised absolute power over world affairs.'[7] Yet Brundage's personality and predilections unquestionably had an enormous influence on the development of the Games during these critical years. A profoundly conservative man, Brundage saw himself as the guardian of sacred traditions, not an innovator tasked with adapting the Olympic Games to a changing world. His determination to hang on to the ways of the past ensured that any radical agendas put forward, in Rome and elsewhere, were forestalled.

The Rome Games did represent a significant consolidation of the relationship between the Olympic Games and television. Fraught with repercussions for commercialization, professionalization, the scale of the Games, and the financial capabilities of international sports organizations, the expansion of live coverage and the television revenues that Rome inaugurated were highly consequential. In other respects, the Rome Olympics merely bore witness to the continuing growth of problems that bedeviled every postwar Games. In 1960, doping was becoming more widespread and visible, and hence harder for international sports authorities to ignore, but it was not a new problem, nor did 1960 prompt truly novel solutions. The proportion of athletes running afoul, usually covertly, of strict amateur rules continued to grow, but the obdurate Brundage responded by grasping more tightly at outmoded standards. Commercialization proceeded apace, with no significant leaps in 1960. The political dimensions of the Olympic Games, present from the beginning, had grown more acute with the entry of the Soviet bloc into Olympic participation at the 1952 Helsinki Games. Ongoing dilemmas over the participation of apartheid South Africa, which would culminate in the country's exclusion from the Games beginning in 1964, divisions over China and Germany, and the entry of newly decolonized nations: all continued in 1960 to perplex, entertain, and frustrate just as they had before and would again after the festivities in Italy. Far from representing something new under the sun, the ills, dilemmas, and tensions of the Rome Games were all too typical.

Television

Television is the lynchpin for Maraniss's claims that the 1960 Games marked a watershed. The events in Rome were the first commercially televised Summer Olympics, shown in 21 countries, including Japan and Eastern Europe.[8] Television coverage unquestionably transformed the nature and scope of the Olympics in dramatic ways. The medium produced tangibly different experiences of the Games for consumers, far removed from radio coverage or live attendance. The televised Olympic Games, Kristina Toohey and A. J. Veal note, are 'enhanced, compacted, interpreted, interrupted and replaced with a distortion of time and space.'[9] The growth of television coverage expanded the audience for the Games, enabling them to reach truly global audiences, and furthered commercialization and the pressures for professionalization of high-performance sport.

The process by which the Olympic Games became a televised spectacle of potentially gigantic proportions occurred over several decades, in which 1960 marked a major step forward. Television had made its first appearance at the 1936 Berlin Olympic Games, with closed-circuit format allowing spectators in special television venues in Berlin to view faint, grainy images of the events. At the next Olympics, in London in 1948, a television network for the first time paid for broadcasting rights. For about US$3000, the British Broadcasting Corporation provided live and delayed coverage aimed at the roughly 80,000 television sets in the London area.[10] In Melbourne in 1956, organizers clashed with television and cinema newsreel executives over whether the Olympics constituted news or entertainment. Television executives argued that because the event was news, they were entitled to the same free and open access to the Games that the print media enjoyed. As yet lacking technology to broadcast events live over long distances, they felt the footage would be dated and of limited value. As a result international television coverage of the 1956 Games was minimal.[11]

When the Organizing Committee of the Rome Olympics sold the US broadcast rights to the Columbia Broadcasting System (CBS) for US$600,000, and European rights to the European Broadcasting Union for US$668,000, it constituted a significant change.[12] The windfall set off protracted wrangling over revenue sharing among the IOC, host city organizing committees, and international sport federations. In 1958, the IOC had formalized a policy on television rights that called for the host city's organizing committee to negotiate the sale of live television rights while the IOC decided how to distribute revenues from the sale.[13] Yet the Rome organizers, citing earlier rules, forwarded only 5% of net proceeds to the IOC.[14] Only gradually did the IOC gain control over the distribution of television revenues, which amounted to US$10 million in 1968 and then doubled or tripled during every Olympiad until topping an astronomical US$2.5 billion in Beijing in 2008. At Rome, television revenues amounted to US$1 of every US$400 it cost to host the Games. By 1972, the ratio was 1:50 and by 1984 it was 1:3.[15]

For the first time, large numbers of people could watch the Games in real time while comfortably ensconced on the sofas of their living rooms. Eurovision provided almost 94 hours of live television coverage to a total of 18 European countries. In the United States, CBS was able to show Olympic highlights only slightly delayed, flying films via commercial trans-Atlantic flights in time for morning events to be seen on the evening news.[16] The immediacy of the viewing experience provided a significant boost to the popularity of the Games.

Television was transformative not only for the sporting events but also for the IOC. Before the sale of broadcast rights flooded the IOC's coffers with millions of dollars, the organization had few sources of revenue other than the small streams from contributions from host cities and membership fees. In the 1950s, the IOC was chronically underfinanced, suffering from what one member called an 'everlasting lack of funds.'[17] It was a tiny organization with a miniscule permanent staff and a small budget that teetered on the brink of insolvency. Top leaders paid for most of their own expenses, and Brundage personally subsidized some of the administrative costs.[18] Television revenues dramatically reversed the organization's financial status. By 1974, 98% of its income came from television.[19]

Yet in other respects 1960 was not a dramatic watershed. Television revenues did not immediately solve the IOC's financial problems. The income from television amounted to tens of thousands of dollars in the 1960s, hardly enough to cover the organization's exploding administrative workload. By 1967, the IOC was deeply in the red, and it was not until 1972 that television rights brought in a large sum of money.[20] Later technological innovations arguably affected popular reception of the Games as much as the onset of live coverage. In fact satellite broadcasting, which began in 1964, was possibly even *more* important in enhancing the marketability and consumer appeal of the Olympics by providing live viewing of events even in places far removed from the action. Color television, an important enhancement for viewing sports events, was introduced in Olympic broadcasts in 1972.[21] In 1960, moreover, television coverage was still small-scale and relatively primitive. As Maraniss found, CBS newscaster Jim McKay wrote his own scripts for the broadcasts, using the *Encyclopaedia Britannica* for background on athletes. The CBS crew in Rome was a tiny group compared with the hordes required to cover the televised mega-events of later years. A mere 50 crew members were able to handle coverage in Rome, whereas later crews would comprise thousands of personnel.[22]

Even as the Olympic Games became big business, television's potential to expand the commercialization of the Games was mostly unrealized in Rome. Commercialism was hardly new: the 1932 Los Angeles Olympic Games had seen a relative frenzy of sponsorships and product tie-ins spurred by American advertising expertise.[23] Commercialism expanded in Rome, but only on a limited basis. Forty-seven companies hopped on the Olympic bandwagon, providing free goods or services in exchange for association with the Olympic 'brand.' Fiat loaned cars, Gillette donated thousands of razors, Nestlé distributed coupons, and the Ceylon Tea Bureau donated 400 tons of tea.[24] But it was hardly the kind of leap that occurred at the next Olympic Games in Tokyo, when 250 companies developed marketing relationships with the Olympics.[25]

Politics and sport

'Almost every action in Rome,' Maraniss claims, 'was viewed through the political lens of those tense times.'[26] The downing of American pilot Francis Gary Powers as he flew a U-2 reconnaissance plane over

Soviet territory just a week before the opening ceremony inflamed Cold War tensions. Contrary to Maraniss's overheated rhetoric, however, the incident had little discernible effect on the Olympics. In fact the Cold War tensions swirling around the Rome Olympics were marginal compared with the turmoil Melbourne had seen in 1956. There the Games had been rocked both by the Suez crisis and the Soviet invasion of Hungary, prompting boycotts, defections, and the famous, bloody Soviet–Hungary water polo match that became an icon of political conflict manifested in sport.[27] Compared, too, with the political events that disturbed subsequent Olympic Games, the 1960 Olympics look remarkable not for the expression of Cold War tensions but for their relative insulation from external events.

The rivalry between the Soviets and Americans that provided so much of the drama of Cold War Olympics was muted in Rome. As it had in 1956, the Soviet Union won the most medals, leading some Americans to talk woefully about their failure to counter the 'Red sports offensive.' But the key sporting match-ups in Rome rarely pitted Soviets against Americans, and the personalities of the athletes and the atmosphere of the Games produced few moments of high tension. Decathletes Rafer Johnson and Vasilii Kuznetsov, two of the most high-profile athletes, enjoyed an easy friendship. The KGB officers who carefully monitored the Soviet team were less obtrusive than they had been in Melbourne, and when the Soviet delegation visited the American team's quarters, the two groups sipped Cokes, smiled, and traded pins.[28] As one historian notes, Soviet and American athletes 'seemed, almost as if by prepared script, to wish each other good luck before their contests and to rush tearfully into one another's arms after them.'[29] After the passions and high tempers of the 1956 Games, Rome was notable for unusual levels of international accord.

The major political issues that beset the 1960 Olympics were the same ones that kept the IOC fretting for decades: growing public clamor over the discriminatory sports policies of apartheid South Africa, the participation of communist East Germany and North Korea, and the virulent and heated competition between Taiwan and the People's Republic over which one represented China. In dealing with these problems and their inevitable political implications, Brundage's IOC often displayed naivete and ignorance. As IOC member Dick Pound later put it, as a part-time organization operating with 'no particular international status,' it simply 'was not equipped, either organizationally or by disposition,' to deal with issues outside the realm of sport.[30] Its responses were *ad hoc* and reactive, and often ill-informed. Above all, the IOC's decisions on important international issues made a mockery of Brundage's claims that sport was apolitical. Decisions made on political issues were necessarily politicized.

Apartheid South Africa made its final appearance on the Olympic stage in 1960, a fact that suggests not the rise of a new order in Rome but the last gasp of the old. South Africa's overt racial discrimination was the most volatile political issue the IOC confronted. Yet when South Africa fielded an all-white Olympic team in 1960, flagrantly violating the Olympic Charter's nondiscrimination rule, Brundage happily accepted the South African Olympic Committee's assurances that blacks simply did not have the athletic skills to make the team.[31] In his view the Olympic Charter's nondiscrimination clause applied only to the question of whether athletes of Olympic caliber were allowed to participate in the Games, not whether internal discrimination had stunted opportunities for black South Africans to reach that caliber.[32] Although Norway and the Soviet Union had begun agitating against South Africa in the late 1950s, throughout his presidency Brundage fought to keep the apartheid regime in the Olympic fold and unmolested. His public stance on the issue was encapsulated in a 1966 statement: 'We cannot penalize a National Olympic Committee for something its government does, or we will not have any left, since the perfect government has not yet been invented.'[33] It was only the pressure exerted by a multitude of decolonizing nations in Africa that pushed the IOC to exclude South Africa from subsequent Games and to make the ban permanent in 1970. In the case of South Africa, the 1960 Games looked to the world of the past instead of anticipating the world of the future.

The solution the IOC applied to Germany in 1960 was also backward looking. Germany, in political terms now firmly divided into a communist East and a capitalist West, fielded a united team in 1960. The arrangement, first put in place in 1955 as a condition of East Germany's entry into the Olympic Games, did not proceed without difficulty, with disagreements flaring over which flag to march under and how to apportion representation. The disputes were eventually settled, and at the opening ceremony in Rome, a rapturous Brundage told Italy's President Giovanni Gronchi that in political terms German unification had proved impossible – 'but in sport, we do such things.'[34] However much the joint team satisfied Brundage's longing to foster political settlements he deemed appropriate, the arrangement ignored political realities, which by 1968 dictated the fielding of separate German teams. Brundage's similar effort to force a deeply divided Korean peninsula into a joint team produced nothing but failure. The cooperation of two countries that had just concluded a bitter, bloody war in which millions had died was profoundly unrealistic, and North and South Korea unsurprisingly failed to reach an agreement on a joint team. As a result, South Korea competed in 1960, but North Korea did not.[35]

Another perennial political hot potato for the IOC, as it was for the United Nations and other organizations, concerned the representation of China. Since the 1949 Chinese Revolution, Taiwan and the People's Republic of China (PRC) had each claimed to be the legitimate representative of 'China.' In 1959, the IOC pushed Taiwan's national Olympic committee to withdraw its title as representative of 'China' and compete under the name 'Taiwan' – a move that accorded with the simple political reality that Taiwan had no control over sports on mainland China – but controversies over the name and the political legitimacy it conferred continued to bedevil sports administrators. Furious at the decision, the Taiwan delegation held up an 'Under Protest' sign at the opening ceremony in Rome.[36] In the United States Brundage was vilified as a communist sympathizer by the right wing, which viewed the ruling on Taiwan as a capitulation to 'the Reds.'[37] The flap over the alleged politicization of the Games was refuted in the UK by the *Manchester Guardian* in a 1959 article on the controversy. 'When are politics non-political?' the *Guardian* asked. The answer, it aptly noted, was: 'When they happen to be your own. It is always the other fellow who defied the purity of your organization by being partisan.'[38]

Communist China initially seemed eager to participate in the Games, and in the years before 1960 had participated in other international sports events. But the PRC's representative at the IOC, Dong Shouyi, insisted that it would send a team only if Taiwan were ousted. Outraged at Brundage's insistence on leaving Taiwan in, which Dong labeled politically motivated, the PRC withdrew in 1958, concluding that Brundage had 'no qualifications to be IOC President' and that further cooperation while he was president was impossible.[39] Not until the 1976 Montreal Games – five years behind the United Nations – did the IOC succeed in fashioning a compromise, admitting the PRC as representative of China and Taiwan as the Chinese Taipei Olympic Committee.[40]

In conjunction with the expansion of the communist bloc and the explosive growth of independent nations as the Third World shook off the colonial yoke, the significance of the Olympics as a means for nations to gain international recognition and legitimacy grew exponentially in the postwar decades. At the same time, however, both the Olympic Games and the IOC offered only limited and narrowly circumscribed opportunities for non-Western nations to claim equal representation in the international order. When Indonesia's President Sukarno founded the Games of the Newly Emerging Forces (GANEFO) in 1963 as an alternative to the Olympics, he attacked the IOC as an imperialist organ through which one quarter of the world's population attempted to control the other three-quarters.[41] The IOC itself was an all-male, virtually all-white institution, dominated by wealthy European businessmen and an assortment of lords, counts, and other aristocrats. Its Executive Board consisted of seven Europeans, an American, and an Egyptian.[42] Although in 1960 the IOC was just a few years from admitting its first black member, it was still decades from admitting a woman. It hardly bears out Maraniss's claim of 'a new world coming into view.'[43]

The IOC's membership did not reflect the increasingly diverse and global scale of the Olympics. In its original conception, the organization was to comprise one or two (or, very rarely, three) members from every country with a recognized National Olympic Committee, with members chosen by the IOC itself rather than by the national organizations. However, as new National Olympic Committees proliferated in the postwar years, many new countries failed to gain representation on the IOC itself. Long-standing Olympic participants like Finland had two IOC members, while newer entries like Ethiopia had none.[44] Many countries participating in the Olympics were thus left without decision-making power in the IOC. In 1960, the IOC's 65 individual members included 11 from Latin America, eight from the Soviet bloc, three from Asia, and a handful from Africa, the Indian subcontinent, and the Middle East. Thirty-eight – almost 60% – were from Western Europe and North America.[45] Dissatisfaction with Western European dominance would begin to bubble over at the end of the 1950s as the Soviets, hoping to gain more power for the communist bloc, started to push for radical restructuring, but Brundage vehemently opposed any reforms that might lead to a one country, one vote system.[46]

Maraniss points to harbingers of change. Of the 95 countries recognized by the IOC in 1960, 83 attended the Games, the largest number to date. Morocco, Tunisia, Sudan, and San Marino appeared for the first time. More significantly, African athletes ascended the victory podium for the first time. Ghana's Clement 'Ike' Quartey became the first black African to win an Olympic medal, taking a silver in boxing. Abebe Bikila of Ethiopia won the marathon; Abdesiem Rhadi ben Abdesselem of Morocco won silver in the same event. Here, as Maraniss notes, the Rome Games were a portent of the coming dominance of African runners.[47]

The outdated amateur ideal

In the postwar years the Western cultural landscape pushed elite sport inexorably in the direction of professionalization, but the more the world changed, the more tightly Brundage clung to anachronism. A man of 'rock-like conservatism,' Brundage brought such rigidity and narrowness to Olympic rules on amateurism that one scholar has called the Brundage presidency the years of 'rabid' amateurism.[48] Believing himself charged with a sanctified mission, Brundage promoted amateurism with the fervor of a religious zealot. The amateur code, he declared in a 1964 speech, 'embraces the highest moral laws. No philosophy, no religion, preaches loftier sentiments.'[49] 'Slavery Avery,' as athletes sometimes called him, had stark and simple views on amateurism. For 'sport to be sport [it] must be amateur,' and to be amateur it must be 'nothing more than recreation... The moment that financial, commercial, or political considerations intrude,' an athlete ceased to be an amateur.[50]

Olympic founder Pierre de Coubertin had adopted the British concept of amateurism in setting up the modern Games. From the first Games in 1896, athletes participating in the Olympics were required to be 'pure amateurs': not simply athletes who did not earn a living from sport (in the British aristocratic ideal, an amateur was not supposed to earn a living at all), but athletes whose participation in sports was free from financial interest. Brundage's interpretation was exceptionally strict. In 1957, he argued for the exclusion from Olympic competition of any athletes who had 'capitalized in any fashion on their athletic prowess,' including by accepting gifts or subsidies, in addition to 'those who make a business of sport.'[51]

His position was profoundly out of step with the sporting world. High-performance sport required many hours of specialized training; participation in elite competitions required lengthy absences from work. As demands increased, financial temptations multiplied, particularly as the expansion of commercial television into sports in general offered new sources of revenue. Olympic athletes found ways to circumvent the strict rules, accepting under-the-table payments (sometimes called 'boot money' because cash-filled envelopes would be stuffed into their shoes) and excessive appearance fees.[52] Some 'amateur' runners were said to earn as much as US$10,000 a year for appearances – at a time when the annual salary of the US Secretary of Defense was US$25,000.[53] Covert payments for the time lost from work due to competition, known as 'broken time,' were common. Endorsement fees were another temptation. At the 1960 Olympic Games, for example, Puma reportedly paid top German sprinter Armin Hary a bonus of 10,000 German marks for wearing the company's shoes when he won the 100-m race, but Hary cleverly played both sides by showing up at the medal ceremony wearing footwear by rival shoemaker Adidas.[54]

Maraniss argues that Rome was 'the beginning of the end' for the ideal of pure amateurism in the Olympic Games.[55] Professionalization was without doubt increasing. As *L'Equipe* editor Gaston Meyer wrote, 'there [have] never been so many flagrant violations of the rules of amateurism than those seen in Rome. State athletes are increasing in number, [and] others are assisted in all conceivable ways.'[56] With the entry of the Soviet bloc into Olympic competition in 1952, Brundage and the IOC turned a blind eye to systemic violations of the amateur rule, tolerating the participation of athletes who received state-subsidized training, salaries, and other benefits as long as Soviet officials mouthed the right principles.[57] As a Soviet sport official admitted in 1989, the Soviet sport system 'covered professionalism with the figleaf of amateurism.'[58]

Yet far from marking the 'beginning of the end' for amateurism among Western athletes, 1960 marked a high point of the IOC's efforts to enforce strict amateur rules. The sports federations charged with enforcing the rules did so with extraordinary rigidity, in part due to pressure from the IOC. British equestrian Pat Smythe was barred from working part-time as a sports reporter; American decathlete Bob Mathias was deemed ineligible because his 'television and movie contracts depended upon his athletic reputation.' The US Amateur Athletic Union slapped a one-year suspension on Lee Calhoun, a prospective Olympic decathlete, for getting married on a television show called *Bride and Groom*.[59] Armin Hary's shoe deals remained secret at the time, but the German track federation suspended the sprinter for a year when it learned that he had submitted false travel expenses for transportation to a track event. The international track federation supported the move, despite the expectation (not borne out) that it would lead to revocation of his Olympic gold medals.[60] The year 1960 thus saw no dramatic changes in the uneasy relationship between Olympic amateurism and the reality of semi-professionalism in the West and the Soviet bloc. Not until 'Slavery Avery' retired from the IOC presidency in 1972 would the system that increasingly amounted to sham amateurism begin to be formally dismantled.

The rise of an anti-doping regime

Taking stimulants and tonics to improve performance is a practice as old as sport itself.[61] At the 1904 St. Louis Olympic Games, the marathon winner, American Thomas Hicks, collapsed after the race from the effects of drinking brandy, raw eggs, and strychnine, a common mixture used to increase endurance. By the 1930s, many athletes were turning to caffeine, heroin, cocaine, and amphetamines to enhance performance.[62] The use of such substances at the 1936 Olympic Games led the IOC in 1938 to issue its first official condemnation of 'drugs [and] artificial stimulants.'[63] By the 1950s, Soviet and American weightlifters had begun using testosterone and other anabolic steroids.[64] The Soviet Union built an official program for the development and administration of performance-enhancing drugs, and by the 1970s doping – most notoriously in the case of East German athletes – had become a major headache for international sports bodies.[65]

Although the harmful effects of many drugs were mostly unknown at the time of the Rome Games, the press and the sporting public were aware of doping's rising significance and regarded it as a form of cheating that undermined sport.[66] As Britain's *Daily Sketch* remarked before the Games, there was 'a growing suspicion that some of the 1960 Gold Medals will be won in the chemist shop.'[67] IOC regulations at the time were very loose, consisting merely of a prohibition not backed by any enforcement mechanism: 'The use of drugs or artificial stimulants of any kind is condemned and any person offering or accepting dope, in any form whatsoever, cannot participate in the Olympic Games.'[68]

The death of a Danish cyclist in the 100-km race at the Rome Olympics convinced the IOC that the Olympics had a doping problem that needed to be confronted. After collapsing near the end of the race, Knud Enemark Jensen died the same day. The temperature in Rome that day had been a sweltering 100°F (38°C), and the official autopsy report, released seven months later, listed heatstroke as the cause of death. But rumors that European cyclists used vasodilators and amphetamines linked the death to doping in the public mind.[69] It was commonly acknowledged at the time that drugs were widely used in sports such as cycling. After retiring in 1954, champion Italian cyclist Fausto Coppi said that he had used amphetamines 'only when strictly necessary' – which was, he said, 'most of the time.'[70]

Jensen was the first athlete to die during the Olympic Games from possible drug use, and the fatality pushed the IOC to create a medical committee in 1961. Brundage began to make public statements calling for more attention to doping and for the application of penalties against it, and by 1964, one IOC member was calling for blood testing.[71] Yet to say, as Maraniss does, that the international drug testing regime 'traces back to the moment in the hot August sun when Knud Enemark Jensen wobbled on his bike and collapsed to the cement' overstates the case by a considerable margin.[72] The IOC did not implement drug testing for another eight years; the first list of prohibited substances was issued only in 1967. Throughout the 1960s, doping remained low on the IOC's list of priorities. Compared with the amount of attention paid to professionalism, doping was a marginal issue, one Brundage rarely spoke or wrote about.[73] His attitudes and views kept doping on the IOC's back burner.[74] It was not the 1960 fatality, but the public outcry at the death of another cyclist, Britisher Tom Simpson, who suffered an amphetamine overdose in the 1967 Tour de France – and whose collapse was broadcast on television – that brought public and IOC attention to doping to new levels.[75] The introduction of drug testing of athletes at the 1968 Mexico City Olympic Games was arguably a far more significant milestone.

Asked to name defining moments in Olympic history, observers are likely to cite Jesse Owens's four gold medals, which stunned Hitler at the 1936 Olympic Games; the bloody aftermath of the 1956 Soviet–Hungarian water polo match; Juan Carlos and Tommie Smith raising their fists in the Black Power salute at Mexico City in 1968; the deaths of 11 Israeli athletes in a terrorist attack at Munich in 1972; the tit-for-tat boycotts in 1980 and 1984, first against Moscow and then against Los Angeles; or the Dream Team's appearance in Barcelona in 1992. Rome's Olympic Games provided no such defining moment and left no iconic Olympic image.

Continuities reigned. The IOC remained financially strained. Members continued to pay their own expenses to attend annual sessions, and the IOC administration still comprised only a few staff members. Instead of coping with bidding frenzies by world cities eager to host the Games, the IOC president often tried to drum up interest among potential candidates, in part because costs were rising quickly and revenues remained low.[76] The ancient splendors of Rome had provided a magnificent backdrop to the sporting events during the warm summer of 1960, but at the end of the day city organizers faced a large deficit. Despite setting a record in receipts at US$5 million, the Games attracted fewer international visitors than expected and could not recoup the billions of lire poured into construction and renovation of sports facilities.[77] The number of competing athletes was fewer than the contingent that had gathered the last time the Games had been held in Europe: 5313 in Rome compared with 5429 in Helsinki in 1952.[78]

Commercial television was a portent of a new and different future, but one as yet unrealized. Wilma Rudolph's fleet, graceful style (in winning the women's 100 meters), the light heavyweight boxing medal won by future celebrity Cassius Clay, Armin Hary's record-breaking finish in the

100-m dash, and the stunning performance of the Soviet women gymnasts, who won 15 of 16 medals, all were significant moments in the world of sport, but not ones that broke the mold. In the key realms of doping, professionalization, and commercialism, the 1960 Games looked little different from those before and after. The 1960 Summer Olympics did not dramatically change the Games or the IOC, much less the world.

Notes

1. David Maraniss, *Rome 1960: The Olympics that Changed the World*, New York: Simon and Schuster, 2008.
2. David Maraniss, 'The Road from Rome,' *Newsweek*, 26 July 2008, available at http://www.newsweek.com/id/148999 [accessed 11 December 2009].
3. Maraniss, a Pulitzer Prize-winning writer and editor at the *Washington Post*, makes little effort to substantiate the argument in the book, most of which narrates stories about athletes and their feats.
4. On 1932, see Barbara Keys, 'Spreading Peace, Democracy, and Coca-Cola: Sport and American Cultural Expansion in the 1930s,' *Diplomatic History* 2004, vol. 28, pp. 165–96; on 1984, see Alan Tomlinson, 'The Commercialisation of the Olympics: Cities, Corporations, and the Olympic Commodity,' in Kevin Young and Kevin B. Wamsley, eds, *Global Olympics: Historical and Sociological Studies of the Modern Games*, Sydney: Elsevier, 2005, pp. 179–200.
5. Robert Creamer, 'The Embattled World of Avery Brundage,' *Sports Illustrated*, 30 January 1956.
6. David Margolick, 'Passing the Torch,' *New York Times*, 13 July 2008.
7. Creamer, 'Embattled World.'
8. Organizing Committee of the Games of the XVII Olympiad (1960), *The Games of the XVII Olympiad (Rome)*, Rome: Organizing Committee of the Games of the XVII Olympiad, 1960 [hereafter *Official Report*], vol. I, p. 398.
9. Kristina Toohey and A. J. Veal, *The Olympic Games: A Social Science Perspective*, Wallingford: CABI Publishing, 2000, p. 124.
10. Robert K. Barney, Stephen R. Wenn, and Scott G. Martyn, *Selling the Five Rings: The International Olympic Committee and the Rise of Olympic Commercialism*, Salt Lake City, UT: University of Utah Press, 2002, pp. 51–8.
11. Barbara Keys, 'The 1956 Melbourne Olympic Games and the Postwar International Order,' in Carole Fink, Frank Hadler, and Tomasz Schramm, eds, *1956: European and Global Perspectives*, Leipzig: Leipziger Universitätsverlag, 2006, pp. 304–6.
12. Barney et al., *Selling the Five Rings*, p. 74; 'C.B.S.-TV to Cover Olympics on Tape,' *New York Times*, 10 June 1959.
13. Barney et al., *Selling the Five Rings*, pp. 68–9; Marannis, *Rome 1960*, p. 133.
14. Barney et al., *Selling the Five Rings*, p. 74.
15. Maraniss, *Rome 1960*, 409; 'Beijing Olympics TV Rights Revenue Top US$2.5bn,' OnScreen Asia, 19 May 2008, available at www.onscreenasia.com [accessed 10 January 2010].

16. Maraniss, *Rome 1960*, pp. 133–6.
17. Prince Axel of Denmark, quoted in Barney et al., *Selling the Five Rings*, p. 67.
18. See, e.g., *Brundage to Hugh Weir*, 21 August 1956, Correspondence 1952–1956, International Olympic Committee Archives, Lausanne; Ramond Gafner, *The International Olympic Committee: One Hundred Years. The Idea, the Presidents, the Achievements*, Lausanne: International Olympic Committee, 1994, vol. II, p. 152.
19. Toohey and Veal, *The Olympic Games*, p. 130.
20. Gafner, *The International Olympic Committee*, II, p. 154.
21. Toohey and Veal, *The Olympic Games*, p. 130.
22. Maraniss, *Rome 1960*, p. 409.
23. Barbara Keys, *Globalizing Sport*, Cambridge: Harvard University Press, 2006, pp. 101–4.
24. *Official Report*, I, pp. 661–3.
25. International Olympic Committee Marketing Department, Olympic Marketing Fact File, 2008 Edition, available at multimedia.olympic.org/pdf/en_report_344.pdf.
26. Maraniss, *Rome 1960*, p. xii.
27. Keys, 'The 1956 Melbourne Olympic Games,' pp. 288–98.
28. Maraniss, *Rome 1960*, p. 80.
29. Allen Guttmann, *The Games Must Go On: Avery Brundage and the Olympic Movement*, New York: Columbia University Press, 1984, p. 155.
30. Richard W. Pound, *Five Rings over Korea: The Secret Negotiations behind the 1988 Olympic Games in Seoul*, Boston, MA: Little Brown & Co., 1994, 18.
31. Ibid., pp. 88, 402; Espy, *Politics of the Olympic Games*, pp. 69–70.
32. Espy, *Politics of the Olympic Games*, p. 70.
33. Brundage to Reginald Stanley Alexander, 3 May 1966, quoted in Maraniss, *Rome 1960*, pp. 402–3.
34. Quoted in Guttmann, *The Games Must Go On*, p. 155.
35. Richard Espy, *The Politics of the Olympic Games*, Berkeley, CA: University of California Press, 1979, pp. 66–7.
36. Guoqi Xu, *Olympic Dreams: China and Sports, 1895–2008*, Cambridge: Harvard University Press, 2008, p. 93.
37. 'Brundage Denies Pressure by Reds,' *New York Times*, 4 June 1959.
38. Quoted in Xu, *Olympic Dreams*, p. 92.
39. Susan Brownell, *Beijing's Games: What the Olympics Mean to China*, New York: Rowman & Littlefield, 2008, p. 134; Espy, *Politics of the Olympic Games*, pp. 62–3.
40. Espy, *Politics of the Olympic Games*, pp. 62–6, 145–54.
41. David B. Kanin, *A Political History of the Olympic Games*, Boulder, CO: Westview Press, 1981, p. 85.
42. *Official Report*, I, p. 13.
43. Guttmann, *Games and Empires: Modern Sports and Cultural Imperialism*, New York, Columbia University Press, 1994, p. 134; Wolf Lyberg, *Fabulous 100 Years of the IOC: Facts, Figures, and Much Much More*, Lausanne: International Olympic Committee, 1996, pp. 31–2.
44. *Official Report*, I, p. 13.
45. Ibid.

46. Guttmann, *Games and Empires*, pp. 134–6. For a thorough discussion of the Soviet initiative, see Jenifer Parks, 'Red Sport, Red Tape: The Olympic Games, the Soviet Sports Bureaucracy, and the Cold War, 1952–1980,' Ph.D. Dissertation, University of North Carolina, 2009, pp. 115–24.
47. Maraniss, *Rome 1960*, pp. 401–2.
48. Hart Cantelon, 'Amateurism, High-Performance Sport, and the Olympics,' in Young and Wamsley, eds., *Global Olympics*, p. 89.
49. Quoted in Allen Guttmann, *The Games Must Go On*, p. 116.
50. 'Avery Brundage on Amateur Sport and Broken Time,' *Olympic Review* 1954, pp. 20–1.
51. Cantelon, 'Amateurism,' p. 93.
52. Ibid., p. 94.
53. Maraniss, *Rome 1960*, p. 406; see Robert McNamara's 1961 salary in 'Before D.C., Robert S. McNamara Called Ann Arbor Home,' *Michigan Daily*, 9 July 2009.
54. Barbara Smit, *Sneaker Wars: The Enemy Brothers Who Founded Adidas and Puma and the Family Feud that Forever Changed the Business of Sports*, New York: Harper Perennial, 2008, pp. 48–50.
55. Maraniss, *Rome 1960*, p. 407.
56. Gaston Meyer, 'At the Olympic Games of Rome, Amateurism Has Been Flouted Worse Than Ever Before,' *Bulletin du Comité International Olympique*, no. 72 (November 1960), p. 70.
57. M. Iu. Prozumenshchikov, *Bol'shoi sport, bol'shaia politika*, Moscow: Rosspen, 2004, pp. 15–17; see also the exposé published by a Soviet émigré, noting practices already developing before the Second World War: F. Legostaev, *Fizicheskoe Vospitanie i Sport v SSSR*, Munich: Institut po izucheniiu istorii i kul'tury SSSR, 1952.
58. K. Romenskii, quoted in Robert Edelman, *Serious Fun: A History of Spectator Sport in the U.S.S.R.*, New York: Oxford University Press, 1993, p. 227.
59. Maraniss, *Rome 1960*, pp. 328–9.
60. Ibid., p. 405.
61. Gafner, ed., *The International Olympic Committee*, II, p. 165.
62. Toohey and Veal, *The Olympic Games*, p. 143.
63. Quoted in Paul Dimeo, *A History of Drug Use in Sport, 1876–1976: Beyond Good and Evil*, New York: Routledge, 2007, p. 50.
64. Daniel Rosen, *Dope: A History of Performance Enhancement in Sports from the Nineteenth Century to Today*, London: Praeger, 2008, pp. 15–16, 26.
65. Paul Dimeo, 'Good versus Evil? Drugs, Sport and the Cold War,' in Stephen Wagg and David L. Andrews, eds, *East Plays West: Sport and the Cold War*, London: Routledge, 2007, p. 157.
66. On attitudes toward doping, see Rosen, *Dope*.
67. Quoted in Stephen Wagg, ' "If You Want the Girl Next Door...": Olympic Sport and the Popular Press in Early Cold War Britain,' in Wagg and Andrews, ed., *East Plays West*, p. 110.
68. *International Olympic Committee: Fundamental Principles*, Lausanne: International Olympic Committee, 1958, p. 96.
69. On the disputed autopsy, see Maraniss, *Rome 1960*, pp. 138–42.
70. George Vecsey, 'A Sport Can No Longer Peddle Denial,' *New York Times*, 27 May 2007.

71. Gafner, *The International Olympic Committee*, p. 165.
72. Maraniss, *Rome 1960*, p. 142.
73. Guttmann, *The Games Must Go On*, p. 123.
74. John Hoberman, 'Olympic Drug Testing: An Interpretive History,' in Young and Wamsley, eds, *Global Olympics*, p. 252.
75. Toohey and Veal, *The Olympic Games*, p. 144.
76. Barney et al., *Selling the Five Rings*, p. x.
77. '84 National Flags Carried in Parade,' *New York Times*, 12 September 1960.
78. Toohey and Veal, *The Olympic Games*, p. 25.

Index

Abbas, Zaheer, 242
Abdesselem, Abdesiem Rhadi ben, 295
Abzug, Congresswoman Bella, 219
Accrington FC, 35, 42
Ackland, Norman, 64
Adidas (sportswear), 297
Aeolian League, 73
African National Congress (ANC), 188
Afrikaner Nationalist Party, 189, 197
Alcock, Charles, 16, 34, 35, 37–8, 43, 45, 47, 49
Alcott, Louisa, 238
Alcott, William, 108
Ali, Muhammad (formerly Cassius Clay), 160, 188, 203, 215, 299
All-American Girls Baseball League, 116
Allen, Gubby, 190–1, 194, 195, 199
Althusser, Louis, 248
Alvarez, Lili de, 125, 126
Alvechurch FC, 73
Amateur Football Association (AFA), 46, 59
Amateur Sport (magazine), 69
American Association for Health, Physical Education and Recreation (AAHPER), 209
American Civil War, 82, 107, 111, 225
American League (baseball), 12, 113, 115
Ames, Les, 190
Amiss, Denis, 245
anabolic steroids, 141, 143–6, 148–9, 298
Anderson, Benedict, 118, 264
Anderson, Lindsay, 188
Andrews, Peter, 33
Ann Summers (adult shops), 269
apartheid, 185–9, 192–3, 197–200
Appadurai, Arjun, 245
Arlott, John, 187, 189, 200
Arnold, Thomas, 107

Arsenal FC, 61, 64
Arthur Ashe Courage Award, 170
Arthur Dunn Cup, 59
Arthur, President Chester, 109
Ashton United FC, 71
Associated Students, 159, 169–71, 174, 182, 208
Association of Intercollegiate Athletics for Women (AIAW), 209
Aston Villa FC, 34, 38, 40, 45
Athenian League, 71–2
Athletic News, 32, 36, 37, 40, 41, 42, 47, 51, 52
Australasian Football Council, 21
Australian Cricket Board (ACB), 240, 242–6, 253
Australian Football League (AFL), 13–14, 24–6
Australian Rules Football, 8–26

Baddiel, David, 265
Bahrke, Michael S., 144
Bailey, Norman, 35, 48–9
Bailey, Trevor, 64, 65, 68, 69
Baldwin, Baldwin M., 126
Bannister, Roger, 1–2
Barlow, Eddie, 199
Barnet FC, 58, 64, 73
Barnett, Marilyn, 204, 218
Barthes, Roland, 2, 150–1
Bartkowicz, Jane 'Peaches', 210
Barzun, Jacques, 119
Bass, Amy, 168
Bateman, Anthony, 248
Battle of the Sexes (Billy Jean King v Bobby Riggs), 204–5, 213–17
BBC (British Broadcasting Corporation), 289
Beamish, Rob, 148
Beamon, Bob, 162
Beauvoir, Simone de, 125
Bederman, Gail, 81–2

Bedford Avenue FC, 58
Bedser, Alec, 190
Beijing Olympics (2008), 290
Bell, Duncan, 270
Bell, Gen. Franklin, 112
Bell's Life in London, 20
Bell's Life in Victoria, 9
Berg, Moe, 116
Berkshire Football Association, 45
Berlin Olympics (1936), 148, 161–2, 289, 298–9
Betts, Morton Petto, 47–8
Beveridge, Senator Albert, 111–12
Bikila, Abebe, 295
Billie Jean (biography of Billie Jean King), 204
Billie Jean King National Tennis Centre, New York, 203
Billie Jean: Portrait of a Champion (documentary), 205
Billig, Michael, 269–70, 275
Billingham Synthonia FC, 58
Birley, Derek, 45
Bishop Auckland FC, 59–61, 63, 66–9
Bishop's Stortford FC, 57–8, 63
Bjurstedt, (later Mallory) Anna 'Molla', 125, 129, 131–2, 136–7
Blackburn Olympic FC, 40
Blackburn Rovers, 33, 35, 39, 40, 42, 43, 63
Blackmore, S. Powell, 134–5
Black, Sydney, 74
Blitz (bombing of London, 1940–1), 2, 272
Bloomfield Road football ground, Blackpool, 133
Bloxam, Matthew, 11
Bodyline controversy (1932–3), 186
Bolton Wanderers FC, 37, 39, 41
Bonacossa, Count Alberto, 125
Book of American Pastimes, 107
Bowen, Andy, 234
Bowl Championship series (BCS), 81
Boy Scouts of America, 237
Bradman, Don, 243
Bride and Groom (TV Programme), 297
British Football Association (BFA), unofficial group, 37, 39–43
British Union of Fascists, 190

British Women's Amateur Athletic Association, 149
Brookes, W. P., 152
Broudie, Ian, 265
Browne, Mary, 134
Brown, Gordon, 6
Brown, H. Rap, 162
Brownlow, Charles, 21
Brown-Sequard, Charles-Edouard, 143
Brundage, Avery, 147, 153, 160–1, 288–90, 292–9
Bryman, Alan, 249, 251
Buckinghamshire Football Association, 45
Bush, President George H.W., 118
Bush, President George W., 118
Butler, Nicholas Murray, 86

Calamity Jane (film), 132
Calder, Angus, 2
Calhoun, Lee, 297
California Afro-American Museum, 169
The Call (novel), 9
Camp, Walter, 85, 95
Cancer Research, 268
Carlos, John, 5, 141, 159, 161–2, 164, 167, 170–4, 188
Carlsberg (lager), 268
Carmichael, Stokely, 162
Carpenter, Edward, 129
Carr, Donald, 190, 193, 196, 198
Carrington, Ben, 266, 272
Carroll, Jimmy, 234
Cartwright, Alexander, 107
Cartwright, Tom, 186, 193, 196–8, 200
Casals, Rosie, 210
Casuals FC, 48–9, 58–9, 64, 70–2
Caught Behind: Race and Politics in Springbok Cricket (by Murray and Merrett), 188
Cazaly, Ciannon, 10
CBS (Columbia Broadcasting System), 290–1
Centenary Test (1977), 239–42
Ceylon Tea Bureau, 291
Chadwick, Henry, 107
Chaka Demus (song), 263

Chalke, Stephen, 196
Chambers, Mrs Dorothea Lambert, 123, 125, 129, 131
Chambers, W.H., 50
Channel Nine (Australian TV), 240–2, 242–7, 249, 251–3
Chappell, Greg, 252
Chappells (Ian and Greg), 245, 251
Charltons (Jackie and Bobby), 272
Chatham FC, 59
Cheetham, Jack, 191–2, 199
Chesham FC, 74
Chesterfield, Trevor, 198–9
Chicago Black Sox scandal (1919), 115
Chicago Daily Tribune, 235
Chicago Defender, 164
Chicago Tribune, 165
Choynski, Joe, 234
civil rights movement(s), 170–3, 175, 208
Clapham Rovers FC, 35
Clapton Orient FC, 64
Clark, Robert, 160, 168
Clegg, Charles, 50
Cleveland, President Grover, 109, 235
clotheslining (in American football), 101
C'Mon Aussie C'Mon (song), 249–50
Coakley, Jay, 154
Cockfield FC, 61, 68
Cofield, J.H., 50
College Football Association, 81
Collins, Tony, 51
Columbia University, 80, 85, 87, 93, 98
Colyer, Evelyn, 137
Comiskey, Charles, 113
Commonwealth Immigrants Act (1962), 23
Consolidated Press Holdings, 240
Coolidge, President Calvin, 115
Cooperstown, Cooperstown ballpark, 8, 11–12, 25
Corbett, James J., 232–7
Corinthian Casuals, 70–2
Corinthians FC, 36, 43, 48–9, 70
Cosell, Howard, 161, 216
Coubertin, Baron Pierre de, 8, 124, 142, 151–3, 296
Court, Margaret, 211–14

Courtneidge, Cicely, 133
Cowdrey, Colin, 186, 190, 192–3, 195–6, 198
Coy, Arthur, 190–1, 194–5, 199
Crawley, Aidan, 199–200
Creamer, Robert, 288
Crook Town FC, 60, 67, 68
Crump, Charles, 36, 38, 49–50
Crystal Palace, 62, 152
cultural pedagogy, 6, 267, 272, 274–5

Daily Express, 134, 136, 197, 200
Daily Mail, 71, 72, 128, 135, 136, 190, 192, 273
Daily Mirror, 127, 133, 135, 136, 137, 241
Daily Sketch, 126, 133, 135, 136, 298
Daily Telegraph, 64, 193
Daley, Arthur, 165
Dalton, Judy Tegart, 210
Dare to Compete: The Struggle of Women in Sports (documentary), 205
Darwen FC, 33, 37, 40, 45
Davis Cup, 189, 207
Dawson, James, 10
Day, Doris, 132
Debord, Guy, 249, 266
Deford, Frank, 203–4
Dewhurst, Evelyn, 134
Dexter, Ted, 186, 199
Dimeo, Paul, 143–4, 146–7, 153
Disney, Disneyization, 6, 249–51, 253, 255
Division of Girls and Women's Sports (DGWS), 208–9
Dixon, George 'Little Chocolate', 235
Dod, Charlotte 'Lottie', 122, 129
D'Oliveira, Basil, 5, 185–200
Donovan, Mike, 232, 234
Doubleday, Abner, 8, 11–13, 25, 80, 111
Douglas-Hume, Sir Alec, 191, 194
Doust, Stanley N., 135
Dreiser, Theodore, 237
drug taking, drug testing (at the Olympics), 141–55, 297–300
Duffus, Louis, 195, 199
Dunning, Eric, 48–9

Dupre, Judith, 172–3
Durham Football Association, 68, 73

Eastbourne FC, 65
Eastbourne United FC, 65
Ecru (T shirts), 268
Education Amendments (to US Constitution), 208
Edwards, Harry, 160, 166–9, 172, 175
Eisenhower, President Dwight D., 117
Eliot, Charles, 87
Encyclopaedia Britannica, 291
Enfield FC, 74
Engelmann, Larry, 125, 131
England and Wales Cricket Board (ECB), 254
Ephron, Nora, 218
Equal Employment Opportunities Act (in US), 208
Equal Rights Amendment (to US Constitution), 208, 217
ESPY (Excellence in Sports Performance Yearly), Award, 170
Essex and Thurrock Gazette, 69
Evans, Lee, 160, 170
Evert, Chrissie, 211
Evesham Standard, 62
Evesham Town FC, 62–3
Before the Eyes of the World (by Kevin Witherspoon), 168

FA Amateur Status Committee, 72, 74
Fairbanks, Douglas, 133
Federation Cup, 207, 210
Felsin, Jan, 217
Feminist Review, 220
Fiat (cars), 291
Fiechter, Jacques, 167
FIFA, 42, 68
Fimrite, Ron, 166
Fingleton, Jack, 199
Fists of Freedom (documentary), 169, 171
Fitzsimmons, Robert, 234
Flanagan, Martin, 9, 26
Football Association (FA), 16, 32, 35–51, 57–60, 62–75, 130, 264, 269
Football Field (magazine), 37–40, 43–8

Football Record, 21–3
Foot, David, 196
Ford United, 73
Foreman, George, 162, 167
Fox, Richard Kyle, 94, 234
Frazier, Joe, 215
Freedom Association, 190
French Championships (tennis), 122
French Tennis Federation, 136

Gambon, Michael, 186
GANEFO (Games of the New Emerging Forces), 295
Garland, Charles 'Chuck', 127
Gehrig, Lou, 264
Gemmell, Jon, 192, 199
General Strike, 61
Gentleman Jack (play), 233
Gera, Bernice, 208
Gila River Camp, Arizona, 116
Gilbert, W.S., 127
Gillette (razors), 291
Gilligan, Arthur, 190
Gillmeister, Heiner, 126
Gilmour, Gary, 250
Gilroy, Paul, 272
Giroux, Henry, 273–4
Gleneagles Declaration, 190
Godfree, (nee McKane) Kitty, 128, 137
Godkin, E. L., 233
Gog's Game, 25
Goolagong, Evonne, 211
Graham, Philip, 2
Grant, Gen, Ulysses S., 224
Graves, Abner, 11
Graydon, Jan, 220
Gray, Ken, 189
Grays Athletic FC, 69
Great Lever FC, 36
Great Split (in rugby football), 52
Great White Fleet (US), 112
Greaves, Jimmy, 264
Green, Geoffrey, 39, 45, 65, 75
Greenidge, Gordon, 242
Greig, Tony, 242, 245
Grenoble Winter Olympics (1968), 149
Griffin, Booker, 165
Griffith, Billy, 190, 192, 194–5, 200

Griffith, Clark, 106
Grook, Marn, 9–10, 12–13, 26
Grotz, Erik, 170–1, 174
Grow, Robin, 16
Guardian (newspaper), 189, 195–6, 294
Guillotte, Joseph Valsin, Mayor of New Orleans, 235
Gutierrez, Alberto, 171

Hain, Drake, 198
Hain, Peter, 189, 198
Hall, G. Stanley, 95, 226–7
Halliwell FC, 36
Hall, John, 163
Hall, Lesley A., 130
Hall, Stuart, 262, 265
Hall, Wes, 187
Hampden Park football ground, Glasgow, 133
Hantze, Karen, 207
Harding, President Warren G., 115
Harding, William Edgar, 231
Hardisty, Bob, 69
Hardman, Mr, 47
Hargreaves, Jennifer, 123
Harper's weekly, 86, 100
Harrison, H.C.A., 11
Harrison, President Benjamin, 106, 235
Harris, Prof. Cobie, 170
Harris, Ron, 167
Harriss, Ian, 254
Hartmann, Douglas, 168–9, 173–5
Harvard University, 80–1, 83, 85–8, 91–5, 97–8, 167
Hary, Armin, 296–7, 299
Havelock Ellis, Henry, 129
Hawthorne, Julian, 97
Hawthorne, Nathaniel, 97
HBO (Home Box Office), 169, 171, 205, 206
Healey, Chris, 270
Healey, George J., 37, 41
Hearst, William Randolph, 83, 86, 96
Heldman, Julie, 210
Helem, John, 164
Helsinki Olympics (1952), 60, 289, 299

Hendon FC, 62, 72
Herald Sun (Melbourne newspaper), 23
Hibbins, Gillian, 9, 17
Hicks, Thomas, 297
Higginson, Thomas Wentworth, 107
Highbury Stadium, north London, 61
Hill, Urla, 174
Hillyard, Cdr. George, 135
Hindle, Thomas, 40, 45
HMV Studios, Middlesex, 133
Hobsbawm, Eric, 3, 11, 14, 26, 267
Hoffman, Bob, 144
Hogg, Quintin, 197
Holding, Michael, 242, 245
Holland, Gerald, 144
Holmes, Oliver Wendell, 93
Holt, Richard, 123–6
Honest Hearts and Willing Hands (melodrama), 232, 235
Hooksey (David Hookes), 250
Hoover, President Herbert, 116
Hopkins, Sir Anthony, 186
Howard, Geoffrey, 195–6
Howard University, 162
Hughes, Robert, 154
Humphrey, Vice President Hubert, 168
Hunter, Archie, 34
Hurricane Katrina, 118
Hurst, Geoff, 272

If I Can Dream (song), 268
ILTF (International Lawn Tennis Federation), 207–8
The Independent (US newspaper), 93, 98
Insole, Doug, 69–73, 190–3, 196
Intercollegiate Athletic Association of the United States (IAAUS), 80
Intercollegiate Football Association, 80
International Cricket Council (ICC), 254
International Olympic Committee (IOC), 124–5, 141–2, 149–50, 152–3, 160–1, 165, 168, 189, 287–8, 290–5, 297–300
The Invention of Tradition (by Hobsbawm and Ranger), 11
Isthmian League, 60, 70

Jackson, N.L., 36–9, 45–7, 49
Jackson, Peter, 234
James, Brian, 73
Jameson, Fredric, 248
Jamie T, 263
Jeffries, Jim, 94–5
Jensen, Knud Enemark, 145–6, 298
Johnson, Jack, 95
Johnson, Rafer, 292
Jope, W. H., 38, 50
Jordan, David Starr, 94
Jordan, Edward S., 94
Journal of Clinical Endocrinology, 144
Judge (humour magazine), 98
Jules Rimet trophy, 265–6

Keating, Frank, 196
Kellner, Douglas, 263, 274
Kelly, Mike 'King', 109–10
Kenyon, Don, 190, 191, 193
KGB (Committee for State Security, Soviet Union), 292
Khan, Imran, 242
Kidd, Bruce, 124
Kilrain, Jake, 230–5, 238
Kim, Gooyong, 263
King, Larry, 207, 213
King, Martin Luther, 188
King (nee Moffitt), Billie Jean, 5, 203–20
Kinnaird, Arthur, 45, 49
Kissinger, Henry, 190
Knight, Barry, 193, 195, 200
Knott, Alan, 242
Kruif, Paul de, 143–4
Kuznetsov, Vasilii, 292

Laird, Bruce, 251
Lancashire Cup, 35, 42
Lancashire Football Association, football clubs, 32–51
Landis, Kenesaw Mountain, 116
Lang, James Joseph, 33
Larcombe, Ethel, 127
Laver, Rod, 211, 219
Law, Denis, 272
Lawn Tennis: The Game of Nations (by Suzanne Lenglen), 131

League of Nations, 114
Lenglen, Suzanne, 4, 122–38
L'Equipe, 297
Lewis, Jim, 69
Lewis, Rob, 50
Leyton FC, 63, 68
Leyton Orient FC, 60
Leytonstone FC, 60, 64, 65, 68, 70
Lichtenstein, Grace, 211, 216, 218, 219–20
Life (humour magazine), 98
Life (magazine), 159, 203, 205
Lightning Seeds (band), 265
Lillee, Dennis, 239, 243, 245, 250
Lindsay, Vachel, 238
Lineker, Gary, 266
Linton, Arthur, 143
Lipsyte, Robert, 169, 208
Little League Baseball, 208
Liverpool FC, 64
Liverpool Football Association, 39
Lloyd, Clive, 243
Loakes Park, Wycombe, 64
Lodge, Henry Cabot, 93
Lomax, Michael E., 160
London, 2012 Olympic bid, 271
London Football Association, 47
London, Jack, 95
London Olympics (1948), 289
Los Angeles Olympics (1932), 287, 291
Los Angeles Olympics (1984), 169, 287, 299
Los Angeles Sentinel, 163, 165
Los Angeles Tennis Club, 206
Los Angeles Times, 163, 166
Lowenthal, David, 172
Lowerson, John, 48
Lumpkin, Angela, 203
Lyttleton, Charles (Viscount Cobham), 191, 194

Macaulay, Lt. Col. Duncan, 128
MacCracken, Henry M., 80, 87
Madison Square Garden, 228
Maine Road football ground, Manchester, 74
Major League Baseball, 115, 117, 205
The Male Hormone (by Paul de Kruif), 143–4

310 *Index*

Malveaux, Julienne, 174
Mandela, Nelson, 186
Mandel, Ernest, 248
Manila Times, 112
Maraniss, David, 7, 145, 284, 287, 289, 291–2, 295, 297–8
Marble, Alice, 206
Marciano (Marchegiano), Rocky, 117
Margolick, David, 288
Marindin, Major, 49
Marsh, Rodney (Marshy), 250, 252
Maskell, Dan, 133
Mason, Tony, 34, 45, 50
Mathias, Bob, 297
Matrimonial Causes Act (1923), 130
May, Elaine Tyler, 149
May, Peter, 190
McAuliffe, Jack, 235
McBrien, L.H., 22
McCain, Senator John, 4
MCC (Marylebone Cricket Club), 185–6, 190–1, 194–200
McDonald's, 252, 268
McDowell, Malcolm, 188
McGraw, John, 113
McKay, Jim, 291
McKibbon, Tom, 167
McLure's (journal), 85, 94 [McClures]
McQueen, Humphrey, 23
McTeague (novel by Frank Norris), 97–8
Meanjin (magazine), 10
Melbourne Cricket Ground (MCG), 10–11, 239
Melbourne Olympics (1956), 289, 292
Melville, Kerry, 210
Mendes, Sam, 186
Merrett, Christopher, 188, 197, 200
Metcalfe, Richard, 67
Metropole Hotel, Cannes, 125
Metropolitan Amateur Football Association (MAFA), 22
Mexican-American War (1848), 108
Mexico City Olympics (1968), 141, 145–7, 149, 153, 155, 159–63, 174, 188, 299
Meyer, Gaston, 297
Mhara, Peter, 234
Miandad, Javed, 242

Middlesbrough FC, 59, 63
Middleton Cricket Club, 187
Milliat, Alice, 124
Mills Commission (on the origins of baseball), 111
Mitchell, Charlie, 230–1
Modern Lawn Tennis (by Lili de Alvarez), 127
Moffitt, Randy, 205
Montreal Olympics (1976), 145, 294
Moore, Bobby, 265–6, 268, 272
Moore, Gregory de, 10
Moore, Harold, 87, 88, 93, 95, 96
Moore, Kenny, 169
Morgan, J.P., 2377
Morley, Ebenezer, 35
Ms magazine, 212
Muldoon, William, 231
Munich Olympics (1972), 263–4, 299
Murdochization, 255
Murdoch, Rupert, 244, 255, 266
Murray, Bill, 24
Murray, Jim, 166
Murray, Prof. Bruce, 188, 191, 195, 197, 200
Muscular Christianity, 15, 93, 107
Myer, Billy, 234–5
Myers, Kevin, 186
myth, concept of, in history, 1–2

Nastase, Ilie, 213
The Nation, 233
National Association of Baseball Clubs, 107
National Collegiate Athletics Association (NCAA), 80, 81, 168
National Football League (NFL), 100–2
National League (baseball), 12, 109–11, 113–15, 117
National Police Gazette, 94, 228, 231, 233–4, 236
Needham, Henry Beech, 85, 90, 94
Newcombe, John, 213
New Road cricket ground, Worcester, 200
News Orleans Times-Democrat, 227
New York American (magazine), 86, 87, 96

New York Athletic Club, 232
New York Clipper, 226
New York Herald, 235
New York Knickerbockers (baseball team), 107
New York Picayune, 231, 234
New York Sun, 230
New York Times, 165, 169, 205, 237
New York Tribune, 225
New York University (NYU), 80, 85, 87, 98
Next (clothing), 268
Nicklaus, Jack, 72
Nixon, President Richard M., 117
Norkunas, Martha K., 172
Norman, John, 69
Norman, Peter, 161, 172
Norris, Frank, 97
Northern League (football), 60, 73
Northwestern University, 98
Norworth, Jack, 109
Nottingham Daily Express, 42
Not the Triumph But the Struggle (by Amy Bass), 168
Nullarbar Plain (south Australia), 191

Obama, President Barak, 203
Oborne, Peter, 185, 190–3
Observer Sport Monthly, 186
Ogilvie, Canon George, 25
Ohio State University, 81
Old Carthusians FC, 58, 59
Old Malvernians FC, 59
Old Trafford cricket ground, Manchester, 193
Old Trafford football ground, Manchester, 133
Olsen, Jack, 174
Olympic Club, New Orleans, 232, 235
Olympic Project for Human Rights (OPHR), 160–2
Olympic Review, 147
Oosthuizen, Tiene, 195
Outing (magazine), 94
Owens, James 'Jesse', 161–2
Oxford City FC, 65

Packerization, 255
Packer, Kerry/'Packer Affair', 6, 239–55
Pan African Congress (PAC), 189
Pascoe, Len, 250
Pascoe, Rob, 15, 18, 24
Patterson, Gerald, 127
Pawson, Tony, 59, 74
PBL Marketing, 246, 253
Peabody, Endicott, 90
Pegasus FC, 60, 65, 66, 70, 72
Peverelly, Charles, 107
Phelps, William Lyon, 236
Philip Morris (tobacco company), 213
Pickford, Mary, 133
Pierce-Dix, William, 51
Pigeon, Kristy, 210
Pollock, Peter, 199
Porritt, Sir Arthur, 147, 154
Poulter, Jim, 12
Pound, Dick, 292
Powers, Francis Gary, 291
Presley, Elvis, 268
Preston North End FC, 35, 42–3, 48–9
Princeton University, 80–1, 85, 87, 113
Probyn, Elspeth, 220
Proctor, Mike, 242
Prokop, Ludwig, 146
Pulitzer, Joseph, 83, 94
Pye, Brad, 163, 165

Quartey, Clement 'Ike', 295
Queensberry, Marquis of/Queensberry Rules, 100, 227–8, 233–4

Race, Culture and the Revolt of the Black Athlete (by Douglas Hartmann), 168
Randall, Derek, 239
Ranger, Terence, 3, 11, 14
Ranson Mr, 48
Rational Dress Society, 130
Reagan, President Ronald, 117–18
Redfield, Marc, 264
Redpath, Ian, 251
Renan, Ernest, 26, 270
Rice, Clive, 242
Richards, Barry, 242
Richards, Huw, 189
Richards, Vivian, 242, 245, 250

Richey, Nancy, 210
Riggs, Bobby, 204–5, 211, 213–18
Rigo, 23 (Ricardo Gouveia), artist, 171
Ritchie, Ian, 148
Riviera tennis circuit, 124–5, 133
Roberts, Andy, 242, 245
Robertson, John, 72
Roberts, Selena, 204, 206, 212
Robinson, Jackie, 117, 203
Robinson, Stuart, 254
Robins, Walter, 195
Rome Olympics (1960), 7, 284–300
Romford FC, 65
Roosevelt, Kermit, 90–2
Roosevelt, President Franklin D., 116
Roosevelt, President Theodore, 4, 80–3, 85–6, 88, 90–5, 98, 112–13
Roosevelt, Ted, 85, 90–2
Rosenbaum, Art, 166
Rosenfeld, Alvin H., 172
Rothmans (tobacco company), 195
Rous, Stanley, 60
Rover, Constance, 128
Rowbotham, Sheila, 130
Rowe, Arthur, 70
Royal Artillery (Portsmouth) FC, 67
Rudolph, Wilma, xi, 299
Rugby Football Union (RFU), 17–19, 51–2
Rugby School, 8, 10–11, 15–18, 107
Ruth, Babe, 8, 115, 203
Ryan, Elizabeth, 134
Ryan, Paddy, 227

Safe, Olivia, 266
Sage, George H., 244
Sainsbury's (chain store), 268
St Albans FC, 64
St George's Cross, 269, 271
St Louis Olympics (1904), 297
San Francisco Chronicle, 166
San Jose City Council, 169
San Jose State College, 159, 162, 168, 170, 172, 173–5
Savage, Rt Rev Gordon, 193
Schoeman, Ben, 198
Scottish Football Association, 34
Seagren, Bob, 167
Selfridges (London store), 133

Sengstacke, John, 164
Serfontein, J.H.P., 197
Seton, Ernest Thompson, 237
Sex Disqualification (Removal) Act (1919), 130
sex testing, xi, 141, 145, 149–50
shamateurism, 59, 66–75, 207
Sharpeville Massacre, 187–8
Sheard, Kenneth, 48–9
Shearwood, Ken, 65
Sheffield FC, 15, 50
Sheffield Football Association, 15, 16, 18–20, 35, 50
Sheffield Heeley FC, 33
Sheffield Wednesday FC, 33
Sheffield Zulus, 34
Sheppard, Rev David, 192, 194, 199
Silk, Denis, 199–200
Simons, J. J., 23
Simpson, Tommy, 146, 299
Sixty Six (film), 268
Skelly, Jack, 235
Skelmersdale FC, 74
Skinner, Frank, 265
Slavin, Frank, 234
Smith, Ed, 254
Smith, Tommie, 5, 141, 159, 161, 164, 167–71, 173–4, 188, 299
Smythe, Pat, 297
Snickers (chocolate bars), 273
Sobers, Garry, 199
Soccer AM (TV programme), 273
Social Darwinism, 95, 108
Society of Biology (Paris), 143
Something in the Air (song), 188
South African Cricket Association (SACA), 190–2, 195, 198–9
Spacey, Kevin, 186
Spalding, Albert, 109–11, 114
Spanish-American War (1898), 111
spearing (in American football), 101
Speed City track team, 160
Spencer, Nancy, 219
Sporting Life (magazine), 47
Sports Illustrated, 144, 169, 205, 209, 217, 288
Stanford University, 94, 98
Steinem, Gloria, 218–19
Stephens, Angharad, 272

Stiles, Nobby, 266
Stockton FC, 59
Sudell, William, 35, 38, 41, 48–9
Suez Crisis (1956–7), 292
Sullivan, Arthur, 127
Sullivan, John L., 6, 224–38
Sullivan, Louis, 242, 245
The Sullivans (TV drama), 244
The Sun, 268, 273
Sunday Mirror, 196
Sunday Telegraph, 186
Sunday Times, 197
Surrey County Cricket Club, 35, 46, 49
Surrey Football Association, 47
Suter, Fergie, 33
Sutton United, 73
Swanton, E. W., 194, 195, 199, 200
Swarthmore College, Pennsylvania, 85
Sydnor, Synthia, 172

Taft, President William Howard, 4, 106, 108, 110, 112, 113, 118
Taiwan issue at UN, Olympics, 292, 294
Take Me Out to the Ball Game (song), 109
Talbert, Bill, 213
Tarzan/Lord Greystoke, 97–8
Taylor, Matthew, 32, 44–6
Tea money scandal (in English amateur football), 67–8, 71
Tennyson, Alfred Lord, 238
Test and County Cricket Board (TCCB), 200, 243
Thatcher, Margaret, 6, 265
Things Are Looking Up (film), 133
Thompson, Ernest, 237
Thompson, J. B., 15, 17–18, 20
Thompson, L., 22
Thompson, Sir Harold, 66–7, 70, 73–4
Thomson, Jeff, 245
Three Lions, 2010 (song), 266–7
Three Lions (logo), 268
Three Lions (song), 265–7
Thunderclap Newman (band), 188
Thursby, Bob, 69
Tilden, William 'Big Bill', 132–3
Tilzer, Albert von, 109

Time magazine, 205, 215
The Times, 39, 57, 65–7, 127, 130, 132–4, 163
Tinling, Ted, 205, 212, 216
Title IX (US law on gender equity), 209, 215–16
Tlatelolco Massacre, 141
Tom Brown's Schooldays (novel), 18
Tommie Smith/John Carlos Project, 170–1
Toohey, Kristina, 289
Tooting FC, 64
Tooting and Mitcham FC, 72
Topp, Laurie, 62
Tottenham Hotspur, 63, 64, 70
Tour de France, 145, 150–1, 154–5, 299
Turton FC, 33
Twenty20 cricket, 254
Tyus, Wyomia, 167

Umbro (sports brand), 268
Underwood, Derek, 242
United States Lawn Tennis Association (USLTA), 208
United States Olympic Committee (USOC), 160–4, 168, 172
University of California, 98
University of KwaZulu-Natal, 188
University of Southern California (USC), 81
University of Texas, 81
University of Texas at El Paso, 160
University of Wisconsin, 96
University of Wyoming, 174
Upham, Arthur, 234
USSR-Hungary water polo match, Melbourne Olympics, 292, 299
US Tennis Championships, Forest Hills, 131, 136, 211

Vahed, Goolam, 188–9
Veal, A. J., 289
Veblen, Thorstein, 96
Venables, Terry, 268
Venerando, Antonio, 146
Verwoerd, Henrik, 197
Victorian Football Association, 22

Victorian Football League (VFL), 22–3
Virginia Slims women's tennis tour, 204, 206, 210–13, 218
Vlasto, Diddie, 134–5
Vorster, John, 186, 190–2, 194–5, 197–8

Waddell, Tom, 167
Wade, Dr Nicholas, 148
Wade, Virginia, 211
Wagner, Honus, 109, 117
Walker, Max, 245, 251
Walters, Dougie, 251–2
Walthamstow Avenue, FC, 64, 68, 69
The Wanderers (cricket stadium in Johannesburg), 192
Wanderers FC, 47–8
Waring, Frank, 197
Washington, Denzel, 186
Washington Post, 165, 205, 212, 218
Washington Senators (baseball team), 106, 113, 115
Watson, Lillian, 124
Watson, Maud, 124
Wavertree, Lady, 125
Webb Ellis Suite (at Twickenham Stadium), 25
Webb Ellis, William, 8, 11–13, 25
Weiland, Paul, 268
Weisenberg, Barry, 167
Weissmuller, Johnny, 116
West Auckland FC, 62
West End FC, 48–9
Western Australia Football league, 23
West Ham United FC, 64
West Point (US military academy), 117
Wetton, John, 167
When Billie Beat Bobby (documentary), 205, 217
White Lion Hotel, Aldeburgh, 67
Whitney, Caspar, 94, 98
Wightman Cup, 207, 210
Wilkes' Spirit of the Times, 226
Williams, Graham, 45
Williams, J. G. P., 146
Williams, Robbie, 266
Wills/Marn Grook story/tradition, 10, 12–13, 26
Wills, Tom, 9–13, 26

Wilson, Clint, 163–4
Wilson, Don, 198
Wilson, Harold, 189, 191
Wilson, President Woodrow, ix, 113–14
Wimbledon FC, 73, 74
Wimbledon (tennis tournament)/All England Club, 122–9, 132–7, 203, 207
Winslow, Charles, 127
Winter, Bud, 160
Witherspoon, Kevin, 168
WNBA (Women's National Basketball Association), 217
Wolfenden Report (*Sport and the Community*), 70, 74
Wollen, W. B., 8
womenSports (magazine), 204
Women's Sports Foundation, 204
Women's Tennis Association (WTA), 204, 213, 218
Wooden, John, 209
Wood, Keith, 49
Woolaston, C. W., 48
Worcestershire Combination (football), 73
Worcestershire County Cricket Club, 187, 191, 194
World Anti-Doping Agency (WADA), 153–5
World Cup Finals (association football) South Africa, 268, 2010
World (New York magazine), 87–9, 94–6
World Series (baseball), 12, 113–16, 118, 164
World Series Cricket (WSC), 240, 241–53, 255
World Team Tennis, 204
World Trade Center (attack on, 2001), 118
Wright, Howard, 8
Wrynn, Alison, 150
Wycombe Wanderers FC, 61, 64–5

Yale University, 80–1, 85–8, 92, 95, 97, 98, 236
Yesalis, Charles E., 144

York Barbell Club, Pennsylvania, 145
Young Australia League, 23
Young, David, 152
The Young Doctors (TV drama), 244
Young, Harry, 61

Young Men's Christian Association (YMCA), 107, 112

Ziegenfuss, Val, 210
Ziegler, John, 144, 148
Zirin, Dave, 172